APEX OF POWER

356-1
84

APEX OF POWER

The Prime Minister
and Political Leadership in Canada

Second Edition

Thomas A. Hockin, Editor

PRENTICE-HALL OF CANADA, LTD. SCARBOROUGH, ONTARIO

Canadian Cataloguing in Publication Data

Main entry under title:

Apex of power

Includes bibliographical references.
ISBN 0-13-038653-7 pa.

1. Prime ministers—Canada—Addresses, essays,
lectures. 2. Canada—Politics and government—
1945—   Addresses, essays, lectures. I. Hockin,
Thomas A., 1938—

JL99.A64 1977   320.9′71′06   C77-001069-5

Prentice-Hall, Inc., Englewood Cliffs, New Jersey
Prentice-Hall of Australia, Pty., Ltd., Sydney
Prentice-Hall of India Pvt., Ltd., New Delhi
Prentice-Hall International, Inc., London
Prentice-Hall of Japan, Inc., Tokyo
Prentice-Hall of Southeast Asia (PTE.) Ltd., Singapore

Design: Julian Cleva

ISBN 0-13-038653-7

1 2 3 4 5 W 81 80 79 78 77

Printed and bound in Canada by Webcom Limited

Contents

SECTION III
The Prime Minister and Other Sources of Policy Influence

SECTION IV
Reflections and Case Studies on the Uses of Prime Ministerial Power

Preface

This is the second edition of this book. This edition examines, as did the first, the apex of power in the Canadian political process. Nine selections are entirely new additions to this book. Seven of the articles retained are either updated, revised, or shortened, eleven have been retained as they appeared in the first edition. The book focuses on the relationships of the Prime Minister of Canada to the Canadian political and governmental system. It also endeavours to encourage some ideas on the meaning of political leadership at the apex. It is hoped that an examination of the office of the Prime Minister and the executive in the perspective of political leadership will be a useful addition to the study and discussion of Canadian politics and government.

In this edition as in the first, the authors have not been asked to discuss political leadership explicitly. Instead, this volume is intended to be a preparation for conceptualization and application. As Lewis J. Edinger has noted in his survey of the literature on leadership, the contemporary social sciences define political leadership in various ways: sometimes as influence, sometimes as authority, sometimes as power and sometimes as control over others.[1] Even if one definition of leadership were chosen for the purpose of this volume, the operational meaning of the definition would change depending on the context in which leadership would be exercised. Given the embryonic nature of the scholarly understanding of the concept of political leadership, the purpose of this book is not to encourage one conceptualization of political leadership but to encourage thought on many ideas of leadership at the prime ministerial level.

The focus on the Prime Minister is extensive for two reasons. First, an emphasis on the office of the Prime Minister ensures a more precise focus for applying concepts of leadership than would a focus on the Cabinet or the executive as a whole. Second, the treatment of this focus in this book may help the reader to avoid two extreme interpretations of that office in the Canadian political, economic and social system.

One extreme is that which Canadian biographer Donald Creighton in his two-volume study of Sir John A. Macdonald and Stanley Hoffman in his study of General DeGaulle warn against.[2] This is the approach which ignores the impact of the personality of a Prime Minister or a President because the empirical focus is on aggregates, or because an abstract theory is being used, a theory which cannot accommodate units or forces as

---

[1] Lewis J. Edinger, ed., *Political Leadership in Industrialized Societies* (New York, 1966). See his Introduction, especially pp. 5-10.

[2] See Hoffman's chapter in *ibid* and Creighton's two volumes on Macdonald, especially *The Old Chieftain*.

idiosyncratic as the traits of individual leaders. In contrast are important interpretations of political leadership by Leon Dion, John Courtney, and others which emphasize personal efficacy and action.[3] This approach, which emerges most emphatically in the literature of political biography, can also be extended too far. One must avoid oversimplifying either the political process or the requirements of leadership. Such oversimplification can arise from placing excessive expectations on the power, influence, authority and control of one person.[4] The articles by Charles Taylor, Richard Schultz, S. J. R. Noel, George Szablowski, Bruce Doern, Peyton Lyon, Joseph Wearing, and the interviews with Lester Pearson and John Diefenbaker in this volume elicit the restraints and imperatives that can circumscribe a Prime Minister.

It is hoped therefore that some of the analysis and evidence found in this volume will stimulate the reader to pursue other works on political leadership and Canadian political biography. Another hope is that it will also encourage the reader to consider those powers, structures, and processes in the Canadian political, economic, and social system, other than the performance of the Prime Minister and his office, that may be more helpful in explaining political and social change (or the lack of it) in Canada. Too often, those who counsel some pet reform, political renewal, or policy initiative place the blame for inaction entirely on the Prime Minister. In reality any Prime Minister who operated by fiat or without a careful scouting of the basis of his support would quickly become a Don Quixote. Equally dangerous, however, is a tendency to downgrade the role of political leadership and to place the blame for Canada's problems on the political and socio-economic structure alone, when in fact well-placed acts of leadership at the apex could in some instances do much to change that structure.

The insights and evidence in this volume reflect many approaches essential to the study of political leadership in any political society. Without confining their vocabulary to any specific conceptualization of leadership, the authors of articles in this volume discuss the Prime Minister in ways which reflect many dimensions outlined by Lewis J. Edinger in Table 0-1.

The reader is also invited to consider the many concepts of political leadership which are implied in this volume. The emphasis of various articles can be explicitly related to the taxonomy of concepts listed by Edinger in Table 0-2.

Because of the proliferation of literature on policy-making in Canada, and on the role of the Prime Minister in this process, a selected bibliogra-

[3] Leon Dion "The Concept of Political Leadership: An Analysis", *Canadian Journal of Political Science*, March 1968, and John C. Courtney "Prime Ministerial Character: An Examination of Mackenzie King's Political Leadership" *Canadian Journal of Political Science*, March 1976.

[4] I find that this oversimplification occurs in places in Peter C. Newman's *Renegade in Power* (a book about John Diefenbaker), and in *The Distemper of Our Times* (on Lester Pearson).

phy on policy-making in the federal government follows Section III. However, this volume cannot include an annotated bibliography for each
section because the concept of political leadership and the impact of the
executive is too extensive for a comprehensive yet discriminating bibliography. Some key studies can be suggested in this preface, not to restrict
further references but to indicate something of the diversity of the literature which may complement this volume.

TABLE 0-1

The Edinger Table on Approaches to the Study of Political Leadership*

I Focus on the leading actors
  A. Elite analysis—leaders studied as collectivities
    1. Elite identification (recruitment, composition, and circulation of leading
      participants in political processes) [Schindeler, Szablowski, Smiley, Noel]
      a. By position
      b. By reputation
    2. Elite attitudes [Taylor, Dawson, Noel, Fletcher, Doern, Lenoski, Dobuzin-
      skis, Schultz, Szablowski].
    3. Elite behaviour patterns [Taylor, Dawson, Noel, Doern, Sharp, Szablowski,
      Fletcher, Lenoski, Dobuzinskis, Schultz]
  B. The study of individual leaders [Lyon, Dawson, Wright].
    1. Standard political biographies
    2. Psychobiographies
II Focus on interaction between leaders and context
  A. Leaders as subjects (for example, the event-making man) [Lyon, Wright,
    Fletcher, Jackson and Atkinson, Taylor, Smith, interviews]
  B. Leaders as objects of social forces, group norms, organizational structures,
    etc. [Hockin, interviews, Smith, Wearing, Winham and Cunningham, Doern,
    Szablowski, Jackson & Atkinson, Fletcher, Schultz, Lenoski, Dobuzinskis]
  C. Leaders as actors in interpersonal relationships (leader-leader, leader-follow-
    ers, etc.) [Almost all articles]
    1. Systems analysis
    2. Influence analysis [Hockin, Schindeler, Sharp, Neustadt, Doern, inter-
      views, Smiley, Winham and Cunningham, Szablowski, Jackson & Atkin-
      son, Schultz, Lenoski]
    3. Issue analysis [Hockin, Lyon, Doern, Schultz]
    4. Analysis of social movements and small groups [Taylor, Noel, Dawson,
      Lenoski]
    5. Situational analysis (for example, "crisis" leadership) [Lyon, Wright]

* Articles in this volume relevant to each approach appear in brackets.

Source: Lewis J. Edinger, *Political Leadership in Industrialized Societies* (New York, 1966), p. 12.
By permission of John Wiley and Sons Inc.

TABLE 0-2

Selected Concepts and Organizational Criteria for the Study of Political Leadership*

CONCEPT	DEFINITION	OPERATIONAL CRITERIA	ILLUSTRATIVE DATA
Leadership authority	A relationship of inequality sanctioned by the legitimacy of leaders to make and enforce policy.	The nature and extent of legitimating group norms.	Elite and/or mass consensus on rights and duties of formal positions, on means and ends of leadership behavior.
Leadership control	The actual or perceived ability to provide or withhold benefits and apply sanctions.	Extent of leaders' ability to extract conforming group behavior.	Comparing means of control (for example, coercion, manipulation) with compliance on the part of group members.
Leadership autonomy	The extent to which leaders are independent of environmental factors.	Leaders' ability to be their own referent.	Intra- and extra-systemic variables interacting with leadership views and actions.
Leadership skills	The nature possession, and application of methods designed to gain compliance.	Predisposition and capabilities of leaders and receptivity of group members to leadership cues.	Comparing goal orientations of leaders with success or failure to achieve group behavior conforming with goals.
Statescraft	A measure of the successful or unsuccessful exercise of legitimate authority in sovereign entities and sub-components thereof.	Determination of the efficacy of such authority in achieving stipulated goals.	Extent of achievement of stipulated objective or subjective communal goals (for example, political stability, defense of the national interest).
Policy-making	The process of choosing among alternative goals, decision-makers, and courses of action.	a. The ingredients which enter into the process. b. The interaction process between relevant agents. c. The relationship between policy inputs and outputs.	a. Extent of available information, perceived goals and capabilities, emotions, time pressure. b. Rules and interpersonal relations in legislative, judicial, and administrative bodies. c. Comparing demands articulated by voters, interest associations, foreign governments, with behavioral re-

Leadership roles	Three definitions involving inequality between actual or aspiring group leaders and actual or potential followers: a. The position of leaders. b. The behavioral "style" of leaders. c. Orientations toward the incumbents of leadership positions.	a. Offices occupied or sought, rights and duties associated with position. b. Nature of interaction with other relevant actors. c. Determination of reciprocal expectations associated with position.	a. The American presidency and its veto power over legislation. b. The extent to which behavioral congruence is attained through coercion, manipulation, persuasion, etc. c. Perception of representative or delegated functions, degree of conformity with group norms in the view of followers.
The personality of a leader	Individual, as distinguished from collective characteristics which influence attitudinal and behavioral patterns.	Determination of personality syndromes, their source, degree of adaptability and general impact on leader and/or follower.	Instinctive needs requiring satisfaction, learned repression, expression, and want patterns, degree of internalization or cultural norms, etc.
Leadership recruitment	The process of leadership selection	a. The variables which promote or hinder the acquisition of leadership. b. The general process through which leaders are chosen and displaced.	a. Social background, ambition, skills, charisma, respect, material values, connections. b. Electoral processes, career patterns, revolutions, etc.

* Derived from Leadership Literature.

Source: Edinger, *Political Leadership in Industrialized Societies*, pp. 6-8. By permission of John Wiley and Sons Inc.

A good general introduction to political leadership is Lewis J. Edinger (ed.), *Political Leadership in Industrialized Societies* (New York: John Wiley and Sons Inc., 1966). Also helpful for a general introduction to the executive, but in a British context, are A. King (ed.), *The British Prime Minister* and R. Rose (ed.), *Policy Making in Britain* (both Toronto: Macmillan, 1969). I find the appropriate chapters in R. M. Dawson and N. Ward's *The Government of Canada* (Toronto: University of Toronto Press, 1970) and in J. R. Mallory's *The Structure of Canadian Government* (Toronto: Macmillan of Canada, 1971) useful for understanding the history of the development of the cabinet and the executive in Canada. Even more detailed is W. Matheson's *The Prime Minister and the Cabinet* (Toronto: Methuen, 1976). R. J. Van Loon and M. G. Whittington's *The Canadian Political System* (Toronto: McGraw-Hill Ryerson, 1975) also is most helpful, as is R. Crossman's *The Myth of Cabinet Government* (Boston: Harvard University Press, 1972).

The study of the Prime Minister's role and behaviour in cabinet formation in Canada—an important part of his leadership responsibilities—is not included here because an excellent compendium of studies on this subject has been edited by Professor F. W. Gibson for the Royal Commission on Bilingualism and Biculturalism and is published by the Queen's Printer. Professor Matheson's study examines this as well. The existing literature on the relationships between the minister and his department is not very adequate. J. W. Pickersgill's 1972 Clark Memorial lectures and the last two volumes of Lester Pearson's memoirs are pertinent however. Especially useful for the Federal-Provincial context of prime ministerial leadership is Richard Simeon's *Federal-Provincial Diplomacy: The Making of Recent Policy In Canada* (Toronto: University of Toronto Press, 1972). Denis Smith's *Gentle Patriot* (Toronto: McClelland and Stewart Limited, 1974) is a view of Mr. Pearson's premiership from a minister's perspective.

The executive's relationship with Parliament, as discussed in other studies, can be used to supplement the discussion in this volume. Examples are David Hoffman and Norman Ward's report for the Royal Commission on Bilingualism and Biculturalism entitled *Bilingualism and Biculturalism in the House of Commons* (Ottawa: Queens Printer, 1970), Norman Ward's *The Public Purse* (Toronto: University of Toronto Press, 1962), and Robert Jackson and Michael Atkinson's *The Canadian Legislative System* (Toronto: Macmillan, 1975).

The impact of the party leader on his party and on voting behaviour is pursued in a host of studies. This volume can mention but a few examples: J. M. Beck, *The Pendulum of Power* (Scarborough: Prentice-Hall, 1969); P. Regenstreif, *The Diefenbaker Interlude* (Toronto: McClelland and Stewart, 1966); J. Courtney (ed.), *Voting In Canada* (Scarborough: Prentice-Hall, 1968); H. G. Thorburn (ed.), *Party Politics In Canada* (Scarborough: Prentice-Hall, 1968); and J. Meisel, *The Canadian General Election of 1957* (Toronto: University of Toronto Press, 1961) his edition of *Papers On The 1962 Canadian Federal Election* (Toronto: University of Toronto Press, 1965) and his *Working Papers on Canadian Politics* (Montreal: McGill-Queen's University Press, 1974). A good full length study on leader selection is

John C. Courtney *The Selection of National Party Leaders in Canada* (Toronto: Macmillan, 1973).

Students of Canadian politics have been well-served by excellent political biographies and general histories. It would be remiss not to refer the reader to the various biographies on Mackenzie King, notably: R. M. Dawson, *William Lyon Mackenzie King 1874-1923* (1958); H. B. Neatby, *William Lyon Mackenzie King: The Lonely Heights, 1923-1932* (1963); J. Pickersgill and D. Forster's volumes of *The Mackenzie King Record* (Vol. I: 1960, Vol. II: 1968, Vol. III: 1970). All five King biographies mentioned above are published by the University of Toronto Press. J. L. Granatstein's *The Politics of Survival* (Toronto: University of Toronto Press, 1967) and Roger Graham's study of Arthur Meighen, especially *Arthur Meighen*, Vol. II (Toronto: Clarke Irwin & Co. Ltd., 1963) are useful for penetrating various dimensions of party leadership. James Eayrs' *The Art of the Possible: Government and Foreign Policy in Canada* (Toronto: University of Toronto Press, 1961) and his volumes *In Defence of Canada* (Toronto: University of Toronto Press Vol. 1, 1964; Vol. 2, 1965; and Vol. 3, 1972) include much that will inform the reader in search of documentation of prime ministerial and ministerial behaviour. Also useful here are M. Hamelin (ed.), *The Political Ideas of the Prime Ministers of Canada* (Ottawa: Les editions de l'Universite d'Ottawa, 1969); Peter Newman, *Renegade in Power* (Toronto: McClelland and Stewart, 1963; and *The Distemper of Our Times* (Toronto: McClelland and Stewart, 1968), and C. B. Power (edited by Norman Ward), *A Party Politician* (Toronto: Macmillan, 1966).

Although the polemics on political leadership (or the lack of it) in various periodicals such as the *Canadian Dimension* and the *Canadian Forum* are frequently informative, the role and meaning of political leadership for comprehensive social and political change and the impact of the Canadian power structure on the Prime Minister and Cabinet are not confined to polemics. Surely John Porter's *Vertical Mosaic* (Toronto: University of Toronto Press, 1966), Chapter XV, Charles Taylor's *The Pattern of Politics* (Toronto: McClelland and Stewart, 1970) and Wallace Clement's *The Canadian Corporate Elite* (Toronto: McClelland and Stewart, 1975) should be consulted, as should Robert Presthus's *Elite Accommodation In Canadian Politics* (Toronto: Macmillan of Canada, 1973) and his *Elites In the Policy Process* (Toronto: Macmillan of Canada, 1974).

I wish to thank the late Right Honourable Lester B. Pearson and the Right Honourable John G. Diefenbaker for extending the interviews which appear in this volume and for their care in improving the transcripts. I am grateful to many contributors who wrote expressly for this edition: Fred Fletcher, Laurent Dobuzinskis, Richard Schultz and Gerry Lenoski. I wish here to thank Michael Pitfield of the Privy Council Office and the *Canadian Journal of Public Administration* for permission to reprint his article in the book. I wish to thank Mr. Gordon Smith, also of the Privy Council Office, for his advice and help in updating various parts of this edition. Finally, I wish to acknowledge with thanks Macmillan of Canada for permission to reprint from R. Jackson and M. M. Atkinson *Canadian Legislative System*.

T.A.H.

APEX OF POWER

The Prime Minister and Cabinet Government in Canada

This section serves as an introductory part of this book. The first article outlines some of the important aspects of political leadership for the Canadian Prime Minister. Fred Schindeler's article introduces the development of the office in a historical context and presents a thesis concerning that development.

The next two papers elaborate and reflect on some of the themes raised by Professor Schindeler in the concluding section of his article. The third selection was prepared by the Privy Council Office early in 1975. The fourth selection, a speech delivered by Mr. Michael Pit field, Clerk of the P.C.O. and Secretary to the Cabinet, looks at the subject from a broader perspective. Both these articles update the perception of, and reasons for, the shape of government organization at the apex as of the end of 1975. They postdate other discussions of the same subject by Mr. Gordon Robertson of the Privy Council Office and by Mr. Marc Lalonde, then of the Prime Minister's Office, which were published earlier in the Canadian Journal of Public Administration. A minister's observations of the Cabinet's mode of decision-making over the years conclude this section.

1

The Prime Minister and Political Leadership: An Introduction to Some Restraints and Imperatives*

THOMAS A. HOCKIN

One curiosity of Canadian attitudes to politics is the readiness with which they assume that their Prime Minister enjoys great influence on the future of the country. In a Gallup Poll published August 8, 1970, in the *Toronto Daily Star*, Canadian and British respondents were asked: "How much influence would you say these groups have on the country's future—the Prime Minister, Cabinet Ministers, the average M.P., 'big business', labor unions, people like yourself?" The results are shown in Table 1-1.

Even though Canada is a fairly decentralized federal state in terms of jurisdiction, Canadians believe that their Prime Minister wields more influence than Britons believe their Prime Minister wields in Britain, though Britain is a unitary state. Even though Canadians are frequently told of American and certain economic class influences on political leaders, a great number of Canadians persist in attributing great influence to the Prime Minister.

In addition to this perception, there has been considerable speculation since the prime ministership of Pierre Trudeau, about the "presidential" nature of his exercise of power. This "transformation" of Canada's system of government has been faithfully explored at least monthly in Saturday newspaper supplements and the subject is opened for scrutiny at least annually in Canada's national magazines. Much of this speculation has been provoked by the trappings of office, not the substance. The trappings continue to fascinate and they seem to enjoy unusual visibility since the prime ministership of Mr. Trudeau. This, plus the growth in the size of the Prime Minister's office, his heavily publicized trips, tours and speeches, and the national and international notoriety of his personality, can confuse the observer who wishes to assess the actual power and influence of the Prime Minister.

---

* Written for this volume.

TABLE 1-1

	Great Influence	Some Influence	Little or No Influence	Can't Say
The Prime Minister				
Canada	56%	27%	11%	6%
U.K.	49%	22%	23%	6%
Cabinet Ministers				
Canada	29%	48%	13%	10%
U.K.	30%	40%	20%	10%
Average MP				
Canada	10%	44%	35%	11%
U.K.	9%	41%	39%	11%
Big Business				
Canada	67%	20%	5%	8%
U.K.	48%	28%	9%	15%
Labor unions				
Canada	53%	28%	11%	8%
U.K.	55%	29%	9%	7%
People like yourself				
Canada	7%	21%	67%	5%
U.K.	6%	15%	71%	8%

The purpose of this article is to serve as a small antidote to these tendencies by introducing to the beginning students of Canadian politics and government some of the institutional decision-making restraints that confront the Canadian Prime Minister in his task of political leadership in Parliament, in his party, in the Cabinet and before the public. The purpose here is to discuss some features of the Prime Minister's job not discussed elsewhere in this volume. The purpose is not to erect a "thesis" about the overall power and influence of the Prime Minister; to do so would require an examination and assessment of more variables than space allows here. It would require, above all, an assessment of the impact of the socio-economic power structure. Nor can this article identify the congruency of the office of Canada's Prime Ministers with some definition of cabinet government, presidential government or prime ministerial government. These concepts are discussed more thoroughly in other articles in this volume, notably those of Fred Schindeler, Denis Smith, Joseph Wearing, George Szablowski, and Laurent Dobuzinskis.

It seems clear that in Canada manifestations of several different forms of executive-legislature relations seem to exist at present. As Denis Smith points out, some of the plebiscitarian assumptions of the "Liberal model" of parliamentary government are closer to presidential assumptions than most parliamentary assumptions. The recent advance of standing committees and reforms of the Liberal party caucus (permitting it a modicum of influence on legislation in that many bills are presented to caucus before they go to second reading in the House) seem to be based on a blend of congressional and early parliamentary assumptions. Fred Schindeler argues that Canadian government has evolved from the predominance first of the Governor, then of the Cabinet, then of the public service, to a form of government which he designates as "prime ministerial" instead of cabinet government. This final stage can also be perceived as a system of government which is less than prime ministerial but which depends for its success on the Prime Minister to act as a kind of generator, to try continually to insure that various sources of opinion and policy (such as task forces, the Prime Minister's Office, cabinet committees, parliamentary party caucus, public debate, etc.) are made manifest and kept working. This new system reflected by the Trudeau approach is in contrast to a system which leans almost exclusively on the policy proclivities of the public service or the Cabinet and occasional royal commissions. In order for these manifold sources of opinion and policy to emerge and function, they must be encouraged by the Prime Minister; to this extent the system depends on him. But he cannot dominate all these sources, and, therefore, to some extent he unleashes forces even he can not control. (Recent ministerial complaints about House of Commons Committee independence since 1966 and parting broadsides from resigning ministers about a so-called inner coterie of public servants who dominate policy-making are examples of this.)

The Complexities of Party Leadership

It has frequently been argued that the Prime Minister's exercise of authority over his political party, and over his parliamentary party in particular, has steadily increased. The development of nation-wide mass parties, the extensions of the franchise and the development of the mass media are said to have changed the nature of the general election and made the Government parliamentary party obedient to the Prime Minister's wishes. A cogent theoretical exploration of these tendencies in mass parties in western industrialized societies is found in Jean Blondel's *Introduction to Comparative Government*. This theory is pursued in my *Government in Canada*. This obedience is said to derive in large measure from the emphasis put on the party leader during elections. The Winham and Cunningham article shows in fact that the image of the party leader did play a significant role in their sample constituency in the 1968 federal election. Professors Murray Beck, Peter Regenstreif and others have argued similarly for overall national voting in other federal elections.[1] None of these interpre-

---

[1] See the references in the preface of this volume.

tations describe the Canadian federal election simply as a gladiatorial contest between party leaders, but it is easy to slip from a heavy emphasis on the leader into such an interpretation. It would also be easy to assume from such an emphasis that the only mandate given by the electorate to an M.P. is to support his leader. The Winham and Cunningham article, however, shows that this would be an inaccurate inference for a majority of voters in the constituency they examined. It is always worth remembering, for example, that some regional and even class voting patterns persist in spite of the images of party leaders.

Regardless of how "presidential" the electoral campaign may have been or how disciplined his party in the House, some complexities of party leadership remain and must be acknowledged. For example, many government Members of Parliament have regional and constituency interests that they know must be articulated to caucus, to Ministers and to the Prime Minister or to the Prime Minister's Office. No matter how attractive or influential is the personality of the Prime Minister during elections, or how influential the rationality of optimal decision-making in the bureaucracy and Cabinet, government M.P.s will never muffle all their opinions. Some M.P.s who hope for advancement to the Cabinet may be circumspect with their criticisms in order to build a reputation of loyalty, since the Prime Minister has at least 70 important jobs to offer his M.P.s (such as cabinet posts, parliamentary secretaryships, and committee chairmanships in the House). But Hoffman and Ward show in their study that only 31.6 per cent of back bench Liberals in 1964 were interested in advancement to a cabinet post some time in the future.[2] It would be foolish, then, to expect that all M.P.s are forever circumspect in private because of private ambition. In addition, the 1969 reforms of the Liberal caucus which require the Cabinet to submit its legislative plans to the caucus at least one month in advance of presentation in the House plus the reform that insures that caucus committees will be appraised of ministerial proposals in cabinet committees can be seen as another way for back bench Liberals to make their opinions heard *before* they are asked to support the government bill in public or in Parliament.

Complexities of parliamentary party leadership will also vary with time, circumstance and party. If the New Democratic Party forms the Government in Ottawa in the future, and if it houses both ideological enthusiasts and bureaucratic minds within it, there can be little doubt that an N.D.P. Prime Minister will have to watch his caucus very carefully. The Progressive Conservative Party has always had representatives of opposed emphasis on many such key issues. Therefore, a future P.C. Prime Minister will not be able to ignore his caucus no matter how closely his Cabinet agrees with him. Liberal Prime Ministers from King to Trudeau may have governed as the "triumphant center" of Canadian

---

[2] See J. D. Hoffman and Norman Ward, "Bilingualism and Biculturalism in the Canadian House of Commons", a report for the Royal Commission on Bilingualism and Biculturalism (Ottawa, 1970).

politics, or even as "the political face of the public service" (as some people charge) but on many policy issues their caucuses have shown a disparity of emphasis on such controversial issues as Medicare, conscription, NATO and more lately arctic sovereignty, aid to cities, and continentalism. To picture any of the three major parties as a monolith and each party caucus as a united choir in private (as well as in public) would be to overlook actual restraints on prime ministerial leadership in the party caucus.

The key question, however, remains: when does the caucus matter or when do M.P.s' opinions receive the attention of the Prime Minister or the Cabinet? Prime Ministers often overcome cleavages and differences simply by refusing to initiate policy on contentious questions unless forced to do so.[3] Even if a posture of policy quiescence is considered to be a form of leadership, however, it must be recognized that it can, on occasion, be a reaction to the complexities of party leadership, not the opposite.[4] Government parties are not tamely subservient to the will of the Prime Minister on all issues. They are, in short, federal and social unions within Canada's overall federal and social union and hence reflect many of the factions and are divided over many of the long-term policy objectives that the country itself is subjected to. There are occasions then, during the life of any Government, when only the modicum of ideological agreement, the "distributive" (everyone receives something) nature of policy outputs and an instinct for self-preservation expressed through disciplined voting in the House, keep a party united in times of fierce internal disagreement.

As Fred Fletcher's article in this book shows, another complexity of party leadership comes from the contemporary mass media. Television allows the Prime Minister to be seen and to be heard in more Canadian homes than ever before, but it also makes Cabinet Ministers more visible than ever before. Cabinet Ministers never receive the same publicity or exposure as the Prime Minister, but, thanks to television, some are more familiar to the public as personalities than could possibly have been true before the vast diffusion of television after 1951. This exposure may increase still further if the meetings of the House or its committees are televised. Some Ministers, therefore, can attract public attention to their views in a way only a well-known regional spokesman in the Cabinet could do before the advent of television. However, the cabinet committee system, by forcing each Minister to defend or compromise his ideas with four or five other ministers and several deputy ministers along the way, may have a tendency to diminish the uniqueness of ministerial ideas in public. This may make it more difficult for a Minister to become identified with one clear policy position in distinction from other Ministers.

---

[3] See J. W. Pickersgill, *The Mackenzie King Record* (Toronto, 1960), Introduction.

[4] An illuminating discussion of this is found in J. Courtney, "Prime Ministerial Characters: An Examination of Mackenzie King's Political Leadership", in *Canadian Journal of Political Science*, IX, No. 1 (March, 1976).

Occasionally there are rumours of plots to force a leader to resign. These may be more numerous while a party is in opposition, such as those that faced Robert Borden, Arthur Meighen, R. B. Bennett, Robert Manion and John Diefenbaker as Conservative opposition leaders, but rumours of party plots have occurred during a Prime Minister's tenure as well. Leon Dion has argued that "the real test of leadership" is its "influence on the core of the faithful"[5] not simply the influence of the leader with masses. It is wise then to recognize the restraints and imperatives of the party. As Dion suggests, these emerge as demands for the leader to be both an agent of innovation, as well as an agent of conservation. "The leader's role as innovator will be accepted only after he has given proof of his absolute loyalty to the group."[6] J. L. Granatstein's excellent study of the Conservatives shows this restraint on party leaders during the Second World War.[7] This said however, it has been argued that party leaders seem less secure within their party when public disenchantment with the leader is also obvious. The party, in this view, is reflecting something of the public view, not simply its own. Rumours of plots and counter-plots should not, therefore, be summarily dismissed, but neither should they be exaggerated. A student of Canadian politics must not assume that the life of a Prime Minister is one in which he is constantly embroiled in ministerial and caucus manoeuverings to replace him. To recognize their occasional occurrence is not to suggest frequent regularity. To recognize their possibility is to be reminded again that all Canadian Prime Ministers know they are the object of suspended judgement not only in the country and in the Cabinet, but in their party as well.

The Prime Minister and the Cabinet in Parliament

Since the "institutional" process and structure sets some of the limits within which a party leader can operate, it is important to examine something of the impact of Parliament on the Prime Minister and Cabinet. Parliament imposes many compelling conventions or customs: all major policy must first be announced in Parliament if Parliament is sitting; the Cabinet is answerable in Parliament for the actions of the executive; and Parliament's "rights" must be protected. These are all examples of how the operation of Parliament affects the Prime Minister and the Cabinet. In fact, to evaluate a Prime Minister's performance as a political leader through his behaviour in, and attitude to, Parliament may be to judge him in an arena where much of his orientation and technique is limited by the nature of the arena. Since Confederation, and in most provincial assemblies before then, the procedure of lower Houses has been basically a procedure for the Opposition, if not to frustrate the Government, at least

---

[5] See Leon Dion "The Concept of Political Leadership: An Analysis", *Canadian Journal of Political Science*, II, No. 1 (March 1969), p. 4.

[6] *Ibid.*

[7] J. L. Granatstein, *The Politics of Survival* (Toronto, 1967).

to criticize it. Regardless of how knowledgeable or partisan opposition members might be, it is they who carry the attack and set the tone of debate, questions and scrutiny in the House. The Government, and especially the Prime Minister, may command more visibility and more public relations advantages than the Opposition outside of Parliament, but inside the House of Commons the Opposition dominates the debate. The reforms of the Canadian House of Commons in 1913, 1925, 1927, 1965 and 1969 have added some time restraints to the activity of the Opposition but no qualitative shift has occurred.[8] Despite limits on some speeches and on some debates, the Opposition has always perceived the House of Commons as its most potent forum for exposing, embarrassing and puncturing Governments, in short, for waging its part of the continuous election campaign between elections. (The Opposition can also go quite far in this activity since the misdrafting of Standing Order 75C in 1969 leaves the Government with no unilateral guillotine procedure short of closure.)

Prime Ministers and Cabinets often appear, therefore, as if their performances in the House of Commons were essentially holding operations. The atmosphere of the House is not unlike an adversary proceeding, with the Government almost always on the defensive. In this context, then, standards for leadership are clearly different from standards for leadership outside of Parliament. On television, on campaign tours, the Prime Minister knows he is speaking to some floating voters; in the House, he knows there are no floaters (except in some minority Government situations). In Cabinet, the Prime Minister knows that well-placed acts of initiative may alter a policy. He knows however that in the House few M.P.s decide policy; they are there primarily to defend or attack stated or promised policy. In discussions with non-political groups or with public servants, the Prime Minister can be openly receptive to suggestions; in the House, he can only occasionally be receptive to opposition ideas. In countless other contexts, the Prime Minister is to portray himself as a leader for all of the people; in the House his role as a partisan party leader is crucial for the morale of his supporters and for his parliamentary prestige. The requirements of political leadership in the House of Commons, in short, are different both in degree and in type from the requirements in most other contexts.

Some men thrive on these parliamentary demands. Edward Blake,[9] Arthur Meighen[10] and John Diefenbaker were party leaders who were so successful in meeting the partisan requirements of the House that their followers could be forgiven for failing to notice the erosion of their support outside of Parliament. The claustrophobia of Parliament can intoxicate as well as repel. If one were to generalize, however, the Prime

---

[8] See T. Hockin, "The Reform of Canada's Parliament: The 1965 Reforms and Beyond", *University of Toronto Law Journal*, 1966.

[9] See G. Ross, *Getting Into Parliament and After* (Toronto, 1913), Chap. iv on Blake.

[10] See Roger Graham, *And Fortune Fled* (Toronto, 1963), pp. 313-17 for example.

Ministers most noted for their affection for the House—Arthur Meighen and John Diefenbaker—were primarily of an opposition temperament[11] and very often their style as Prime Minister was less to defend their Government than to attack the Opposition or to expose the folly of the previously defeated Government. The House is the cockpit of the continuous election campaign; its adversary proceedings are tailor-made for those with contentious and opposing temperaments. There is a danger that Prime Ministers and Ministers who have had little experience in Parliament will grow restless and impatient with the politics of contention, the procedure of Opposition. It may be difficult for a Government to be at home in the atmosphere of the House of Commons when, for example, the Cabinet is composed of Ministers who have sat in the House only three to five years before they were named Privy Councillors. (This, for example, was the background of most of the Trudeau Cabinet when it took office in 1968.)

According to John Diefenbaker, the most important parliamentary occasion, the one which "makes or unmakes Governments" is the oral question period.[12] The formal role of the Prime Minister and of Ministers in this 40 minutes each day is to accept accountability for the performance of the Government and to answer accordingly. While accepting these requirements, however, a Minister can be extremely vague in his responses. For example, he can assert that the matter is "under study", or he can take a matter as "notice". For example, of 1,119 oral questions asked in the House January 22 to April 23, 1968, 103 or 9.4 per cent were ruled out of order; 167 or 15 per cent received no answer at all.

Even with these various "escapes", the oral question period affords the Opposition, in MacGregor Dawson's words, with "one of the most formidable devices which it has at its disposal".[13] It "draws the acts of government out into full publicity and threatens at all times to submit the most obscure happenings to a sudden and unexpected scrutiny".[14] For example, during the first four months of 1968, opposition M.P.s asked 97.3 per cent of all of the oral questions. The Official Opposition asked 61 per cent, the N.D.P. asked 33 per cent; other parties the rest. Of the 263 members sitting in the House during the second session of the 27th Parliament, most of the Opposition members (120 of 130) asked questions. There is a natural tendency, however, for certain opposition M.P.s to dominate the period. N.D.P. leader T. C. Douglas asked 40 questions during the first four months of 1968, seven M.P.s asked between 26 and 35 questions, 13 between 16 and 25, nine asked between 11 and 15 questions, 25 between six and ten and 65 M.P.s asked at least one to five questions.

---

[11] See *ibid.*, p. 317 for Meighen's brilliant demolition of the Government's ill-fated "Peterson Contract".

[12] Interview with John Diefenbaker, May 7, 1970, Ottawa by this author.

[13] R. M. Dawson and N. Ward, *The Government of Canada* (Toronto, 1968), p. 404.

[14] *Ibid.*, p. 405.

If the procedure and organization in the House of Commons are dominated by a majority Government in a legislative sense, they are not so dominated in the realm of political rhetoric and debate. In other words, many complaints about "the decline of Parliament" are really complaints about the Government's ability to pass everything it wants to pass through Parliament sooner or later. But in terms of political rhetoric and debate, the Opposition carries the attack subject to a few time restraints. [In fact, Stanley Knowles's suggestions for parliamentary reform outlined in Section IV of this book are posited on this reality.] In short, the House is a place where Governments go to to defend their policies and occasionally to attack the Opposition. Political leadership by the Prime Minister and the Cabinet can perhaps be best described then as the task of reconciling a desire for expeditious passage of their legislation and for avoiding political embarrassment in defence of their policies without giving the appearance of either ignoring Parliament, or more precisely, of ignoring the right of its critics and of the Opposition to question and criticize. The Opposition, however, should be aware of its own behaviour; it should be aware of the electoral penalty it may invite if it over-extends its rights by continually preventing government bills to come to a vote after a tolerable amount of debate.

The most important implication of all this should not be missed. Since Parliament is the legal and symbolic sovereign institution in the political process, dramatic failure to provide leadership in this institution can, on occasion, be disastrous for the Prime Minister and the Cabinet. The pipeline debate in 1955 to 1956 is an example of such a disaster. However, the power of the House of Commons over the fortunes of the Prime Minister and his Cabinet also comes from an accumulation of small mistakes by those on the Government benches. Ministers are tested daily in the House and much of their public reputation flows from their performance in the House. Ministers seldom contradict each other, but in the cross-fire and debate in the House and the scrutiny in House Committees contradictions and confusions sometimes emerge. Tempers flare in the House and unfortunate things can happen. One such episode during the Pearson years was its decision to open the Munsinger scandal. It is doubtful if this scandal would have emerged if Justice Minister Lucien Cardin had not lost his temper (when he was being mercilessly taunted by the Opposition) one warm day in the House of Commons. It is equally doubtful, for example, if critics of the Government and its policies could sustain public attention to an issue such as sovereignty in the north or starvation in Biafra, if the Government did not have to face opposition questions and criticisms on these subjects day after day. The House of Commons even if dominated by disciplined parties, is therefore frequently a catalyst and if it does not register in vote switching in the House it is still a theatre for political upheavals and for erosions of party and personal reputations. Abject failure in Parliament has a way of being transmitted to the public at large.

Another feature of the House which may set limits, as well as change the context in which the Prime Minister and Cabinet make and explain policy, is the increased activity of House standing committees in examining Bills and Estimates and in conducting general studies.[15] The price of this activity has been a perceptible increase in expertise and even collegiality in committees. In 1966, in the second session of the 27th Parliament, standing committees began to take the "committee stage" of a number of bills. They examined all parts of seven government bills and the subject matter of parts of six other bills. Three years later, 23 government bills were examined in standing committees. By 1977 most government bills go to standing committees and, in committee, many bills are changed to some degree. In examining the broadcast legislation in 1966, for example, the Government allowed 22 of the 35 amendments in the House Committee to pass, and although most changes were minor, though the P.C.s and N.D.P. were given credit for moving only three of these successful motions, many of the successful motions were originally their ideas. It is notable, too, that the Government back bench members of the committee found their energies worthwhile: they amended their own party's bill 19 times. Similar examples of committee alteration of bills on details are not difficult to find since 1966 as well.

Standing committees have also gone beyond mere refinement. Standing committees in the 28th Parliament have amended the Government's proposed bills on substantive matters such as the Languages Bill, breathalizer legislation, and parliamentary representation on C.I.D.A. for example. These have been striking and important changes in government bills, and in all cases it was clear that the Cabinet was less than pleased with this manifestation of committee independence. The Cabinet, in cases like this, is confronted with either accepting the amendments to its basic policy or changing the bill back to its originally expressed policy before the vote on third reading. To do the latter is to ignore its own party members in the committee; to do the former is to accept a bill which is not totally, even in its important features, an expression of the executive's policy. Either choice is difficult for any Cabinet. Time will tell if committee independence on the policy in bills will be allowed to increase.

Another impact of committees on the Government is their use as a kind of "parliamentary royal commission". In the first session of the 28th Parliament, for example, there were a number of "parliamentary enquiries" or "'general studies". The Standing Committee on External Affairs examined Canada's relationships with Europe and Latin America as well as the air defence of Canada. The Finance, Trade and Economic Affairs Committee studied the White Paper on Anti-Dumping, conducted an enquiry into rising interest rates and by February 1970 had launched into a major study of the Benson White Paper on Tax Reform. The Transport and Communications Committee examined transportation in the Atlantic Provinces. The Fisheries and Forestry Committee enquired into the seal industry in the

---

[15] The content of the next four paragraphs summarizes some of the findings of T. Hockin, "The Advance of 'The Standing Committees of Canada's House of Commons'", *Canadian Public Administration*, xiii, No. 2 (June 1970), pp. 185-202.

Gulf of St. Lawrence and fisheries and forestry problems on the west coast of Canada. Some committees, however, such as Justice and Legal Affairs; Agriculture; and Broadcasting, Films and Assistance to the Arts conducted a general study of policy areas under the guise of examining proposed Government legislation.

General enquiries in standing committees can have an unusual effect on committee members. Party partisans have noted how in some standing committees a collegial attitude across party lines has been induced. For example, the report of the Standing Committee on Indian Affairs and Northern Development in January 1970, calling for a Canadian declaration of sovereignty over the arctic archipelago, was supported by members of all parties in the committee even though the Government did not agree with the report. The Minister of Agriculture and the Minister of Justice spent many hours in the summer of 1969 consulting with committee members on proposed legislation, thus recognizing the political reality that the Agriculture Committee and the Justice and Legal Affairs Committee were developing attitudes of their own, attitudes sometimes at variance with government policy. The price to a Government of a standing committee becoming conversant, even expert, in a policy area may be the establishment of a policy-idea source which is independent of party and of the public service. The price of excessive collegiality might be to break down party lines on policy altogether. Certainly this has not yet happened to any alarming extent. But the way to arrest excessive collegiality without harming standing committees is to stimulate more vigorous and informed party caucus committees. It is hoped that this will be the Government's response rather than to weaken the committees by refusing them the right to conduct general enquiries or by refusing them the assistance of staff and expert and technical assistance.

These recent parliamentary reforms are relevant to the Prime Minister in several ways. For example, insofar as the activity of some members of standing committees is devoted as much to a policy influence strategy as to a partisan strategy, policy ideas can be explored by such committees and this could in time add another input, thereby lessening the Prime Minister's dependence on the public service and on some Cabinet Ministers. However, M.P.s also engage in much partisan activity in standing committees. By embarrassing Ministers and unearthing inconvenient evidence, these committees can also make life difficult for the Prime Minister and his Cabinet.

One general concluding note about the impact of the House on the Prime Minister and his Ministers. Prime Ministers and Ministers can become impatient with the House not simply because of the adversary atmosphere of the House, or because their interest in politics may be more managerial than political, or because the opposition is dragging its feet in passing government bills, but because of the lack of clear ideological and philosophic differences between the two major parties on many issues. This forces the House to spend an inordinate amount of time bickering over procedural, personal, and tactical questions or over comparatively minor issues which might divide the major parliamentary parties. This suggestion needs further study. Although sometimes deep, and therefore interesting, differences do emerge between Liberals and Conservatives in House debates, very often they do not. In fact, if deep differences exist in political society some of the differences are very often reflected *within* the two major parties more than between them (as the free vote on capital punishment in 1976 showed). Therefore, party leaders or caucus committee chairmen feel they must discourage many sharp, unequivocal articulations of certain complaints or reforms because prior party caucus agreement cannot be reached. If this dampening of political debate does occur, the Prime Minister and his Cabinet become aware that much of the debate itself is something less than a sharp and candid exchange of views and therefore less arresting intellectually or politically.

The Prime Minister And His Cabinet: Beyond the Transactional Interpretation

The traditional transactional interpretation of prime ministerial-cabinet relations emphasizes each Minister's personal (mostly regional) "representative" role in getting into the Cabinet and in explaining his leverage within it. (See the article by George Szablowski in this volume.) This interpretation is reflected by Macgregor Dawson in his *Government in Canada* and by many of the essays in *Cabinet Formation and Bicultural Relations* (edited by F. W. Gibson for the Royal Commission on Bilingualism and Biculturalism) on selected federal Cabinets up to and including 1948. It may be in keeping with S. J. R. Noel's identification of the necessary attributes of the Canadian consociational political network in this volume. Yet George Szablowski in this volume questions whether this transactional dynamic is not threatened in Cabinet by a policy-making system which, with the aid of programme budgeting and clear leadership from the Prime Minister in the Cabinet Committee on Priorities and Planning, emphasizes rationality and the supra-regional functions of policy.

There should be little doubt, however, whether in the transactional interpretations or the optimal policy process outlined by Szablowski, that the Prime Minister is more powerful than any of his cabinet colleagues. Since 1867, the Prime Minister's power to appoint and dismiss Ministers has always conferred considerable influence to him in his daily dealings with his colleagues, as well as in deciding government policy. It must be remembered that this power is not new; it is as old as the office. Conversely, however, Ministers can resign of their own free will and if enough Ministers do resign, a Prime Minister is in trouble. Prime Minister Mackenzie Bowell discovered this in 1895 when the resignation of seven of his Ministers ultimately led to his own resignation, and John Diefenbaker almost faced a somewhat similar dilemma in 1962. In the transactional model of prime ministerial-cabinet relations, the emphasis is on the fact that the Minister enjoys an independent source of power outside of

Parliament and his resignation can be harmful to the Prime Minister's control and influence in cabinet and in the party. Therefore according to this view, Cabinet Ministers who are acknowledged spokesmen for a significant regional or cultural group (such as French Canada), or an economic group (such as prairie farmers, labour or the business world) are colleagues a Prime Minister can ignore only after a careful scouting of the consequences. In the transactional model, the type of group that can threaten a Prime Minister through its cabinet "representative" will vary according to party and circumstances. Some might argue that the dominant French-Canadian spokesmen in some of this century's Conservative Governments have enjoyed less power than their counterparts in Liberal Cabinets, and vice-versa for spokesmen from the west since 1957.

There are, however, some obvious problems with taking the transactional interpretation too literally, even on its own terms. In most cases, Ministers are aware that a threat of resignation is a tricky weapon to use on a Prime Minister. A Minister's resignation over a dispute with the Prime Minister is usually an act which belongs to the politics of extremity; it is not a regular feature of most administrations. Also, the norm of collective responsibility of the Canadian Cabinet can strengthen a Prime Minister's power. By insisting that all members of Cabinet openly agree on policy, the Prime Minister is able to count on a unified public posture from his Cabinet. It is true that in the process of getting the Cabinet to agree on a policy or a position, a Prime Minister may find that he must accept a collective cabinet decision at some distance from his original hopes, but in some cases if the Prime Minister can set the vocabulary, research and priorities in which the decision is to be made, Cabinet will not stray too far from his wishes. (This is clearly implied in Bruce Doern's and George Szablowski's articles in this volume.) It must also be recognized that a Cabinet Minister is (if not institutionally or formally, at least psychologically) "responsible" to the Prime Minister since the Prime Minister chose him to be a Minister, and since the Prime Minister is the leader of the "vehicle" (the party) and represents the "phenomenon" (e.g., the Prime Minister's personality or the party ideology or platform) which put the Minister into office in the first place. It can also be argued that the Prime Minister deserves fidelity because he, too, will be responsible for the Ministers' actions.

All of this may be true, but this emphasis overlooks one fundamental reality about the transactional or optimal policy-making interpretations. Ministers, in fact, are institutionally responsible to the Cabinet, not to the Prime Minister. If a "presidential" system was to be installed in the place of present cabinet-prime ministerial relations, Ministers would be made responsible to the Prime Minister alone and not to the Cabinet at all. Deputy Ministers could report to the Prime Minister instead of to their Minister, and so on. In fact, in Canada Ministers have always been responsible to the Cabinet or its committees on most policy and public servants to their Minister; this remains true under Prime Minister Trudeau. Some of the centripetal forces this implies are explored in part in the articles by Mr. Schultz and Mr. Lenoski in this volume.

Perhaps it could be argued instead that Trudeau's approach to his office is a blend of the transactional and the optimal models. The huge increase in the size of the P.M.O. and P.C.O. since Mr. Trudeau took office is obvious to everyone. Those who believe that a blend is being pursued argue that this increase in staff is not a means of elevating the Prime Minister, but is a necessity if the Prime Minister is not to end up less an elected monarch than a constitutional monarch, reigning but not ruling. Officials working on regional problems in the Prime Minister's Office argue that their responsibilities are not meant to circumvent M.P.s or frustrate "political rationality," but are meant to give M.P.s more access to the Prime Minister's Office and, therefore, to the Prime Minister and the Cabinet.[16] Officials in the expanded Privy Council Office argue that their function is as much to help cabinet committees as it is to help the Prime Minister.[17]

Another way in which "political rationality" and "transactional" considerations may become important is through decision-making in times of a crisis. The Prime Minister is as captive as anyone else by crises; both he and the Cabinet must often make policy in circumstances not of their choosing. Prime Ministers can use crises to their advantage, as Gerald Wright shows in his study of Mackenzie King in this volume. However, Prime Ministers are more frequently made captive by events. For example, the Trudeau Government's action in March 1970 to prevent the sale of Denison Mines to an American company had to be decided at an emergency full cabinet meeting, without discussion in a cabinet committee and without the context of an overall Government policy toward the problem of foreign ownership of strategic resources.[18]

A broader complication is the influence of the public service over both the Prime Minister (and his P.C.O. and P.M.O.) and Ministers. The Prime Minister can be the recipient of as much information on a policy proposal as any Minister. But he may not have time to digest it all and most information reaches him after it filters through more intermediaries than even a Minister or a Deputy Minister would have to tolerate. Donald S. Macdonald, Government House Leader, revealed something of the extent of this information flow from July 1, 1968 to June 30, 1969, when in a statement to the House he said that the full Cabinet had met 70 times, cabinet committees had met 378 times, and 1315 cabinet documents had been considered in all. Some of this information will be dominated by the values of the optimizers (P.C.O., Treasury Board, etc.). Some will be dominated by those responsible for policy and administrating in departments. The Prime Minister must, therefore, be aware of the inclination of briefs to skew data in order to justify the choice that was initially preferred by the authors of the briefs. (See Mr. Chrétien's comments on this in Section III of this book.)

---

[16] Interview with members of the Prime Minister's Office and the Privy Council Office February 22, 1970, by this author. See also the last two articles in Section I of this volume.

[17] Ibid.

[18] Ibid.

The bias of information reaching the Prime Minister may arise from the optimizing values of the rationalists but they will also emerge from bureaucratic realities such as the policy inclinations of public servants in departments and from the imperatives of "sunk costs" where many programmes (such as many social welfare programmes) have a history and structure that make radical departures too time-consuming, too expensive, and allow for too few bureaucratic allies.

The Prime Minister and Federal-Provincial Relations

Another important set of limits within which the Prime Minister must operate are the policy patterns implied by the jurisdictional patterns of Canada's federal system. These are part of both the "institutional setup" and part of the "formula for political legitimacy" in the political system.[19] No Canadian Prime Minister or Federal Cabinet can make policy which clearly lies within the exclusive jurisdiction of the provinces unless all of the provinces agree to this intervention, or, as occasionally happens, the provinces affected make it clear they will tacitly accept not to define federal policy as interference. The amendment to the British North America Act to give the Federal Government jurisdiction over unemployment insurance in 1941 is an example of the first—the provinces' acceptance of funds for capital construction of hospitals or for post-secondary education may be examples of the latter. Of course, only infrequently are the Prime Minister and the Federal Government greeted with such provincial cooperation.

These are the more obvious and the more inflexible limits of federal-provincial realities on the Prime Minister. Yet there remains the vast unchartered region, the Prime Minister's style of operation within these limits. This style will vary but some regularities within these limits are worth hypothesizing. As Mr. Pearson reveals in the interview in this volume, he felt that his role as Prime Minister at conferences with Premiers was to "act more in a diplomatic capacity than in a political negotiating capacity". There is little doubt that it is imperative for the Prime Minister to play a diplomatic role in these conferences, regardless of the personality of the Prime Minister; he cannot view himself as a hierarchical leader primarily, if at all. These conferences have become a regular part of the Canadian political formula since 1945, and it seems that increased economic interdependence and improved communication between the provinces have made it more difficult to disregard the inter-relationship between not only the provincial governments and the Federal Government, but the relations between the provinces themselves. This leads to more federal-provincial meetings at all levels as well as at the heads of government level. The smoothest meetings may be those which discuss

---

[19] See Stanley Hoffman, "Heroic Leadership: The Case of Modern France", in (ed.) Lewis J. Edinger, *Political Leadership in Industrialized Societies* (New York, 1966).

incremental changes, technical questions or distributive policies[20] (these are policies which disaggregate the stakes and give something to everybody); but these meetings usually occur below the premier-prime ministerial level. At the top level, the debate and discussion seem to center on issues and proposals which the provinces tend to see as redistributive. And redistribution controversies rarely involve more than two sides, the money-providing and the service or subsidy-demanding. The rhetoric and argument of almost all provincial Premiers since 1945 in these conferences have centered (with varying degrees of intensity) on perceived redistributions, whereas distributive technical questions have in general been left to Ministers or public servants to work out.

This atmosphere places the Canadian Prime Minister not only in a defensive diplomatic capacity, as Mr. Pearson indicates, but it also implies other roles, orientations and techniques. For example in order to prevent, or at least to temper, redistributive perceptions by Premiers, the federal Prime Minister will usually try to couch federal proposals in "national unity" or "distributive" language or offer side payments to the non-indulged in order to lessen the possibility of a phalanx of provincial positions against the Federal Government's proposals. The Canadian Prime Minister knows that it is in meetings with Premiers that special attention will be given to perceived or real redistributions. These decisions are the most politically controversial of all federal-provincial issues and no Federal Government could allow them to be settled at a lower level without at least consent at the highest level. Therefore, the Canadian Prime Minister becomes involved in redistributive federalism although he may not have to become involved in distributive and technical questions of federal-provincial relations. The task of political leadership in the redistributive arena is one which places a high premium not only on diplomacy, but on handling emotional, even "quasi-separatist" threats. The style of politics at the redistributive level is not the quiet, technical, mutual non-interference style so characteristic of distributive politics.[21] (Since distributive policy is so hospitable and catholic it arouses less controversy.) An attempt to gain political capital in their home province and the nature of redistributive politics both imply that generalized federalist complaints, even veiled threats of separatism, will be a regular feature of the performance of certain Premiers in federal-provincial negotiations. A Canadian Prime Minister, as Prime Minister Trudeau intimated after the elections of the Bourassa Government in Quebec (April 26, 1970), may wish to turn all federal-provincial meetings into business-like conclaves of experts and reasonable men,[22] but the nature of redistribu-

---

[20] For an extended discussion of policy types, see T. J. Lowi, "The Functions of Government," in (ed.) R. Ripley, *Public Policy and Their Politics* (New York, 1966), pp. 29-30. Donald Smiley has suggested this in his examination of federal-provincial relations on such policies. See his *Canada In Question* (Toronto, 1975).

[21] *Ibid.*

[22] Toronto *Globe and Mail*, April 27, 1970, p. 1.

tive federalism will always make this difficult (even inappropriate). These imperatives may justify why the Federal Government seldom advertises or offers dramatic redistributions unless forced to do so; and it also indicates the necessity for any federal Prime Minister to define a sense of purpose and national mission in order that the non-indulged province will be willing to make the sacrifice. It should always be remembered here, however, as Michael Stein has pointed out,[23] that the federal Prime Minister has sources of support on these questions in the political system beyond the jurisdictional or tax authority given to the Federal Government in the B.N.A. Act. He need not rest solely on legal and constitutional defences. He can draw upon the power relationships in the informal structure of politics (e.g. the national appeal of his political reputation and of his party, the national organization of groups, and the national feeling in various regional, provincial and cultural groups). He can remind provincial Premiers that a proposed federal government "bargain" with the provinces is not a bargain offered by one government against ten, but a bargain which may have considerable support in the informal political structure and opinion within each of the provinces.

One concluding note about the Prime Minister's role in federal-provincial relations remains. The overall federal balance or "bargain" in Canada implies one cruel paradox for the Canadian Prime Minister. This structure has had a tendency to mute and discourage great national debates and resolutions on major questions of public policy and national purpose. Efforts by a Canadian Prime Minister to assert standards or to define programmes in advance of considerable preparatory agreements with provincial governments often submerge what might have been an educational and nation-defining exercise into a weary confused jurisdictional wrangle with the provinces. But to wait for this prior agreement is often to wait too long or to qualify the expectation of agreement so that few forceful or concrete proposals can be advanced by the Federal Government or by the Prime Minister. Leadership in presenting "bold and radical new proposals" by the Prime Minister or his Ministers on pressing national issues such as poverty, pollution, education, labour, agriculture, transportation, urban renewal, or economic regulation, if not impossible, is a delicate exercise because the provincial governments have concurrent, partial or almost complete jurisdiction in each of these areas. This said, however, the Prime Minister must try to play a persuasive role on national problems and this imperative is given further study in the article by Mr. Fletcher in this volume.

The Prime Minister's Unique Role As Public Persuader

A brief introduction to the various contexts of the Prime Minister as political leader will be given here. Any introduction would be incomplete,

---

[23] See M. Stein, "Federal Political Systems and Federal Societies", in (ed.) P. Meekison, *Canadian Federalism: Myth or Reality* (Toronto, 1968).

however, without recognizing the office's most unique resource and imperative—the Prime Minister's power to command national attention. All his other powers, including his power to appoint, to make policy initiatives, to call elections and to grant patronage, are seldom as absolute as they seem. His power to command national attention both during and between elections, if not absolute, is usually more potent than that of any other political leader in Canada and there are times when his words are greeted with an unusual amount of emotional intensity. Whether he likes it or not, the Prime Minister and his Government are objects of various emotional responses from the public. Intimations of this can be seen in Professors Winham and Cunningham's article in this volume.

The intensity of these emotional responses is sometimes astonishing. Writing of college students' attitude toward such leaders as university presidents, A. M. Nicholi has traced the frequent "implacable hostility, the uncontrolled rage" of students to the lack of leadership implied by the "remote, distant" university president.[24] Some of these intense feelings may emerge also in public responses to a Prime Minister because the "remote, distant" leader may provoke several categories of emotional responses apart from, and in addition to, the feelings caused by the political issues themselves. For example, frustration can be caused by a leader's lack of response to an issue and by his failure to understand the depth of feelings surrounding an issue. Leaders also can be subject to an increasingly intense distortion and vilification of motive, the more remote and invisible they are on an issue. Prime Ministers can make themselves and their Governments less remote not only by personal visits to the site of a crisis or a challenge but also by timely appearances on television. Murray Edelman has written in his *Symbolic Uses of Politics* how concern over symbolic issues can be lessened, even removed, by symbolic responses of the Government, by acknowledgments and the appearance of emotional involvement by the Government in the issue.[25] Edelman argues, however, that the depth of feeling over material issues can never be significantly lessened through symbolic acts. On material issues, Prime Ministers and Cabinet Ministers must not confuse expressions of concern with an effective response. In fact, these are precisely the issues on which Nicholi and others argue that a careful outline of the difficulties and restraints hedging a leader should be publicly outlined by the leader or, as Charles Taylor would argue, the leader must not rest on making acknowledgments or outlines of difficulties, but instead force his party and the bureaucracy to prepare radical change.

It should not be surprising, therefore, that two seeming functions of the speeches outside of the House of Commons by Pierre Trudeau in his years of office are to educate and to be symbolic. His speeches have ranged from abstract dissertations on responsibilities of levels of govern-

---

[24] A. M. Nicholi, "The Ordered University: A Challenge to Adult Leadership", *Harvard Bulletin*, November 16, 1970, pp. 29-30.
[25] See Murray Edelman, *The Symbolic Uses of Politics* (Illinois, 1964).

ment, to problems of national priorities, to specific arguments about clearly defined issues at a time and place carefully chosen for maximum effect. The Prime Minister then becomes a teacher on subjects which are often very general. (In fact, Prime Minister Trudeau seems to have used public appearances for this type of activity more than any previous Prime Minister.) There are also other explanations. Only the Prime Minister of Canada may reasonably expect that his speeches on general themes will be reported in the national media. Secondly, he may be trying to set the stage and to prepare his audience for actions on policy that he knows must soon follow. A general educational speech by the Prime Minister in the House of Commons will attract close media attention only in a time of crisis or over a controversial issue. However, the occasion of a personal visit and of a public address by the Prime Minister will likely attract more media attention than a similar speech in the House even if his theme is general and not topical. Ministers or M.P.s who deliver general educational speeches have difficulty in attracting media attention unless they are in the midst of a controversy or proposing solid policy. Only the Prime Minister, it seems, can command media attention for general public dissertations in an effort at broad persuasion.

The Prime Minister will use public appearances for obvious symbolic purposes. For example, speaking May 18, 1969 before a university audience in New Brunswick, he referred to the University of Moncton as "the living symbol of the resurgence of the French-speaking minorities, to whose support the government, which I lead, is firmly resolved to contribute". The symbolic value of the Prime Minister's appearance before the National Conference on Price Stability (February 9, 1970) was obvious and was meant to be obvious. When Timmins, Geraldton, Thunder Bay and Blind River received personal appearances from the Prime Minister September 26 and 27, 1969, these towns and cities in Northern Ontario were being singled out as a symbol of the Prime Minister's concern for these oft-forgotten parts of Ontario. The Prime Minister's visit to the north a few months after the "declaration of sovereignty crisis" was an investment of almost one week in a highly symbolic exercise. The Pacific tour of Mr. Trudeau was a self-confessed symbolic act. The purpose of these symbolic appearances may be to signify resolve (as in Moncton or on the topic of price restraint) or to show to a region or group that the Federal Government, and the Prime Minister's party in particular, can influence their lives.

In conclusion, then, the power of the Canadian Prime Minister in this one respect may not be unlike Anthony King's assessment of the powers of the British Prime Minister. After quoting Harry Truman, who while President of the United States said that the "principal power the President has is to . . . try to persuade people to do what they ought to do without persuasion", Professor King concluded, "for all the differences between the two countries and their political systems, that is almost certainly what the powers of the [British] Prime Minister amount to, too".[26]

Canada's Prime Minister, like the United States President and the British Prime Minister, has a unique responsibility and some capacity to persuade. It is in his use of the persuasive powers of the office that his performance may be the most important. His other powers are hampered by the restraints and imperatives of Canada's federal, social, economic and parliamentary system. If he is to dominate these contexts, any Canadian Prime Minister who fails to try to persuade both publicly and privately will be neglecting the very source of his potential for political leadership in Canada. In this sense, Presidents and Prime Ministers are similar. In this sense, all political leadership depends on the power of persuasion as much as on anything else. But even this persuasion is not without its restraints in Canada.

Compared with the British Prime Minister, the Canadian Prime Minister must be even more sensitive to sectional and limited identities. And compared to the United States President, the Canadian Prime Minister, being merely the head of the Government without authority as Head of State, must persuade not as a symbol of the nation but as the most important symbol of the Federal Government.

---

[26] A. King, ed., *The British Prime Minister* (Toronto, 1969), p. xii. Prime Minister Trudeau has not found this easy of course. His efforts at persuasion on complex topics such as the limits of the "free market economy" (in 1975) or the basis of the air controllers' settlement (in July 1976) have provoked as much increased tension as amelioration.

2

The Prime Minister and the Cabinet: History and Development*

FRED SCHINDELER

Introduction

To a very large extent Montesquieu's comment that "la constitution de l'Angleterre elle n'existe point" applies equally well to Canada when it comes to describing the place of the Cabinet in our system of government. The documentary part of our constitution is of no help whatsoever: the British-North America Act does not so much as mention this most important institution. And, while the non-documentary part of the constitution does at least describe the various parts of the executive branch of government, the relationships between these institutions are still evolving.

In this article, I would like first to define what is meant by terms such as the Cabinet, the Ministry, the Privy Council, and then go on to discuss the relationships between these various elements of the executive branch and their place in the total governmental system.

While the institutions by which we are governed are constantly changing their natures, usually one can understand something of their essence by discovering their origins in history. It would not be a complete travesty of history to say that effective power in Britain has passed from the monarch to Parliament; from Parliament to Cabinet; from Cabinet to public service; and now, from public service to Prime Minister. Certainly a similar pattern has evolved in Canada and a description of this evolution is perhaps the best way to begin defining terms.

Prior to the granting of responsible government in Canada in the mid-nineteenth century, the colonies of British North America were largely governed by a modified monarchical system. The Governor General, as the monarch's representative, ruled with the advice of an executive council which he appointed and which was responsible only to him. The

* Written for this volume.

acquisition of responsible government initially meant that the executive council would be drawn from the elected representatives of the people and that it would be responsible to those elected representatives. By 1867, when the provinces of Canada, Nova Scotia, and New Brunswick "expressed their Desire to be federally united into One Dominion under the Crown of the United Kingdom of Great Britain and Ireland, with a Constitution similar in Principle to that of the Kingdom", the principle of responsible government was firmly established. Both the British monarch and the Canadian Governor General retained only the right to be consulted, to advise and to warn. Only in dire emergencies, such as on the death of a Prime Minister, did the Governor General have any effective power and then only the power to choose a Prime Minister who still had to obtain the support of a majority in the House of Commons in order to remain in office. This "prerogative power" of the Governor General has only been exercised in Canada on two occasions: in 1873 when Lord Dufferin asked Alexander MacKenzie, as opposed to Edward Blake or Alexander Galt, to form a new ministry to replace that of Sir John A. MacDonald, and in 1926 when Lord Byng chose Arthur Meighen to form a new government instead of allowing William Lyon Mackenzie King a dissolution of Parliament.

The Letters Patent appointing the new Governor General in 1867 indicated that while it was not normal usage for the Governor to sit with his executive council it was not entirely improper for him to do so. When the draft Letters Patent of 1875 implied that the Governor General still had this right, the Minister of Justice pointed out that the precedents of over 20 years were clearly against such a practice.

Thus, there has never been a time in the history of the Canadian Federation when a Governor General ruled the country as the Monarchs of Britain once did. However, the Lieutenant Governors of the provinces have on occasion exercised considerable power and influence and have even taken a direct hand in government. The most notable example of this was during the early years of the province of Manitoba when the lack of parliamentary experience created a vacuum that was effectively filled by the first two Lieutenant Governors of that province for the first six years of its existence.[1] Following the "King-Byng thing" in 1926—when Governor General Lord Byng refused William Lyon Mackenzie King's request for a dissolution of Parliament—even the right to *advise* the Prime Minister was curtailed, at least during the quarter-century that Mackenzie King remained in office. An example of King's assessment of the restricted powers of the Governor General occurred during the conscription crisis of the Second World War when the Prime Minister received a letter from Major General, the Earl of Athlone, concerning certain correspondence between the Prime Minister and Colonel Ralston who was resigning from the Defence portfolio. The Governor General's letter included these two sentences: "There is actually nothing in the letters which could not be

---

[1] M. S. Donnelly, *The Government of Manitoba* (Toronto, 1963), p. 109.

published with the exception of references to certain meetings of the Cabinet. I read in the press, however, that you will make a statement on the whole subject and I hope this will satisfy the general public." That night, Mackenzie King put the following note in his famous Record:

This is the first time since his appointment as Governor General, that His Excellency has ventured to advise me even indirectly of the course to be followed in a matter for which I have full responsibility. I confess I felt some annoyance on the receipt of this letter for the reason that I am as sure as I am dictating that it has not been written by His Excellency without His Excellency having sought and acted upon advice from some other source. . . . [I]t looks very much to me as if the communications I have shown His Excellency have been communicated to London and that something had come back from that source. The purpose obviously is to assist Ralston in the immediate disclosure of what he has written and thereby to help his aim and make the situation more difficult and embarrassing for General McNaughton and myself. It is something new. . . . [2]

It is generally assumed that when effective power was removed from the hands of the Monarch (and in Canada from the Governor General) it was transferred to Parliament. However, Parliament is an unwieldy body to have responsibility for governing a country and if pure "convention government" or "parliamentary government" ever did exist in Canada it was only for a short period of time. The legislative assemblies of some of the provinces, on the other hand, have actually operated without direction from Cabinet for short periods of time. For example, during the first session of the first Parliament in Ontario, private members were more active than members of the Cabinet in bringing forward legislative proposals and, unbelievable though it may seem today, their proposals were passed. However, this was such a notable exception to the rule even in those unhurried days that the editor of *The Globe* was moved to remark:

If the Attorney General [the Prime Minister] is not careful it will soon become a doubtful point whether he or Sir Henry Smith [a private member] is to lead the House, and direct its legislation. [3]

In place of "parliamentary government" we developed a system known as "cabinet government". As the title denotes, under this system of government, effective power lies with the Cabinet, but what is this thing called the Cabinet?

Formally, the Cabinet may be described as a committee of the Privy Council and, happily, provision *is* made for this latter body in our Constitution:

There shall be a Council to aid and advise in the Government of Canada to be

[2] J. W. Pickersgill and D. Forster, *The Mackenzie King Record*, 1944-45 (Toronto, 1968), II, 208. This quote reprinted by permission of the University of Toronto Press and Mr. Pickersgill.

[3] F. F. Schindeler, *Responsible Government in Ontario* (Toronto, 1969), p. 177.

styled the Queen's Privy Council for Canada; and the Persons who are to be Members of that Council shall be from time to time chosen and summoned by the Governor General and sworn in as Privy Councillors and Members thereof may be from time to time removed by the Governor General.

It may very well be asked whether or not that provision adds anything to our understanding of the executive branch of government. The point is, of course, that the Governor General does not "choose", "summon" or "remove" any members of the Privy Council *except* on the advice of the Prime Minister.

Prior to Confederation, the colonial "Cabinets" had been styled "Executive Councils" and resignation from office had carried with it no continuing title of precedence; that is, contrary to British practice, a Minister who resigned his portfolio ceased to be a member of the Executive Council and hence lost his title of "Honourable." This is still the case in the provinces of Canada. However, at the federal level, once a person has been appointed to the Cabinet he retains the title of "Honourable" for life, just as those appointed to the British Cabinet retain the title "Right Honourable" for life. At the federal level, this also means that once a person has been appointed to the Cabinet, that is, to the Privy Council, he remains a Privy Councillor for life. Hence, the Privy Council is composed of current members of the Cabinet and all former Cabinet Ministers. From 1867 to 1891, none other than a Cabinet Minister was appointed to the Privy Council in recognition of services to the country in various walks of life, as was the case in Britain. Then, in 1891, two former speakers of the House of Commons and three former speakers of the Senate were sworn to the Canadian Privy Council. This became the normal procedure and in 1912 the practice was broadened by the appointment to the Privy Council of two members of the House of Commons who were supporters of the Conservative Government but did not hold ministerial posts. At that time, the *Toronto Globe* remarked: "The present innovation costs the country nothing and enables the Government to recognize some of its long and faithful supporters hitherto unrewarded."[4] Since that time the practice has been broadened further by the inclusion of prominent statesmen from other parts of the Commonwealth, members of the Royal Family, retiring Governor Generals, retiring provincial Premiers, and even the former leaders of opposition parties. According to the *Parliamentary Guide* for 1970 there were 130 members of the Canadian Privy Council, whereas the Cabinet itself has never numbered more than 30.

Obviously, a body such as the Privy Council can have no real role to play in governing Canada. It is the committee of the Privy Council known as the Cabinet which is usually considered to be the mainspring of government. The classic definition of the Cabinet was given by Walter

---

Toronto Globe, January 1, 1913, as quoted in Margaret A. Banks, "Privy Council, Cabinet and Ministry in Britain and Canada: A Story of Confusion", *The Canadian Journal of Economics and Political Science*, XXI, No. 2 (May 1965) p. 196.

Bagehot in the year of Canada's Confederation. He described it as "a combining committee—a *hyphen* which joins, a *buckle* which fastens, the legislative part of the state to the executive part of the state."[5] However,[*] in spite of its popularity, this definition is entirely misleading. The formal executive (in Canada, the Governor General) has devolved into such insignificance as to hardly warrant consideration in a discussion of the modern Cabinet. For all practical purposes, the Cabinet is the final seat of power for the authoritative allocation of values in the Canadian federal political system. A good start towards a definition of the place of the Cabinet in the modern parliamentary system was given by the Machinery of Government Committee in Britain in 1918 which gave as the functions of the Cabinet:

(1) the final determination of the policy to be submitted to Parliament;
(2) the supreme control of the national executive in accordance with the policy prescribed by Parliament;
(3) the continuous co-ordination and delimitation of the authorities of the several Departments of State.[6]

I have suggested as one reason why the Cabinet became the crucial institution of government that Parliament itself was too large and unwieldy to initiate and integrate policies in such a wide variety of areas. But, if Parliament was too big for the job, in a sense the Cabinet has proven too small. Members of the Cabinet are expected to sit in Parliament, take an active part in debate and answer the questions of members. In addition, they are expected to do long-range planning, initiate specific policy proposals, administer their respective departments and represent Canada in various international relations. The bare mentioning of the onerous responsibilities of the Government in office is enough to demonstrate that no Cabinet could possibly perform them all equally well.

Thus it was that during the Second World War and in the years since there has been another shift of power away from the Cabinet and to the permanent public service. In order to make intelligent policy decisions, the members of the Cabinet had to have a great deal of information and this could only come from the permanent civil servants. However, with information often goes power and, with the myriad of decisions confronting the Cabinet, those who had the information were more and more drawn into the actual process of policy formulation. Canada has been fortunate in being able to attract some of the brightest minds in the country to positions of power and influence in its civil service and it is entirely appropriate that these public servants should want to play a creative part in the development of the policies governing the country.

The point is that there are so many fields of government jurisdiction that demand a high degree of expertise that it is quite impossible for the Cabinet Ministers to have sufficient information to make intelligent

---

[5] Walter Bagehot, *The English Constitution* (London, 1867), p. 12.
[6] *Report of the Machinery of Government Committee*, Cd. 9230/1918, p. 5, as quoted in Ivor Jennings, *Cabinet Government* (London, 1959), p. 232.

policies. Those who have the information, namely, the public servants, are the ones who in many cases in fact make the policies. The impossibility of making policy without adequate expert information is well illustrated by Will Rogers' suggestion for getting rid of the German submarine menace during the First World War. "All we have to do," he said, "is to heat up the Atlantic to 212° fahrenheit then the submarines will have to surface and we can pick them off one by one. Now some damn fool is going to want to know how to warm up that ocean. Well, I'm not going to worry about that. It is a mere matter of detail, and I am a policy maker."[7] Someone else has suggested that a Deputy Minister is a civil servant who makes policies but does not get caught at it.

Senior civil servants perhaps reached the apex of their power vis-à-vis the Cabinet under the premierships of Louis St. Laurent and Lester B. Pearson. Instead of the Cabinet first coming to collective decisions as to policy, then shepherding the policy through Parliament and finally, supervising its implementation by the civil service, almost the reverse became the rule. Policy was initiated in a given department, or in the various departments concerned if it was not in the jurisdiction of any one department, and only when the senior civil servants had a firm proposal to make did it come to the attention of the appropriate Minister who then presented it to the full Cabinet. Having had little or no opportunity to evaluate the merits of the proposal before it was presented in Cabinet, the other members of the Cabinet usually confirmed the recommendation of the Minister primarily concerned with the policy. Senator Maurice Lamontagne, who served as a member of the Cabinet from 1963 to 1965, has said,

Generally speaking, at least until recently, when the Establishment [i.e., the senior civil service] was united behind or against a certain policy, its advice was accepted by the Cabinet; when there was a division of opinion between the officials of a particular department and those of the Department of Finance, including the Treasury Board, then the views of the latter would prevail at the Cabinet table.

I have seen situations when two important groups of the Establishment had not been able to reconcile their views on vital policy issues; in those circumstances, the Cabinet failed to act.

The special position of influence of the Establishment was underlined again not long ago when a minister was asked to resign by the Opposition for having consulted outside experts and when another minister had to resign for having reached a decision without proper consultation with his civil servants.[8]

The pre-eminent position that the senior bureaucrats occupied for a number of years in Ottawa is humorously illustrated in the story of the ambitious young man who wrote the Prime Minister asking that he be

---

[7] The Honourable Darcy McKeough, "The Relations of Ministers and Civil Servants", *Canadian Public Administration*, XII, No. 1 (Spring 1969), pp. 2-3.

[8] Maurice Lamontagne, "The Influence of the Politician", *Canadian Public Administration*, XI, No. 3 (Fall 1968), p. 265.

given a position in the Cabinet. The Prime Minister replied to the effect that he did not feel that the member had the depth of experience, the breadth of knowledge and the intellectual vigour required for such an exalted position. Undaunted, the young M.P. wrote back, "My dear Prime Minister, I believe that you misunderstood the nature of my request; high as my ambition can aspire, I do not expect to become a *Deputy* Minister; I merely want to be a Minister."

Since the accession of Pierre Elliott Trudeau to the position of Prime Minister, we have entered yet another stage in the evolution of our parliamentary system of government. In order to give the Cabinet some independence of the permanent civil service, Mr. Trudeau has enlarged the Office of the Prime Minister and the Privy Council Office (i.e., the Cabinet Secretariat) to a total complement of over 500 and has organized this enlarged staff into areas of specialization. In addition, the Privy Council Office has become the focal point for a number of task forces and royal commissions which have been charged with the responsibility of investigating certain areas of government responsibility and making recommendations thereon. Thus, for the first time in Canadian history, the Prime Minister has a source of policy initiation that is independent of the permanent civil service. Civil servants in the regular line departments can and do still make policy proposals but the important point to note is that these proposals can now be evaluated by experts who do not have the same points of view or vested interests as members of the regular departments.

The crucial question is whether or not this new independence afforded the Cabinet leads to an enlargement of the role of the Cabinet Ministers and, indirectly, to more responsible government or simply to prime ministerial government. Obviously, giving the members of the Cabinet a source of information and advice independent of the regular departments does give them a new position of power in relation to the permanent officials. However, the expansion of the Cabinet Secretariat in the Privy Council Office and particularly of the Office of the Prime Minister could also be used to give the first Minister an even greater position of strength vis-à-vis the Cabinet, so denying much of the essence of responsible government and turning our parliamentary system into a presidential form of government.

An observer of the British political scene believes that the doctrine of collective cabinet responsibility has already been turned inside out in that country. He notes that when Walter Bagehot wrote his classic, *The English Constitution*, collective responsibility meant the responsibility of a group of equal colleagues for decisions taken collectively, after full, free and secret discussion in which all could participate. He continues, "It now means collective obedience by the whole administration, from the Foreign Secretary and the Chancellor downwards, to the will of the man at the apex of power."[9]

When responsible government was granted to the Dominions in the nineteenth century, it meant essentially that the Cabinet was to be drawn from the popular assembly and that it should remain in office only so long as it could command a majority in Parliament. Each Minister was responsible for the administration of his own department, but the Cabinet as a whole was collectively responsible for all matters of policy. If the Cabinet could not remain united or if it lost the support of Parliament, the whole Cabinet, including the Prime Minister, was to resign. The fact that the Prime Minister could be removed from office at any time has always been considered to be the prime distinguishing feature of the cabinet form of government as compared to the presidential form of government where the President has a fixed term of office. However, Crossman and others now argue that the Prime Minister in a parliamentary system of government is in such a powerful position that he cannot be removed from office against his will by public, constitutional procedures. This seems to be the case in Canada, even when the governing party does not enjoy a majority in the House of Commons. Minor parties support the Government to assure their own survival and to avoid the costs of an election. As Professor Denis Smith has pointed out, when the minority Pearson Government was defeated in the House by its own carelessness in February 1968, the Prime Minister simply chose not to treat defeat as a matter of confidence, whipped in his followers and gained Creditiste support in order to command a majority.

What is it that gives the Prime Minister this power over the Cabinet and the House of Commons?

Some idea of the basis for the pre-eminent position he occupies may be gained from an official statement of his functions. The most recent minute of the Privy Council on this subject is P.C. 3374 of October 25, 1935, which reads as follows:

The Committee of the Privy Council, on the recommendation of the Right Honourable W. L. Mackenzie King, the Prime Minister, submit the following Memorandum regarding certain of the functions of the Prime Minister—

1. *A meeting of a Committee of the Privy Council is at the call of the Minister and, in his absence, of that of the senior Privy Councillor, if the President of the Council be absent;*

2. *A quorum of the Council being four, no submission, for approval to the Governor General, can be made with a less number than the quorum;*

3. *A Minister cannot make recommendations to Council affecting the discipline of the Department of another Minister;*

4. *The following recommendations are the special prerogative of the Prime Minister:*

---

[9] R. H. S. Crossman, "Introduction to Walter Bagehot, *The English Constitution*" (London, 1964), p. 53, as quoted in Denis Smith, "President and Parliament: The Transformation of Parliamentary Government in Canada", a paper presented to the Priorities for Canada Conference, Niagara Falls, Ontario, October 10, 1969, and appearing in this volume.

Dissolution and Convocation of Parliament: Appointment of—
Privy Councillors;
Cabinet Ministers;
Lieutenant-Governors;
(including leave of absence to same);
Provincial Administrators;
Speaker of the Senate;
Chief Justices of all Courts;
Senators;
Sub-Committees of Council;
Treasury Board;
Committee of Internal Economy, House of Commons;
Deputy Heads of Departments;
Librarians of Parliament;
Crown Appointments in both Houses of Parliament;
Governor General's Secretary Staff;
Recommendations in any Department.
The Committee advise that this Minute be issued under the Privy Seal, and that a certified copy thereof be attached, under the Great Seal of Canada, to the Commission of each Minister[10]

While this official statement is useful, it is far from complete. To gain a fuller understanding of the Prime Minister's position, one must examine the political context within which he gains and occupies that position.

In the first place, he is chosen by a popular convention of a major party and therefore can usually count upon the support of party stalwarts in the Cabinet, in the House of Commons and across the country. Removing a party leader is no easy task—as the Conservative Party found when it decided to be rid of John Diefenbaker. However, this does not explain how even a minority government is able to maintain itself in office. While there are many small ploys that the Prime Minister can use, such as the distribution of patronage, his fundamental weapon is the power of dissolution. Elections are expensive in terms of time, energy and money, and even at the best of times they are a risk. Certainly members of a party enjoying the fruits of office are not going to chance this for frivolous reasons. Similarly, while opposition parties may sound as though they want to go to the people, in reality few of them are keen to put their own careers and pocketbooks on the line much more frequently than at the conventional four-year intervals. William Lyon Mackenzie King understood this power of the Prime Minister all too clearly. During the conscription crisis mentioned above, he noted in his diary:

On the question of going to the people, Ralston has not reckoned at all, nor had he seen what two months' election campaign is likely to mean. British parliamentary practice is very sound in giving to the Prime Minister the right to appeal at any

---

[10] Quoted in "Cabinet Government in Canada: Developments in the Machinery of the Central Executive", *The Canadian Journal of Economics and Political Science*, XII, No. 3 (August, 1946).

time. It brings home to Ministers where their authority and power really come from.[11]

And, when he asked for and received Ralston's resignation he noted "[t]here was no comment at all" from the Cabinet.[12]

To end this introduction to the meaning of cabinet government, it may be useful to attempt to summarize the discussion thus far by means of pictorial models of the various stages through which our system of government has evolved. Of course, none of these models is in any sense an accurate reflection of the system it is meant to represent. They are meant simply to portray the main shifts in power relations as has been outlined above. For didactic purposes, I have assumed that Britain was first ruled by an absolute monarchy, in which effective control of the Privy Council (including the First Minister), the Parliament, the Public Service and the people was vested in the Monarch. This model of government may be depicted as follows, where the solid lines represent effective control and the dotted line represents the right to advise.

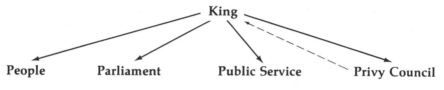

FIGURE 2-1

Monarchial Model

It has been argued that next we entered upon a brief period of Parliamentary Government (depicted in Figure 2-2).

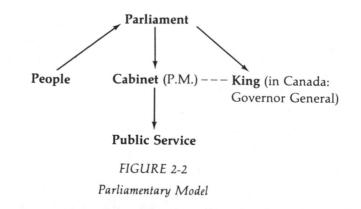

FIGURE 2-2

Parliamentary Model

---

[11] Pickersgill and Forster, *Mackenzie King Record*, II, 141. Reprinted by permission of the University of Toronto Press and Mr. Pickersgill.

[12] *Ibid.*, p. 194.

If not at its inception, certainly early in its history, Canada moved to a system of government wherein responsibility for the final allocation of values in those areas under federal jurisdiction was effectively lodged with the Canadian Cabinet.

Cabinet (P.M.)
Parliament
Public Service
Governor General
People

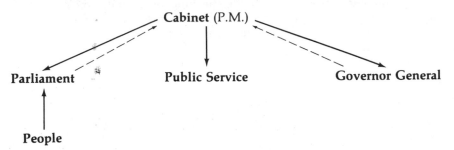

FIGURE 2-3

Cabinet Model

Complexity of government in the modern age meant that the Cabinet became increasingly subordinate to the Public Service which was the only institution large enough and expert enough to cope with the myriad of demands made upon government. Some have argued that this trend went so far that we in fact had a form of bureaucracy, or rule by the bureaucrats.

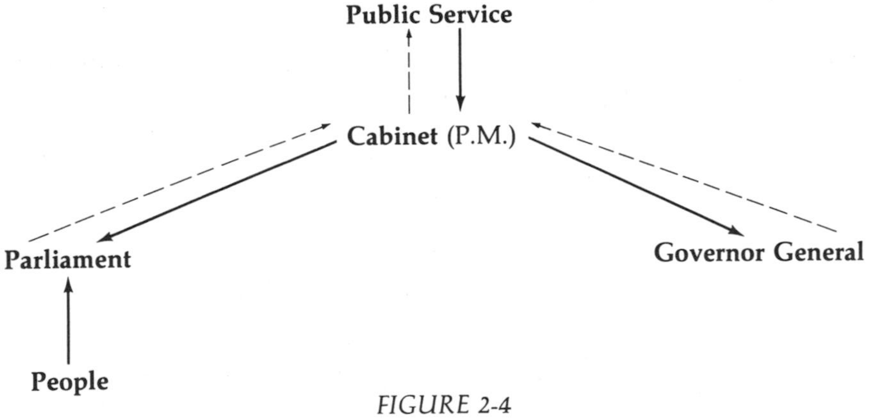

Public Service
Cabinet (P.M.)
Parliament
Governor General
People

FIGURE 2-4

Bureaucratic Model

Now Crossman and others say that we have moved to something like a presidential system where not only final executive power but also effective legislative power lies in the hands of one man, the Prime Minister.

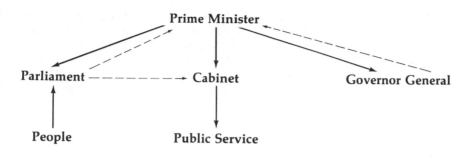

FIGURE 2-5

Prime Ministerial Model

Of course the problem with all of these models is that they are too static; they do not depict the dynamism of the system as a whole or the intricacies of the interrelationships between the various parts of the models, and therefore none of them can be said to be an accurate representation of reality. Perhaps dropping the Governor General, whose functions are for all practical purposes formal and ceremonial, adding political parties and putting the whole complex in a circular model gives a closer approximation of actual power relationships.

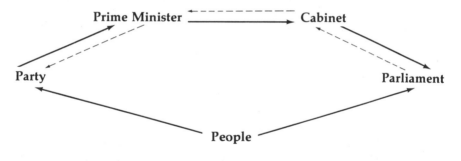

FIGURE 2-6

"Mod" Model

But, if the previous diagrams were less than accurate representations of the real world, this one is so confusing as to be meaningless. However, before we get inside this model to see what really makes it tick, we must understand the composition of the Cabinet: who is in it and why.

Representation

In view of the crucial role that is ascribed to the Cabinet in our system of government, it is extremely important to understand the considerations that determine which Canadians are chosen to participate in its deliberations. Although the Cabinet is not the combining committee that Bagehot thought it to be, certainly one of the roles that has been assigned to the Canadian Cabinet has been that of combining the interests of the various geographical regions of the country. In addition to these regional considerations, the evidence suggests that in choosing his cabinet colleagues the Prime Minister consciously attempts to make the Cabinet as representative as possible of the various social divisions within the country. But, by the time attention has been paid to the geographical, ethnic, educational, religious and occupational divisions in the country, how much room is left for consideration of such factors as talent and experience? In this section, the Cabinet's role as a representative institution is examined in order to evaluate not only how well it performs this function but also to suggest how efforts to succeed in this regard have affected the other roles that the Cabinet is expected to play.

Prior to Confederation, the colony of Canada had a long series of double-headed premierships which symbolized the bicultural fact of that Dominion. But in 1867 a new dimension was added by the inclusion of the Maritime provinces and dualism as a method of accommodation was no longer applicable. In its place, the principle of regional representation was explicitly accepted. For example, the delegates to the Westminister Conference of 1867 reached agreement not only on the size of the first Cabinet but also on the number of places to be allotted to each province; Nova Scotia was to have two, New Brunswick two, Quebec four, and Ontario five.[13] As new provinces have been added, the principle has been extended and conventions have grown up until now it is assumed that—with the possible exception of Prince Edward Island—each province ought to have at least some representation in the Cabinet.

From the beginning, certain portfolios were deemed to be more relevant to some regions and interests than to others. Thus precedents were established and expectations were built up which a Prime Minister could ignore only at his peril. For example, Marine and Fisheries came to be associated with the Maritimes while Agriculture went to western Ministers from 1911 to 1966. From 1888 until it ceased to be a department of government, the Department of the Interior was considered to be a western portfolio and when it gave way to Mines and Resources, the same practice was followed. The Labour portfolio has traditionally gone to a Minister with some knowledge of trade union organisation and so went to the Minister from the province with the largest number of organized workers, Ontario, from 1909 to 1950. Similarly, Trade and Commerce went to an Ontario Minister eleven out of seventeen times up to 1966

[13] Frederic W. Gibson, ed., *Cabinet Formation and Bicultural Relations: Seven Cases*, report presented to the Royal Commission on Bilingualism and Biculturalism, May 1966, II, 420. Much of the material in this section is taken from this report and from Richard Van Loon, *The Structure and Membership of the Canadian Cabinet*, Internal Research Project of the Royal Commission on Bilingualism, October 1966.

while, Postmaster General, Public Works and Justice have been identified with French Canadians.[14]

In the early days of Canadian history, the population was very small and the prevailing political philosophy held that Government ought to be responsible for the waging of war or the maintenance of peace in foreign affairs, the preservation of law and order and the grudging provision of those public works that could be provided in no other way. It was not until the concept of the positive state gained general acceptance that Government was charged with making broad social policy. In the early years, federal politicians were concerned with holding the country together and maintaining a working majority in the legislature. The distribution of patronage was conducive to both these ends and so it was that "the distribution of patronage was the most important single function of government."[15]

At first, the patronage in the hands of federal politicians consisted of many small items in a number of departments and it made good sense to apportion the portfolios to Ministers who could most effectively allocate the various types of patronage. This confirmed the tendency for certain portfolios to be associated with various regional groupings of political power. However, from the very beginning and even more noticeably since the advent of the positive state, certain forms of patronage have been national in scope. In particular, the business elites have been less concerned with the petty patronage of the broad service departments and more interested in matters of national policy affecting their ability to exploit the resources of the country. The considerations they sought from Government were preferential access to natural resources, tariff adjustments, government guarantees for corporate bond issues, subsidies and subventions, tax concessions and even trade treaties. The departments concerned with dispensing this kind of patronage were Finance, Trade and Commerce, and Labour, and it is not surprising that these portfolios have always gone to eminent members of the Canadian business community and usually to English-speaking representatives from Toronto or Montreal. When one considers the fact that French Canadians have never been accepted into the business elite of the country, it comes as no surprise that they have seldom held these portfolios. The Finance portfolio, for example, has never been in French Canadian hands. Of the first 24 men who held the portfolio, eight were from Ontario, six were from Quebec (all of them English-speaking), six were from Nova Scotia, two from New Brunswick and one each from Alberta and Saskatchewan.[16]

On the other hand, certain portfolios have consistently been held by French Canadians: Postmaster General, Public Works, Secretary of State, President of the Privy Council, Solicitor General, Marine and Fisheries,

---

[14] Gibson, *Cabinet Formation*, p. 402-3.
[15] O. D. Skelton, *Life and Letters of Sir Wilfred Laurier* (New York, 1922), II, 270. Quoted in Gibson, *Cabinet Formation*, p. 412.
[16] Gibson, *Cabinet Formation*, p. 405.

and Justice. Hoffman and Ward, in their study of legislative behaviour, learned that French Canadian M.P.s were much more constituency-oriented than were their English-speaking counterparts and that their constituents looked upon the provision of patronage as a much more important part of their role. Perhaps this explains why French Canadians have traditionally sought portfolios such as Postmaster General and Public Works, the two departments with the largest amount of petty patronage.

The fact that Canada has a dual system of law—the civil code in Quebec and British common law in the rest of Canada—has made the Justice portfolio of special interest to French Canadians from Quebec. This is the most prestigious of the seven portfolios that have consistently been held by French Canadians. It is the Minister of Justice who conducts all litigation for or against the Crown, who advises the departments on legal questions and advises the Governor General in council on the exercise of the important executive powers. The giving of royal assent, the disallowance of provincial legislation, the granting of petitions of rights, the prerogative of mercy and the appointment of judges all fall under the authority of the Minister of Justice.

In addition to having a certain number and type of portfolios assigned to French Canadians, certain English-speaking Prime Ministers have had a French Canadian as their principal lieutenant or co-Prime Minister. The practice began with Georges Cartier in Macdonald's Cabinet but perhaps this was not so much because he was French as because of his past relations with Macdonald in the Cabinets of the Province of Canada for a dozen years and his general weight and influence. When he passed from the scene no French Canadian Minister rose to take his place. Then, when the Liberal period of dominance began in 1896, there was no need for a French lieutenant since the Prime Minister was himself a French Canadian. But Sir Wilfred Laurier did not need an English co-leader either and instead treated his English Canadian colleagues as spokesmen of their respective provinces and sections, reserving for himself the position of chief spokesman for "La Belle Province".

In 1923, Ernest Lapointe became the federal leader of the Liberal Party in Quebec under Prime Minister William Lyon Mackenzie King and by 1935 he was firmly established as King's principal lieutenant, influencing the whole range of government activity and not solely those aspects of government activity pertaining to Quebec. When Lapointe died, King went outside of the officials of the hierarchy and recruited a Montreal corporation lawyer, Louis St. Laurent, to be his new lieutenant. Over the next seven years King groomed St. Laurent as he had groomed Lapointe so that St. Laurent's succession to King in 1948 was really a foregone conclusion.

The closest anyone has ever come to being an English Canadian lieutenant to a French Canadian Prime Minister was C. D. Howe under St. Laurent. But, while there can be no question about the pre-eminent position occupied by Howe during the St. Laurent regime, it appears likely that as the senior Minister from Ontario and, more generally, "the Minister of everything" he would have been a confidant and lieutenant to any Prime Minister, French or English Canadian.

Although their relative share of cabinet positions has varied over the years, French Canadian representation in the Cabinet has recently increased. In the first Cabinet, the French Canadians received three places out of 13, or 23 per cent, much below the French-speaking population of Canada. Adherence to the principle of proportionality would have required that the French be given three and one-half Ministers. But, as Professor Morton has observed, while all Cabinet Ministers are not in fact equal, they are persons and "it is impossible to employ persons as vulgar fractions."[17] For over a quarter of a century, the French Canadian proportion of the Cabinet remained fairly constant, usually somewhere between 21 per cent and 23 per cent. Borden kept the same number of French Canadian Ministers, but, by increasing the number of western Ministers, he reduced the French Canadian share to 16 per cent. For a period of almost three years, from 1917 to 1920, French Canadians had only one Minister in a Cabinet of 22, giving them only 4.6 per cent of the total. In 1920, Meighen restored the number of French Canadian Ministers to three but this was still only 14 per cent of the Cabinet when the French constituted 28.4 per cent of the total population. This situation was rectified when Mackenzie King took over with the French Canadian M.P.'s constituting a majority of his party. He appointed five French Canadians at first and then added another from New Brunswick giving a total of six or 33 per cent when the French share of the population was still only 28.8 per cent.

French Canadian representation fell back to three under the next Conservative Prime Minister, R. B. Bennett, but it was restored to five out of sixteen (31 per cent) with the King ministry of 1935. Prime Minister St. Laurent attempted a balance in the Cabinet that reflected the numerical size of the two groups of the population at large but, generally, French Canadian representation fell slightly below that ideal.

The Conservative Prime Minister, John Diefenbaker, started out in 1957 with only one French Canadian out of 17 Ministers but this increased to two out of twenty during his first term of office. In 1958, he added a third French Canadian and in 1959 a fourth was added in a Cabinet that usually contained 23 or 24 members. Thus, for most of his term of office, Diefenbaker gave the French Canadians approximately 17 per cent of the cabinet seats.

When the Liberals returned to office under Lester Pearson the number of French Canadian positions in the Cabinet was increased to an all-time peak: ten out of 26 ministers or 38 per cent. In addition, the French Canadian representation was distributed over a wider geographical area than ever before: six from Quebec, two from Ontario, one from New Brunswick and one from Manitoba. Pierre Elliott Trudeau has maintained similar proportions so far as French Canadian representation is concerned; his major innovation has been the fact that he has assigned a number of important portfolios to his French Canadian counterparts.

But the French were not the only ethnic group in Canada which sought and gained representation in the Canadian Cabinet. In 1871 the Irish constituted the second largest ethnic group, and for generations it

---

[17] W. L. Morton, "The Cabinet of 1867", in Gibson, *Cabinet Formation*, p. 41.

became vital to have an Irish Catholic representative in the Cabinet. For example, Arthur Roebuck advised Mackenzie King that "it would be a great mistake to take Paul Martin in preference to McCann as representative of the English-speaking Catholics. Martin was preferable as a man but we could not pass over that large section of the country." When Mackenzie King had telephoned Dr. McCann about the appointment, he recorded his misgivings in his diary:

... [H]is manner was anything but the kind of manner I like. Unfortunately he is really the only Irish Catholic sufficiently outstanding to bring into the government. Paul Martin would be regarded as a French rather than as an English-speaking representative.[18]

For at least a half-century, the Scottish Canadians constituted approximately 15 per cent of the population and usually managed to fill approximately 25 per cent of the seats of the House of Commons and a similar proportion of the cabinet posts available. However, they have either so melted into the Canadian social structure or have so taken over that they are no longer considered to be a peculiar ethnic group. In any case, the fact that over half of the non-French Canadian Ministers now prefer to be known simply as Canadians seems to indicate a decreasing tendency for the fragmentation of the Canadian political elite along ethnic lines.[19]

The growing ethnic heterogeneity of the Canadian population, particularly since the Second World War, is illustrated by the fact that groups hitherto unrepresented in the Cabinet are now seeking and obtaining representation. For example, during the Diefenbaker era, much was made of the fact that Michael Starr represented in the Cabinet the interests of the Ukrainian community.

So far as the representation of religious groups is concerned, the most obvious conclusion is that the Catholics have been slightly under-represented. According to Professor Van Loon,[20] they have held only 34.8 per cent of available cabinet seats while their mean proportion of the population has been 41.5 per cent. Up to the time of his own research, 87 of the 88 French Ministers had been Catholic. But only 11.4 per cent of the English oriented Ministers had been Catholic, compared to 23.3 per cent who were Anglican, 21.2 per cent who were Presbyterian, 27.8 per cent Methodist and the United Church, 13.9 per cent who belonged to various other Christian groups and .4 per cent who were non-Christian. The Anglicans have always been over-represented, having never had less than 17.3 per cent of the seats in the Cabinet but never constituting more than 16.1 per cent of the population. Similarly, until they joined the United Church in 1921, the Presbyterians always held at least 20 per cent of the

---

[18] Pickersgill and Forster, Mackenzie King Record, I, 364 and 370.
[19] Richard Van Loon, The Structure and Membership of the Canadian Cabinet, Internal Research Project of the Royal Commission on Bilingualism, October 1966, p. 49.
[20] Ibid., pp. 77-86.

available portfolios while constituting only approximately 16 per cent of the population. The most over-represented have been the members of the United Church and earlier the Methodists and Congregationalists who have constituted from 13.6 per cent to 20.1 per cent of the population but who have held no less than 30.6 per cent of the English ministerial posts and, since the War, 40.4 per cent.[21] And perhaps the most under-represented have been the Jews who received no recognition in the Cabinet until Herb Gray was appointed Minister Without Portfolio in 1969.

A close study of the patterns of religious representation at the federal level and in the Province of Ontario[22] indicates that religious representation in Canadian Cabinets fairly accurately reflects representation in the popular legislatures but the legislatures, in turn, do not accurately reflect the religious composition of the population as a whole. Apparently geographical, socio-economic and ethnic factors in the make-up of the House of Commons and likewise in the composition of the Cabinet result in a disproportionate representation of the dominant Protestant religions in the key positions of the political elite structure. Certainly the under-representation of Catholics has not been the result of discrimination on the part of Protestant Prime Ministers: ministerial appointments by Catholic Prime Ministers were 29.8 per cent Catholic whereas those by all of the Protestant Prime Ministers have been 36.5 per cent Catholic.

So far as occupation is concerned, the traditional road to a political career in Canada has been through the professions and particularly through law. Among English-speaking members of the Cabinet, 55 per cent to 60 per cent have followed professional careers. Among French-speaking Ministers the proportion has been fully 90 to 95 per cent. Before the Second World War, 70 per cent of French Canadian Ministers were lawyers and since that time the proportion has only fallen to 60 per cent. Professions apart from law have contributed 10 to 13 per cent of our Ministers.

Among English Canadian Ministers the merchandizing trades have always had a substantial representation and, as Canada has become more industrialized, the manufacturers have slowly increased their representation from 1.6 per cent to 9.4 per cent of the English posts.[23] The finance and insurance fields have held a steady if small proportion of cabinet posts whereas the service industries have had only negligible representation. The public service and labour have negligible representation and agriculture has been steadily under-represented at the federal level, although it has had strong representation in some of the provincial Cabinets. With increased urbanization, the representation of agricultural interests in the Cabinet is bound to decrease. Before 1896, 14.1 per cent of all Ministers were urban born, whereas since 1948 30.4 per cent have been born in urban areas.

---

[21] *Ibid.*, p. 81.

[22] Fred Schindeler, *Responsible Government in Ontario*, pp. 37-8.

[23] Van Loon, *Structure and Membership*, p. 91.

While it may not be a significant factor in the minds of the Prime Ministers who appoint the Cabinet, previous political experience would conceivably be an important factor in the success with which a Cabinet Minister performed his various functions. It is therefore interesting to note that only 23.5 per cent of all federal Cabinet Ministers have had municipal political experience and only 30.2 per cent of the French Canadians and 40 per cent of the English Canadian Ministers have had provincial legislative experience. But even these figures are exaggerations. When the Federal Government was created in 1867, almost everyone in the federal House of Commons who had had previous legislative experience had gained it at the provincial level and this situation continued for some time whereas, since the Second World War, only 18.4 per cent of the English and 8.5 per cent of the French Ministers had such experience.[24] Thus, while it might seem logical on the surface, it appears that progression from local, through provincial to federal political office is not the most popular route to federal political office. And this is even more true of French Canadian Ministers. Indeed, it seems that would-be French Canadian politicians must first choose whether they are going to try to make their mark in the federal or the provincial arenas for there does not seem to be very much movement between the two.

Efficiency in Decision-Making

Earlier, I listed the functions of the Cabinet as they were seen in 1918 by the Machinery of Government Committee in Britain but this really gave only a hint of the responsibilities of the Cabinet. Since the end of the Second World War, demands for an increasingly positive involvement on the part of government in the affairs of the country have increased the Cabinet's burden enormously. The problems attendant upon rapid urbanization and industrialization have also created new technical problems that did not confront Cabinets of an earlier day. Indeed, the workload facing the Cabinet today is such that there is some doubt as to whether or not it will be able to carry it out or whether some of its work will simply be passed on to others by default. In 1968, Mr. R. G. Robertson, the Clerk of the Privy Council and Secretary to the Cabinet, made this assessment: "It seems to me that without changes from present methods there is a real risk of a steady reduction in the efficiency of government in coping with growing needs together with a shift of effective decision-making from the ministers, where it ought to be, into the hands of civil servants."[25]

Perhaps the most visible aspect of the Cabinet's work is the direction that it must give to Parliament. The legislative proposals coming before Parliament are of two types: private bills and public bills. As their names suggest, private bills deal with specific matters of concern to only a small

---

[24] *Ibid.*, p. 112.
[25] R. G. Robertson, "The Canadian Parliament and Cabinet in the Face of Modern Demands", *Canadian Public Administration*, XI, No. 3 (Fall 1968), p. 276.

portion of the population, such as bills for the incorporation of companies, etc. The Cabinet has no particular role to play with respect to these bills and the current practice is for the bulk of them to be introduced by Senators in the Upper House. The public bills are of two types: financial and non-financial. Financial bills can only be presented to the House by a Minister of the Crown, whereas non-financial bills may be introduced either by a Minister, in which case they are called government bills, or by ordinary members of the House of Commons, in which case they are called private members' bills. These latter take up a relatively small proportion of the time of the House and have very little chance of success. All of the other public bills, both financial and non-financial, are government bills and reflect government policy. The preparation of these bills and their defence through three readings in the House of Commons is a large part of the legislative work of the Cabinet.

Once Parliament has passed a bill it becomes an Act of Parliament and some idea of the growth of government functions may be gained by comparing the number of bills in two five-year periods, 1957-1962 and 1963-1967. In the first five-year period Parliament never sat for more than 174 days in any session and never passed more than 64 bills in any session. In the five-year period 1963-1967, the House sat for as many as 250 days and in the last session of the period it passed 97 bills. The largest printed volume of statutes in the first period had 583 pages of legal text but by 1966-67, the statutes passed took up 1,273 pages of text.

But for Parliament to pass an act is not sufficient. The act is usually only a very general statement of Parliament's intent and before it can be given real effect a great deal more work must be done to make it applicable in specific cases. This work is usually done by means of minutes or orders in council, which are basically rules and regulations passed by the Cabinet. Ordinarily there are 5,000 or 6,000 of these orders in council passed each year and the preparation and discussion of these must be considered a part of the legislative role of the Cabinet.

Another well-known part of the work of members of the Cabinet is answering Members' questions each day in the House of Commons. In Canada, it is possible for Members to ask questions without giving previous notice of their intention to do so and this means that Cabinet Ministers must be prepared to answer questions on a wide variety of government activities under their respective jurisdictions. While the actual time spent in the House answering the questions is not great, the preparation of answers to expected questions is a time-consuming matter for Ministers, even with the expert assistance of their civil servants.

A second major function of Cabinet Ministers it to administer the various departments and agencies of government and to ensure that their activities are somehow co-ordinated. Often a number of departments will have programmes that relate to common problems, and it is no small task to avoid useless duplication and ensure that all of these programmes serve a common end.

In recent years, there has been a more concerted effort to maintain continuing liaison with the provinces to ensure the co-ordination of related efforts and to avoid disputes, or at least to resolve them should they arise. So important and continuous a function has this become that in 1969 the old railroad station across from the Chateau Laurier in Ottawa was refurnished to provide a permanent meeting place for federal-provincial and inter-provincial conferences, and a special section of the Cabinet Secretariat has been set up to deal with this aspect of the Cabinet's work.

Canada's relations with foreign countries are also the responsibility of the federal Cabinet Ministers and as Canada continues to assume a larger role in world affairs this aspect of the work of the Cabinet becomes increasingly important.

But, in addition to all of these general areas of responsibility, members of the Cabinet are first and foremost politicians who must maintain their positions in their party and also keep in close touch with their constitutents. When all these pressures are taken into account, it is no wonder that people close to the centre of power wonder whether or not it is possible for the system of government we enjoy to survive. To end this section, recent steps taken to make our cabinet system a more efficient decision-making institution will be described.[26]

One of the earliest reforms in Cabinet decision-making was the creation of a system of standing committees. Cabinet as a whole could only meet for so many hours in each week and it was therefore impossible for the whole Cabinet to review all policy recommendations and proposals for legislation or orders in council. The result was that policies were worked out by the senior officials and the Minister of one department and were presented to the full Cabinet only in the very final stages of their development. Other Ministers were thus effectively cut off from participation in the development of the policy but were nevertheless expected to provide collective support for it. This system also made it difficult for the Cabinet to perform the co-ordinating function that logically falls to it. A system of cabinet committees enables Ministers to participate in the collective decisions of Cabinet in a much more meaningful way than was previously the case.

Committees were first used to a significant extent during World War II but the system fell into disuse again following the war. It was revived under the premiership of Lester B. Pearson and was formalized and improved under Prime Minister Pierre Elliott Trudeau. The Prime Minister appoints members to the nine standing committees of Cabinet and, while some Ministers are members of more than one committee, it is usually possible for at least two committees to meet at the same time. Virtually every proposal to go before Cabinet has first been discussed in a committee which has its own staff. Other Ministers are allowed to attend if they have an interest and, in any case, they are informed of the deliberations of all committees through the circulation of documents.

---

[26] The following information has been garnered by means of personal interviews with a number of senior public servants and Cabinet Ministers.

Once a committee has come to a decision on a matter, it is usually communicated to the Cabinet by means of a cabinet document submitted at a regular meeting. Unless there has been a division of opinion in the committee itself or unless some other minister challenges the committee's recommendation, its proposal is confirmed by Cabinet. Since all proposals are circulated to members of Cabinet prior to their meetings, ministers have time to give notice of any objections they may have. Normally approval is routine, allowing the Cabinet to process in a very few minutes items that previously would have involved lengthy discussion, so freeing the cabinet to discuss matters of larger policy import. To a large extent, the co-ordinating function of Cabinet is also carried out by the committees.

The Privy Council Office provides staff for the nine committees and senior officials of the various departments are sometimes invited to attend meetings. Perhaps the most important standing committee of Cabinet is the Priorities and Planning Committee which is chaired by the Prime Minister and serviced by a staff of four members of the Privy Council Office who report to the Deputy Secretary of the Cabinet (Plans). Sometimes referred to as the "Inner Cabinet", this committee attempts to set priorities for the government and to plan for the orderly development of integrated policy. It is also charged with the evaluation of ongoing programmes.

The Federal-Provincial Relations Committee is also chaired by the Prime Minister and has a staff that reports to the Deputy Secretary of the Cabinet for federal-provincial relations. A third committee of Cabinet, the Treasury Board, is a statutory committee established under the Financial Administration Act. It is empowered "to act on all matters relating to finance, revenues, estimates, expenditures and financial commitments, accounts, establishments, the terms and conditions of employment of persons in the public service, and general administrative policy in the public service." It carries out continuous economic analyses and presents these and its economic forecasts to the Priorities and Planning Committee. The other committees of Cabinet are the Economic Policy and Programmes Committee, the Social Policy Committee, the External Policy and Defence Committee, the Legislation and House Planning Committee, the Culture and Information Committee and the Science Policy and Technology Committee which is also a statutory committee. With the exceptions noted above, the secretaries of the committees are usually assistant secretaries of Cabinet.

In addition to the nine standing committees of Cabinet there are a number of special committees, some of which are relatively permanent but which meet on an ad hoc basis as circumstances dictate. For example, the Special Committee of Council meets to pass routine orders in council; the Labour Relations Committee deals with serious strikes that require some kind of government response; the Tax Reform Committee worked on the White Paper on Taxation that was released in 1969 and will remain fairly active until those policies have been implemented; and the Committee on Western Grain will probably remain active in the foreseeable future.

The head of the Cabinet Secretariat is both the Clerk of the Privy Council and the Secretary to the Cabinet. However, the purely formal functions that have traditionally been associated with the Privy Council Office are now performed by the Assistant Clerk of the Privy Council who is responsible for such matters as checking the statutory authorities for orders in council and serving as a formal communication link between the Governor General and the Cabinet. The Secretary of the Cabinet is thus free to serve much more "political" functions.

The Cabinet Secretariat is divided into two main divisions: one for operations and one for plans, each headed by a Deputy Secretary to the Cabinet. There is also a Deputy Secretary of the Cabinet for federal-provincial relations. The Operations Division of the Secretariat itself has four sections, each headed by an Assistant Secretary of the Cabinet: the Economic Section, the Social Policy Section, the External Policy and Defence Section, and the Cultural and Information Section. The assistant secretaries to the Cabinet in these sections serve as the secretaries of the relevant cabinet committees. In addition, they usually have three or four assistants who maintain close contact with the departments in their respective areas of responsibility, attend inter-departmental meetings and ensure the close co-ordination of policy development and administration in other ways. These contacts with the departments put them in good positions to ensure that the Office of the Prime Minister is informed on a wide range of specific topics.

Given the pre-eminent position of the Prime Minister within the total system and the crucial importance of the Cabinet as a whole, the relationships between the Office of the Prime Minister and the Privy Council Office are perhaps the most important in the whole process of government in Canada. The very fact that the two offices occupy contiguous space is indicative of the very close relationship that exists between them. The Office of the Prime Minister (P.M.O.) needs to be informed at all stages in the development of policy and also seek the opportunity to directly influence the determination and administration of policy when it sees fit. The P.M.O. is thus not only concerned with questions of planning and priority but also with ongoing governmental programmes. To ensure that the P.M.O. inputs are present at the very earliest stages of policy formulation, representatives of the P.M.O. sit on various inter-departmental committees that are struck for various purposes and on the committees of the Privy Council Office (P.C.O.). However, the liaison between the two offices is not left to these informal channels of communication; there are a number of regular meetings which ensure a close working relationship between the two offices. Perhaps most important is the meeting that the Prime Minister holds each day with two members of the P.M.O., including the Principal Secretary, and two members of the P.C.O. This group discusses day-to-day problems and serves as a general co-ordinating committee for the two offices. Once a week there is usually a larger meeting, involving at least three representatives of the two offices, which is concerned with planning.

The Principal Secretary is a political appointment and is therefore not a part of the regular civil service. However, at approximately $60 000 per annum, he is one of the highest paid public servants in Canada and his position is one of the most influential in the country. He attends the senior staff meetings of the P.C.O. every week, although no representative of the P.C.O. attends the thrice weekly staff meetings of the P.M.O. Thus, the Prime Minister's point of view is continually and directly expressed in the Cabinet Secretariat. The senior staff meetings of the P.M.O. are quite "political" in nature and are attended by the Prime Minister's Parliamentary Secretary whereas the P.C.O. senior staff meetings tend to be less concerned with political strategy, giving their attention more to policy and administrative matters.

The P.M.O.'s general position is that any attempt to create formalized policy groupings within that office would be a useless duplication of effort because they are able to call upon the resources of the policy groups in the Cabinet Secretariat of the P.C.O. There are, however, at least three people in the P.M.O. who are primarily concerned with policy generation. Some members of the P.M.O. do develop specialisations but these flow from the personal talents and interests of the people involved and from the government priorities at any given time.

In addition to creating a close working relationship with the Privy Council Office and with the departments of government, the Office of the Prime Minister must maintain close liaison with outside groups and the party in office. To assist it in this task, the P.M.O. first created "regional desks" for Quebec, the Maritimes, the West and for Ontario. (The desk for Ontario was finally established in 1970.) These were to keep the Prime Minister in touch with M.P.s and party workers in the various areas to serve as trouble shooters for the Prime Minister. They were to be the Prime Minister's means of communication with various interests and with groups who want to be certain that the Prime Minister is aware of their views but who, at the same time, can be used by the Prime Minister in a variety of ways. Because these desks have been perceived by some to downgrade Members of Parliaments' regional roles, this work is not now done officially by "desks" per se in the P.M.O.[27] At the same time, as has already been mentioned, the centre of power and influence has shifted away from Parliament and to the Cabinet and the Prime Minister so that interest groups are no longer satisfied with contacts with M.P.s. However, it is physically impossible for every interest group to have a direct access to the Cabinet, let alone to the Prime Minister himself. Thus, the "regional desks" were set up to create a new vehicle of communication between Government and people, guaranteeing that the views of important segments of the community get to the heart of the decision-making process. Naturally, Members of Parliament, and particularly opposition

---

[27] Editor's Note: This sentence has been added by the editor.

Members, opposed this extension of the Office of the Prime Minister as an infringement of their sphere of operations. Similar criticisms were levied against Information Canada which was set up following the recommendations of the Task Force on Government Information Services in an attempt to improve the flow of information from government to citizens and to encourage the participation of citizens in federal government decision-making. Opponents to the development did not question the need for improved communication with the people but insisted that the improvements ought to have come in the system of representation through the provision of additional staff to M.P.s to man constituency offices and to deal with the complaints, questions and suggestions that they receive in Ottawa. Supporters of the agency claimed that the improvement in the position of the Member of Parliament through a restructured committee system and increased research assistance would give Members of Parliament a positive role to play, albeit a much different role than had traditionally been assigned to them.

The relationships between the Office of the Prime Minister and the central office of the party in power in many respects parallel the relationships between the P.M.O. and the P.C.O. At least once a week there is a meeting of members of the P.M.O. staff, the President of the Liberal Federation and the Parliamentary Secretary to the Prime Minister. These meetings ensure that the P.M.O. is constantly informed of the opinions of the extra-parliamentary party. Of course, the resources of the P.M.O. are also of tremendous assistance to the Liberal Party when it comes to manning the party machinery and planning party meetings. When such political meetings are held, there is usually someone from the P.M.O. in attendance. Perhaps the most important method for ensuring some kind of responsibility to the extra-parliamentary party and insuring that the party receives the information and support it requires are the special meetings of the "Cabinet" and party. These are not to be confused with regular cabinet meetings. They are not organized by the P.C.O. but by the P.M.O. and, in addition to the Ministers, the chairman of the parliamentary party caucus and the head of the extra-parliamentary party attend. These are purely "political" meetings aimed at setting overall goals and priorities.

Another interesting method of maintaining liaison between the Prime Minister and the Cabinet, on the one hand, and the extra-parliamentary party, on the other hand, are the various regional "troikas". Each troika is composed of a Minister from that region, a representative of the Liberal Party caucus from that region (if there is one) and a representative of the Liberal Federation. They usually meet at least once a month and, to ensure that the Prime Minister's point of view is known and that the discussions of the troikas are communicated to the Prime Minister, someone from the P.M.O. attends each of these meetings.

Given all of the resources of the Office of the Prime Minister and of the Privy Council Office, the organization of which is depicted in the following article, and the relationships that exist between these institutions and with the extra-parliamentary party, one is better able to assess the role of the Prime Minister in our system of government. Elected by a national party conference, supported by a majority in Parliament who are largely dependent upon him for their continued existence in office, supported by a Cabinet selected by himself and holding office at his pleasure, able to call upon the resources of the well trained and well paid professional staff in the Cabinet Secretariat, informed and advised by the extra-parliamentary party hierarchy and assisted by an elite personal staff, the Prime Minister occupies a position of power in some ways unrivalled even by the President of the United States.[28] We may call it parliamentary · government or cabinet government but in fact we have prime ministerial government in Canada. How, and to what extent this Government is kept responsible to the people is one of the most important questions to be studied by political scientists in Canada today.

---

[28] R. Neustadt, "White House and Whitehall" and "Some Canadian Notes on 'Whitehall and White House'", by T. Hockin, both in this volume.

3

Policy Planning and Support for Ministerial Decision-Making in Canada*

PREPARED BY THE PRIVY COUNCIL OFFICE, OTTAWA,
1975

The Policy Planning Process

Within the context of Cabinet government individual Ministers are responsible for identifying issues of future concern and for planning the development of policy responses for matters falling within the mandate of their particular departments. This individual responsibility is transformed and shaped into governmental policy in the Cabinet where Ministers fulfil their collective responsibility for the Government of Canada. The Prime Minister and his colleagues work together to ensure the compatibility of particular proposals and to take a broader view of such proposals in an effort to provide direction and lend coherence to the work of government. Individual Ministers are assisted by their departments to identify issues of future concern. The Cabinet receives similar assistance from the Privy Council and Federal-Provincial Relations Offices.

The identification by government departments of issues or concerns related to responsibilities within a given portfolio is perhaps the more traditional method of identifying issues. The recognition of future concerns of this kind tends to be part of the normal, on-going activities of the department undertaken in the course of administering a given policy or program. Such concerns can, under most circumstances, be taken account of by adjusting or redirecting existing programs. In some instances, where the issue raised is significant, a new policy or program or a substantial review of existing policies or programs may be required.

---

* This paper was prepared by the Privy Council Office early in 1975. The extract here begins at page 6 of that paper. The editor wishes to thank the Privy Council Office for permission to publish this material.

48

The process by which Ministers collectively identify future concerns is more complex due to the variety of institutional, political, social, personal, and bureaucratic forces with which a Minister must deal. To assist Ministers in this regard, a responsive procedure for planning at the Cabinet level has evolved that endeavours to reflect and make use of the general attitude of Ministers towards overall policy in an effort to identify or at least indicate the policy areas or issues that warrant action by the Government.

The planning procedures help in translating Ministers' views on the longer term objectives and priorities of the Government as well as on current issues and problems into concrete policies and proposals. This is easier said than done. The collective development by Ministers of an agreed overall appreciation of their concerns is a difficult undertaking, as is the organization and selection of areas or sectors where major specific and significant change is desired—i.e., setting the Government's priorities. The priorities serve as a guide for the activities of the Government and as a means of responding to the requirements of particular problems, although they must themselves be changed as the political, social, or economic climate alters.

Ministers collectively are assisted by the Plans Division in the Privy Council Office in formulating a general orientation, and in identifying future concerns and considering the importance and priority of such concerns. Each year an attempt is made to bring together in a single memorandum proposed priorities for the Government. The sources for this paper include the following:
- individual interviews with all Ministers in order to gather their views as to the desired direction in which the Government should be moving, and to gather their perceptions of pending issues and concerns;
- concerns and issues identified by Ministers in Cabinet and Cabinet Committee meetings, and by general contact and liaison with the advisory staffs of the Prime Minister and Ministers;
- the proposals of the Party holding office (made in an election or resolutions passed at a Party policy convention); and,
- legislative items of an essential, urgent nature and those carried over from previous sessions of Parliament.

An additional means of gathering Ministers' perceptions of this sort has been to hold an informal, day-long meeting of Ministers. No background papers or formal agenda are prepared. The meeting provides Ministers with an opportunity to discuss their political program and identify issues of future concern. The conclusions reached at such meetings are recorded and form part of the process of arriving at an agreed program for the development and implementation of policy proposals.

It is usual to summarize and synthesize Ministers' perceptions and other proposals relating to priority problems in a Memorandum to the Cabinet. This Memorandum looks at changes and modifications in the Government's on-going activities, suggests new lines of endeavour, assesses the progress achieved in meeting established priorities and attempts to provide an appreciation of future needs.

Usually this memorandum also draws upon the findings of Cabinet Planning Studies, which, at the direction of Ministers, endeavour to ascertain whether governmental action is required over the longer term in a particular area of national importance. The memorandum summarizes the status of each of these studies and suggests additional studies or other changes based upon the views of Ministers, experience of other Cabinet Planning Studies, and an appreciation of future concerns. Following consideration by the Prime Minister, the memorandum is presented to Ministers for discussion.

After discussion in Cabinet the document together with any additional changes is presented to Deputy Ministers, who are asked to respond by describing how existing programs, or variations of such programs, might contribute towards the Government's priorities, and by proposing new programs. Following further detailed consideration by Cabinet of the responses of Deputy Ministers, Ministers will usually agree to a set of priorities to extend over the next two to four year period. In this way it is hoped to ensure (i) that departments are aware of the Government's priorities, and (ii) that the Government's priorities can be given practical expression in the form of new programs or alterations to existing ones. The priorities are reviewed every six months to determine whether they continue to reflect Ministers' concerns and are adapted to changing circumstances. At the same time progress in achieving the priorities is reviewed. The priorities affect the allocation of new government expenditures, the order of the legislative program, the development in departments of new policies, and the direction of existing expenditures and programs.

An attempt is made to ensure the continuing applicability of the Government's policies and programs through an instrument known as a Cabinet Evaluation Study. These studies, instigated by Ministers, examine whether on-going policy and programs are operating effectively and efficiently and continue to reflect Ministerial concern and the Government's priorities.

The process of identifying issues, developing policies, and marshalling priorities is only useful if it serves to enhance the development and implementation of programs. To the extent that government is a reactive undertaking it is particularly important that aids to planning be developed as fully as possible to provide a workable framework that can assimilate the imperatives and unforeseen events of society in general with the activities of government in particular. The procedures serve a particularly important need in helping to improve the effectiveness of Ministers, and, by extending their control of, and influence over, the direction of policy, they help to clarify the nature of Ministerial concerns and their relative priority.

The Privy Council Office and the Federal-Provincial Relations Office

The Cabinet and its Committees (both standing and *ad hoc*) are serviced by a series of Secretariats, which together compose the Privy Council (or Cabinet) Office, which is headed by the Secretary to the Cabinet, who is the senior public servant and the principal source of official advice for the Prime Minister. Within the Privy Council Office there is an organizational division between Operations and Plans that parallels the Cabinet Committee system. The separate Federal-Provincial Relations Office, headed by the Secretary to the Cabinet for Federal-Provincial Relations, contains a Secretariat that serves the Cabinet Committee on Federal-Provincial Relations. The sectoral committees of Cabinet are serviced by individual secretariats located within the Operations Division. The Cabinet Committee on Priorities and Planning and the Cabinet Committee on Legislation and House Planning are serviced by Secretariats located within the Plans Division.

The recently created Federal-Provincial Relations Office is headed by the Secretary to Cabinet for Federal-Provincial Relations, who has the full rank of a senior Deputy Minister and reports directly to the Prime Minister. In addition to providing the Secretariat for the Cabinet Committee on Federal-Provincial Relations, the Federal-Provincial Relations Office is responsible for co-ordinating the federal government's relations with the provinces and assists in the continuing process of constitutional review and development.

The Privy Council and Federal-Provincial Relations Offices (a) provide secretariat services to the Cabinet and its committees, (b) advise the Prime Minister as to the manner in which specific issues complement or conflict with overall policy, and (c) because of their central location act in inter-departmental and advisory and co-ordinating capacities. They facilitate the development of policy by assisting Ministers and their departments to co-ordinate their efforts, and attempt to make available an evaluation of particular proposals based on the perspective from their vantage point at the crossroads of Cabinet where all new proposals must meet.

There is a real but subtle distinction between the Prime Minister and the Cabinet in the services provided by the Privy Council Office. As noted, the Office provides the Prime Minister with advice keyed not so much to the specifics of the proposals set forth by individual Ministers as to endeavouring to ensure that they are compatible with the overall orientation of the Government and with related policies and programs. In servicing the Cabinet and its Committees the Privy Council Office fulfils a secretariat function, having only an informal role in responding to requests for advice from these bodies. In some instances, however, the Privy Council Office prepares briefings of an advisory nature for the chairmen of Cabinet Committees, similar to those provided to the Prime Minister. As a central agency the Office frequently services, chairs, or is represented on interdepartmental committees established to report to the Prime Minister or to Cabinet on specific issues of concern to a number of departments even though the substance of such an issue may be substantially the prime responsibility of one department. Similar services and advisory activities are fulfilled by the Federal-Provincial Relations Office.

In addition to the Cabinet Committee Secretariats located in the Privy Council and Federal-Provincial Relations Offices, the Prime Minister himself has available other sources of official advice in the Privy Council and Federal-Provincial Relations Offices. The Machinery of Government section, which is part of the Plans Division, has special responsibility for advising the Prime Minister on matters involving government organization that fall within the terms of his prerogative to allocate functions between Ministers, and to oversee periodic reorganizations of the government, subject if necessary to Parliamentary approval. The Prime Minister is also served by special sections that advise him on constitutional questions, and on senior governmental and quasi-governmental appointments for which he and his colleagues are responsible.

The Prime Minister's Office

The Prime Minister's Office and the offices of individual Ministers provide advice of a more political nature and means of co-ordinating Ministerial perceptions of what the Government should be doing and how well it is performing. The Prime Minister's Office is headed by the Principal Secretary to the Prime Minister and contains a number of professional advisers, who, working in co-operation with the Privy Council Office assist the Prime Minister in developing proposals with regard to priorities for discussion in Cabinet. The Office contains a policy planning unit headed by an Assistant Principal Secretary to the Prime Minister. The unit provides political advice to the Prime Minister on major policy issues. The unit has a close working relationship with the Privy Council Office, and it places most of its emphasis on an understanding of what the Government wants to achieve during its mandate and on an appreciation of the likely public perception of, and reaction to, proposed government policies and programs. The Prime Minister's Office also liaises with the offices of other Ministers with regard to general governmental and political matters. There is considerable potential to develop these offices more along the lines of providing general advice on policy matters in the context of the philosophical approach of the political party whose members form the Government.

Ministries of State

It has not always been possible for central mechanisms such as the Privy Council Office and the Treasury Board's Secretariat to provide the degree of co-ordination necessary in defined fields of particular complexity that cut across individual department mandates. Because of the growing complexity and multi-departmental involvement in particular policy sectors (for example, science and technology and urban affairs) responsibility for the development of policy advice in such areas has been given to separate Ministers of State. These Ministers are members of the Cabinet, but the Ministries they head have no program functions and their role is strictly limited to the development of policy advice in order to assist the development and co-ordination of the programs of individual departments. Their credibility depends upon their awareness of particular issues as they affect different departments of the government, and upon their ability to offer departments a persuasive means of grappling with such issues. It is most desirable that they be staffed not only by sector policy experts, but also by officials with experience of central agencies, who are aware of the limitations of any one sector when juxtaposed with others, and who maintain close contacts with officials of central agencies who have a broader appreciation of overall trends and requirements. The Ministries have no control over budgetary allocations similar to that possessed by the Treasury Board for purposes of financial management. They do, however, provide the Treasury Board with an evaluation of departmental budgets pertaining to the areas of the particular Ministry's policy concern.

Conclusion

The support and coordination of the processes whereby Ministers set priorities for government and decide the content and means of implementating programs described in this paper have been evolved over time as part of the larger effort to meet the requirements of governing a modern state in accordance with the principles of parliamentary and Cabinet government. It is important that the procedures be responsive so that government may adapt readily to new demands and unforeseen circumstances. Although the procedures are dynamic, evolving constantly, they also provide and continue to provide continuity, which itself provides licence for experimentation and innovation. This responsiveness founded in continuity lies at the heart of Cabinet government.

4

The Shape of Government in the 1980s: Techniques and Instruments for Policy Formulation at the Federal Level*

MICHAEL PITFIELD

Recent Developments

To forecast what might be coming in terms of techniques and instruments for policy formulation at the federal level in the 1980s, it is perhaps useful to cast back and consider recent developments in this field and the options for the future such developments may have opened or closed.

Scarcely ten years ago, our "Chairperson" today was Chairman of the Economic Council of Canada and Ministers and officials were still digesting his First Annual Review. Ten years is not a long time and yet the last decade has seen a great number and a wide variety of techniques and instruments for policy formulation brought into play at the federal level.

Whatever appearances may sometimes have been, these developments were not as ad hoc as some might think. The federal government long ago recognized the need to come to grips with the modern problems of big and complex government but it opted to meet this requirement in an evolutionary rather than a revolutionary manner. Government had little doctrine to guide it and very little public acknowledgement of the need for change to support it. It considered the requirement for change unavoidable, but was determined that changes should be consistent with the

---

* This selection, with the omission of prefatory remarks and a few other pages, is a speech delivered by Mr. Michael Pitfield, the Clerk of the P.C.O., on August 30, 1975, to the annual meeting of the Canadian Institute of Public Administration and subsequently published in the Institute's journal. The editor wishes to thank Mr. Pitfield and the Journal for permission to republish here.

genius of our system and sensitive to the existing political and administrative climate.

Subject to these parameters, new techniques and instruments of policy formulation were badly needed for at least four reasons:

— first, for greater efficiency: the tendency of growth in government was seen to be too easily responsive to demands as they arose and too ad hoc in terms of simply adding this or that to the already existing structure.

— second, for greater effectiveness: the ad hoc and responsive tendency of growth in government was seen as a further complication for Ministers and officials in dealing with already complex problems. There was little, if any, view of the whole. Important, but not always obvious, inter-relationships were ignored, with results that were frequently wasteful, sometimes counter productive, and on occasion even undermined the basic tenets of the system.

— third, the massive and complex mechanism that resulted from these tendencies was less and less subject not only to political direction but even to political control. The need for efficiency and effectiveness sometimes became itself a justification for by-passing political control. The sheer size of government gave rise in some quarters to doubts of its susceptibility to political direction.

— fourth, and finally, the development of new techniques and instruments was necessary to more clearly define the objectives of government. Big and complex government led to a muddling of objectives. Each Minister or official coming to the well often sought to answer every possible objection along the way, to bring with him the widest possible support, so that in the end his proposal appeared to be all things to all men and its original purpose was obscured.

Objectives

The search at the federal level in recent years for greater efficiency, greater effectiveness and greater political control and direction has been paced by an effort to more clearly define objectives and to ensure that government programs are more tightly related to objectives.

In talking about objectives, I do not want to get into a debate about the desirability of planning, the utility of abstract goals, and whether or not intellectual sophistication has any place in something as strictly practical and realistic as politics and government. Suffice it to say that I am talking about objectives simply in the sense of a government knowing what it wants to do in the over-all. With this in view, the defining of priorities—that is, of objectives set in their relationship to one another— has evolved during the past ten years through a number of forms, each more clearly a process of iteration than its predecessor.

The process has a number of aspects:

First, it is a process of Ministers talking to one another and trying to define what they, as the Government of the day, are trying to accomplish. This is a highly political discussion. It encourages the relationship of the government's objectives to the ideas of the party in power. To support them in their deliberations Ministers individually rely upon their advisers and collectively, upon their party organization and the Prime Minister's Office. In this connection, one of the important developments in recent years has been the increasing recognition of the Prime Minister's Office as clearly apart from the Privy Council Office, with its own distinct staff and mandate.

Second, it is a process of Ministers talking to the bureaucracy: reconciling short-and long-term objectives, clarifying the linkages between objectives and programs, considering ways and means, distinguishing between the possible and the impossible, more often than not between what can be afforded and what cannot. In this aspect of the priorities process, the key roles of the Privy Council Office, the Treasury Board and the Department of Finance are obvious and there have been important developments in these departments in recent years. No less crucial is the increased importance of the role of each deputy minister as the senior policy adviser to each Minister. I will return to this subject later on.

As the priorities process reaches out to the bureaucracy and beyond, it becomes more and more a question not merely of knowing what it is the government wants to do, but of the government communicating and dialoguing with regard to its objectives. Thus,

Third, the priorities process involves discussions between Ministers and their supporters, particularly the members of the House of Commons and of the Senate. The role of the Parliamentary Secretary has been developed for this amongst other purposes and there has been greater use of the caucus, with various techniques being established for consultation with that body and its committees.

Fourth, the development of the priorities process is influenced by debate between the government and the Opposition. It has played a part in the development of Parliamentary procedure in recent years, particularly in the use of committees. It has also been furthered by new arrangements for the funding of research by political parties and by the development in the Parliamentary Library of research facilities available to Members of Parliament and Senators.

Fifth, the priorities process has brought to the fore the need for much greater consultation between the government and the public and here a host of techniques and instruments, new and old, have been tried. Bills introduced for discussion but not passage, White Papers, Green Papers, Task Force Reports and a wide variety of study papers have been published. Advisory Councils have been set up in virtually every department and considerable use has been made of periodic meetings of Committees of Ministers with national associations, and of Commissions of Inquiry, not only in particular cases but also on a more or less standing basis, as in the case of Indian claims and food prices. During the past ten years a Science Council has been put in place along with the Economic Council and funds have been set aside for the development of the independent Institute for Research on Public Policy. New approaches have been taken to grant-giving, as in the case of Opportunities for Youth and New Horizons, and grants of all kinds to voluntary organizations and to individuals, not only for support in service to the community but also for research and for dialogue with the government on the development of public policy, have grown enormously. The desire of government to include as much input as possible from the private sector has not been the only factor in the use of consultants and the increasing bias of government towards buying rather than making, but it has been an important element in this trend.

Some of these techniques and instruments have served more than the single purpose with which I identify them. Increased facilities for Members of Parliament and Senators in terms of travel, offices and supporting services, have—for example—furthered at least two of the purposes I have mentioned. Some of the techniques and instruments have not succeeded and a number—like Information Canada, for example—are still in the course of being worked out. But their overall thrust has generally been a positive effort by government to define its objectives more clearly and to communicate its objectives more thoroughly.

Implementation

Lying behind general efforts to define and to communicate are a series of more detailed changes that have significantly affected the organization and process for decision-making, for departmental administration, for senior personnel management and for intergovernmental arrangements.

With regard to the organization and process for decision-making, the principal developments have been extensively documented in papers prepared some years ago by my predecessor, Mr. Gordon Robertson, and by the then Principal Secretary to the Prime Minister, Mr. Marc Lalonde.

One significant change was the increase in the size of the Cabinet. Some argued that the Cabinet should be smaller and therefore, supposedly, more efficient. In going in the opposite direction, it seems to me that government opted for a larger political interface with the bureaucracy and the greater capacity to control and direct that it was hoped this would permit.

Closely associated with the increase in size was the decision to rationalize the substantial number of Cabinet Committees that existed ten years ago into a design of 4 coordinating committees (i.e. Priorities and Planning, Federal-Provincial Relations. Treasury Board and Legislation and House Planning) and five operating committees (i.e. Economic Policy, Social Policy, External Policy and Defence, Science, Culture and Information, and Government Operations). The number of special and ad hoc Cabinet Committees was drastically reduced and has been kept to a minimum. By sub-dividing a large Cabinet into sub-committees with this specialized structure, it was possible to obtain many of the benefits of a smaller, tiered Cabinet without having to try to duplicate the British system, which is not really appropriate or workable in Canada with its federal structure, regional identifications and geographical distances.

These changes in the Cabinet Committee system cannot really be appreciated except in the context of related processes: agendas that are circulated to all Ministers ahead of time, documents that examine a full set of alternatives, and the attendance of senior officials at the committees, permit all Ministers and their most senior advisers to be aware of what is going on, and also encourage a degree of countervailance in the advice Ministers receive and the debate given to ideas before they are accepted.

It will also be recognized that the techniques chosen for the expansion of the Cabinet permitted the introduction into decision-making at the highest level of a number of new ministers and departments for what have since become recognized as major concerns of government: Energy, Mines and Resources, Regional Economic Expansion, Consumer Affairs, and the Environment, to name a few. In the concept of the Ministry of State, an effort was made to develop a mechanism without program responsibilities which would be essentially a secretariat, possibly of a temporary nature, for policy advice on a particular problem of a multidepartmental character.

You will note that as one speaks of the organization and process of decision-making, one is drawn inevitably into matters of administrative process and organization. In this area, it seems to me that government during the past ten years has sought to maintain a neat balance between reinforcing the authority of the great departments of state as lead departments, while at the same time encouraging a degree of countervailance by more specialized departments increasingly equipped with the back-up in expert skills necessary to the effective presentation of their points of view. I should emphasize the use of departments rather than the creation of more or less independent agencies. In keeping with the essential genius of our Constitution, the federal government has chosen to maintain a Cabinet-oriented system of decision-making rather than resorting to a more administrative and quasi-judicial, a less political system.

Thus, Finance has been maintained as the department responsible for stabilization policy and a court of last review for economic policy, while at the same time there have been created a number of new economic departments, such as Regional Economic Expansion, Manpower and Immigration, Consumer and Corporate Affairs, Energy, Mines and Resources, Environment—each with its own expert skills. Likewise, External Affairs has been maintained as the lead department of foreign policy, while the Interdepartmental Committee on External Relations has been established as a forum for departments whose fields of interest have important foreign policy aspects. The Department of Justice has been maintained as the Government's principal legal adviser, while the Department of the Solicitor General and the Department of Consumer and Corporate Affairs have been established as quasi-legal departments: the one with an orientation towards problems of anti-social behaviour and the other with an orientation towards economic law. The Department of National Health and Welfare has been increasingly developed as a lead department in social policy, and the Treasury Board has been created as an independent body with considerable authority over the whole process of resource allocation.

The Treasury Board is the crucial forum for ensuring that programs are closely related to objectives, for making sure that the government's policy levers are in fact connected with the rest of the machine. The concern is not only for the allocation of dollars but of manpower. During the last ten years, it has been recognized in government that personnel resources are every bit as important and in some respects much more important than financial resources. With regard to both we have seen the full bloom of the seeds of the Glassco Commission. A real effort has been made to let the managers manage.

In taking this path, it is clear that government at the federal level has opted for a strong and professional public service active not only in administration but in important aspects of policy. Rather than the development of a sizeable partisan sub-strata in the bureaucracy,—of in-and-outers responsible to a particular political party for policy development and the control and direction of the civil service—we have seen the development of the Senior Executive category and, to monitor certain aspects of its administration, a committee of private sector executives first under the chairmanship of Mr. J. V. Clyne and now headed by Mr. Allan Lambert. The Lambert Committee, as it is now known, has also played a vital role in monitoring the administration of what is known as the GC category, that is, all the appointees of the Governor in Council.

In recent years a lot of care and attention has been given to the GC category. In this group lies the key to better administration and better policy development. Occasional appointments to the GC group from the private sector are made to provide a vital leavening of rare skills and fresh outlooks, and this is a good and necessary thing, but the very large majority of appointments remains, as it should, from within . . . .

Looking Forward

Looking forward, then, I expect that a process of iteration aimed at the definition and communication of government objectives, such as the priorities exercise, will continue to develop. I believe this will happen whatever Government is in power, for though the results of the process are intended to bear the stamp of the Ministry of the day, the process itself is not partisan. Its sole purpose is to ensure that big government will have,

— for communication with the public, a focus for discussion;
— for its decision-making process, a basis for coordination;
— for its administrative process, a basis for resource allocation, for management and for policy and program evaluation;
— for its personnel process, a basis for the designation in our system of

government of individual responsibility and authority, and for performance assessment; and,
— for the intergovernmental process, a basis for consultation.

As regards more particular forecasting, the techniques and instruments that we will need for policy formulation can perhaps be envisaged better in their purpose than in their actual design.

In relation to the decision-making process and organization, it seems to me that we have yet to really come to grips with our most difficult problem of scarce resource allocation, namely the effective use of Ministers' time. The developments of the last ten years have been costly in terms of what they have detracted from the performance of ministerial duties in other than policy-making: communicating with the public, representing their constituencies, and administering their departments, for example. However great the importance of policy, it seems to me no more important in the total scheme of things than these other duties and if they are not to suffer it is vital that we find means of helping Ministers discharge them.

The same problem emerges in another form when dealing with the administrative process and its organization. The time of Deputy Ministers is also a rare and valuable commodity. The events of recent years have increased enormously the demands upon them as policy advisers and departments have not yet fully developed mechanisms for supporting the policy-making process.

A deputy minister is by definition both policy adviser and administrative head. Few people are greatly endowed with both skills. One of the dilemmas of senior personnel policy is to determine the balance of each that a job requires. It is difficult to find someone with the precise qualifications, and what fits today can be entirely contradicted by events tomorrow. It may be that in recent years administrative skills have not received all the recognition they deserve. I suspect that some of the concern now being expressed about the effectiveness and efficiency of departmental administration is rooted in the emphasis upon policy formulation in the last few years. Equally, however, I believe that that concern reflects uncertainty as to the rules governing accountability in this day of big government—not so much uncertainty as to what the rules are but as to what they should be. I expect that hard thinking is going to have to be done with regard to the accountability of senior officials both in terms of whom they are accountable to, and of what they are accountable for. We are brought back to the question of objectives, for accountability presumes criteria against which to measure success or failure and criteria presume that objectives have been identified and communicated.

We have been through a period of considerable organizational change and I would hope that the next few years will be largely a time of consolidation that will permit the changes of recent years to work their way through the system. As regards dealing with the growth, the magnitude and complexity and pressures of government, many important options have been taken that would in any event seem to discourage experimentation with more drastic organizational changes such as have been tried in other countries. I have in mind such measures as the creation of tiered Cabinets, of super departments or of the hierarchical structuring of central agencies to actually control departments. Recent changes in the techniques and instruments for policy formulation at the federal level have been at pains not only to preserve but to reinforce the subtle interplay of individual ministerial and collective ministerial responsibilities that are the essence of our system of government. Ours is a confederacy of institutions coordinated by various techniques for common objectives, not rigidly commanded but enriched by a certain degree of built-in countervailance. In this sytem I would suggest that new techniques and instruments for policy formulation during the next few years will benefit from an emphasis on a more efficient process and a higher quality of personnel.

I would stress particularly greater concern for personnel—selection, training, promotion and *demotion* are in the final result as determinant in policy formulation as techniques and instruments are likely to be. We have to become better personnel managers and, indeed, we must expect that, in some respects, personnel policies will themselves become instruments of policy as, for example, in the case of bilingualism, of equal opportunities for women, and perhaps even of management-labour relations generally.

Finally, in terms of the intergovernmental process, I suggest that what we have seen in the problems of bigness and complexity posed for one government, we have really yet to entirely perceive in the relationship of all our governments acting and reacting upon one another. Today, and indeed for some years past, it has been the provincial and municipal governments that have been setting the pace in growth. A recent speech by the former Deputy Treasurer of Ontario has underlined the degree to which federal, provincial and municipal actions can be at odds with one another. In this context, the increasing frequency of federal-provincial conferences in recent years can perhaps be seen as more or less of a realization of the need for intergovernmental agreement as to what governments are trying to do and the communication of that message to the people. To the extent that this is so, we will doubtless be seeing in the years ahead increased efforts at a multi-government process of identification of objectives, not entirely unlike that which I have described as going on at the federal level.

Some Questions

What the techniques and instruments for dealing with all these problems will be could be very much influenced by how much the practitioner and the theorist can get together. There are a host of matters on which we could benefit from some hard and thorough thinking.

On objectives, there is, for example, the fact that the time frame for decision-making in big government more and more surpasses the traditional term of a government in power, so that those who face election today must pay for long-term benefits to the public at the very real cost of perhaps not being elected.

In matters of decision-making, there is the problem of confidentiality which on the one hand has never been more important within the Cabinet, and yet on the other hand, is preserved at great costs, not only in terms of credibility with the public, but also in terms of getting criticisms and suggestions from those concerned with public policy and public administration. Not far removed from the problem of confidentiality is the question of the role of the Member of Parliament: is he in a time of big government a participant in decision-making or a censor of the decision-maker?

In matters of the administrative process, two technical problems of enormous and practical impact upon government occur to me: first, the question of what lines and standards of accountability should apply to senior officials in a system which also requires the interplay of ministerial and collective responsibilities in a parliamentary forum; and, second, the question of how to decentralize government institutions across the country while maintaining meaningful standards of accountability for Ministers and, as the case may be, their officials. In relation to communications, what techniques and instruments are we to develop to supplement the politician in communicating with the people, without at the same time turning the official into a partisan?

In terms of the personnel process, is it really justifiable to apply the traditional protections of tenure to executives paid at rates comparable to those earned by their opposite numbers in the private sector who, theoretically at least, are much more subject to the consequences of failure. Indeed, can a large bureaucracy have a meaningful system of performance assessment if it does not have the ready sanction of getting rid of those who do not perform?

Finally, basic to the whole question of government in the 1980s is the question of the continued growth of government: How long can the public sector take on functions and manpower from the private sector before the latter loses its vitality and not only our system of government but the whole structure of society is irrevocably changed?

Conclusion

The roots of these questions, like the design of techniques and instruments for developing policies to deal with them, lie not only in politics but also in the technical subject matter of public administration. Just as government has never been bigger or more complex, so it seems to me the challenge to the practitioners and theorists of public administration has never been greater.

I suggested earlier that the development of techniques and instruments for policy formulation in the 1980s should be an evolutionary process if consistency with the genius of our system is to be retained.

I would go further and argue that we have not viewed government sufficiently as a total system. We tend to look at parts in isolation or, at most, in the context of their most obvious sub-systems. We increasingly lose sight of the comprehensive web of inter-relationships whereby the total system, while giving to each part a unique role, maintains the democratic equilibrium of the whole.

I venture to suggest this criticism applies both to theorists and to practitioners. It is a worrisome situation, not only because it can lead to erroneous analysis, inappropriate and wasteful prescriptions, but also because it can cause us to subvert the system and open the way to forces that are destabilizing and even undemocratic.

The development of new techniques and instruments for policy formulation requires that we understand inter-relationships and the indirect consequences of any proposals for change that may be advanced. This demands not only sensitivity to the political and administrative environment within which government has to operate but also an understanding of and respect for the history of our system. If I were to leave those who study public administration with only one message it would be simply a plea that in developing new techniques and instruments for policy formulation for the 1980s, we do these things and I hope this paper will be helpful in that regard.

5

Decision-Making in the Federal Cabinet*

HON. MITCHELL SHARP

Let me begin immediately by a description of decision-making at the cabinet level as I have observed it over a period of many years, while I was in the public service and since I became a Minister. I shall not attempt the sort of formal presentation that has been made so well by Gordon Robertson and more recently by the present secretary of the cabinet, Michael Pitfield. My comments will be much more personal, subjective, and impressionistic.

I begin by remarking on the extraordinary changes that have taken place in the decision-making process at the cabinet level during the time that I have been part of the process, either as a civil servant or as a minister. I arrived in Ottawa while Mackenzie King was prime minister and just a few years after Arnold Heeney had succeeded in establishing minimum documentation for cabinet meetings. The tradition was an oral one, and the recommendations of ministers were seldom rejected. Cabinet agenda were reasonably flexible so that matters could be raised of which notice had not been given. Very few records were kept. There were few formal cabinet committees except Treasury Board, the Defence Committee and, for a time, the Wheat Committee. Proposals by ministers came before cabinet in the first instance and only in the event of disagreement were they referred to ministerial committees which were more often than not ad hoc.

At that time, interdepartmental committees of officials were more numerous than ministerial committees. I can recall particularly the interdepartmental committee on economic policy, chaired by the deputy minister of finance, where the main lines of government economic policy during wartime were hammered out. This economic committee was succeeded after the war by functional interdepartmental committees. When I

* This paper was originally presented at a seminar at York University, September 29, 1975. Reprinted by permission of *Canadian Public Administration*.

arrived in Ottawa at the beginning of 1942, I recall Dr Mackintosh's account of how he had been instructed to prepare a statement for Mr King to use when announcing on the radio the over-all price ceiling which came into effect towards the end of 1941. He showed his draft to the prime minister who, after reading the opening paragraphs, looked up and said: "This is important, isn't it, Dr Mackintosh?" I couldn't imagine Mr Pearson or Mr Trudeau being so unaware of the momentous consequences of introducing over-all price controls.

Decision-making became somewhat more formalized in Mr St-Laurent's time, partly because government business became more complex and partly because the prime minister himself was a well co-ordinated chairman. One difference between Mr King and Mr St-Laurent will illustrate the point. Except for the political aspects of sensitive questions and, of course, foreign affairs, I am informed that Mr King let his ministers take the lead, and he only intervened to settle disputes. I am informed that in his prime Mr St-Laurent's technique was, after private discussions with the ministers, to take the initiative, invite discussion, sum up the case pro and con, express his preference, and ask if there was any difference of view.

Cabinet committees tended to remain ad hoc rather than systematized during Mr St-Laurent's time, and interdepartmental committees of officials continued to flourish. Proposals were made directly to cabinet and documentation by present standards was brief. Indeed, I couldn't imagine ministers of that day agreeing to read the numerous and voluminous cabinet papers we are presented with from week to week.

I can't speak with much authority about the Diefenbaker régime. I remained in Ottawa only during the minority government of 1957-8. The accounts I heard of what went on confirmed my impression from those first few months that the process of decision-making did not change enough and was centred to a very great extent in the Prime Minister. Full cabinet met more frequently then than before.

Certainly when Mr Pearson succeeded as prime minister in 1963, I did not detect any significant departures in the decision-making process inherited through the cabinet secretariat from the former régime, except some gradual growth in the number of committees.

Under Mr Pearson, the cabinet committee structure began to be elaborated in earnest and an effort was made to prevent the introduction of items on the cabinet agenda without notice, an effort which did not always succeed. Only proposals that were contentious or involved detailed examination were referred to committees. Usually, but not invariably, papers were distributed in advance, and for the most part these papers were reasonably short. The cabinet secretariat endeavoured to promote some uniformity in presentation, but the rules were flexible.

At this point, let me digress for a moment to describe the form in which cabinet decisions are made. First, it may come as somewhat of a surprise to learn that cabinet decisions rarely take the form of orders in council. About the only orders in council approved in cabinet are those relating to appointments or proclamations. Other orders in council are approved by the special committee of council of which I happen to be chairman.

Most cabinet decisions take the form of a record of decision authorizing ministers to take certain actions or to make certain announcements. They are reached, as I believe you are aware, by consensus and not by the taking of votes. In the case of Bills to be introduced into Parliament, approval of cabinet is signified by the prime minister's signature on the face of the Bill.

I come then to the process of cabinet decision-making under Prime Minister Trudeau. This process has undergone development and modification over the seven years since Mr Trudeau assumed the leadership in 1968, and I shall not have time to describe these changes in detail, although I may refer to some of them incidentally.

The main characteristic of the Trudeau Cabinet in my judgment has been the application of the principle of collegiality, the practical application of the concept of joint responsibility. In the Pearson government of which I was a member throughout, we discussed and agreed to or disagreed with recommendations of individual ministers and accepted responsibility for the actions of our colleagues resulting from cabinet decisions. However, Mr Pearson did not require ministers to document their proposals fully and did not, generally speaking, require detailed scrutiny by other ministers, although of course there were exceptions in matters of major political concern.

Under Mr Trudeau all proposals must be fully documented, their conclusions and recommendations based on a careful consideration of alternatives and presentation of the arguments pro and con. Lengthy documents must be accompanied by a summary in both official languages. Where appropriate, financial implications must be specified. Caucus consultations must be described or reasons given if these have not taken place. Effects on federal-provincial relations must be described, and if an announcement is to be made, the arrangements for publicity must also be specified.

The general rule, to which there are extremely few exceptions, is that proposals are referred in the first instance to cabinet committees for consideration and decision or, failing decision, report to cabinet.

Cabinet committees are carefully structured, care being taken to achieve geographical as well as departmental balance in the membership. They meet regularly on specified days, the agenda being circulated in advance, together with the appropriate documentation. Officials attend at the invitation of their ministers. Privy Council Office provides the secretariat.

When cabinet committees reach agreement on a proposal, the resulting decision appears on the cabinet agenda at a subsequent meeting and the prime minister calls each committee decision to ascertain whether there are any differences of view in the full cabinet. When cabinet committees cannot agree, they report the matter to cabinet for decision.

Most cabinet ministers are on about three cabinet committees and thus spend a good part of their time in meetings with their cabinet colleagues. Personally, I spend twelve to fifteen hours a week in cabinet or cabinet committees.

I have been describing the process of decision-making from the time of the presentation of a proposal by a minister until final disposition. As you will see, it is highly formalized, detailed, and documented to a degree never even approached under earlier administrations.

Let me now describe another important and innovative part of the decision-making process under the Trudeau administration. That is the attempt to establish priorities, to give over-all direction in the field of policy, to give coherence to the government's programme. This effort has gone through several phases with varying degrees of success, because it is inherently a most difficult exercise and is always subject to being sidetracked by the emergence of crises or unforeseen developments, which by the very nature of things demand the full attention of the government and disrupt priorities.

In a sense what is being attempted is to reverse the usual process of decision-making, which typically begins with a particular proposal from a minister and ends as a cabinet decision. The priorities exercise is an attempt to set a general course which will be implemented later by particular ministerial proposals. Recently, for example, we have been looking at our defence policy as a whole, beginning with consideration of the objectives and the priority to be attached to each of these objectives.

The Trudeau approach to decision-making in the cabinet has had many consequences. Perhaps one of its most significant has been to require ministers to become knowledgeable, even expert, to an extent that was not required of them in the past. The very fact that all proposals have to be fully documented imposes a discipline upon the sponsoring minister. And at least the more conscientious ministers are educated in the affairs of departments other than their own by having to read and discuss the documents. Prior consideration in cabinet committee where officials are present reinforces the process of education.

My impression is that for these reasons ministers are not as dependent upon their principal civil servant advisers for policy guidance as they were in earlier administrations and that interdepartmental committees, while they remain numerous, are not as significant in the decision-making process as they once were. I have to add, however, that while ministers have become more expert, the problems have become more complex, and there remains plenty of scope for the exercise of the analytic powers and judgment of senior permanent advisers.

How has this systematized process of decision-making affected the role of the prime minister? One point will I hope be clear from the description that I have given: Mr Trudeau would not have initiated this kind of system had he wanted to concentrate decision-making in his own hands. What he has achieved, however, is the reinforcement of cabinet solidarity and the principle of collective responsibility, and that is sometimes mistaken for the centralization of power in the hands of the prime minister. There has been a good deal less 'shooting from the hip' by ministers and perhaps less entertainment value in their performances. Certainly ministers have had to spend a good deal more of their time in Ottawa and in cabinet and cabinet committees than they would prefer, perhaps to the detriment of the political interests of the government and of the party.

Finally, a word or two about the input into decision-making by government supporters in Parliament. Along with the systematization of decision-making in Cabinet has gone a similar process of caucus consultations. In the past, I think it is fair to say, the principal purpose of government caucus had been to afford an opportunity for government backbenchers to express their grievances against the ministry, and this remains an important function of caucus today, particularly in the view of some backbenchers. Nowadays, however, many backbenchers insist on making a much more substantial contribution to decision-making and insist upon prior consultation and opportunity for full discussion of important and sensitive subjects before government positions are taken. I have already mentioned that ministerial proposals must include reference to caucus consultations, past or future. This kind of caucus consultation has also, I believe, improved the level of debate when bills are before Parliament or when other motions are being debated, at least on the part of government supporters.

Parliament remains the final decision-making body. Because of the zeal with which our government works, the enthusiasm of some of the ministers to take action, and the machinery which has been created for decision-making, we tend to overload Parliament, which is not organized to deal with such a press of public business. Some further systematization of parliamentary procedure, parallel to the systemization of government decision-making is, I think, inevitable and I hope will not be too long delayed.

The Leader, His Party, and Politics in Canada

This section examines several dimensions of the Prime Minister's political contexts. The first article explores the nature of mass legitimate political parties in Canada and suggests implications for the party leaders. Then Fred Fletcher provides an extensive look at what is key but seldom examined in the political science literature, the Prime Minister's role as public persuader. Donald Smiley examines the Prime Minister's recruitment and choice by his party. Gilbert Winham and Robert Cunningham study the Prime Minister's impact on voting behaviour. The selection included here introduces their methodology of research and follows with their discussion of the independent effect of leaders' images on voting behaviour in their sample from a constituency chosen for study. A little understood but growing part of the political apparatus of the executive in Ottawa, ministers' staffs, is outlined by Gerald Lenoski. Prime Minister Trudeau's idea of the participant party is introduced through several of his own statements. Finally, MacGregor Dawson, Charles Taylor and S. J. R. Noel discuss some diverse approaches to the Prime Minister's responsibility of political leadership.

6

Canada's "Mass Legitimate" Parties and Their Implications for Party Leaders*

THOMAS A. HOCKIN

What are the differences between Canadian political parties? What kind of parties are they? Although clearly class voting exists, it can be misleading to press analogies of European or American ideological voting attitudes too far in Canada. Ideology in the European sense is flawed (or perhaps muted is a better word) in Canada. The centrist Liberal Party and the Conservative Party (officially known as the Progressive Conservative Party since 1942) do not appear to be clear ideological enemies, yet party competition remains intense. The most frequent explanation in most analyses of the Canadian party system and of Canadian voting behaviour has been to emphasize the impact of regionalism on voting behaviour. Although studies have indicated that there is significant class voting in some Federal constituencies and definitely in provincial elections, the dominant impression in the voting behaviour literature is that, on the whole, regionalism has greater impact on voting behaviour than class. Canada has seen minor regionally based parties arise to contest the dominance of the two major parties; the Progressives in 1921; in 1935 the Social Credit and the Cooperative Commonwealth Federation, and since the mid-1960s the Social Credit, then le Ralliement des Créditistes in Quebec. The single-member, single-plurality electoral system, too, combines with regional preferences to produce heavy representation of one party in certain provinces, such as the near-monopoly of seats given to the Liberals in Quebec during most of this century, and the virtual capture of parts of the prairies by the Conservatives since 1958. Opportunity to build leverage for various regions is thus afforded by the large representation of some regions in their Federal Party caucus. This may also help to entrench

* From Thomas A. Hockin, *Government in Canada* (Toronto: McGraw-Hill Ryerson, 1976). Reprinted by permission.

regional affiliations within certain parties in Ottawa (for example, Quebec in the Liberal Party and Alberta in the Conservative). It has been suggested that although the socio-economic change that accompanies industrialization leads to more class voting, or what voting behaviour students in Western democracies call 'nationalization' or 'realignment', this process is not so evident in Canada because of a host of resistant factors. Prominent explanations for explaining this resistance are: the disinterest in cross-regional alliances of certain 'functional' social groups in Quebec owing to Quebec's concern with its own culture; other regional identities fostered in part by metropolitan centres oriented to provincial more than national economic growth, and the high visibility of provincial governments in their publicized struggles with Ottawa; and, to some extent, provincial boundaries reflect different types of economic activity and priorities in Canada.

Given the regional differences in voting behaviour and the amount of significant social and economic fragmentation in Canada, why isn't Canada similar to the Netherlands, where a vast number of parties win seats and majority Governments are now remote? The prevailing academic explanation for the cohesion and broad base of Canada's two major political parties has been their supposed ability, especially in the case of the Liberals, to act as 'brokers'. The brokerage theory suggests that a party attempts to balance and reconcile divergent interests by such strategies as regional compromises in policy outputs and by granting regional representation in the cabinet. This theory emphasizes the subordination of party to social forces. Other explanations give more emphasis to party superordination. Another explanation of Canadian parties emphasizes both party and elite superordination; this is the explanation from the left in Canada, which focuses on selected elites to explain how non-left parties dominate election results. These theories have many variants but all of them are not too dissimilar to the analyses by Ralph Miliband of Western democracies or by C. Wright Mills of the American power structure. These theories insist that the business and other elites in Canada dominate the two major Canadian political parties, the mass media, party finance and a host of other arenas of political power and perception in the country. Party competition, so the theory goes, is conducted between the two major parties (sometimes the other parties are also included in this conclusion) on the basis of personality-oriented appeals. Policy debate becomes carefully orchestrated and permits furious arguments over comparatively minor (and certainly non-revolutionary) policy distinctions. This leads to 'contrived', 'dilettantish', 'bourgeois pragmatic' party competition which safely keeps the major parties in the ascendancy and retards the growth of class-based politics.

Yet similar conditions exist in other countries, and these have not prevented the emergence of huge class parties. Why is Canada so different? Part of the answer may lie in the relatively conservative belief system of a majority of Canadians and in the fact that Canadian politics cannot be expected to unfold in a way similar to Europe. Equally important, however, is the impact of the Canadian state dynamic, which may also help to keep class conflict from dominating Canadian politics through the state's ability to command considerable social allegiance to the given state and political structure. The state is allowed to unfold and to penetrate society thanks to the peculiar nature of Canada's centre parties, which appeal to the mass in such a way as to permit the state system considerable autonomy. Part of the explanation for this may lie in what Arend Lijphart has called the 'operation of a cartel of elites' which, although representing quite different interests, agree to work together. This produces what Lijphart has called a 'consociational democracy'.[1] Its operation seems evident in Switzerland and in other fragmented political societies, and it helps to explain why these countries hold together when a national consensus is weak and mass social integration is lacking. Various business, agricultural, labour, educational and other key elites cooperate; and this may be sufficient. S. J. R. Noel explains the point further in this book. Under a consociational system agreements in a political society can be made and compromises reached among political leaders which would not be possible if they required popular ratification.

For it to function successfully, those who occupy positions of political leadership must understand the perils of political fragmentation and be committed to the maintenance of the national system; they must also be able, within their respective subcultures, to accommodate divergent interests and demands. For the masses, on the other hand, all that is required is that they be committed to their own subcultures and that they trust and support their respective elites. Since the more contact and interaction there is between the masses of the subcultures the greater the likelihood of friction between them, Lijphart suggests, 'it may be desirable to keep transactions among antagonistic subcultures in a divided society . . . to a minimum.' In theory, there is no reason why a consociational democracy could not function satisfactorily even if among the masses of the different subcultures there was absolutely no attachment to the national political system and no sense whatever of a national identity. In actual systems, however, some degree of popular national sentiment is invariably present. The distinguishing feature of a consociational political system is the relative weakness of popular national sentiment and the overcoming of this weakness through a process of elite accommodation.[2]

To some extent the integration of the state and the dependence of parts of society on the state is the structural outcome of this consociational collaboration. After a while, structures and policy programmes already in existence become a cause for more collaboration. Conditions allowing this collaboration can also be traced to the mass legitimacy of Canadian political parties.

---

[1] See A. Lijphart, 'Cultural Diversity and Theories of Political Integration', *Canadian Journal of Political Science*, IV, No. 1 (March 1971).

[2] See S. J. R. Noel's 'The Prime Minister's Role in a Consociational Democracy', Chapter 12 in this volume.

To explain this it is necessary to introduce the notion of 'mass legitimate' and 'group legitimate' parties to the Canadian scene.

In any political society, groups can be placed analytically on a continuum. At one end are communal groups which 'embody social relationships' and on the other associational groups which are those bodies 'constituted to pursue a goal'.[3] Blondel suggests something further about these* two types of groups: the 'legitimacy' of the communal group comes from the members' tie to the aims of the group and from the fact that 'they are achieving and want to achieve something in common'. Communal groups can seldom be equated with interest groups. Since the 'aim' of the communal group is the well-being of its members, such groups translate, select and interpret the interests of the group. These interests may vary over time, and 'interpretation of what these interests are is likely to be left, to a great extent, to the leaders and to the pressure of circumstances'. Associational groups, however, are 'coexistensive with demands'.

The distinction between these two groups helps us to understand better the structure of Canadian parties and the role of parties in Canadian policy-making. One can easily find Canadian examples of these two types of groups, especially if one recalls their origins. The importation of new people into a community can give rise to a new communal group and/or change the goals of a previous group. For example the concentration in Canada of Ukrainian and Italian immigrants gives rise to new communal groups, and in the first case perhaps changed the goals of what communal reality there was in 'Manitoba' as a communal group. Communal groups can also emerge from political or administrative structures. Provinces such as Alberta and Saskatchewan, which may have had little or no communal legitimacy at their birth, developed this as experience with provincial political institutions grew. The St. Jean Baptiste Society in Quebec is probably a perfect example of a communal and associational group, its communal base resting, perhaps, on the characteristics of the larger communal group, a large number of French Canadians in Quebec.

If the bond of allegiance between members and their group exists, in the case of communal groups, in the members themselves, and 'the goal' exists in the case of associational groups, both groups will allow transfers 'of support or of legitimacy' to a party in elections if the group is widely accepted by its members, and if its members recognize the importance of the group. For example, in Canada it may have been possible for French Canadians, because of their high communal legitimacy, to shift support from one Federal party to another in the first fifty years after confederation without, in most cases, endangering the group. Immediately after confederation, Nova Scotian MPs (many of whom were against the terms of the confederation agreements) felt free to vote as they pleased, for the communal legitimacy of Nova Scotia was hardly in doubt.

When a party draws support from the electorate indirectly, through the allegiance which members have to the groups which have helped to

[3] Jean Blondel, *Introduction to Comparative Government* (London, 1969), Chapter 5.

constitute the party, there is, in Blondel's definition, no element of 'massness' at the basis of party support. A 'mass legitimate party' is one with direct mass support. Mass legitimate parties, however, are usually begun or 'put into orbit' by groups in the first place. Blondel notes that legitimate mass parties have tended to develop more quickly where parties have emerged from a class-based group. But, he notes, if parties have become legitimate before class-based loyalties have become strong, the legitimate mass party can spring from any one of the broad communal groupings (including even clientele organizations). For example, the Federal Liberal or Reform party was launched by a number of associational, communal and clientele groups; the most prominent perhaps in Ontario was the 'Clear Grit' group and its associational attitudes, reflecting, in the opinion of one observer:

... a deep and abiding suspicion of the commercial and transportation monopoly of Montreal; and a belief in egalitarianism and rugged individualism, in free trade and free land, in representation by population, and in strict supervision of, if not limitation on government support to business enterprise. The Clear Grits were almost exclusively Protestant, and their latent anti-Catholicism found expression and stimulation in the writings of [their first leader] George Brown.[4]

The French Canadian part of this uneasy Reform coalition was composed of cross-cutting communal and associational groups, made up primarily of those who were Catholic yet against the ultramontane attitudes of the clerical hierarchy, and of those who were suspicious of certain business interests and the Conservatives in general. The Conservatives' coalition was made up of spokesmen who emerged from the Montreal commercial and industrial interests, a major part of the ecclesiastical hierarchy which represented and led perhaps the largest communal group in Quebec (the Church-led communities of Quebec), the United Empire Loyalists, the Orange lodge, and moderate Reformers who earlier had followed Robert Baldwin. It is difficult to describe this collection of disparate forces as anything more than a coalition. The largest coalition also depended on floating MPs, mainly from the maritimes and the west, who would vote for the ministry, and any ministry would do if it proved profitable for the constituency and province.

For the first decade after confederation, Canadian parties were not therefore as mass legitimate as they were group legitimate. They were creatures of a host of associational and communal groups. The Conservative coalition was sustained in large measure by the astute leadership of Canada's first prime minister, Sir John A. Macdonald. In those days, when government was less complex and 'public policy' by definition was primarily patronage, Macdonald was able to disaggregate the stakes and keep his coalition together through the distribution of patronage. Most regions and constituencies in the coalition were indulged. He also attempted to

4 George Hougham, 'The Background and Development of National Parties', in H. Thorburn (ed.), Party Politics in Canada, (Scarborough, Ont., 1967), p. 5.

attach the budding associational labour groups to his party by supporting a progressive labour code. If he could avoid zero-sum decisions and keep attention on selected nation-wide needs, so as to capture the national imagination, he could sustain the coalition until the communal or associational groups changed. He did the latter through his audacious but courageous all-railway route to the west coast, and his 'National Policy' which, with the railway, provided tariff protection and other measures for an integrated transcontinental economy. The Riel Rebellion, however, was the zero-sum decision which eventually forced Macdonald to choose between the English and French. Macdonald decided to execute the Indian-French or Métis leader Louis Riel (because Riel under the authority of his self-proclaimed 'provisional government' had executed an Orangeman acting as an Agent of the Dominion government). This began the erosion of Macdonald's support among French Canadian communal groups, even if it was not immediately condemned by the associational business and clerical groups in Quebec.

Even if the major parties were originally highly dependent on certain groups as intermediaries for their appeal to the mass, it seems evident that, in Blondel's terms, each major party eventually became increasingly 'mass legitimate' rather than merely 'group legitimate'. Macdonald's party to 1891, and then Laurier's from 1896 to 1911, were able to reach directly to the mass through the dispensation of favours and patronage, through the production of broad and sometimes nationally integrative policies. The ability of either one party or the other to gain support from most of the major newspapers in the country, and the monopoly of Parliament by these two parties, may also have helped to shift public opinion to the view that these two parties were the viable national political parties.

As a result of these developments, Canada's two major parties were "placed in orbit," in Blondel's terms, and a key parallel process of 'legitimacy transfer' took place. Once parties are so launched, they are then able to make appeals to the mass directly, and not simply through groups. When this occurs, Blondel suggests, broad communal groups begin to see that they must alter their strategy and not place their hopes in owning a political party but in supporting new associations with their specific goals. For example, rural regions attempt to work through farm associations. Parties then alter their strategy toward groups and begin to aim at 'aggregating' or mediating the interests represented by these associations, while not on the whole attempting to modify the goals of society. As they become increasingly independent of the broad communal groups, parties and associations will come to have an increasing number of specific reciprocal relationships. The pure type of a wholly legitimate party in Blondel's definition is one which ceases to have any special relationship with any communal group and 'comes to have relations with all associations on the basis of the intrinsic importance of their demands'.[5]

Today we see all sorts of evidence of this in Canada. The two major

---

[5] Blondel, *Introduction to Comparative Government*, p. 129.

Federal parties—especially the governing party—allow for almost constant contact of the Federal state with an immense array of associations: business, farm, professional, labour, and governmental (provincial and even municipal); contact with communal groups becomes less and less frequent. Communal groups in fact articulate increasingly through associational groups. The New Democratic Party has also developed more into a mass legitimate party than a simple 'group legitimate' (i.e. labour union supported) party. It too is in constant contact with a host of associations. It does, however, view itself in large measure as a 'particular type' of mass legitimate party, more reminiscent of European left-wing parties. Its Federal leader in 1972 puts it thus:

There is a mistaken view of the original purpose and concept of our party's association with labour unions. I have never believed that because a local union by majority decides to support the party ... that all its members would support the party in every election, or even that those who vote for affiliation will support the party in every election. To assume that is very naive. ...

I think the value of the association has been very definitely an identification of the average working man and woman in Canada with the New Democratic Party as being their party—even when they vote against us, they still admit the fact that the NDP is the worker's party. ...

That was the purpose of the association and that is still true.[6]

The essential condition which allows the two major parties to gain a fair degree of mass legitimacy is the presence of what is so often assumed to be absent in Canada: consensus. There is a broad (though not unanimous) consensus that the Canadian collectivist-capitalist system is not in need of dramatic change. Supporters for the major Canadian parties cannot be called supporters for dramatic social change if their opinions on policy issues in 1968 are any guide.[7] As Blondel suggests, when 'there is no, or little, conflict of goals in the political system, the dependence of groups on political parties will be small' (as in the United States) and 'the level of dependence at any given moment' can be measured 'by the extent to which the party is legitimate in the community'. Blondel's hypothesis suggests, therefore, that if there has been relatively little conflict in the majority of the political community about the proposition that the Canadian collectivist-capitalist system is not in need of revolutionary change, then the business community need not depend on one of the two major Federal parties but can support either, and it could, no doubt, survive a government formed by the more left-wing third party, the New Democrats. Similarly, individuals or groups who do not believe in a radically different economic and social system (and this category could include a host of groups, including teachers, unionized and non-unionized workers, lower-middle class workers, etc.) no doubt also feel free to oscillate among the major parties. John Meisel's data show considerable correlation

6 *Globe and Mail*, 21 January 1972, p. 7.
7 See John Meisel, *Working Papers on Canadian Politics* (Montreal 1972).

between certain statistical groups and certain parties. Hence only a minority of Canadians may oscillate in their voting preference. But it has been quite a sizable minority and it is crucial to victory. This part of the electorate may feel free to oscillate because it feels the major parties are open to communication with most groups when in power. S. H. Beer has explained, in his *British Politics In the Collectivist Age*, the openness of the British Labour and Conservative parties by pointing to the inherent necessity of state contacts with a host of 'functional' groups if the government is to manage Britain in the collectivist age. Something similar seems true for Canada. Most interest groups in Canada try to remain openly non-partisan. Most of them also remain ready to communicate with the Federal government of the day regardless of party. Their willingness to write briefs, to pass comment on embryonic legislative proposals, and to appear before parliamentary committees, give ample proof of this readiness, and perhaps the necessity, for them to interact with the major parties, or with the state under the auspices of the major parties.

All this might also help to explain the curiously pragmatic and untheoretical character of Canadian politicians. It has been suggested by Dorothy Pickles in a study of French politics that 'overindulgence in a national predilection for argument about ideas rather than about practical policies' is characteristic of political parties in that country. What a contrast this is to Canada! Of all the things that can be said to characterize Canadian political parties, a 'predilection for argument about ideas' is not one of them. The attraction in France for theories, doctrines and distinctions of principle is foreign to the world of Canadian political parties. The closest Canada comes to this French penchant for theoretical debate is in its publications on the left, especially in Quebec. Yet even here there is as much emphasis given to practical problems of public policy, to concrete examples—most of them markedly regional—of failures or abuses of the major parties as to theory. English-Canadian and much of the French-Canadian tradition of social science—especially historical—scholarship is heavily empirical, cautious about offering general explanations and well-known for its suspicion of almost all broad theories. In this respect it cannot be said that Canadian political parties lag behind the intellectual attitude of the most advanced thinking in the land. Canadian political parties almost never deduct their electoral policy platforms from elaborate theoretical prolegomena. Canada's major parties appear to pride themselves on their 'pragmatism'. To foreign observers the more socialist New Democrats may also appear to be unusually pragmatic, considering their perennial opposition status at the Federal level. This party is intensely empirical in its electoral strategy. The party platform seldom belabours theory: it concentrates on policy prescription.

Communication and Canadian Party Leadership

It is no doubt true that leaders and leadership groups in most party systems are the main channels through which parties are linked to the people. This, of course, is not to say that party leaders and leadership groups are the main channels through which all public policy is made. As we have seen in other chapters, the complex and systematic work of the public service, boards and commissions makes them probably more important in countless areas of policy than political leaders. But political leaders are important for linking parties to the people. This is true for group-dependent, as well as mass-legitimate, parties. All party leaders probably have dark moments of doubt about how closely their party is involved in the real world of community concerns. At least annually they exhort their party to participate more in the life of local communities, to seek 'roots closer to the people'. Yet when election time comes in Canada, the relationship of the mass to the leader and to leadership groups in the party become vitally important in the formation of popular perceptions of political issues and political parties.

This is especially true for mass legitimate parties which, because of their perceived independence from any communal group and their readiness to communicate with all associations on the basis of their intrinsic demands, are thereby considered not to be group-dominated, and are able to emphasize the party leader, or leadership group, as the object of attention. His or their utterances, attitudes and styles then become important for defining the nature of the party. This may be part of the explanation for the heavy emphasis given to the personality and style of the party leader in the mass media, and why party publicists respond with similar personality-oriented appeals in their campaign strategies. This type of politics is intrinsic to the nature of mass legitimate parties, rather than evidence of a contrived restriction of political debate by party publicists frightened of the public's hunger for something else. When parties are able to be perceived as mass-legitimate, a symbiosis emerges between public notions of what is relevant and what party leaders say and do. This symbiosis, of course, will always strike that part of the electorate which is alienated from the mass legitimate parties as empty and cruelly irrelevant; hence perhaps the despair and cynicism of a large minority of the population who vote for the smaller parties or the 25 per cent who do not vote at all. Yet the business of mass-legitimate parties as defined by Blondel is to gain political power, and thus their mode of appeal will centre instead on the constituency which can provide this.

The business of building a direct appeal to the mass makes modes of communication through the press, radio, television, parliamentary debate, and party campaign literature vital to all parties but especially for mass-legitimate parties. 'Direct contact with the mass' becomes heavily dependent on how political messages are communicated. The ways in which the mass media define and publicize issues, the way they ignore some issues and concentrate on others, are matters of considerable importance to mass-legitimate parties. If the mass media are hostile, the mass-legitimate party, like the group-legitimate party, will have to depend heavily on its party canvassers, volunteers and advertising to overcome this handicap. Also, leaders of the three major parties are not without considerable exposure in the mass media. At one time Canadian newspapers were stridently partisan, and many urged their party choice on their readers from the front page. It is fair to say that although most Canadian dailies now suggest their choice on the editorial page, they at least give better than token coverage to what all the major party leaders say and do during an election campaign. The Canadian Press wire service also strives to report in a balanced way and this service is used by most Canadian newspapers. The Canadian Broadcasting Corporation supplies time on television for the major parties each week and after its reporting of prime ministerial or ministerial statements it usually allows time for opposition opinion to be expressed as well. All this helps to facilitate communication from the major Federal parties to the mass and thereby helps them in their efforts to become increasingly mass-legitimate. There are some disquieting features, however, about the concentration of media ownership in Canadian communities, and this may narrow somewhat the diversity of political opinion heard in various communities. The first volume of the Senate Special Report on the mass media found that in their 103 surveyed communities there were sixty-one where groups or independents own two or more of their community's media outlets, thirty-four communities where groups own two or more radio outlets, and thirty-one where groups have common interests in both radio and television stations. Although radio and television licences are granted under a fairly independent licensing commission, there have been rumours of political influence.

Another feature of Canadian political life which may help major parties to dominate disparate and unorganized political dissent and opinion is the dialectic of Parliament. With its orchestration of debate and with the importance given by the media to statements made by party leaders, the diversity of views the electorate is able to hear can become somewhat narrow. The loosening of the Government's control over some Commons committee activity may be increasing diversity to some extent, however.

Finally, the more successful a party looks likely to be, the greater is its ability to raise enough money for its advertising and for campaigning. It is argued, therefore, that dependence on the financial contributions of businesses to maintain the party apparatus between elections and to wage election campaigns makes them less mass-legitimate than they seem. (The chairman of the Federal Liberal Party's Finance Committee stated on CTV television on 30 April 1972, that the bulk of his party's funds for operating the central office of the Federal Party between elections came from 95 firms, and from about 350 firms for Federal election campaigns.) It is a well known but as yet unproven axiom in Canadian politics that many large businesses split their contribution to the Liberals and Conservatives with slightly more going to the governing party. (For more documentation on the dynamic and history of party finance in Canada, see the publications of the Advisory Committee on Election Expenses, Ottawa, 1966.) Analytically, however, this question of sources of party funds should not be understood as a direct indication of the degree of dependency of recipient parties on certain parts of the business world. This whole question can be placed in a more comprehensive perspective by realizing that these sources of funds permit first of all the two major parties to finance a nationwide appeal. Yet this appeal becomes far more than a mere partisan appeal on behalf of one part of society. Just as the New Democrats claim that their dependency on union funds does not make their party a party only for labour unions, business-financed parties claim a similar catholicity. In fact, as we have suggested earlier, it is imperative for the three major parties to reach beyond the partisan interests of their benefactors if they are to grow increasingly mass legitimate and to attain or remain in office. Only if a society is significantly split between the advocates of capitalism and its enemies, will the partisan benefactors insist on pure partisan use of governmental power. Even that insistence could prove suicidal to the party that provides it. It is difficult to maintain that in Canada there exists a high level of consciousness of such a split in society. Generally, the major parties have been careful not to emasculate their mass legitimacy by fostering a perception of such a split.

The peculiar mass legitimacy of Canada's major parties has some important implications for party leadership and policy-making. Although an iron law of oligarchy may limit the number of key decision-makers that can coexist in mass-legitimate parties, the more a party becomes mass legitimate, the greater is the openness in its choice of leaders and the more frequent is the rotation of leaders. The three major parties have chosen their leaders by convention since 1919 in the case of the Liberals, since 1927 for the Conservatives, and since the founding of the party in the case of the CCF-NDP. The choice of leaders by convention rather than by the parliamentary caucus helps to make leadership selection more open if one assumes that parliamentary caucuses would have been disposed to choose leaders with long records of Federal elective office. Of the twelve leaders chosen by convention by the P.C.s and the Liberals, three (Bracken, Drew and Stanfield) were provincial premiers with no Federal legislative experience; four (King, St Laurent, Trudeau and Clark) had six years or less in the House of Commons; and only two—Manion and Diefenbaker—were in relative terms parliamentary veterans.

For example, John Diefenbaker was chosen as Conservative Party leader in 1956, though his support was greater outside the identifiable party oligarchy than within it. Equally instructive were the soundings made by the Federal Conservative party association's president, with the party outside the party leader's apparatus in Ottawa. These enabled him to discover the demand for, and later organize the engineering of, the passage by his party of a request for a leadership convention. This was done in the teeth of the wishes of the incumbent party leader from 1966 to 1967. Although mass-legitimate parties in opposition often appear to be more open in leadership choice than mass-legitimate governing parties, it is by no means evident that this need always be true. National leadership can exhaust men. For example, Lester Pearson voluntarily stepped down after five years as prime minister and twenty years in the cabinet. Furthermore, the exercise of government can diversify a party's direct contact with the mass because the party headquarters' national apparatus and the party caucus cannot monopolize the contacts with the electorate or with active party supporters. A host of other agencies, offices and manifestations of governmental power build up contacts with various clienteles as well. It is interesting to note, therefore, that Liberal leaders since that party first began to govern with longevity, under Laurier from 1896 to 1911, have been chosen from the cabinet. Equally interesting is the way the Conservative party, which has been in opposition for forty-four of the fifty-six years since 1921, has chosen leaders from outside the Federal caucus, to lead the party in three of its five leadership conventions since 1942.

The powers of leaders of mass-legitimate parties frequently give rise to allegations of elite dominance in Canada. But, once again, the notion of the mass-legitimate party helps us to see the tendencies of the leaders of the Federal Liberals and Conservatives (and to some extent the NDP) to insist on decisive power to make vital policy decisions and also on the right to control the party apparatus. These traits are not unique to Canada but are characteristic of mass-legitimate parties everywhere. Of course such leaders do not exercise power in a vacuum. They must accept the broad, non-revolutionary goals of their party and they must tailor their policies to the influence of electoral defeats and to deeply felt divisions in the party over policy. In office they are also limited by the traditions of collective cabinet government, by the rigidities of bureaucratic structures, and by Federal-provincial relations. These restraints on an Opposition leader may be weaker but also the incentives for him to make hard policy may be weaker and thus the temptation to remain at rhetorical generalities strong.

These restraints and imperatives on leaders are real; yet in Canada's Federal Liberal and Conservative parties, as in mass-legitimate parties in other countries, the leader can seldom allow party congresses, party policy conventions, or party 'thinkers' conferences' (now a frequent feature of all three major parties) to dictate party policy. Blondel has asserted that for mass-legitimate parties everywhere,

It may be shown that leaders are often, particularly in large parties of a competitive type, nearer to the views of the mass of supporters than the most extreme and more ideological regulars who speak on party platforms . . . even if in practice, party policy comes to be more representative because party leaders 'flout' Congresses, the fact of flouting congresses is far from being uncommon and is only relatively rare because leaders appear sufficiently skilful in preventing internal opposition from becoming overt or at least from assuming significant proportions.[8]

For example, by the end of 1971 the Federal Conservative party in its annual meeting, and the Federal Liberals one year before, completed what was probably the most extensive process of formulating policy resolutions

---

[8] Blondel, p. 136.

in either party's history. From the summer of 1968 to their November 1970 policy convention, the Liberals (and some non-Liberals) formulated policy papers and debated them in policy seminars organized by constituency, regional and district associations. These papers and debates set the stage for the Liberals' 'National Policy Rally' or Convention in November 1970. The result, 'Directions for the Seventies', was distilled from more than four hundred resolutions dealt with at the convention. The Conservatives also produced a 'votation book' of 260 resolutions for vote at its December 1971 policy meeting. Delegates debated the resolutions, then marked 'yes, no, or undecided' by every resolution in the 47-page votation book, and the results of the voting were released early in 1972. Delegates to these two conventions were chosen from constituency and other local associations and by the party headquarters. Most, but not all, delegates were party supporters. As one reporter noted, however, 'many members are still confused about the ultimate purpose of this technique' of passing opinions on policy.[9]

Little confusion was evidenced by party leaders about the purpose, however. The Liberal leader and prime minister, Pierre Trudeau, agreed that his Government would be glad to come before party conventions and account for its actions if certain resolutions were not implemented; but he made it clear that 'in respect of some [resolutions], the Government will not be able to proceed in accordance with the delegates' wishes. The Conservative opposition leader, Robert Stanfield, took a similar position before his party's policy convention. 'We still have much to do before our final programme is ready', he told the delegates. In fact, the first page of the votation book warned that 'resolutions presented here are not intended to be statements of party policy', but are voted on 'to assist the leader and caucus by ascertaining the opinion of delegates'.[10]

Nor does the operation of the Liberal or Conservative parliamentary caucus ensure anything like complete control over the leadership. Full caucus meetings sometimes vote on policy. More often, however, they also provide an occasion for back-bench advocacy of policies or of political strategies before the party leader and (in the case of the governing party) the cabinet ministers. Caucus committees have become active since the mid-1930s under King for the Liberals, and since 1942 under John Bracken for the Conservatives, but these have always had to defer to the leader and to the full caucus. Although caucus influence may have increased since 1968 owing to the requirement that ministers consult with the Liberal caucus before legislation is presented to the House, complaints continue that ministers are not greatly affected by the representations. One Liberal back-bencher has suggested that caucus meetings are so 'loaded' with ministers' legislation that there is no time to discuss 'general directions of the party'. The NDP claims to operate with less leader dominance of its caucus (similar perhaps to the British Labour party), but its small parlia-

---

[9] *Toronto Star*, December 9, 1971, p. 9.
[10] *Ibid.*, April 1, 1972, p. 16.

mentary membership affords a much greater opportunity for the leader and the other caucus members to discuss policy informally. The three major parties also maintain permanent party headquarters in Ottawa which, especially in the case of the opposition parties, churn out policy research and are sometimes deployed as intellectual allies of certain forces in the party. Notable about the Conservative research work under George Drew, John Diefenbaker, Robert Stanfield, and Joe Clark as leaders of the official opposition, is the fact that close liaison is maintained between the research office and the party leader.

In Canada, a party leader as prime minister has five weapons by which he can assert his supremacy. He has the power to dismiss, appoint and shuffle ministers. He can manage, within very few limits, the agenda of the full cabinet and to some extent the cabinet committees. He organizes and controls a great many of the patronage decisions of government. He can shuffle the personnel at top levels of the public service. He can appoint to key positions on boards, commissions, task forces and parliamentary committees.

The Canadian prime minister may, if he wishes, run a loose ministerial form of government. This seems to have been Lester Pearson's style. Or he can insist on a large number of collective cabinet decisions (this, on a number of issues, was John Diefenbaker's style). Or he can move to varying degrees of prime ministerial government based on heavy policy control from his Privy Council Office staff, and close political monitoring from the Prime Minister's Office (as under Pierre Trudeau).

A prime minister cannot always exercise all of these options, however, not because his will has failed, or because his colleagues have mounted a spontaneous mutiny (although both seem to have happened twice in Canadian history, once in the last year of Mackenzie Bowell's prime ministership in 1895, and once in the last year of John Diefenbaker's in 1962). Instead, the failure to exercise his options and powers more frequently comes when he has lost the authority because of declining personal popularity in the country. To some extent, the same may be true for opposition party leaders, although the indicators of popularity are frequently less reliable. It is the prime minister's position as the key link between the mass (not simply the groups within it) and the state that is significant. It is not his power to make policy in detail which defines the prime minister's role. As selections in this book suggest, most of this activity is done primarily by public servants, by ministers, and occasionally by backbench MPs. It is the tendency of mass-legitimate parties to push the essential decisions on vital political judgements to the prime minister, especially on controversial national issues, and the concomitant tendency of the electorate to look to the prime minister for responses in crises, which make him the symbol around which the mass reacts to the Government of the day. Before this pivotal and symbolic state can be attained, however, a party leader must keep his party mass legitimate by maintaining its perceived independence from a handful of communal or associational groups. He can do the first primarily through orchestration of the representation in his cabinet. This is a time-honoured necessity for all Canadian prime ministers. Due representation must be given to Quebec, and so on. Yet he must now go further in an age when the growth of the state and of provincial visibility demands more extensions of the same principle. The prime minister, therefore, gives positional power to various representatives of communal and associational groups through appointments to other key administrative positions. He will also indicate a willingness to acknowledge group interests not simply through policies, but through Federal-provincial conferences, speeches, personal visits, and so on.

That the Federal cabinet ought to be representative of Canada's major regions is a long-standing imperative in Canada. Yet, as Professor Szablowski suggests in Chapter 17, this may be of more symbolic than policy-making importance given the many forces that operate in Ottawa against instituting a system of regional strongmen centred in the cabinet. Thanks in part to jet travel and television the leaders of the Federal parties are able to communicate directly to regional electorates without going through Federal regional power brokers. Federal departments are organized less to emphasize regional interests than to emphasize industrial, social and other clientele structures which are seldom completely coterminous with regional interests. Ministers, as spokesmen for departments and working through cabinet committees with functional mandates for 'economic policy', 'social policy', 'external policy', 'technology', etc., are, in effect, encouraged to supersede regionalism. All of this helps to make the Federal party in power and the public service agents of state direction somewhat superordinate to many regional imperatives.

All this must be intelligently orchestrated in Canada if the prime minister is to keep his party relatively mass legitimate. (In fact, the failure of successive Liberal prime ministers to do this intelligently for the west in Canada since 1953 has decreased the extent of the governing party's mass legitimacy there.) All these are obvious preconditions. If this is done adequately, the prime minister can find himself in a position of sufficient independence from such groups that he and his administrative machine can then approach associational groups (with their cutting edges of specific demands) on the basis of their intrinsic utility for the prime minister's political strategy and the administrative apparatus's policy-making imperatives.

A group-legitimate party leader supported by a majority of the society which is at one with the group in power need do little but forward the group's interests. This may be possible in some provinces. But federally, where such a majority group consensus does not seem to exist, the prime minister then has the most crucial role of all, that of giving cognitive leadership to the public on key issues, persuading the public to accept the state's inclinations and his own. This points to his most influential role in the state's relation to society, that of shaping public cognitions and perceptions. It is a role also played to a lesser degree by the leaders of the other parties.

Government plays an important function in shaping perceptions about political issues and public policy problems. There are several conditions that facilitate governmental influence upon perceptions. One condition is the public's difficulty in examining a source of anxiety empirically, because it involves a situation expected to occur in the future. Another is that "conspicuous, publicized governmental actions either explicitly assert or clearly imply a factual state of affairs"[11] and the public can never be sure if the assertions are accurate. Canadians became especially aware of these conditions during the FLQ crisis in October 1970. Mr. Trudeau's allegations about the extent of the uprising, the size of the FLQ and the potency of the War Measures Act went far to shape the views of Canadians during this crisis. The power of the prime minister to contribute to the shaping of public opinion on political issues is not, however, confined to such dramatic occasions. In fact almost weekly the second condition is exploited by the prime minister (and by the other Federal party leaders.) This is perhaps one of the most potent powers of the state. Its exploitation by the prime minister of Canada is perhaps one of his most powerful tools for helping to shape public perceptions.

In the long run, the extent of the state's influence on society may not depend greatly on which type of party dominates Canadian political life. Both contribute to penetration. The group-dependent party does so in a group-engineered way. The mass-legitimate party with a detailed policy mandate would do so in a way based on the political energy of the cabinet and the caucus. The mass-legitimate party without a detailed policy mandate would penetrate in a way congenial to the imperatives of the public service and to the political executive's assessment of what outputs are needed to maintain or to enhance the party's image.

Let us note in conclusion, then, that the function of mass-legitimate parties in Canada is to foster political stability and integration. The ability of the mass-legitimate parties to communicate directly with the mass, their openness to communication with almost all associational groups, especially when the party is in office, and the party's basic intelligence and soundings of communal grievances, have all helped the governing party of the day to achieve a fair measure of mass legitimacy. This gives it the ability to appeal directly to the mass, primarily through the leader. This can contribute to stability because it can allow the public servant in Ottawa to communicate with all associations necessary to ease the state into new activity and to monitor the needs of these groups. It also gives the Federal state an aura of mass legitimacy and support to rival the legitimacy given to provincial state systems. All this has given Ottawa confidence to expand its relationships with the provinces and thereby to help integrate the overall state system.

---

[11] Murray Edelman, *Politics As Symbolic Action* (Chicago, 1971), p. 174.

7

The Prime Minister as Public Persuader*

FREDERICK J. FLETCHER

The Prime Minister and Public Opinion

I got into politics mainly to have a platform for some ideas, some views on the country, on society, and in a sense I knew that the Prime Minister had a higher platform, one from which he could speak more loudly. But I still see the job as one in which no government can do anything that people can't be led to accept, can't be instructed or educated to accept.

—Pierre Elliott Trudeau
Maclean's, *October 20, 1975*

Despite his considerable authority as head of his Government and his party, Canada's prime minister must be able to persuade as well as command to govern effectively. Not only must he be able to persuade his party to accept him as its leader and the electorate to vote for his party, he must also be able to persuade his cabinet colleagues to accept his leadership, his caucus to back cabinet decisions, and the bureaucracy to implement decisions with vigour. On occasion, he must also try to persuade special publics, such as business or labour, independent agencies, provincial governments and foreign leaders to follow his lead. In performing his persuasive function, the prime minister does not, of course, rely solely on his logic and charm.[1] The authority of his office provides him

---

* Written for this volume.
I wish to express my gratitude to several informants who provided me with information and suggestions for this paper and especially to Anthony Westell who commented thoughtfully on an earlier draft.

[1] This argument runs along lines suggested by Richard E. Neustadt: "A President concerned for leeway inside government must try to shape the thoughts of men outside. If he would be effective as a guardian of public standing, he must be effective as a teacher to the public." See his *Presidential Power: The Politics of Leadership* (New York, 1960), pp. 34 and 99-100.

with rewards and punishments, such as appointments and disappointments, which he can use to seek compliance. But an important source of influence is his standing with the general public. The prime minister's colleagues and competitors in Ottawa, the provincial capitals and elsewhere pay attention to it and their responses to his initiatives are conditioned by it.

Despite the obvious importance of the prime minister's role as persuader, little systematic research has been done on it. In this necessarily speculative essay, we can do little more than set out some of the relevant dimensions of such an analysis. The emphasis here is on the prime minister's role as public persuader, on the assumption that the prime minister's popular support is an important resource when he confronts other members of the elite for attempts at private persuasion. In the crucial field of federal-provincial negotiations, for example, Richard Simeon concluded that "perhaps the most important political resource—or constraint—for negotiators . . . is the degree of support they believe they have in the underlying population, or at least among attentive publics."[2] The argument is that if the public supports the federal government, generally or on a specific issue, the provincial governments are likely to make concessions to the federal position for fear of losing popular support themselves. Thus a popular prime minister or one who can lead public opinion on a particular issue is strengthened in his negotiations with the provincial premiers. The important thing, of course, is what negotiators think public opinion is. Frequently the views of press commentators are seen as representative. Thus, the prime minister's capacity to convince journalists of the wisdom of his policies becomes important, not only because they can influence the attentive public, but also because their opinions may be taken by influential people to represent those of the public.[3]

Just as provincial premiers may be influenced by the appearance of public support, so may business and labour leaders, cabinet colleagues, senior civil servants, and other elites. In elections and between elections, in the words of John Meisel, "acceptance or rejection of a government . . . depends not only on what it does (or ignores) but also on how it presents and defends its policies."[4] Senator Maurice Lamontagne, a former cabinet minister, has commented on the importance of public standing: "if [a minister] enjoys a good press, he will be envied or respected and feared by his colleagues. . . . And, if he has a bad press, he is in serious trouble,

---

[2] Richard Simeon, *Federal-Provincial Diplomacy* (Toronto, 1972), p. 204.

[3] Though widely used, public opinion is in fact a difficult concept. Only a small number of people (the attentive public) regularly pay attention to public affairs generally, though there are special publics who pay attention to particular issues. Governments are usually concerned primarily with the opinions of those people who care enough about an issue to express views on it.

[4] John Meisel, *Working Papers on Canadian Politics* (Montreal, enlarged edition, 1973), p. 226.

because he will be viewed even by his own associates as a political liability, in spite of the qualities he may have."[5] This observation applies as well to prime ministers, who owe their positions as party leaders in large part to the expectation that they could command wide public support. It was John Diefenbaker's loss of standing outside of government, in the press and public, as well as his government's internal problems, which threatened his control of his cabinet, his caucus and the civil service in the early 1960's.[6] In short, the prime minister's image may be almost as important as his acts.

Development of the Prime Minister's Persuasive Role

National leaders have always had to rely on persuasion to govern effectively. The capacity to persuade mass publics has increased in importance in the western democracies in this century with the extension of the franchise and the development of new technologies of transport and communications. As Anthony Westell has put it, "in the age of TV and the jet, people [have come] to expect more direct personal contact with their national leader."[7] The general tendency toward closer ties between leaders and their publics, mediated by the mass media, has been observed in all democratic states.[8] People have come to identify the government with its leader, resulting in a growing personalization of politics and the inevitable pre-eminence of the chief executive. It is generally agreed that the impact of television has been to shift attention (and power) from legislatures to executives. The prime minister's status has been enhanced "by the fact that television producers and reporters want him on camera, answering the questions, so that he becomes almost the sole government spokesman on key issues."[9] The ability to use television effectively has become virtually a prerequisite for party leadership. The prime minister has always been a key communicator in parliamentary systems, as chief government spokesman, but his pre-eminence has been greatly enhanced by public expectations and media patterns.

Several developments in the late 1960's confirmed the international trend in Canada. Three of the most important, all reflecting the impact of television, may be cited. One of these was the decision of Lester B. Pearson, then prime minister, to appear on national television in February,

---

[5] Maurice Lamontagne, "The Influence of the Politician," in *The Canadian Political Process*, eds. Orest M. Kruhlak, Richard Schultz and Sidney I. Pohbihushchy (Toronto, rev. ed., 1973), p. 464.

[6] See Peter C. Newman, *Renegade in Power: The Diefenbaker Years* (Toronto, 1963), esp. Chs. 18, 24 and 25.

[7] Anthony Westell, *Paradox: Trudeau as Prime Minister* (Scarborough, Ont., 1972), p. 114.

[8] See Elmer E. Cornwell, "Role of the Press in Presidential Politics," in *Politics and the Press*, ed. Richard W. Lee (Washington, 1970), p. 16; Khayyam Z. Paltiel, *Political Party Financing in Canada* (Toronto, 1970), pp. 76-91.

[9] Walter Stewart, *Shrug: Trudeau in Power* (Toronto, 1971), p. 219.

1968, to explain why his government was not going to resign over its accidental defeat in the House of Commons, despite the parliamentary convention that a government must resign when an important bill is defeated. "Able to see and hear their political leaders on TV," as Westell has put it, "the public were less willing to leave day to day decisions to their elected MPs. A prime minister could appeal over the head of Parliament directly to the public, and Parliament would feel the public reaction within hours."[10] The decisions to seek a vote of confidence instead of resigning and to have the prime minister explain his action directly to the public were both to a degree precedent-setting. A second important development was the impact of the televised leadership conventions which chose Robert L. Stanfield as leader of the Progressive Conservative Party and Pierre E. Trudeau as leader of the Liberals. Both became national figures in a very brief period.[11] Trudeau's intriguing personal style during and after the 1968 federal election campaign was a third factor which accelerated the trend. His popular appeal attracted considerable media and popular attention and made it difficult for other political figures, friend and foe alike, to make an impact on the public mind during the 1968 to 1970 period.

The pressures on the prime minister have made it difficult for him to opt out of the role of chief public persuader for the government. It appears that the leader who fails to use the arts of public relations to build up his image will come under pressure from his party colleagues who need his popularity and will find his standing with other elites eroded. Attempts to delegate the role to lieutenants have met with only moderate success, despite the theory that the prime minister is only the first among equals in the parliamentary system. Prime Minister Trudeau's attempts in the 1972 campaign to employ his ministers as political substitutes worked poorly because neither the public nor the media would pay as much attention to them as to the prime minister. A survey of newspaper coverage of the 1974 campaign found that more than three-quarters of the front page stories on the election focussed on the party leaders (i.e., the prime minister and the challengers for the job).[12] Marc Lalonde has summed up the situation:

The Prime Minister's contacts with the public will continue to expand because of the

---

[10] Westell, *Paradox*, p. 87. For Pearson's account of these events, see *Mike: The Memoirs of the Right Honourable Lester B. Pearson*, ed. John A. Munro and Alex I. Inglis (Toronto, 1975), Vol. III, pp. 316-322.

[11] One political scientist has argued that "if anything has accelerated the trend to presidential politics in Canada it has been the adoption of televised leadership conventions." Denis Smith, "President and Parliament: The Transformation of Parliamentary Government in Canada," in *Apex of Power: The Prime Minister and Political Leadership in Canada*, 2nd ed., ed. Thomas A. Hockin (Scarborough, Ont., 1977), p. 308.

[12] For details of this study, see Frederick J. Fletcher, "The Mass Media in the 1974 Canadian Federal Election," in *Canada at the Polls*, ed. Howard R. Penniman (Washington, 1975).

changing nature of public needs, expectations and demands. As a consequence, his symbolic, motivational and pedagogical roles will inevitably increase in importance.[13]

In short, the prime minister cannot escape the roles of spokesman, inspirational leader and public educator.

The Prime Minister's Persuasive Resources

The authority and visibility inherent in the prime ministerial role confer impressive persuasive resources on the incumbent. The prime minister can use these resources to build his personal support, manage the news, influence the agenda of public political discussion, appeal to special publics for support on specific issues, and prepare the citizenry for new policies.

Among the prime minister's most important resources are those which permit him to command national attention. He can increase the visibility of an issue at the expense of others by commenting on it or simply by having a report released. He can also speak directly to the public by asking for national radio or television time to make a statement. In recent years, the prime minister has made such statements on a variety of subjects: the economy, inflation, national unity, the October (1970) crisis and the energy crisis, among others. Less dramatically, the prime minister is so newsworthy in his own right that virtually any speech, interview or press conference he chooses to give will be extensively reported. Each year, the prime minister gets thousands of invitations to speak and hundreds of requests for interviews. He can thus choose the time and the place for any announcement to have maximum impact. (However, he must for political reasons maintain a balance between French and English, among the regions and among the news media in his appearances and interviews.)

The prime minister can and does use his attention-getting capacity to draw attention away from other news. For example, it is a common strategy in House of Commons debates and, from time to time, during election campaigns for prime ministers to schedule important announcements to draw attention away from statements by the leaders of the opposition parties. Trudeau did this several times during the 1974 campaign. Through his co-ordinating role in government, the prime minister can also orchestrate government announcements for maximum advantage. It has been suggested that Trudeau tabled a letter announcing that the federal government would not challenge Quebec's controversial Official Language Act (Bill 22) in the courts at the same time one of his ministers was announcing the postponement of the United Nations crime confer-

---

[13] Marc Lalonde, "The Changing Role of the Prime Minister's Office," *Canadian Public Administration*, XIV, (1971), p. 529. Lalonde was then principal secretary to the Prime Minister.

ence in Toronto, which representatives of the Palestine Liberation Organization were to attend. Whether intentional or not, the news coverage of the announcement swamped that of the letter.[14]

The prime minister's co-ordinating role and his access to information are also important resources. The parliamentary tradition stresses centralized control of information and this control has been strengthened in recent years by the increased authority of the Prime Minister's Office (P.M.O.) and the Privy Council Office (P.C.O.). Officials in Canada are more reluctant to release information to reporters than their United States counterparts and less discretion is left to departments.[15] The prime minister has access to the vast informational capacity of the civil service and, working through his staff, can co-ordinate the release of information and announcements for maximum persuasive effect. The PMO advises ministers on both the content and timing of announcements. A frequent tactic of Canadian prime ministers is to release tentative policies to permit them to assess public reaction before making a final decision. When the prime minister announces a major policy, he rarely discusses its disadvantages or presents the arguments marshalled against it during the internal policy debate. He selects the supporting evidence for release.

The prime minister also has considerable capacity to influence the activities of the news media. At one level, he can generally get easy access to editors and publishers to explain his case. Private briefings are common. In time of crisis, he can call upon their patriotism to influence coverage. The most recent example is the care with which the CBC handled the October crisis.[16] On a day-to-day basis, reporters are susceptible to influence. The prime minister can influence not only news reports but also columns and commentaries through judicious use of personal interviews, background briefings, selective leaks to friendly journalists and the like. Well-known commentators have often been used as unofficial spokesmen for government policies. For example, Peter Dempson of the now defunct *Toronto Telegram* and Richard Jackson of the *Ottawa Journal*, both traditional Conservative newspapers, performed this function for John Diefenbaker. Mackenzie King also had his favorites and various journalists have been reported as playing this role for St. Laurent and Pearson. Trudeau has lacked such a confidante, though his aides have had close ties with some journalists.[17]

Less directly, the prime minister can pick and choose reporters for

---

[14] See column by Marjorie Nichols, *Vancouver Sun*, July 23, 1975.

[15] See Anthony Westell, "Access to News in a Small Capital: Ottawa," in *Secrecy and Foreign Policy*, ed. Thomas M. Franck and Edward Weisband (New York, 1974), p. 270.

[16] For a discussion of the pressures on the CBC, see Gertrude J. Robinson, "The Politics of Information and Culture during Canada's October Crisis," in *Studies in Canadian Communication*, ed. G. J. Robinson and Donald F. Theall (Montreal, 1975), pp. 150-158.

[17] See Westell, *Access*, pp. 255-56, and Larry Zolf, *Dance of the Dialectic* (Toronto, 1973), pp. 15-16 and 113 f.

interviews. Requests greatly exceed available time. Access can be given to reporters likely to be sympathetic and denied to those who have been hostile. This has the immediate effect of producing friendly coverage and the long-run effect of discouraging reporters, who are expected to produce the occasional interview with the prime minister, from doing critical reporting.[18] One former Ottawa reporter has commented that the cumulative effect of background briefings (which he calls "brainwashing") and the need to make friends to get information "mean that each government for the most part has its press gallery reporters in the palm of its hand."[19] The activities of the prime minister are covered almost exclusively by the parliamentary press gallery, made up of about 150 reporters and columnists representing most major news organizations. Walter Stewart, with the print journalist's disdain for broadcasters, argues that television reporters are most vulnerable to manipulation: "the producer doesn't want the reporter's face on his screen all the time, he wants the politicians, especially the Prime Minister's. Television reporters soon learn to ask only the obvious questions. . . ."[20]

Stewart gives another instructive example of the way in which a prime minister can influence coverage. Because there is no television or radio in the House of Commons, the prime minister is often able to turn the Question Period from an ordeal to an advantage. Trudeau's pattern, for example, has been to have an aide relay the questions reporters want him to comment on as he leaves the House. He may agree to repeat (and perhaps elaborate) his answer for the cameras and the tape recorders or he may refuse to do so. If he refuses, the issue will often receive only routine treatment, unless the opposition has come up with something genuinely dramatic. If he agrees to answer, he does so without the challenges he would face in the House. "What the viewer sees is the Prime Minister answering, fully and openly, the questions put to him; what he doesn't see are the issues he declines to discuss. . . ."[21] Stewart's analysis may be excessively conspiratorial, since the prime minister may refuse to answer not only to avoid issues on which he feels vulnerable, but also because he feels the responsible minister should deal with the issue or simply because he has other business to attend to. Nevertheless, the prime minister does have considerable capacity to influence coverage, especially television coverage.[22]

---

[18] Officials in the prime minister's office argue that their primary concerns in granting interviews are the size and appropriateness of audiences and balance among media, regions and languages. For a detailed account of U.S. practice, see Timothy Crouse, *The Boys on the Bus* (New York, 1973), Chs. IX and X.

[19] Frank Jones, "The Watchdogs on Parliament Hill," in *A Media Mosaic*, ed. Walt McDayter (Toronto, 1971), p. 96.

[20] Stewart, pp. 215-16.

[21] *Ibid.*, pp. 218-19.

[22] Researchers and the public tend to agree that television is more influential than the press. See, for example, "The Media and the People," a report by Martin Goldfarb Consultants, in Special Senate Committee on Mass Media, *Report*, Vol. III.

In short, the prime minister's persuasive resources, derived from his authority and visibility, are magnified by the mass media. While Canadian prime ministers have not been nearly as sophisticated as their British counterparts or U.S. presidents in their use of the media, the potential for news management is clearly there.

Constraints on the Prime Minister's Persuasive Powers

The prime minister does not, however, have a clear field for his persuasive messages. The operation of the parliamentary system, for example, limits his capacity to speak unchallenged. The convention is strongly held in Canada that parliament has the right to hear about government policy and to ask questions before the press or the public. Trudeau has shown himself even more reluctant than some of his predecessors to bypass parliament.[23] This convention provides an opportunity for the opposition parties to challenge prime ministerial statements and to send out competing messages immediately. The Question Period permits the opposition to seize the initiative and put the prime minister on the defensive by questioning government policies, raising important issues or exposing scandals. Unlike the U.S. system, the opposition in Canada is highly visible and institutionalized. The news media tend to follow parliamentary conventions: it is standard operating procedure for accounts of government statements, especially those made by the prime minister, to include reactions by opposition spokesmen. This holds true even for statements made outside the House. Some of the larger newspapers try to give opposition statements prominence equal to government statements, but others often "bury" them at the end of their stories.

Some critics have argued, however, that the government maintains a great and growing advantage over the opposition. Walter Stewart has put it colourfully:

With the advent of television, the government lead has lengthened; for every goodie to be dropped into the public craw there is a friendly government spokesman waving his wand at the camera, followed in due course by three opposition spokesmen who have, apparently, nothing good to say about anything.[24]

Frank Jones, former head of the *Toronto Star* Ottawa bureau, takes the view that

most opposition criticism is regarded by the public as sour grapes carping. The result in media terms is that the government can command the headline or the lead item much more easily than the opposition. It does not take reporters long to realize, after invariably making page one with a tidbit from a minister as opposed to page 67 with

---

[23] Trudeau has, according to Anthony Westell, "old-fashioned views about the rights of Parliament to hear about government policy and ask questions before information [appears] in the press." *Toronto Star*, September 5, 1975.

[24] Stewart, pp. 201-02.

a landmark speech by an opposition member, that their paper and presumably the readers are far more interested in what the government has to say.[25]

The result of these patterns is that the media magnify the traditional government advantage of being able to propose action where the opposition parties can only oppose it. Nevertheless, the institutionalized opposition usually provides more competition for the prime minister than the rather disorganized congressional parties do for the United States president. For example, Robert Stanfield was able to get good coverage of his proposal for wage and price controls to combat inflation in 1974, much more than congressional leaders usually get for their alternatives to presidential initiatives.

The prime minister also faces competition for attention from a variety of other sources, such as major interest groups, political commentators and provincial premiers. Within their own provinces, the premiers often attract more media attention than the prime minister, especially outside Ontario, and they frequently send out messages contradicting those of the prime minister. With few exceptions, Canada's news organizations have a local or provincial orientation. National messages do not always get through.[26] Regional identities are strong, especially outside Ontario, and in several provinces a significant proportion of the population feels a sense of grievance against the federal government. Such feelings are well entrenched in Quebec and the Prairie provinces, for example. Canada's regionalized politics inhibit the capacity of the prime minister to frame effective political appeals for the nation as a whole. Regional climates of opinion are such, for example, that inflation may be the major issue in one area (say Ontario) and unemployment in another (say the Atlantic provinces). Or a prime ministerial campaign against high oil and gas prices may go down well in Ontario but not in Alberta. The prime minister's difficulties are increased when provincial premiers take advantage of the climate of opinion to score points off the federal government, as they often do. The 1975 Ontario election, in which the premier blamed the federal government for problems in the economy, was a classic case, though the pattern has been more common in other provinces.

Two instances of news coverage of the prime minister and his competitors illustrate relative strengths and weaknesses. In the 1974 federal election campaign, the competitors were the other national party leaders. Despite the fact that the news media are more alert to the need for balanced coverage during a contest for votes, the prime minister was the clear victor. He was featured in at least one front page story in more than half of the 192 editions (of 16 newspapers) surveyed. The figure for his major challenger, Robert Stanfield, was less than one-third. The prime minister also led in front page pictures and in making news apart from his

[25] Jones, p. 93.

[26] See Fletcher, *Mass Media*, and sources cited therein.

TABLE 7-1

Attention to Party Leaders on Front Pages of 16 Daily Newspapers During the
1974 Federal Election Campaign

Leader	Editions Mentioned[a] on Front Page (%)	Pictures on[b] Front Page (%)	Number of Stories on Leader Independent of Party
P. E. Trudeau (LIB)	54	41	30
R. L. Stanfield (PC)	32	30	5
D. Lewis (NDP)	19	24	0
	N = 192	N = 78	T = 35

a. This column does not add to 100% because of multiple mentions.
b. Real Caouette, leader of Social Credit accounts for the remaining 5% of pictures.
Source: Frederick J. Fletcher, "The Mass Media in the 1974 Canadian Federal Election," in
Canada at the Polls (Washington, 1975).

party. (See Table 7-1 for details.) The pattern for radio and television was
similar, but Trudeau's lead was less pronounced, probably because the
broadcast media were more concerned about partisan balance than the
newspapers. The prime minister's victory in the contest for media attention reflects the traditional incumbent's advantage, the capacity to
announce decisions and to take actions, as well as Trudeau's colourful
personal style and the Liberal party's highly effective campaign, in which
reporters were given a steady diet of headline grabbing "happenings" and
hard news. The Trudeau campaign made heavy use of the prime minister's access to civil service studies to keep policy announcements flowing
throughout the latter half of the campaign.[27]

In the second instance, the prime minister's major competitors for
attention were the provincial premiers. A survey of the news coverage of
the federal-provincial conference on energy, March 27, 1974, in seven
major daily newspapers disclosed that of 568 references to political figures, nearly a third were to the prime minister.[28] In all but one province,
Alberta, the prime minister was quoted more often than the provincial
premier in the local newspaper(s). Nevertheless, the provincial spokesmen
taken together got more attention than the prime minister, and the premier of Alberta was quoted widely (24% of all references). It is notewor-

[27] This study of media coverage is reported in detail in *Ibid.*
[28] This content analysis carried out by Daphne Gaby, then an honours student in political
science at York University, covered at least one newspaper in each of Canada's five
regions and included analysis of the two issues published immediately before the
conference, the issue on the day of the conference, and the two issues immediately
following. The *Toronto Star* was included as the Ontario paper because of its local
orientation, the *Globe and Mail* because of its pretensions to national coverage and the
Ottawa Journal for a national capital perspective.

thy also that the prime minister was quoted three times as often as other federal spokesmen, despite the fact that the energy and finance ministers played significant roles in the negotiations. Even more important perhaps was the fate of the federal opposition leaders. They were the forgotten men, ignored entirely by four of the seven newspapers and accounting for only three per cent of all references. (See Table 7-2 for details.)

In both these cases, the prime minister got more media attention than his competitors. And he had different competitors in each case. No other political figure can match his attention-getting capacity. But in neither case was he without challenge. In the energy conference case, he received less attention in Alberta than the premier of that province. That outcome is also likely in other cases where the premier is in direct conflict with Ottawa. The prime minister's advantage is clear but it is by no means absolute.

Besides competing political messages, the prime minister faces a number of other barriers in trying to persuade the public. To begin with, getting media attention does not guarantee public attention. Only a small proportion of the population pays regular attention to political news. For example, only one-quarter of a national sample of citizens reported a good deal of interest in politics in a 1965 survey and, in a 1968 survey, only 44 per cent said they were very much interested in the federal election.[29] In general, the public will not pay attention to prime ministerial messages unless they are either dramatic or obviously relevant to their personal interests. As Richard Neustadt has put it with regard to the U.S., "Without a real-life happening to hoist it into view, a piece of presidential news, much like the man's own voice, is likely to be lost amidst the noises and distractions of the day."[30] This is particularly true in a highly regionalized system such as Canada.

Even when he can get his message through, it may have little impact. For example, research shows that media audiences tend to ignore or misunderstand messages that they find disagreeable or which challenge previously established opinions. Audiences also have preconceived notions about any particular prime minister and knowledge of his past actions which will colour their reception of his messages. For example, Trudeau may have had more difficulty in persuading English Canadians to accept measures to promote French than a prime minister less closely associated with French Canada might have, especially given the fact that some English-Canadian voters originally supported Trudeau as a leader who could deal with Quebec's demands. The Official Language Act has not been fully accepted in English Canada. Rumblings of discontent have continued to emanate from the civil service, spilling over into electoral politics in the Ottawa area, and there has been a good deal of misunder-

---

[29] These data are from the 1965 and 1968 national election studies carried out by John Meisel and others and were provided by the Institute for Behavioural Research, York University.

[30] Neustadt, p. 102.

TABLE 7-2

Attention to Political Spokesmen in News Coverage of the Federal-Provincial Conference on Energy, March 27, 1974, in Seven Daily Newspapers[a]

Spokesman	St. John's Evening Telegram (%)	La Presse (Montreal) (%)	Ottawa Journal (%)	Toronto Star (%)	Toronto Globe & Mail (%)	Edmonton Journal (%)	Vancouver Sun (%)	Total (%)
Prime Minister	27.0	44.7	30.9	28.4	23.7	30.8	35.4	30.1
Other Federal	15.3	–	14.7	8.8	20.3	6.7	5.1	11.1
Local Premier[b]	17.0	15.8	1.5	10.8	5.1	39.4	2.5	13.6
Other Local	3.4	–	–	2.0	4.2	1.0	–	1.8
Other Premiers	37.3	39.5	51.5	50.0	39.8	14.4	57.0	40.5
Federal Opposition	–	–	1.5	–	6.8	7.7	–	3.0
N	59	38	68	102	118	104	79	568

a. All quotations counted.
b. In one case, a cabinet minister represented the premier.

Source: Calculated from data collected by Daphne Gaby for an honours seminar in political science at York University, 1975.

standing of and hostility to the bilingualism policy in English Canada. Trudeau has felt this failure of persuasion sufficiently to blame the press for failing to explain the Act adequately to the public. Press spokesmen replied that Trudeau and his Cabinet had done little public persuading themselves.[31] This is, however, an area where prime ministerial persuasion is not easy. For unilingual civil servants, self-interest and fear are involved. For the general public, the language issue involves questions of personal and national identity. In these circumstances, minds do not change easily.

The distorting lens of partisanship is also a factor. The prime minister invariably gets much higher support ratings from supporters of his own party than from other citizens. His partisan supporters are also much more likely to be receptive to his persuasive messages than other citizens. Surveys tend to show that a Liberal prime minister's position will have much more support among Liberal partisans than among other citizens.[32] This cuts two ways, however. While Liberals are likely to be most receptive to a Liberal prime minister, they also expect him to represent certain views and interests. The positions a prime minister can take are constrained by the views of his followers. Abortion and bilingualism are, for example, touchy issues for a Liberal leader because of the traditional dependence of the party on French Catholic support.

The prime minister is also, of course, at the mercy of events. Not only must he use favourable events to promote his views, he must also react to unfavourable ones. There are, in effect, environmental constraints on the prime minister's persuasive powers. External events, such as inflation or recession, which impinge on the lives of large numbers of citizens, limit the effectiveness of any public relations campaign and are not easily explained away. But their impact can be blunted if the prime minister can influence the way in which they are interpreted. In the 1974 election campaign, for example, it appears that the argument offered by the prime minister and his ministers that the high rates of inflation were caused by events beyond government control were quite widely accepted, despite the contrary arguments of the opposition parties.[33] However, the prime minister can rarely escape having to deal with such events.

The Prime Minister and the Press

The fact that the prime minister must use the mass media as a major channel for communicating messages to the public is also an important constraint on his persuasive powers. Although the prime minister can influence news coverage, as we have seen, the fact remains that there is a natural conflict of interests between the prime minister and the press. Reporters want easy access to information on government decisions, pre-

---

[31] See Paul Stevens and John Saywell, "Parliament and Politics," *Canadian Annual Review 1969*, ed. J. Saywell (Toronto), 1970, pp. 10-11. See also Westell, *Paradox*, p. 17.

[32] See, for example, Meisel, chs. 1 and 2.

[33] See chapters by William P. Irvine and Lawrence LeDuc in *Canada at the Polls*.

ferably before they are taken; the prime minister wants to feed out information selectively for maximum persuasive effect. Reporters want to report the conflicts of personalities and ideas within government; the prime minister seeks to protect the privacy of cabinet discussion and to protect the confidentiality of the advice civil servants give to cabinet, in line with parliamentary tradition. The government also, of course, wants to cover up internal divisions to avoid providing ammunition for the opposition, to stress successes rather than failures and to avoid scandals. Reporters and editors, in contrast, regard failures, corruption and back-room deals as more newsworthy than successful policies, honest government and open debate of issues. In some journalistic circles, there is a "culture of disparagement" which leads to constant questioning of government motives and sincerity. There is a tendency to compare prime ministers to some vague ideal of an omnipotent leader who can solve all problems and to find them wanting. To the extent that reporters take this view, or regard themselves as an unofficial opposition, the prime minister's capacity to speak through them undistorted is reduced. This pattern is not as well-established in Canada as in the U.S. and, indeed, some critics would say that Canadian political reporting is too uncritical. Other Canadian journalists respond that the critical scrutiny of the executive can be left in Canada to the official opposition, whereas in the U.S. the press must perform this function.[34] In any case, the news media are not simply a passive channel for the prime minister to use.

Political leaders frequently complain that the news media shape the kinds of messages they can send. Instead of explaining government policy, they complain, the media concentrate on conflict or on trivia, such as the name of the prime minister's latest son. Journalists find personalities more interesting than events and events more interesting than speeches. Thus, while the prime minister can get press attention with a general speech aimed at educating the public on a complex issue, for example, it must be striking in style or substance to get extensive coverage, and it is likely to be simplified (and perhaps distorted) as presented. Effective communication through the media requires that messages be brief, relatively simple and dramatic or colourful. Trudeau's penchant for philosophical speculation has frequently led to misunderstandings and irritation on both sides.[35] The late Prime Minister Lester Pearson complained:

Newspaper editors are always bleating about the refusal of politicians to produce mature and responsible discussion of the issues. The fact is, when we do discuss policies seriously, we are not reported at all, or reported very inadequately. Reporters

---

[34] See James C. Strouse, *The Mass Media, Public Opinion, and Public Policy* (Columbus, Ohio, 1975), p. 129. See also discussions in Westell, *Access* p. 268; Stewart, pp. 203-24 and 214; Cornwell, *Role of Press*, p. 18; and for a more general treatment, Frederick J. Fletcher, "Between Two Stools: News Coverage of Provincial Politics in Ontario," in *Government and Politics of Ontario*, ed. Donald C. MacDonald (Toronto, 1975), pp. 259ff.

[35] See Westell, *Paradox*, p. 132.

do not appear even to listen, until we say something controversial or personal, charged with what they regard as news value. And audiences normally confirm the reporters' judgement by obvious boredom with reasoned argument. . . . People want a show, and the competition for their attention is savage. So show it must be, with excitement, headlines, personal attacks, and appeals to prejudice or fear or other emotions.[36]

One consequence of these patterns has been for prime ministers to give up on the mass media for serious communication and simply to project their personalities and to hope that a popular personal image will gain support for their policies (if not understanding).

The process of prime ministerial press relations has changed dramatically in recent years. Prior to 1957, prime ministers used a few privileged reporters from sympathetic newspapers as channels to the public. Other reporters had to rely on these insiders for information. Major cabinet ministers had their own insiders and the whole information process was somewhat haphazard.[37] The first prime ministerial press secretary was appointed in 1957 by John Diefenbaker, but Diefenbaker placed little confidence in him and continued the old system of leaking news to favoured journalists. The first effective prime ministerial press office was established by Lester Pearson in 1963. The press secretary, Richard O'Hagan, was an effective spokesman and adviser, who facilitated the prime minister's persuasive role and the work of reporters. Pearson also continued informal relations with journalists. Westell believes that prime minister-press relations were "as close as they have ever been" in the 1963-67 period.[38]

When Trudeau became prime minister in 1968 he continued the process of institutionalizing the press office. By 1975, it consisted of a press secretary (one of four senior officers in the P.M.O.), three assistant press secretaries, an advance man to handle press logistics on prime ministerial tours and three secretaries. The office performs a wide variety of services for the prime minister and the reporters who cover him: issuing press releases on announcements and statements by the prime minister; arranging press conferences and interviews; answering inquiries from the press and public; preparing transcripts of all prime ministerial speeches, news conferences, television and radio appearances and interviews for release to the parliamentary press gallery (simultaneous with publication or broadcast); assembling briefing materials for the prime minister before news conferences and interviews; preparing summaries of editorial reaction to government policy. The press secretary also serves as

---

[36] Lester B. Pearson, *Mike: The Memoirs of the Rt. Hon. Lester B. Pearson, Vol. III: 1957-1968*, ed. John A. Munro and Alex I. Inglis (Toronto, 1975), p. 205.

[37] Westell, *Access*, p. 257, notes that the Canadian system was less structured than the British system which he had previously experienced, requiring more work to get the story, but also permitting more cross-checking.

[38] *Toronto Star*, September 5, 1975.

the prime minister's chief adviser on press relations. The press office tries to have an officer with the prime minister during all encounters with reporters to assist him and to tape all exchanges for the record. This formal apparatus is intended to serve the reporter's need for information and to regulate the flow of information for the prime minister. In fact, however, reporters complain that the Trudeau administration is excessively secretive and that even innocuous information, such as the prime minister's vacation plans, is often unavailable.[39]

Despite the formal apparatus, there is an important personal dimension to prime ministerial press relations. John Diefenbaker, colourful and dramatic in parliament and on the hustings, had a good press in 1957 but his peevish reaction to press criticism once in office eroded the goodwill and by 1962 there was much bitterness toward him in the press gallery.[40] Lester Pearson always had good press relations, though some reporters thought him too dull and insufficiently dynamic. Trudeau, like Diefenbaker, started off with a highly supportive press corps but soon developed bitter enemies in the press gallery.

Commentators writing before 1970 frequently noted Trudeau's masterful use of the media and some complained that the press corps treated him uncritically.[41] By the time of the 1972 campaign, however, the general mood among Ottawa reporters was one of bitter hostility. It has been suggested that Trudeau neither likes nor respects the mass media and that "he feels no particular need to explain himself or his government to [reporters]."[42] He holds himself aloof from the press gallery and has used his press office from time to time "as a shield between himself and reporters,"[43] although he has not been inaccessible for formal interviews. Unlike previous prime ministers, Trudeau appears to have no personal friends among Ottawa reporters. Diefenbaker had both friends and enemies in the gallery and would frequently wander through the press section of his plane or train while on tour, telling anecdotes, answering questions and sometimes berating individual reporters. His relationships were as personal as Trudeau's are impersonal. Pearson seemed to enjoy the company of reporters and often held off-the-record chats at his resi-

---

[39] The information in this paragraph and the one following is derived from Lalonde and from personal interviews with Ottawa reporters and press office personnel. In 1976 Richard O'Hagan joined the P.M.O. as special adviser on communications, taking on some of the functions of the press secretary.

[40] See Newman, *Renegade*, ch. 18.

[41] Denis Smith commented in 1969 that Trudeau had "made brilliant use of the public opportunities of a party leader, in convention, in the general election, and in his continuing encounters outside Parliament. He has recognized that the public responds first to personalities, not to issues, and so he campaigns for the most generalized mandate," *President and Parliament*, p. 323. Stewart and Jones are among the critics. See their works, cited above.

[42] Anthony Westell, *Toronto Star*, September 5, 1975.

[43] Westell, *Access*, p. 264.

dence or invited reporters to his hotel room for drinks while on tour. Trudeau has tried similar tactics but with little conviction or success. He also tends to "give tart answers to what he [regards] as stupid or unfair questions. . . . "[44] In short, Trudeau has shown little inclination to manage the news by managing reporters. Instead, he has resorted to tours, television appearances and radio hot-lines to reach the public, whenever he has had an important case to make.

Some observers have suggested that Trudeau has made fewer efforts to manage the news than his predecessors, finding the process degrading. There have been fewer calculated leaks and few direct attempts to influence reporters, at least by the prime minister himself. He appears to prefer to leave the backgrounding briefings to others and to avoid the use of leaks altogether, yet he appears to place little confidence in his press aides.[45] Trudeau has not generally used the press to set the stage for policy initiatives, as Pearson appears to have done by stirring up controversy over proposals for a new Canadian flag so a compromise could be reached.[46] He seems to prefer more direct appeals to the public through television and in person.

The Trudeau Image

Trudeau's failure to cultivate the press gallery may have been a significant factor in the decline of his public support in the 1968-72 period, though the economic situation and his tendency to blurt out tactless remarks in blunt language were also factors. In any event, he was tagged by the news media as arrogant, aloof and inaccessible and, the polls suggest, a large segment of the public agreed. Except for a sharp resurgence of popular support in 1970, after the October crisis, the polls showed a fairly steady decline in Trudeau's popular image over the 1968-72 period.[47] The shift in Trudeau's image from that of "an attractive, exciting, resolute thinker-doer" to a "proud, temperamental, impatient ruler" which resulted in part from the work of a hostile press gallery had a good deal to do with the Liberal party's near-defeat in 1972.[48] However, his behaviour after the 1972 election brought another image change: in a Gallup poll taken late in 1973, 57 per cent of a national sample said Trudeau had changed his attitudes since the 1972 election; 35 per cent saw him as less arrogant and 30 per cent as less aloof (showing more concern for people).[49] The prime

---

[44] Ibid., p. 265.
[45] This observation is supported by several Ottawa reporters. See, for example, Westell, Toronto Star, September 5, 1975.
[46] See Westell, Access, p. 259, and Peter C. Newman, The Distemper of Our Times (Toronto, 1968), ch. 19.
[47] See, for example, Lawrence LeDuc, "The Measurement of Public Opinion," in Canada at the Polls, figure 3.
[48] The quoted phrases are from Meisel, p. 229.
[49] Paul Stevens and John Saywell, "Parliament and Politics," in Canadian Annual Review 1973, ed. J. Saywell (Toronto, 1974), p. 96.

minister's improved image, which no doubt helped the Liberals win the 1974 election, did not last and, as will be seen, his popular support hit new lows in 1976. The implications of these image shifts are not completely clear but it is reasonable to suggest that the decline of Trudeau's "image capital" contributed to his difficulties in selling his bilingualism and voluntary anti-inflation policies to the special publics involved, despite personal appeals in print and on television. Certainly his shifting image did little for his general credibility.

The Prime Minister as Public Educator

Trudeau is one of those prime ministers who have taken the role of public educator seriously. When he set up the Task Force on Government Information soon after taking office, he was concerned with providing the information necessary for public involvement in government. According to Anthony Westell, "his objectives were to ensure that the federal Government would have a strong presence in the minds of all Canadians, particularly in Quebec, and to provide the basic facts about government programs without which participation would be impossible."[50] His own behaviour reflected these goals and his early popularity has been attributed to "his ability to make contact with the voters."[51] In a variety of public forums, he tried to educate the public on the necessity for government to set priorities. "The Government," he told one audience, "cannot build harbours, roads, airports everywhere. We have to choose."[52] He urged citizens not to ask for more than the country can afford. The prime minister commented in 1972 that

It is necessary periodically to force the attention of the citizen on national questions: what kind of Canada do you want? And I think that an election is the only period, barring major crisis, when he has to ask himself that question.[53]

Trudeau did in fact run his 1972 re-election campaign in these terms, seeking a general mandate. Larry Zolf has termed it Trudeau's search for a "dignified dialogue," suggesting that "the ego of post-charisma Trudeau demanded a reasoned, pragmatic endorsement by the Canadian people of a reasonable, pragmatic government."[54] Most of Trudeau's campaign speeches were low-key lectures on the problems of government, the duties of citizens during elections and the general goals of the Trudeau administration, stated in terms of national integrity, economic growth, social justice and individual fulfillment.[55]

---

[50] Westell, *Paradox*, p. 121.

[51] Paul Stevens and John Saywell, "Parliament and Politics," in *Canadian Annual Review 1970*, ed. J. Saywell (Toronto, 1971), p. 175.

[52] *Ibid.*, p. 176.

[53] *Toronto Star*, September 2, 1972.

[54] Zolf, p. 41.

[55] Paul Stevens and John Saywell, "Parliament and Politics," in *Canadian Annual Review 1972*, ed. J. Saywell (Toronto, 1973), p. 51.

However educational these speeches may have been, they were evidently not what the public (or reporters) wanted to hear. The Trudeau campaign was hurt by Statistics Canada's announcement in mid-campaign that both the cost of living and unemployment were up. But the damage appears to have been worsened by the prime minister's decision to stick to his educator role and not deal directly with the announcements or opposition attacks based on them. This stance made him appear aloof and unconcerned about the public's economic worries. No measures were put forward to deal with them and the government appeared either unconcerned or inept.[56] John Meisel has commented that "failure to recognize and debate issues, and the well-held pose that nothing was seriously wrong, convinced majorities, particularly west of the Ottawa River, that Mr. Trudeau was somehow too far from them, too aloof to deserve renewed support."[57] Even many civil servants were no longer convinced that the government deserved their support.

One consequence of the electoral result seemed to be that Trudeau withdrew somewhat from his educator role. During 1972 and 1973, he concentrated on his duties in Ottawa and generally kept a low political profile. When he did go on television, for example, he spoke about more specific issues, such as national energy policy and western alienation.[58] For the 1974 federal election campaign, he revived some of his attention-getting antics of 1968 and also provided a rapid-fire series of concrete policy announcements. He appeared to be trying to project the image of a hard-working leader and a fighting politician. In the event, the Liberals won the campaign and were returned as the majority party. The prime minister had been able to minimize the distorting effect of a hostile press by providing reporters with news they could not ignore and allowing them little opportunity for confrontation.[59]

It is also instructive to trace the prime minister's efforts to influence the behaviour of general and special publics with respect to inflation. As early as 1969, the prime minister went on television to support the campaign for voluntary price and wage restraint begun by Edgar Benson, then Minister of Finance, and John Young, head of the Prices and Incomes Commission. During the following year, he spoke to conferences of union and business leaders, issued statements and made television appearances. In 1971, he went on television to announce a freeze on government spending—a symbolic as well as practical act—but it appeared to have little impact. Business and labour proved unreceptive to signals from Ottawa and no national consensus in favour of price and wage controls emerged. Trudeau's efforts to use his persuasive powers to crush the

---

[56] *Ibid.*, pp. 54-5, 77-8, 85.

[57] Meisel, p. 230. See also p. 226.

[58] See, for example, Fred Lazar, "The National Economy," in *Canadian Annual Review 1973*, ed. J. Saywell (Toronto, 1974), p. 325.

[59] See Fletcher, *Mass Media*.

psychology of inflation proved unsuccessful and by 1971 he appeared to have given up.[60]

In the more recent campaign for voluntary restraint, spearheaded by Finance Minister John Turner, the prime minister took little public part, perhaps having decided that his capacity to shift the national mood was too limited to justify risking his prestige publicly. His limited private efforts and those of Turner appear to have had little success. The point made above that the public takes note of actions as well as words is pertinent here. It seems clear that the prime minister's decision to support a large increase in salary for members of parliament in 1975 seriously weakened the government's campaign for voluntary restraints. Regardless of the justification for such an increase, it was symbolically devastating and could hardly be called leadership by example. As Allan Fotheringham observed, "people with [common sense] do not grant themselves 33-1/3 per cent pay increases while attempting to exhort the grubby unwashed to a policy of restraint."[61]

Late in 1975, the Trudeau administration embarked on a new and dramatic war against inflation, one which involved government controls over incomes, prices and profits in key sectors of the economy.[62] The actions were symbolic as well as practical and, as the prime minister made clear in his national television and radio address on October 13, were aimed as past campaigns had been at changing public attitudes:

Tonight I am making a direct appeal for the co-operation of all Canadians in the practice of individual restraint. . . . I am asking you to live by the fact that all Canadians must restrain their rising demands upon the nation's wealth, so that Canada as a whole will be able to live within her means.

. . . . . .

If I could persuade you of nothing else tonight, I would want to persuade you that no amount of Government control, not even a vast army of bureaucrats operating the most massive restraining machinery, not even a total freeze of all prices and incomes of all Canadians, could permanently cure the disease of inflation.

The only benefit of having restraint imposed by law is that it gives people time to understand and adopt the real cure, which is a basic change in our attitudes—a realization that we cannot expect incomes to continue growing at a faster rate than the economy itself is growing.

. . . . . .

In this struggle, we must accomplish nothing less than a wrenching adjustment of our expectations—an adjustment of our national lifestyle to our means. This change will not come easily, nor soon. It will take time before much smaller increases in

---

[60] See Westell, *Paradox*, pp. 145-64 and Donald Forster, "The National Economy," in *Canadian Annual Review 1969*, pp. 305-318.

[61] *Maclean's Magazine*, October 6, 1975, p. 96.

[62] For a good summary of the program's details, see *Maclean's*, November 3, 1975, pp. 18-20.

prices and incomes are accepted as normal. It takes time for people to change their basic attitudes. But change we must.[63]

Few prime ministers have set themselves a more difficult task of public persuasion. Well aware of this, Trudeau backed up his actions with a major publicity effort which rivalled an election campaign in intensity. The campaign began before the announcement with leaked warnings that the government's anti-inflation program would be "tough", "frightening" and "unprecedented in peacetime". It continued after the announcement on several levels, including the activities in the House of Commons surrounding the introduction and debate of the legislation, meetings with provincial premiers, opposition leaders, leaders of labor, business and farm organizations, news conferences, and radio and television appearances and public speeches by the prime minister and other senior ministers. In the weeks following the announcement, the prime minister spoke and met with interest group officials in several cities, as well as appearing on radio and television and holding news conferences. In Toronto, for example, he spoke to the Rotary Club, taped a local radio interview, met with members of the Ontario Weekly Newspaper Association and held talks with local Liberal party officials. An important element in the campaign was meetings with newspaper editorial boards. The seriousness with which the government viewed the public information campaign was underlined by the recall of Richard O'Hagan, the highly successful press secretary to Lester Pearson, from his job at the Canadian Embassy in Washington, to work on it and the use of eight senior ministers to supplement the prime minister's efforts.[64]

The prime minister's persuasive performance drew mixed reviews. While some observers viewed his initial broadcast as stiff and unimpressive, his early speeches were thought to be effective.[65] However, another observer commented that his "penchant for the putdown" was hurting his persuasive efforts[66] and Geoffrey Stevens wrote that

The Prime Minister . . . tends to lose sight of the fact that the object is to persuade the country to cooperate, not to intimidate it into obeying. In some appearances, Mr. Trudeau's tone is just right—concerned, conciliatory, patient. Other times, however, he lets himself slip into a quite different routine—We kept Telling you People that We didn't Want to Bring in Controls Because of all the Bad Things They would do but You Wanted Leadership and now You've Got it and if You don't go along now

---

[63] These quotations are from a text of the prime minister's address printed in the Toronto *Globe and Mail*, October 14, 1975.

[64] These and other details of the campaign are derived from the *Toronto Globe and Mail* and *Toronto Star*, October 13—November 5, 1975, and from *Time*, October 27, November 3, and November 10, 1975 and from *Maclean's*, November 3, 1975.

[65] See, for example, columns in the *Toronto Star* by Richard Gwyn, October 18, 1975, and Anthony Westell, October 24, 1975.

[66] Tom Gould on CTV national news, October 23, 1975.

with me I'll Clap the Lot of you in Jail. If the Prime Minister does not exercise greater self-censorship, the best efforts of his Cabinet colleagues will be useless.[67]

Even during the early weeks of intensive campaigning, opponents of the program were able to seize the initiative from the prime minister on several occasions. There is every indication that the public relations battle, which has waxed and waned in intensity, will last as long as the programme itself.

Although the prime minister has been able to command national attention and to make the anti-inflation program the major subject of national debate for many months, he has had only limited success in convincing labor leaders, opposition politicians and editorial writers that the controls can slow rising prices. The barriers to effective persuasion include Trudeau's previous position on controls, labor's firm rejection of similar guidelines, the inevitable inequities in such a program, which have been given considerable publicity, and the long-term nature of the program. It has proved difficult for the prime minister to convince the public that conditions have changed since the 1974 federal election campaign when he vehemently rejected controls. There has been a tendency to question both his commitment to the new program and his motives for introducing it.[68] Organized labor rejected similar guidelines in 1971 and earlier in 1975 when the government put them forward on a voluntary basis. The labor movement, which distrusts the Trudeau government and fears that it is being made the scapegoat for inflation rejected the program immediately and the Canadian Labor Congress launched a $500,000 public relations campaign to discredit it, including a one-day national work stoppage on October 14, 1976, the first anniversary of the program. Trudeau and his senior ministers have held several meetings with labor leaders but appear to have had little success in changing their minds. Even the program's initial supporters—business leaders, provincial premiers and some professional groups—have raised doubts about its implementation. Attempts to control profits have angered business groups without placating labour leaders. The government has also been concerned that the controls would affect wages much sooner than prices, creating resentment which could not be overcome by pointing to a reduced rate of inflation.

The prime minister has also been faced with hostile opposition parties and a querulous press. The opposition parties have been working to discredit the program in the House and NDP leader Edward Broadbent has made nation-wide speaking tours to oppose it. Although the consensus of newspaper editorial boards before the announcement had appeared to be in favour of a control program, the major dailies did not give the Trudeau initiative anything like wholesale support. Rather they tended to

---

[67] Toronto *Globe and Mail*, October 29, 1975.

[68] It has been suggested that the prime minister did not commit the full power and prestige of his office to past campaigns. See Westell, *Paradox*, p. 152.

criticize the program for its inconsistencies or inequities and to take the government to task for not cutting its own spending more to set an example. One academic supporter of the program has noted that "few issues in Canadian history . . . have generated in such a short time more whining and complaining, quibbling and cavilling, shouting and defying, searching for loopholes and general hypercriticism [than this one]."[69]

News coverage of the government's campaign has not made the prime minister's task any easier either. The pattern was typical: the prime minister has been able to command the major headlines and the lead items on news broadcasts but his statements were immediately challenged by the leaders of the opposition parties and by labor leaders. Even the coverage of the announcement of the program was not dominated by the prime minister; reaction to the announcement, much of it negative, actually received more newspaper space and broadcast time than the announcement itself.[70] In the weeks that followed, it appeared that opponents of the program dominated the news. Government spokesmen complained that the coverage had been negative and focused excessively on the labor-government confrontation. Business complaints also appear to have received a good airing. It would take a major research project to document such claims but it is clear that the prime minister has not been given a clear field for his persuasive efforts. The news media have tended to treat the program in partisan political terms, despite the best efforts of government spokesmen, and have not accepted the view that the program deserves automatic national support as an emergency measure in the public interest.[71]

On the positive side, there has been some evidence of public support for controls. Justifying the government's change of mind on controls, Finance Minister Donald Macdonald, who succeeded John Turner only weeks before the new program was adopted, commented that while there had been little support for such a program in 1974, a consensus in favor had emerged during 1975.[72] A Gallup poll taken about a month before the program was announced found 54% of its national sample in favor of compulsory income controls, up from 45% in 1974. Support for compulsory price controls was basically unchanged at about 70%. In March 1976, 58% of respondents in the Gallup poll reported thinking that ' "the Federal Government's anti-inflation program is a good thing;" 30% thought it "a bad thing." Even among respondents in union households, a

---

69 William A. Dimma, *Toronto Star*, October 18, 1975.

70 The prime minister's announcement received about 40% of the space devoted to the issue on the front pages of the *Globe and Mail* and *Toronto Star*, on October 14, for example, and about the same proportion of time on the CBC and CTV national news broadcasts.

71 For a fuller discussion of this proposition, see Frederick J. Fletcher, "The Prime Minister, the Press and the Public: The Case of the Anti-Inflation Program," *Queen's Quarterly,* LXXXIII, (Spring 1976), pp. 81 ff.

72 Interview in *Time*, October 27, 1975, pp. 6-7.

majority (52%) favored the program. There appeared to be majority support for the program in all regions and classes. In several surveys, however, respondents showed themselves skeptical about the fairness of the program—about two-thirds reported thinking it unfair—and about its success: only about one-third reported being confident it would reduce inflation significantly. By June 1976 most respondents (85%) still tended to believe that prices would rise faster than family incomes. The public seemed to have taken the view that the program was unfair but inevitable.[73] Analysis of earlier surveys had suggested that support was broad but shallow: few saw themselves making significant sacrifices.[74] The challenge for the prime minister remained to deepen that support and to convince skeptics that the modest sacrifices required by the program are indeed necessary (and apportioned reasonably fairly among the various groups in society). Broad, general support is not sufficient to ensure a program's success when key groups are intensely opposed. This is especially true when one considers the prime minister's larger goal of changing fundamental attitudes.

During 1975 and 1976, the prime minister faced the dual challenge of actually reducing inflation and of dispelling growing doubts about his capacity to inspire public trust. Public approval of "the way Pierre Trudeau is handling his job as prime minister" dropped from a high point of 48% in May 1974 to 42% in October 1975, and dipped to the very low figure of 33% in April 1976.[75] The approval rating for the federal government as a whole dropped from 44% in 1973 to only 27% (21% among English speaking respondents) in June 1976. In addition, the proportion of Gallup poll respondents saying they would vote for the Liberal candidate if a federal election were being held dropped to a near-record low of about 30% during 1976, 13% below the proportion of the vote received by the party in the 1974 federal election.[76] It was clear that, despite majority acceptance of the inflation program, the controversy surrounding it and the bilingualism program had bitten deeply into the general support for the prime minister and his administration.

Although the anti-inflation program seems unlikely to be overturned by labor protests or business complaints, the public relations battle regarding it is by no means over.[77] The prime minister must concern

---

[73] The opinions reported in this paragraph are taken from *The Gallup Report*, selected issues, November 1975 to July 1976. The interpretations presented here are my own.

[74] Richard Gwyn, *Toronto Star*, October 18, 1975.

[75] This is one of the lowest ratings ever recorded by Gallup for a Canadian prime minister. *The Gallup Report*, May 12, 1976.

[76] These data are from *The Gallup Report*, July 7, 1976 and August 4, 1976.

[77] The prime minister's public relations battle with the Canadian Labor Congress may be aided by public response to the union campaign. In a poll taken in March, 1976, 56% of a national sample reported thinking that labor unions were taking an unreasonable attitude towards the government's prices and incomes policy, compared to 28% who thought it reasonable. Even in union households, more respondents thought the attitude unreasonable (49%) than reasonable (39%). *The Gallup Report*, March 30, 1976.

himself not only with his major goal of changing public attitudes towards the economy but also as his term moves along with restoring public confidence in himself and his administration. Observers of all political stripes will be watching to see if he can bounce back as he did in 1974. Even a good record on inflation is no guarantee of success. The battle to influence the public's interpretation of cost of living and unemployment statistics is on now and will continue. The best measure of the outcome may be the next federal election, expected in 1978. Whatever the prime minister's persuasive strategy, he will inevitably remain the central figure in the public relations process.

Some Concluding Comments

As we have seen, the prime minister has been forced into the spotlight as chief spokesman for the government, not only by his traditional centrality in the parliamentary process, but also increasingly by the demands of many in the public who appear to want a symbolic link with government through the prime minister. The mass media, especially television, reinforce these demands. The prime minister's pre-eminent role seems destined to continue, regardless of the incumbent. We have seen that the role of prime minister confers impressive persuasive resources on the incumbent but that he must cope with competing messages, guaranteed by the system itself, and an inattentive citizenry which often shows reluctance to be persuaded.

While it is notoriously difficult to demonstrate definitively the effectiveness or ineffectiveness of government efforts to persuade the public, primarily because of the complexity of the relationships involved, the examples we have examined suggest the severe limitations on the prime minister's persuasive powers. The prime minister appears to be able to raise issues at will but to have more difficulty selling his solutions. For example, the government's decision to issue its green paper on immigration made that subject a major public issue, but the diversity of opinions expressed suggests that selling the public on a new set of policies will be anything but easy. The anti-inflation program is an even more compelling example.

The negative outcome of Trudeau's efforts at public education, at least in electoral terms, might lead one to the conclusion that shrewd leaders should concentrate less on public education and more on image making.[78] But image-making, too, has its limitations. Personal popularity is not always easily transferred to policies or programmes. For example, Samuel Lubell found that John F. Kennedy's very high personal popularity throughout the U.S. in 1962 did not carry over to his programs, many of which could not attract majority support.[79] Though valuable at election

---

[78] Cornwell, *Role of Press*, p. 30.
[79] Cited in Elmer E. Cornwell, Jr., *Presidential Leadership of Public Opinion* (Bloomington, Ind., 1965), pp. 301-2.

time and in such bargaining situations as federal-provincial conferences, image capital needs help from events to sell programs to the public. Indeed, despite his ups and downs, it may not be unfair to say that Trudeau has been more successful at selling himself than at selling his policies.

It would probably be incorrect to conclude from this discussion, however, that Trudeau is an ineffective persuader or that the role of prime minister lacks persuasive clout. The issues of bilingualism and wage and price controls, discussed above, are areas in which personal interests and feelings are strong and persuasion is extremely difficult. The prime minister has had more success in other areas, such as energy, where there has been considerable support for his attempts to cushion the consuming provinces against rising oil prices, and during the October crisis. In the latter case, the prime minister was able to counter the propaganda of the F.L.Q. and the objections of some civil libertarians to the imposition of the War Measures Act with arguments effective enough to win overwhelming support for the government's actions. Although the major explanation and defence of government actions was left to John Turner, then Minister of Justice, it was Trudeau who went on television and "made a moving appeal to the nation for understanding and support."[80] Trudeau's mastery of television and the impact of crisis combined to produce effective persuasion. The prime minister was also successful in regaining the trust of the electorate in 1974, as we have seen. Whether or not he can repeat his 1974 performance and regain the public support lost in 1976 remains to be seen. But the 1974 performance can be cited as evidence that he can do the job. The limitations of his personal persuasive powers—and those of the prime ministerial role—became apparent when we examined issues which were fundamental or highly emotional. Awareness of these limitations should not blind us to the fact that the prime minister has on balance potentially greater persuasive powers over a wider range of issues than any other public figure. The importance of the power to act, which had led a large segment of the public by the fall of 1976 to accept, if not applaud, the government's controls program, should not be underestimated.

---

[80] John Saywell, "Quebec 70: A Documentary Narrative," in *Canadian Annual Review 1970*, ed. J. Saywell (Toronto, 1971), pp. 92-93.

8

The National Party Leadership Convention in Canada: A Preliminary Analysis*

DONALD V. SMILEY

Delegates, Party Leaders, and Candidates: Voting by Successive Secret Ballots

The Canadian party convention can be understood only against the background of its two basic voting rules: (*a*) voting is by secret individual ballot; (*b*) successive ballots are held at short intervals until one candidate has a majority of all votes cast. These procedures predetermine the patterns of relations within the convention and those established prior to it—relations between candidates and delegates, between delegates and provincial and other party leaders, and between candidates themselves. The secret, individual ballot most clearly distinguishes the Canadian leadership convention from its American counterpart. The definitive study of United States national party conventions asserts: "For many purposes, the working unit . . . is the state delegation rather than the individual delegate. The ordinary delegate seldom takes an individual part in the deliberations except in meetings of state delegations."[1] It is quite otherwise in Canada. The individual delegate in the privacy of the voting cubicle is supreme and must be deferred to as such.

The Canadian type of balloting gives a powerful incentive for candidates and their supporters to seek the favour of individual delegates wherever this may be found. Alan C. Cairns has conclusively demonstrated that the Canadian electoral system reinforces regionalism and encourages regional appeals in federal politics, in some cases by virtually shutting out a party from parliamentary representation in a province or region in which it has significant electoral strength and in others by giving a party a regional

---

* Slightly abridged from *Canadian Journal of Political Science*, I, No. 4 (December 1968), and reprinted by permission of the author and the Canadian Political Science Association.
[1] Paul T. Daniel, Ralph M. Goldman, and Richard C. Bain, *The Politics of National Party Conventions* (Washington D.C., 1960), p. 355. Bloc voting by states seems to be decreasing. It has traditionally been less prevalent among Republicans than Democrats and at the 1968 Democratic convention the unit-rule was successfully attacked.

dominance in the House of Commons quite disproportionate to its voting support.[2] The convention voting-rules work in the other direction. The vote of each delegate counts equally, quite independently of the choices made by others from his riding, provinces, or region. When this factor is combined with the heterogeneity of the activists in each party in terms of age, ideology, regional and linguistic identification, and other determinants of candidate preference there are powerful influences on each candidate to make an inclusive appeal to all significant groupings, factions, and tendencies in the party.

The first aim of each candidate for the party leadership is thus to encourage individual delegates to support him and to declare their support so as to influence others. But his subsidiary goal must be to gain the tolerance of candidates overtly pledged to other contenders. The expectation that the leadership will be decided only after several ballots makes candidate strategy enormously more complex than it would otherwise be.[3] If delegate X is committed openly to candidate Y_1 his support may be needed on the second ballot—or even more crucially, on the fifth—by candidates Y_2, Y_3, and Y_4, when Y_1 has been eliminated from the contest, either by the voting rules or his own voluntary withdrawal. Thus every delegate is in a sense "up for grabs" by every serious candidate.

What might be called the successive-ballot expectation leads to an enormous uncertainty in the approach of candidates to individual delegates —a situation in which the delegate has all the advantages. There are many incentives for delegates to commit themselves openly to particular candidates prior to voting but few to give any indication of how they will act if their preferred contender is eliminated. Some delegates may make such first-ballot declarations in the processes of being chosen by their respective constituency or other party organizations. Others no doubt make commitments in gratitude for past, or in hope of future, favours. During the convention itself, organizers for various candidates attempt to establish their supporters as a cohesive bloc by informally commandeering sections of the convention hall, providing entertainment and refreshments for committed delegates, and so on, and it takes a delegate with a highly developed sense of inner-directedness to resist such pressures. Perhaps most importantly of all, a delegate cannot influence others to support his preferred candidate unless he declares himself. There are, on the other hand, positive disincentives for delegates to give any prior indication of how they will act as voting proceeds. Candidates and their supporters strive to create the impression that they are winners and any open discussion of successive preferences is of course an admission of possible defeat. Candidate-blocs are undoubtedly in many cases deeply divided about second and later

---

[2] The Electoral System and the Party System in Canada, 1921-1965," *Canadian Journal of Political Science*, I, No. 1 (March 1968), 55-80.

[3] The number of ballots needed to elect a leader at the ten conventions was as follows: 1919 (Lib.), 3; 1927 (Cons.), 2; 1938 (Cons.), 2; 1942 (Cons.), 2; 1948 (Lib.), 1; 1948 (Cons.), 1; 1956 (Cons.), 1; 1958 (Lib.), 1; 1967 (Cons.), 5; 1968 (Lib.), 4. The 1976 Conservative convention went to three ballots. (Ed.)

preferences and the discussion of these matters would endanger unity. There are thus many influences against delegates giving overt indications of their behaviour as voting proceeds. Furthermore, their voting behaviour is highly unpredictable. Canadian parties do not sustain stable factions: candidates' appeals are inclusive and play down divisions, and thus delegates give their first, second, and successive preferences for quite different reasons. Another element of uncertainty is the extent to which delegates will take their cues as balloting proceeds either from candidates who are eliminated or from provincial or other party leaders.

The voting rules of the Canadian conventions make the influence of provincial leaders over delegates less crucial than in the United States where voting is open and recorded by states. At the Conservative leadership convention of 1967, Premier Robarts of Ontario did not declare himself for any candidate—something that would have happened in an American convention only under the most unusual circumstances. It is significant in this connection that Canadian conventions have not seen anything like American "native-son" candidates—i.e. candidates whose strength is limited to their state but who barter the support of cohesive state delegations as balloting proceeds. However, at the western regional convention of Liberals held some weeks before the 1968 convention, there were some desultory discussions on the possibility of a western candidate running with a Prairie and BC bloc of votes. The party influentials involved in this discussion could not agree on a candidate or, apparently, on whether such a move was appropriate, and the scheme was quickly abandoned.

The expectation that several ballots will be needed to select a leader creates the corresponding expectation among candidates that they may need the support of other contenders as successive votes are taken. There are the utmost difficulties in negotiating such alliances before voting commences. The inherent uncertainties of the situation seem to preclude bargains among candidates, except of the most oblique, and open-ended variety—uncertainties relating, for example, to the relative standing of candidates as voting proceeds and to the ability of eliminated contenders to deliver their supporters. The mythology of the convention favours "no deals," and even the rumour of such arrangements gives candidates so involved unfavourable publicity. Thus such bargaining as takes place must occur for the most part under the extraordinary distracting conditions of the convention floor as balloting proceeds.

The voting rules of the Canadian leadership convention preclude the deliberate creation of the kind of presidential coalition[4] that is so central to American national politics. The Canadian candidate strives not so much for a coalition of party forces, but for an aggregate of individual delegate support on the first and subsequent ballots, and a significant proportion of this aggregate must be won under circumstances of uncertainty, distraction, and publicity.

---

[4] For one of the most interesting accounts of building such a coalition, see Theodore H. White, *The Making of the President 1960* (New York, 1961).

The Convention and Party Leadership

Canadian national politics is profoundly personality-oriented. Peter Regenstreif is perceptive on this matter.[5] According to his analysis "there is relatively little of a long-term group basis to party affiliation that operates to stabilize voters behind a party." The national organization of Canadian parties is "weak and inarticulate" and leadership is crucial in attaining the degree of party cohesion necessary to fight elections successfully and to operate parliamentary institutions. There is, of course, the direct and immediate impact of American presidential politics. The mass media in Canada as elsewhere present a highly personalized view of the political process; in particular, newspapers have almost entirely ceased to be party organs as they were in previous periods and the working reporter is enormously more influential in presenting his perceptions of politics, so long as he makes his copy exciting.[6] It may be too that the biographical character of most contemporary English-Canadian historiography disposes those within the linguistic community to view politics in personalized terms.

In any analysis of the relation between the party convention method of choosing party leaders and the character of that leadership there are two questions. First, does the convention system result in different kinds of leaders being chosen from what would occur under the caucus system? Second, what is the impact of convention choice on the leadership role itself?

One can only conjecture about whether different leaders would have been chosen if caucus selection had been perpetuated in the major Canadian parties. On the basis of the experience of Australia, New Zealand, and the United Kingdom, as well as that of Canada prior to the establishment of the convention system, it seems likely that parliamentary caucuses would have been more disposed to choose leaders with long records of federal elective office. Of the ten leaders chosen by convention, three (Bracken, Drew, and Stanfield) were provincial premiers with no federal legislative experience; three others (King, St. Laurent, and Trudeau) had six years or less in the House of Commons; and only two—Manion and Diefenbaker—were in relative terms parliamentary veterans with 21 and 17 years respectively as MPs. In general, leadership conventions have been more open than caucus selection, thereby making it possible for leaders to be chosen from among other groups than those with long experience in the federal Parliament.

---

[5] *Parties and Voting in Canada: The Diefenbaker Interlude* (Toronto, 1965), pp. 24 and 68-9.

[6] The most perceptive account of the influence of the mass media on contemporary Canadian politics that I know was in an address by Senator Maurice Lamontagne to the annual conference on the Institute of Public Administration at Hamilton in September 1967. So far as I know, this address has not been published. According to one of Lamontagne's interesting arguments, the mass media "do not have a decisive impact on public opinion, at least in so far as politics is concerned." However, most politicians are "newsworms" and their perceptions of themselves, their colleagues, and their competitors are deeply influenced by how much and how favourable is their publicity in the media.

The widespread reporting of recent conventions[7] adds another degree of openness by making it possible for men who have not been national figures previously to become serious contenders for the leadership in a very short time. The experience of 1967 and 1968 is instructive here—six months before the conventions neither Stanfield nor Trudeau was well known even among the activists of their respective parties. It is significant too that both were very late entrants to the leadership contest. There has been a good deal of speculation about the role of the media in the Trudeau victory. According to one extreme version, the media rather than the delegates chose the Liberal leader. The situation was obviously more complicated. One newspaperman, Anthony Westell, has declared that reporters were hearing about the "Trudeau boom" from the grass-roots some time before they were willing to give it credence or publicity.[8] On the other hand, by the time that the convention assembled, the newspapers and television, through the polls they sponsored and other reporting, were picturing the Minister of Justice as front-runner. The impact of the media on the results of the Conservative convention of 1967 is even more difficult to assess. Mr. Stanfield was not a colourful figure, and before the convention Mr. Roblin was most commonly portrayed by the media as the leading contender. However, observers of the convention seem to agree that a crucial point in the convention was the very favourable impression made on both the 400-odd delegates on the Policy Committee and the reporters present by Mr. Stanfield on his Tuesday night speech. Joseph Wearing in a perceptive account of the convention commented, "Next day the three Toronto newspapers agreed that Mr. Stanfield had made the most impressive performance the evening before and this undoubtedly had a considerable impact on the minds of the undecided. In fact, from that point on, the three Toronto newspapers were the only media the delegates could pay much attention to and the Toronto papers said that Stanfield was winning."[9]

The impact of the convention system on the role of the party leader can be looked upon in two dimensions—the relationship between the leader and his parliamentary colleagues and between the leader and the public.

---

[7] According to a report by the Canadian Broadcasting Corporation 14,511,000 people heard or saw part of the seven hours broadcasting of the last day of the Liberal convention of 1968. Of these 13,606,000 had seen television. Le Devoir, March 6, 1968. Although the figures are not directly comparable, it would seem that these figures are similar to those who heard or saw broadcasts of the Kennedy-Nixon debates in 1960 where estimates of the percentage of the U.S. population of 12 years of age or over who saw or viewed each of the four debates was 60, 62, 64, 54. Sidney Kraus, ed., The Great Debates, Background, Perspective, Effects (Bloomington, Ind., 1962), 189.

[8] "Is Charisma the Key to Solving the Trudeau Mystery?" Toronto Globe and Mail, Feb. 12, 1968.

[9] "A Conference for Professionals: The P.C.s in Toronto," Journal of Canadian Studies, II, No. 4 (November 1967), p. 8.

It is reasonable to assume that because the party leadership in Canada is conferred by an extra-parliamentary body the individual so chosen has an influence over his party colleagues in the House of Commons that he would not possess if the caucus selection method were used. One writer has said of Mackenzie King, "On the rare occasions when the parliamentary caucus began to growl, when the party has been in opposition and the going has been hard, he has more than once silenced the parliamentary wolves by emphasizing that he is the representative and leader of the party as a whole, not merely of the parliamentary group. What the parliamentary group did not create, it may not destroy, at least not without ratification by the party 'grass roots.' The leader may appeal beyond the caucus to the party membership."[10] (Mr. Diefenbaker's experience after the November 1966 party convention seems to demonstrate that a leader cannot successfully rely only on the support of the preponderance of his party colleagues in the House of Commons if he has lost the support of those dominant in the extra-parliamentary party.) It may also be true that the acceptance in this decade of the tradition that party leaders are not only chosen by convention but may be so replaced further strengthens a leader in relation to caucus. Thus a leader under sustained attack by his parliamentary colleagues might claim with some justification that the failure of the extra-parliamentary organization of his party to move toward his replacement constitutes an implicit vote of confidence. However, the normal workings of parliamentary government would make it virtually impossible for a prime minister to be sustained in office if he lost the support of his colleagues in the House of Commons and retained the support of the party outside, although an opposition leader might for a time do so.

In any consideration of the impact of the convention system on the role of party leaders the question may be asked as to whether the system is influencing Canadian politics toward a presidential-plebiscitary kind of leadership and away from the normal practices of parliamentary government. Miss Mary Southin, a Vancouver Conservative lawyer, has made a root-and-branch attack on party leadership conventions in Canada and recommended a return to choice by caucus.[11] She asserts, "The American system leads inevitably to presidential tyranny of numbers." But in the United States the president's power may in some crucial circumstances be restrained by Congress. In the Canadian system, according to Miss Southin's argument, the normal traditions of party solidarity leave us without even this restraint. Further, parliamentary government is based on the collective accountability of the cabinet to the House of Commons and is incompatible with a situation in which the prime minister is not effectively accountable to his supporters in the House.

Miss Southin's strictures have a good deal of point. There are several

---

[10] J. Lederle, "The Liberal Convention of 1919", *The Dalhousie Review*, XXVII, No. 2 (May 1948), p. 86.

[11] "Why Do We Need a Leadership Race?" Vancouver *Sun*, March 26, 1968.

deep-seated characteristics of the Canadian political system which make it peculiarly vulnerable to plebiscitary leadership. Howard Scarrow has lucidly summarized these interrelated traits as " ... the absence of policy conflict, the non-partisan posture of organized interest groups, the dominance of non-economic correlates of partisan preference, low image differential, low party identification, low policy polarization among respective , [party] supporters and wide swings of the electoral pendulum."[12] Peter Regenstreif has pointed out the absence of "stable group moorings to political parties" and a situation in which "social reference affiliations are weak mediators of political loyalties."[13] Thus there are few of the social• and political restraints to a highly personalized leadership where the individual relates himself to the political system directly through the leader without the mediations of family and group affiliations, political parties, members of Parliament, the House of Commons and so on. The way in which the convention system works reinforces these tendencies. The creation of a presidential coalition in the United States is a deliberate aggregation of important party and other interests. As we have seen, the successful candidate campaign in Canada relates the contender to the individual delegates in a more direct way.

The changing influences of the parliamentary as against the plebiscitary elements of the Canadian political system can best be seen in comparing the circumstances of the changes in Liberal leadership in 1948 and 1968—the only occasions on which a leadership convention in effect chose a new prime minister. There were certain similarities in the two situations. In each case a senior and distinguished leader retired leaving his party in a relatively weak position in the House of Commons.[14] In each case too the new prime minister faced a new leader of the opposition. The changeovers were, however, made differently and with different results.

First, Mr. St. Laurent did not become prime minister until more than three months after he had been chosen party leader. Mr. Trudeau's accession came just fourteen days after his selection by the Liberal convention.

Second, Mr. St. Laurent did not radically change either the composition or the functioning of the cabinet when he became prime minister whereas Mr. Trudeau did. The St. Laurent cabinet which took office on November 15, 1948, included sixteen of the nineteen members of the previous ministry in the portfolios they had formerly held—including Mr. Gardiner, St. Laurent's only serious opponent for the leadership, in Agriculture.[15] The transfer to Mr. Trudeau involved a much more radical change in the cabinet and several of these changes could be attributed in

---

12 "Distinguishing between Political Parties—the Case of Canada," *Midwest Journal of Political Science*, No. 1 (Feb. 1965), p. 73.

13 *Parties and Voting in Canada*, pp. 6 and 24.

14 The 1945 general election gave the Liberals 125 of 245 seats; that of 1965, 131 of 265 seats.

15 Lester Pearson took office as minister of External Affairs between the time of the Liberal convention and Mr. St. Laurent's becoming prime minister. In the cabinet of November 15, Stuart Garson, the former premier of Manitoba, assumed Mr. St. Laurent's former portfolio of Justice and Robert Winters became minister of Reconstruction, a portfolio

one way or another to the changes in the leadership itself. Two ministers (La Marsh and Winters) had resigned prior to the changeover. Two others (Benson and Sharp) who had been Trudeau supporters were given new portfolios which each presumably desired. Martin, the former Minister of External Affairs and a contender for the leadership, was appointed to the Senate and became minister without portfolio and government leader in that body. Four other new ministers without portfolio were appointed, of whom two had supported Trudeau in his campaign for the leadership. During his first week in office the new Prime Minister announced very basic changes in the way in which the cabinet would function, including a complete reorganization of its committee structure, the naming of Paul Hellyer to be acting prime minister in the future absences of Mr. Trudeau, and the assignment of the ministers without portfolio to responsibilities in specific departments. An even more radical reorganization was made after the general election of 1968 and in this cabinet only two ministers (Cadieux and Hellyer) had the same portfolios as in the Pearson government.

Third, Mr. St. Laurent did not cause an election to be called until more than six months after he came to office while Mr. Trudeau advised dissolution two days after acceding to power. On becoming prime minister Mr. Trudeau apparently found it one of the compelling arguments for an election, as Mr. St. Laurent had not,[16] that both parties had changed their leaders.

In the spring of 1968 the close association between two national leadership conventions and a general election has in the most basic way resulted in at least the temporary dominance of the plebiscitary as against the parliamentary elements in the Canadian political system. Under the normal workings of parliamentary institutions the party leader, whether a prime minister or otherwise, is in a fundamental sense *primus inter pares*. A national party convention is on the other hand a highly publicized trial by combat where there are no equals, only a victor and the vanquished. A general election succeeding quickly after two such conventions is almost inevitably regarded by both politicians and public as not the choice of a House of Commons but a personalized conflict between party leaders.

The Leadership Convention and the Party System

The holding of a leadership convention reactivates a Canadian political party at the constituency and national levels, although the provincial

---

previously held by C. D. Howe who remained as minister of Trade and Commerce. During 1949, St. Laurent made only five cabinet changes, all involving relatively unimportant portfolios (Mines and Resources, Secretary of State, Solicitor General, Postmaster General, and Government Leader in the Senate/Minister without Portfolio). Three of these were made after the decisive election victory of June 25.

[16] Of course, this would have been a winter election and this challenged a fundamental Canadian tradition. However, my reading of the situation in 1948 is that politicians and public had not progressed as far as now in perceiving general elections as primarily personal contests between party leaders.

associations as such are not so deeply involved.[17] A large number of party activists are brought together to make a decision recognized by all to have great consequences for the party and the country. The extensive reportage of the convention and the candidate campaigns preceding it allow the party almost to monopolize public attention and push its competitors for the moment off the political stage.

The institution of the leadership convention serves to strengthen the extra-parliamentary organizations of the national party. The major Canadian parties had their origins in Parliament and extra-parliamentary national organizations were at first, and until recently, dominated by parliamentary leaders.[18] The activity of holding a leadership convention strengthens these national organizations and gives them a degree of autonomy both vis-à-vis parliamentary caucuses and the provincial associations.

The events surrounding a leadership convention reactivate the riding associations also. We have few studies of these local bodies[19] and circumstances undoubtedly vary from region to region, but it appears that for the most part these groups are confined to relatively pedestrian tasks during election campaigns and between elections find little of great interest or consequence to do[20]. For many reasons riding organizations do not ordinarily play active roles in the formulation of public policy, the activity most likely to be attractive to the kinds of people the parties are allegedly anxious to attract into their ranks. However, in their nominating roles of choosing candidates to contest parliamentary seats and as delegates to leadership and other national conventions, the constituency parties come into their own. The 1967 and 1968 conventions were particularly crucial in revitalizing the riding associations because both parties decided that local delegates should be chosen according to the boundaries set up by the 1966

---

[17] In the two recent conventions the provincial Liberal organizations were somewhat more active than the Conservatives: (a) during the campaign period there were four provincial/regional Liberal conferences (Maritimes, Quebec, Ontario, Western) where the candidates for the leadership were heard; (b) provincial Liberal associations were directed in conjunction with each federal member or candidate and each riding organization to arrange the date, place, and hour of constituency meetings to choose local delegates to the Liberal convention. See *Convention Call*.

[18] Cf. F. C. Engelmann and M. A. Schwartz, *Political Parties and the Canadian Social Structure* (Scarborough, Ont., 1967), Chaps. 1 and 12. I think that the authors used Duverger's classification of the cadre parties originating in their government and mass parties originating outside too rigidly. While undoubtedly the Canadian parties owe much to their origins, it seems to me that the authors do not adequately describe or explain the changing relations between extra-parliamentary and parliamentary organs of the Liberals and Conservatives.

[19] Among the best of these studies are Brian Land, *Eglinton: The Election Study of a Federal Constituency* (Don Mills, Ont., 1965) and essays by Peterson and Avakumovic, Perlin, Lemieux, Davis, and Scarrow in John Meisel, ed., *Papers on the 1962 Election* (Toronto, 1965).

[20] According to John Meisel, the parties agree that "the basic function of the constituency organization is to select a suitable candidate and get him elected." This latter is accomplished primarily by making sure that those who are inclined to support the candidate do so rather than by devoting resources to persuade others to support the candidate. *The Canadian General Election of 1957* (Toronto, 1962), p. 81.

redistribution and the necessity of choosing such delegates forced the constituency bodies to reorganize themselves within the new territorial limits.

The holding of a national leadership convention exposes a party to the risks [of] a future disunity. For whatever reasons, the heterogeneous Liberal and Conservative parties have never sustained stable internal factions, and intra-party conflict on ideological or other lines has never been legitimized or institutionalized.[21] Interestingly, none of the ten leadership conventions has resulted in a break-away party like the Roosevelt Progressives of 1912, the La Follette Progressives of 1924, or the Dixiecrats of 1948 where important party groups have refused to accept the leadership choices of American national conventions. The voting rules of the Canadian convention appear to inhibit the development of certain kinds of cleavages which would be difficult to repair. These rules predispose candidates toward inclusive appeals, appeals which are so framed as not to exclude the possibilities of support on the first or subsequent ballots of any important sentiments or interests within the party. The creation of an American presidential coalition almost inevitably excludes certain important party groupings; Canadian circumstances are otherwise. In a nationally televised press interview the day after his selection as Liberal leader Pierre Elliott Trudeau was able to turn a good deal of the discussion to party unity, a matter which he declared was a "first priority" in his attention. Mr. Trudeau's judgment, I believe an accurate one, was that the scars of the convention were for the most part personal rather than ideological in nature and affected supporters of unsuccessful candidates rather than the candidates themselves.

Under the existing circumstances of crisis between English- and French-speaking Canadians, what did the 1967 and 1968 conventions do for this critical dimension of national unity? Paradoxically, the selection of Mr. Trudeau by the Liberals may have broken what some regarded as a fixed tradition in that party that an English-speaking leader should be succeeded by one from the other linguistic community.[22] Although Trudeau's decision

---

[21] This assertion is subject to further research. However, there seems to be nothing comparable to, say the Bow Street group among the British Conservatives or the faction in the Labour party of fifteen years ago led by the late Aneurin Bevan. During this decade Walter Gordon has made unsuccessful efforts to establish a relatively stable left-wing group within the federal Liberal party, and he and his supporters would have preferred Jean Marchand as Liberal leader, presumably because this would have unequivocally forced the party leftward. Joseph Wearing suggests that a relatively cohesive group of new Conservatives emerged during the struggles against Mr. Diefenbaker in 1962-63 and the Fredericton "Thinkers" conference of the latter year. "A Conference for Professionals," pp. 5-6.

[22] Peter Regenstreif has provided some interesting information here in a survey of 215 delegates to the 1968 Liberal Convention: 61 per cent thought the tradition of alternation existed, 28 per cent denied that it did, and 11 per cent were undecided. However, 58 per cent of the entire sample felt that the tradition was not a good one. 24 per cent of the English-speaking delegates in the sample favoured the tradition as against 45 per cent of the French "Changes in Leadership: The Successors to Pearson and Diefenbaker," paper presented to the Annual Meeting of the Canadian Political Science Association in Calgary, June 6, 1968 (mimeo).

to enter the race was apparently motivated in part by his judgment that *some* French-speaking contender should run, he asserted again and again that he should not be regarded as *the* French-Canadian candidate and there was here the clear implication that this affiliation did not give him any claims to the leadership that he would not otherwise have had. The rationale of the open leadership convention is contrary to such deliberate alternation and its seems unlikely that this procedure will in the future be effectively asserted for or against any Liberal candidate. It is significant that in both the 1967 and 1968 conventions Quebec support was widely scattered among contenders. This has not always been so in the past. The secrecy of the ballot precludes certainty on this point, but it seems probable that French Canadians were fairly solidly behind King in 1919, Manion in 1938, and St. Laurent in 1948—and against Diefenbaker in 1956. Although Quebec support was divided in the two most recent conventions it is likely that Stanfield had on all ballots a smaller proportion of Quebec votes than in the convention as a whole and that in Trudeau's case the reverse was true. Another factor of great significance is that in neither convention did Quebec provincial party organizations participate. Premier Daniel Johnson is alleged to have favoured Roblin for the Conservative leadership but it is unlikely that he exerted himself in his favour. The Conservatives as such do not exist at the provincial level in Quebec and many if not most of the Quebec delegates to the Conservative convention represented little in the way of effective party organization or influential political sentiment. This is, of course, a situation which has existed in the Conservative party for a generation. However at the 1968 Liberal convention the provincial Quebec Liberals carried through the logic of the formal separation of the federal and Quebec parties established in 1964. Mr. Lesage and his lieutenants did not attend the convention and the provincial constitution of the national party. Thus the 1967 and 1968 conventions saw a rigorous separation of federal and Quebec politics which does not prevail in respect to the other provinces, a kind of *statut particulier* in partisan-political matters.

John Meisel has pointed out that the Canadian party system has failed to contribute "to the development of a national political culture."[23] It has not in his terms effectively promoted "a sense of national community."[24] A strong case can be made that, more than other Canadian political institutions, the party leadership convention works in the direction of nationalizing Canadian politics. There is here a common national experience in having several thousand partisans assemble under circumstances of great publicity to make a single choice—a choice which has up to now been accepted by all the important elements of the parties themselves in each of the ten conventions that have been held. As I have pointed out, the convention voting rules predispose candidates against regional, ideological, or

---

[23] "Recent Changes in Canadian Parties," in Hugh G. Thorburn, ed., *Party Politics in Canada*, 2nd ed. (Scarborough, Ont., 1967).

[24] "Conclusion: An Analysis of the National (?) Results," in *Papers on the 1962 Election*, pp. 287-8.

other divisive appeals. Although these circumstances undoubtedly inhibit constructive and pointed debate on national issues, leadership conventions seem to work toward alleviating some of the deficiencies in our political system about which Meisel is concerned.

The National Leadership Convention and Party Policy

The various leadership conventions have proceeded quite differently in terms of formulating platforms or statements of party principle. Thus no firmly established traditions have evolved as to the role of these conventions in the processes by which party policy is made.

... The Conservatives in 1967 attempted a very new way for making party policy. Just a month before the convention a conference was held at Montmorency, Quebec, to which about 130 persons were invited—Conservative MPs and members of provincial legislatures along with businessmen, academics, and other individuals with knowledge of specialized policy fields. The chairman of the conference was the Ontario Minister of Education who had already been named as the chairman of the Convention Policy Committee. The conference was divided into eight groups on various public policy areas and in plenary session adopted a series of resolutions, some of a very specific nature and one—relating to English-French relations—highly controversial.[25] The Policy Committee of the convention, which consisted of one representative from each federal constituency and representatives of other party groupings, adopted the Montmorency document without significant change. According to the rules of the convention, this document was tabled in plenary session of the convention and neither discussed nor accepted by the convention as such.[26] In the words of the co-chairman of the convention " ... the report of the Convention Policy Committee represents the deliberations and recommendations of the party membership to the Leader and to Caucus."[27] The exact status of this report is somewhat indeterminate, but it is probably true to say that neither Mr. Stanfield nor his parliamentary colleagues regard themselves as being bound in any explicit way by its provisions.

The Liberal convention of 1968 was the first such meeting in which no platform or statement of party principles was fomulated. There was however a national policy conference of the Liberal Federation of Canada in 1969.

During the past decade the sources of policy inputs in the Canadian political system have become much more fragmented than in the King-St.

---

[25] With all the controversy engendered at the Conservative convention and elsewhere by the so-called "two-nations" resolution there has been little direct reference to the text of the resolution. What presumably is the contentious clause is an assertion "That Canada is composed of the original inhabitants of this land and the two founding peoples (deux nations) with historic rights, who have been, and continue to be joined by people from many lands." Chairman's Report, Convention Policy Committee Meetings (mimeo.), 10.

[26] *Ibid.*, Foreword.

[27] *Ibid.*

Laurent period. In the war and post-war period down to the defeat of the Liberals in 1957 the policy centre of national politics was the cabinet working in collaboration with its like-minded senior advisers in the civil service.[28] The new circumstances have given rise to several new and as yet unco-ordinated sources of policy direction; federal-provincial conferences, policy committees of the parliamentary caucuses, the Quebec Liberal caucus, "thinkers' " conferences and national party conferences not involved with party leadership questions, royal commissions, so-called "task forces," etc. The circumstances of the national leadership convention and in particular the inevitable preoccupation of all those concerned with the choice of a leader would seem to preclude the major parties in the future from attempting serious platform-making at these meetings. Further, the constitutions of these parties provide for regular meetings with precisely the same composition as the leadership convention and able to discuss party organization and policy free of the distractions of choosing a leader.[29] The decision of the organizers of the 1968 Liberal convention that this gathering should not even go through the motions of adopting a platform or statement of party principles seems not to have occasioned criticism, or even much notice, from any quarter. It may well be that an important precedent has here been set.

The National Leadership Convention: Are the Two Parties Different?

There has been a great deal of discussion among students of Canadian politics about the differences between the Liberal and Conservative parties. Such discussion proceeds in terms of (a) characteristics of electoral support —class, occupation, religion, etc.[30] (b) voter-support in terms of characteristics of ridings and as translated into parliamentary seats;[31] (c) long-term ideological and policy commitments;[32] (d) public perceptions of the par-

---

[28] See John Meisel, "The Formulation of Liberal and Conservative Programmes in the 1957 General Election," *Canadian Journal of Economics and Political Science*, XXVI (1960), and J. E. Hodgetts, "The Liberal and the Bureaucrat," *Queen's Quarterly* LXIII, (Summer 1955), 176-83.

[29] The Constitution of the Progressive Conservative Association of Canada provides that the National Association "shall meet normally once in each calendar year." The executive officers of the party may call a special meeting at any time or postpone the general meeting in any year in which a leadership convention, general election or any other circumstances in their opinion justifies such an action. The constitution of the Liberal Federation of Canada provides that there shall be a convention "at least every two years."

[30] Robert Alford, *Party and Society: The Anglo-American Democracies* (Chicago, 1963), particularly Chap. 9.

[31] Cairns, "The Electoral System and the Party System."

[32] Robert MacGregor Dawson, *The Government of Canada*, 3rd ed. (Toronto, 1957), pp. 497-503.

ties.[33] Although there are difficulties in summarizing these analyses succinctly the general outlines are clear—the two major parties do not differ profoundly in the social characteristics of their supporters, their orientations to public policy, or how they are perceived by citizens.

With the importance of leadership in the Canadian party system it is interesting to see how the parties behave in national leadership conventions. Liberal and Conservative conventions do not differ profoundly in composition and procedure. The Conservatives have, however, a tendency to engage in bitter public quarrels at their conventions which is less pronounced in the other party. The Conservative conflicts have indeed been dramatic—Meighen's defence of his 1923 Hamilton speech at the 1927 Convention,[34] the consternation caused by Bracken in 1942 in his insistence that the party change its name and accept what was regarded by some as a radical platform before he would place his name in nomination,[35] the bitter dispute centering about Diefenbaker's decision in 1956 that he would not have a French Canadian second his nomination,[36] and Diefenbaker's attempt to have the 1967 convention reject the "two-nations" policy. The Liberals have been able to avoid such open controversies, although in 1948 C. G. Power used the occasion of his candidacy to deliver a sermon to the party on what he believed were the principles of Liberalism[37] and in 1958 the plenary session of the convention rejected a resolution of the platform committee related to party organization.[38]

When one examines the leadership choices of the Liberal and Conservative parties several important differences emerge. First, and most obviously, two of the four Liberal conventions have chosen as leader French-speaking Roman Catholics from Quebec, while all the six Conservative leaders so chosen have been English-speaking, five of them Protestants and one (Manion) a Roman Catholic. In none of the Conservative conventions has any French-Canadian put his name in nomination. Second, at each of their six conventions the Conservatives have chosen leaders who were veterans of elective office; but at each of the four Liberal conventions a leader with a relatively short service as an MP has been preferred over contenders with an extended period of legislative office. The dates of the first election to legislative office of each of the Conservative and Liberal leaders chosen by the convention are given in Table 8-1.

Third, in the six Conservative conventions three provincial premiers

[33] Scarrow, "Distinguishing between Parties," p. 72. Scarrow's article is a lucid analysis of the matter.
[34] Roger Graham, *Arthur Meighen: A Biography,* II, *And Fortune Fled* (Toronto, 1963), pp. 493-9.
[35] J. L. Granatstein, *The Politics of Survival: The Conservative Party of Canada 1939-1945* (Toronto, 1967), pp. 144-7.
[36] Meisel, *The Canadian General Election of 1957,* pp. 31-3, and Pierre Sevigny, *This Game of Politics* (Toronto/Montreal, 1965), Chap. 3.
[37] *A Party Politician* (Toronto, 1966), p. 398.
[38] Ward, "The Liberals in Convention," pp. 99-100.

(Bracken, Drew, and Stanfield) have been chosen as party leaders while two others (Bennett and Diefenbaker) were former provincial leaders. None of the four Liberal leaders chosen by convention had run for provincial elective office.

Fourth, the Conservatives have chosen three of their leaders (Bennett, Bracken , and Diefenbaker) from the Prairie provinces, one (Stanfield) from the Maritimes, and two (Manion and Drew) from Ontario. Of the four Liberal leaders two (King and Pearson) came from Ontario and two (St. Laurent and Trudeau) from Quebec. The central Canadian orientation of the Liberals was graphically demonstrated in the 1968 convention in which all the five leading candidates on the first ballot held seats in the House of Commons from Ontario and Quebec—four of them from Montreal and Toronto. On the other hand, of the five first ballot leaders at the 1967 Conservative convention two were from the Prairies, one from British Columbia, one from Nova Scotia, and only one from Ontario.

Fifth, the Conservatives have shown a predilection for political professionals, the Liberals for those who have been co-opted into politics after other careers.[39] It is broadly accurate to say that all six of the Conservative leaders chosen by convention were men to whom politics was a preoccupation throughout their adult life. Three of the Liberal leaders (St. Laurent, Pearson, and Trudeau) had been co-opted into political life after pursuing other careers. While Mackenzie King's career is in a sense *sui generis* he had been a civil servant and management consultant prior to his selection as party leader. It is interesting here to note that apart from Trudeau's few months between the election of 1965 and his appointment as parliamentary assistant to the prime minister the next year none of the Liberal leaders had ever sat in the House of Commons as a private member.

Sixth, Conservative conventions have tended to result in rather sharper breaks with the person and policies of the past leader than those of the Liberals. In only one Conservative convention—that of 1942—has the retiring leader had an influential voice in the choice of his successor. Although there is still some doubt as to whom Laurier would have wished to succeed him, King possessed a decisive advantage in the 1919 convention in that he had run for election as a Liberal in 1917 while his major opponent, Fielding, had joined the Unionists. In 1948 St. Laurent was the choice of King and in 1958 St. Laurent appears to have favoured Pearson. While Prime Minister Pearson remained neutral before and during the 1968 convention,

---

[39] For an analysis of the processes of co-option in Canadian politics see John Porter, *The Vertical Mosaic: An Analysis of Social Class and Power in Canada* (Toronto, 1965), pp. 405-15. Porter does not, I think, emphasize enough that co-option to senior political office is a process characteristic of the Liberals rather than the party system as such. The instincts of the CCF-NDP are wholly otherwise and, but perhaps to a lesser extent, this is also true of the Tories. When Mr. Diefenbaker was prime minister he showed a propensity for professional politicians both from the House of Commons and the provinces. Only Wallace McCutcheon and the late Sidney Smith were brought into the Diefenbaker government by co-option.

TABLE 8-1
Legislative Background of Leaders

CONSERVATIVE CONVENTIONS		
1927	Bennett	elected to Legislature of NWT in 1898
1938	Manion	elected to House of Commons in 1917
1942	Bracken	elected to Manitoba Legislature in 1922
1948	Drew	elected to Ontario Legislature in 1938
1956	Diefenbaker	elected to House of Commons in 1940
1967	Stanfield	elected to Nova Scotia Legislature in 1949

LIBERAL CONVENTIONS		
1919	King	elected to House of Commons in 1908 (over Fielding, elected to Nova Scotia Legislature in 1882).
1948	St. Laurent	elected to House of Commons in 1942 (over Gardiner, elected to Saskatchewan Legislature in 1914)
1958	Pearson	elected to House of Commons in 1948 (over Martin, elected to House of Commons in 1935)
1968	Trudeau	elected to House of Commons in 1965 (over Winters, elected to House of Commons in 1945)

he had advanced Trudeau very rapidly after the latter's election to the House of Commons in 1965, first as one of his Parliamentary Assistants and later as Minister of Justice.

Seventh, although one should not generalize too broadly from the 1967 and 1968 conventions, it appears that the Conservatives in their choice of leaders have a mildly patrician bias, while the Liberals are more open to upwardly mobile individuals. It is indeed remarkable how similar were the backgrounds of the three Conservatives (Stanfield, Roblin, Fulton) who led on the first and subsequent ballots—members of families with reportedly significant means and long records of political service in their respective provinces, education in private schools and universities, legal training, etc. There seems to be little of this patrician element in the senior ranks of the Liberal party.

The paths of the top leadership are thus significantly different in the two major parties. An analysis of these paths is far beyond the limits of this paper, but it might be said in passing that Conservatives have been more prone than Liberals to withhold their full support from their leaders. The obvious explanation is, of course, that since the convention system was established the Conservatives have been out of power roughly four-fifths of the time. There are probably other factors involved. The focus of the Liberal party is more distinctly toward the national political arena than that of the Conservatives. It may be that the processes of co-option in the Liberal party accumulate more outstanding political debts to the leader, create more anticipations of future preferment, and cause dissidents to retreat to their other careers rather than do battle with the existing leadership as would those more committed to politics. It is also possible that the groups from which the Liberals recruit their leaders have an ethic of bureaucratic solidarity which is carried over into political life. At any rate, Mr. Diefenbaker showed he possessed an accurate knowledge of the history and predispositions of his party which extended prior to his own period as leader, when at the end of the Conservative convention of 1967 he adjured the delegates to give their support to the leader they had just chosen. . . .

Conclusions

The conventions of 1967 and 1968 indicate profound changes in the structure and functioning of the major Canadian parties. What seems to be developing are organizations which do not conform to Duverger's influential classification of cadre and mass parties.[40] At key intervals surrounding the choices of a national party leader and of party representatives to contest seats in Parliament, there is an enormous increase in party activity. However, many of those who participate most actively in these nominating processes are not motivated toward a similar degree of participation in other party activities, including election campaigns,[41] and at both local and national levels the Liberals and Progressive Conservatives tend to revert to many of the characteristics of cadre parties. These parties are extraordinarily volatile and because a large proportion of their members are not committed firmly either to the party or toward electoral success they may prove increasingly difficult to control by national, provincial, and local party hierarchies.[42]

The new kinds of political mobilization are at present directed to-

---

[40] Maurice Duverger, *Political Parties*, trans. Barbara and Robert North (New York, 1954), pp. 63-71. See also Engelmann and Schwartz, *Political Parties and the Canadian Social Structure*.

[41] The interest generated by the leadership conventions seemed to have carried over into the nominating politics at the local level prior to the 1968 election campaign. Nominations were contested to an unprecedented degree and many more people than ever before attended constituency nominating conventions. I am informed, however, that many of those latter were not available for subsequent chores during the campaign. It also seems true that the increase in nominal membership of the two major parties has not as yet led to them being significantly less financially dependent on corporate contributors.

[42] I am very grateful to Alan Cairns for suggesting the analysis in this paragraph.

wards personalities rather than ideologies. The voting rules of the convention predispose serious candidates against ideological stances which are divisive within the parties and there are few significant ideological differences between the major parties. Peter Regenstreif's survey of delegates to the Conservative and Liberal conventions indicates that the personal qualities of the candidates rather than issues were decisive in determining delegate preferences.[43] Canadian parties thus appear to be evolving in very different directions from those in the United States. Frank J. Sorauf has analysed the increasing importance of ideology in American politics in this decade and has concluded that the parties themselves

... have needed the kinds of skills that the ideologues possess as mass-media campaigning and coffee-hour socializing replace the canvassing and club rooms of the earlier politics.... this new breed of political activist has brought to the party ... his involvements in issues, causes and even an occasional crusade.[44]

Although the underlying conditions mentioned by Sorauf occur in both countries, the new Canadian political activists have as yet been little disposed to "issues," "causes," or even "occasional crusades." Nothing like the Vietnam war or racial relations has ideologically polarized Canadian society and, as is well known, Canadians are less prone to discuss the general role of government in ideological terms. However, the provision in the constitutions of both major parties for regular national conventions other than those convened to choose party leaders makes it at least possible that issue politics will be more important in the future. An indication of what may happen with some frequency occurred when western delegates at the convention of the National Liberal Federation in the fall of 1966 were able to mobilize majority support for a resolution calling for a North American free trade area. Within a few days Prime Minister Pearson and his Minister of Finance had repudiated this proposal, obviously with some embarrassment. The national party conventions of the next two years will indicate whether the extra-parliamentary parties will become more involved with policy, as these meetings will presumably be held under circumstances where there is neither a general election nor a leadership contest in the offing.

The open party convention contributes an influential nationalizing influence to the Canadian political system. Regionalism and localism are endemic to almost all important aspects of Canadian life and many of our political institutions and procedures reinforce these territorially based particularisms—the electoral system,[45] the composition of the federal cabinet, a decentralized federalism, and the over-representation in the Senate and the House of Commons of the least cosmopolitan provincial and local communities. The national leadership convention, on the other hand, has had an important though inevitably sporadic integrative effect.

---

[43] "Changes in Leadership."
[44] "The Rise of Ideology in American Political Parties," in C. J. Wingfield, ed., *Political Science: Some New Perspectives* (El Paso, 1966), pp. 73-4.
[45] Cairns, "The Electoral System and the Party System."

9

Party Leader Images in the 1968 Federal Election*

GILBERT R. WINHAM
ROBERT B. CUNNINGHAM

The literature on electoral behaviour specifies that, in addition to his party identification, the voter's perception of and his affect towards party candidates and leaders are important in determining voting behaviour.[1] In Canada the importance of the party leader's image has been noted by several writers. For example, Mallory speaks of the importance of a party's being in tune with the national mood, which is primarily a function of the leader's personality.[2] Dawson states that "their personalities and qualities often become more decisive factors in the election than the issues themselves."[3] Others such as Beck and Dooley mention the electioneering tactic occasionally employed by Canadian parties of basing the campaign solely on the image of a popular leader.[4]

Party backbenchers in the Canadian Parliament have little voice in determining governmental policies and limited exposure in the mass media, so only occasionally is a politician able to build up an independent

---

* Reprinted in part from the *Canadian Journal of Political Science*, III, No. 1 (March 1970) by permission of the authors and the Canadian Political Science Association. Data for this paper were gathered as part of a Hamilton Election Study Project initiated by the McMaster Political Science Students' Association. Dennis Harrison served as project co-ordinator, and Ron Shimizu, Angela Martinson, and Murray Knox co-ordinated interviewing activities in the three ridings surveyed. Approximately forty students and faculty members conducted the interviews.

[1] See, for example, Peter Regenstreif, *The Diefenbaker Interlude* (Toronto, 1965) esp. Chap. 4; and Angus Campbell, Philip E. Converse, Warren E. Miller, and Donald E. Stokes, *The American Voter* (New York, 1964), Chap. 2.

[2] J. R. Mallory, "Structure of Canadian Politics," in Hugh G. Thorburn, ed., *Party Politics in Canada* (Scarborough, 1967), p. 28-9.

[3] R. MacGregor Dawson, *The Government of Canada* (Toronto, 1956), p. 226.

[4] J. M. Beck and D. J. Dooley, "Party Images in Canada," in Thorburn, *Party Politics in Canada*, p. 82.

base of electoral support. Consequently, it is assumed that the party leader constitutes a focal point in any federal election.[5] This would be even more true for elections where parties are led by charismatic personalities. The literature is rather barren of systematic studies of how Canadian voters perceive party leaders, and how these perceptions relate to background and social characteristics of the electorate. This is a serious omission, since the effect of personality on electoral behaviour is an important question in Canadian politics. In elections where a magnetic personality leads one of the parties, does traditional party voting weaken as a force in determining a person's vote? Are religion, class, and ethnicity still important influences on voting behaviour? Are apathetic or uncommitted voters more likely to support a strong leader than party identifiers?

The 1968 Canadian federal election provides an opportunity to examine closely the dynamics of leader-influence on voting behaviour. In this election it was widely reported that the popular appeal of the Liberal leader, Pierre Elliot Trudeau, was responsible for the strength of the Liberal showing across the country, which resulted in the first majority government for the Liberals in this decade. Trudeau's appeal presents a good case study of leader-image and charisma in electoral behaviour. The Prime Minister's very rapid rise in national politics within an established party suggests that his appeal was not based on political experience or long-standing party affiliations, but was rather a function of something else— perhaps his personal image.

The purpose of this paper will be to analyse the importance of voters' perceptions of party leaders in comparison with other factors which influence electoral behaviour. The paper will also describe certain aspects of the leaders' public images which help to explain the outcome of the 1968 election.

Methodology

Data for the analysis were generated by a pre-election survey carried out in three federal ridings in the city of Hamilton, Ontario. These ridings were Hamilton West, Hamilton East, and Hamilton Mountain. The survey involved direct interviews with 832 Hamilton voters based on a questionnaire which took about forty minutes to administer. The survey was limited to those persons who were eligible to vote, and who declared their intention to vote in the June 25 election. Interviewing was begun three weeks before the election, but the bulk of the interviews were conducted in the ten days prior to June 25.

---

[5] Alford argues that the party leader is more important in non-class based political systems such as Canada than in class based political systems such as Great Britain and Australia. See Robert R. Alford, *Party and Society* (Chicago, 1963), p. 281. Though Alford's argument differs from ours, the common conclusion is that the party leader is a focal point of the system, and that his public image has an important effect on voter behaviour.

The sample was chosen from the lists of registered voters published prior to the election. Sixty polls were chosen at random in each of the three ridings, and five individuals were chosen randomly from each poll. This made a desired sample of nine hundred for the entire three-riding survey. Interviewers were instructed to make at least two call-backs to the respondents selected, and in the case where respondents were unavailable substitute names were randomly selected in the deficient polls.[6] Interviewing was terminated by the election, and the final tally of respondents by riding was as follows: Hamilton East, 296; Hamilton West, 259; and Hamilton Mountain, 277.

A sample from Hamilton cannot be used to generalize concerning all Canadian voters. However, since all three ridings are completely urban, our data represent an increasingly crucial element in Canadian electoral politics: the urban voter. Furthermore, the three ridings are diverse, both in terms of party strength and demographic characteristics. The Liberal party with John Munro easily won in Hamilton East, but in the other ridings, party competition was keen and the results were close. In Hamilton Mountain, Liberal Gordon Sullivan defeated NDP incumbent Dr William Howe, and in Hamilton West, Conservative Lincoln Alexander narrowly won over Liberal Thomas Beckett. The demographic composition of two of the three ridings (Hamilton East and Hamilton West) includes large ethnic minorities, especially Italians and Eastern Europeans. These same ridings also have large disparities in the economic status of voters. On both counts Hamilton Mountain is less diverse, and is characterized by a large group of middle-income, native-born Canadians.

Voter Images of Party Leaders

Party leader image was evaluated by a question which asked respondents whether their impression of each leader was favourable, unfavourable, or in between. Additionally, respondents were asked to give their reasons for this impression.[7] It was apparent from this question that Liberal leader

---

[6] The breakdown of responses and non-responses for the original sample of 900 is as follows: original sample (five from each polling station), 900; completed interviews with persons intending to vote, 59 per cent; contacted, but refused to be interviewed, 11 per cent; not voting (sick, moved, ineligible, will not vote), 9 per cent; not at home after at least two call-backs, 21 per cent. Interviewing only those who intended to vote had two effects on the sample. First, this reduced the response rate (that is, by as much as 9 per cent). Second, it resulted in a sample that was in some respects unrepresentative of the general population of Hamilton. For example, the sampling procedures favoured the inclusion of older voters, particularly the 41-60 age group, since they are more likely to vote than younger individuals. Similarly, there is likely a bias towards higher class voters.

[7] This interviewing procedure had the advantage of directly determining positive or negative affect towards a candidate, while at the same permitting the richness of an open-ended question. The answers to the open-ended questions were coded into various dimensions useful in describing the type of appeal each leader had for the voters.

TABLE 9-1

Impression of Party Leaders
(Percentages; N = 832)

	STANFIELD	TRUDEAU	DOUGLAS
Favourable	34	47	40
In between	39	27	33
Unfavourable	16	18	13
Don't know	11	8	14

TABLE 9-2

Impression of Leader's Qualification*
(Percentages; N = 832)

	STANFIELD	TRUDEAU	DOUGLAS
Personality and image	32	39	22
Ability, judgment	8	8	6
Experience	6	4	3
Policies, ideas	3	10	9
Party	2	2	6
Leadership qualities	3	2	4
Other	1	0	0
No response	45	35	50

Includes positive and negative responses (for example, "candidate has ability" or "candidate has no ability").

Pierre Trudeau was perceived more favourably than either Conservative Robert Stanfield or the NDP's Tommy Douglas (see Table 9-1). Furthermore, voters were more inclined to have positive or negative opinions about Trudeau than about the other leaders, since fewer respondents showed ambivalence or lack of interest ("in between") towards the Liberal leader. This same pattern was observed in the open-ended questions, where more voters had substantive comments, or favourable or unfavourable adjectives, to offer about Trudeau than about Stanfield or Douglas.

The open-ended questions were coded for statements about the leader's qualifications as a candidate, and for the presence of favourable and unfavourable adjectives. The former coding separated general statements about a leader's personality or image from other more objective comments about the leader's qualifications, such as his experience or judgement (see Table 9-2). Statements falling in the personality and image category were often unspecific comments such as "he's a good man," "I think he's insincere," or "a man of integrity." General statements of this sort were most numerous in the open-ended questions, a finding which is consistent with previous voting research.[8]

Table 9-2 indicates that some interesting differences occurred in the voters' perceptions of the party leaders. In Douglas' case, the non-response rate is higher than with Trudeau or Stanfield. This difference is due mainly to Douglas' lower score in the personality and image category, since in the more objective categories there is little overall difference between Douglas and other leaders. It appears that as a candidate Douglas was rated on a par with Trudeau and Stanfield in terms of general performance and ability, but as an individual personality he was more distant from the electorate, particularly when compared with Trudeau.

The differences between Trudeau and Stanfield appear less striking than between Trudeau and Douglas, and the main distinction was in the greater non-response rate for Stanfield, with less frequent references in the personality and image category. Stanfield, as might be expected, was more frequently mentioned in connection with experience and leadership, although his policies or ideas evidently did not make a clear impression on the voter. This presents an interesting paradox of the campaign. Trudeau was frequently accused of talking in vague generalities and failing to deal with issues and policies in his campaign speeches, while, on the other hand, Stanfield was viewed as doggedly keeping to the issues.[9] In the voters' eyes, however, it was Trudeau who was more frequently referred to as having taken stands on policies or issues.

The open-ended questions were further coded for the presence of favourable or unfavourable statements. Codes for these statements were set up as antithetical so that, for example, candidates could be compared according to references to "sincerity," as well as "insincerity." This procedure revealed clear differences in the image each candidate projected to the voters. Both favourable and unfavourable references to candidates were recorded, and therefore it was possible for a respondent to comment both positively and negatively for a given candidate on the same dimension.[10]

... To sum up one of the previous sections of this paper, the data suggest that when party identification—the best determinant of leader impression —was controlled, only ethnic origin showed significant distributions with

---

[8] Campbell et al., The American Voter, p. 25.

[9] See J. Murray Beck, Pendulum of Power: Canada's Federal Election (Scarborough, 1968), p. 405.

[10] While only 10 per cent of the respondents failed to characterize each of the three party leaders as favourable, unfavourable, or in between, 50 to 60 per cent were unwilling or unable to express the basis of their perceptions. It may be disappointing, but it should not be surprising, that the average citizen is unable to articulate the causal underpinnings of his political beliefs. Politics has been shown to have low salience for many people. The respondent may like or dislike a political personality for a reason that seems silly or irrelevant (which causes him not to answer), or he may honestly not know why he feels as he does about the man.

TABLE 9-3

Favourable Perceptions*
(Percentages; N = 832)

CATEGORY	STANFIELD	TRUDEAU	DOUGLAS
Youthful	0	14	0
Personal maturity, age	1	0	0
Initiative, drive	0	6	3
Steady, serious	6	0	1
Sincere, honest	5	2	4
Capable, competent	9	8	5
Speaking ability	2	3	10
Independent, free thinker	0	1	1
None of above	77	66	76

* Positive or negative effect of respondent's perception was judged by coders-in difficult cases the respondent's answer to the question in Table I was used as a guide; in cases where the respondent's answer could be coded in more than one favourable (or unfavourable) category, the first response recorded on the questionnaire form was coded.

TABLE 9-4

Unfavourable Perceptions
(Percentages; N = 832)

CATEGORY	STANFIELD	TRUDEAU	DOUGLAS
Youthful (too young)	0	2	0
Age (too old)	2	0	1
Lacks initiative, drive	5	0	1
Not steady, serious	1	6	1
Insincere, dishonest	2	3	1
Incapable, incompetent	4	2	1
Speaking ability (poor)	3	1	1
Lacks independence	0	0	0
None of above	83	86	94

impressions of Trudeau. Generally these distributions indicated that non-British-Canadians were more likely than any other ethnic category to perceive Trudeau favourably. In a recent article Wilson has pointed to the possible emergence of a class vote which supersedes the importance of ethnic affiliations among voters in Waterloo.[11] The Hamilton data suggest this finding does not apply to the voters' perceptions of the Liberal leader in

[11] John Wilson, "Politics and Social Class in Canada: The Case of Waterloo South," *Canadian Journal of Political Science*, I, No. 3 (Sept. 1968), pp. 288-309.

1968, for ethnic origin was more strongly related to voter's impressions than earlier religion or class.[12]

Voting Behaviour and Impressions of Party Leaders

A final step in the analysis is to determine if a systematic relationship existed between voters' impressions of party leaders and intended voting behaviour. This question is of obvious importance since if a voter's choice is determined by variables such as religion, ethnic origin, or party affiliation, and his impression of party leaders is similarly determined by these variables, then studying perceptions of party leaders is less relevant in the study of voting behaviour. Our findings indicate that perceptions of leaders have an independent influence on voting behaviour beyond the influence exerted by background variables.

The relationship between leader image and vote was tested by comparing a respondent's stated impression of the party leaders with his intended vote in the 1968 election. The results showed a significant relationship between perceiving a party leader favourably and intending to vote for his party. The data also indicated that voters were seen even less disposed to vote for a party's candidate if they felt "unfavourable" towards the party leader (see Table 9-5).

There is a possibility that the above relationship might be influenced by a voter's party affiliation , since identifying with a party might lead a voter both to establish a favourable impression of the party leader as well as to vote for the party. This could have been the case with the Hamilton respondents since 75 per cent of these respondents identified themselves with one of the three national parties, and party identification had a stronger relationship with expected vote than any other single variable.[13] When party identification is controlled, the relationship between impression of leader and expected vote was greatly decreased for those respondents who identified with the major parties. Generally, party identifiers intended to vote for their party regardless of their impression of its leader. Alternatively, they may or may not have had a favourable impression of opposition party leaders, but still they intended to vote for their party.

Among uncommitted voters this pattern did not occur (see Table 9-6). Generally, uncommitted voters stated their intention to vote for parties whose leaders they had perceived favourably. This relationship was significant in the case of Stanfield and Trudeau. For Douglas the relationship was not statistically significant—however, column percentages in Table 9-6

---

[12] The variables education, income, and occupation were used singly as indicators of social class.

[13] In a 1965 study Meisel found 77 per cent of the voters to identify with one of the four major parties. For a reference to this unpublished study, see Allan Kornberg, Joel Smith, and David Bromley, "Some Differences in the Political Socialization Patterns of Canadian and American Party Officials: A Preliminary Report," *Canadian Journal of Political Science*, II, No. 1 (March 1969), p. 74.

TABLE 9-5

Impression of Party Leaders and Intended Vote (Percentages)

		INTENDED VOTE		
	LIB	PC	NDP	DON'T KNOW
Stanfield				
Favourable	25	69	31	46
In between	53	28	42	40
Unfavourable	22	3	27	14
N	323	159	157	102
	$x^2 < .001$			
Trudeau				
Favourable	76	30	32	38
In between	19	35	35	43
Unfavourable	5	35	33	19
N	335	162	165	104
	$x^2 < .001$			
Douglas				
Favourable	31	39	83	44
In between	48	44	15	42
Unfavourable	21	17	2	14
N	303	149	165	102
	$x^2 < .001$			

indicate that over 95 per cent of those uncommitted voters who expected to vote NDP were favourably, or at least not unfavourably, disposed toward the NDP leader. Thus, among uncommitted voters there appeared to be a relationship between voting intention and impression of party leader. This is highly significant in overall election strategy since the respondents who classified themselves as uncommitted voters comprised 25 per cent of the total sample.

A further test was conducted on the uncommitted voters to insure that the relationship between voting and leader preference was not caused by other factors such as ethnic origin and religion. The possibility exists that uncommitted voters, whose impressions of party leaders are not predisposed by party loyalty, may still have their impressions systematically determined by religious or ethnic factors. That is, could not a voter's religious or ethnic background influence him towards preferring Trudeau and voting Liberal, even though the voter had no permanent identification with the Liberal party? The religious and ethnic backgrounds of the uncommitted voters were tested with their impressions of the three national leaders. In all cases there existed no significant relationship between these social characteristics and perception of the party leaders. In addition, religion and ethnic origin were tested with intended vote among the uncommitted voters. Again, no significant relationship was found between these

TABLE 9-6

Impression of Party Leaders and Intended Vote
Among Uncommitted Voters
(Percentages)

	LIB	PC	NDP	DON'T KNOW
		INTENDED VOTE		
Stanfield				
Favourable	33	63	16	43
In between	49	29	42	46
Unfavourable	18	8	42	11
N	66	38	19	57
$x^2 < .01$				
Trudeau				
Favourable	77	37	30	36
In between	20	32	30	48
Unfavourable	3	31	40	16
N	69	38	20	56
$x^2 < .001$				
Douglas				
Favourable	36	43	73	49
In between	48	37	23	39
Unfavourable	16	20	4	12
N	63	35	22	57
$x^2 > .05$ (n.s.)				

variables and intended vote (see Tables 9-7 and 9-8). Thus it appears that among uncommitted voters impressions of party leader are associated with intended vote, while religion and ethnic origin are not associated with intended vote for these same voters.[14]

A final test of the independence of leader preference from other factors in voting behaviour can be made by examining the responses of the voters who deserted their customary party in June 1968. In the Hamilton survey sixty-six respondents indicated that they would vote for a different party than that with which they normally identified. Of these sixty-six party switches, nearly one half (twenty-nine) indicated that they had a

[14] The relationship between social class variables (income, education, and occupation) and intended vote among uncommitted voters was tested, and statistical significance was obtained only in the case of income and vote $(x^2 < .02)$. The Liberal vote was evenly spread through all classes, while the PC vote was proportionately greater in the $10,000 to $15,000 income range, and the NDP drew from those uncommitted voters in the $4,000 to $7,000 bracket. If income is used alone as a measure of social class, it appears that social class has some systematic impact on the voting preferences of uncommitted voters. For elaboration on this point see Cunningham and Winham, "Comparative Urban Voting Behaviour: Canada and the United States," a paper presented at the annual meeting of the American Political Science Association, New York, Sept. 1969.

TABLE 9-7

Religion and Intended Vote among Uncommitted Voters
(Percentages)

INTENDED VOTE	PROTESTANT	ROMAN CATHOLIC
Liberals	34	35
Progressive Conservatives	26	12
New Democrats	11	8
Don't know	29	45
N	113	66

$x^2 > .05$(n.s.)

TABLE 9-8

Ethnic Origin and Intended Vote Among Uncommitted Voters
(Percentages)

INTENDED VOTE	CANADIAN	BRITISH	OTHERS
Liberals	36	40	34
Progressive Conservatives	22	27	8
New Democrats	13	5	12
Don't know	29	28	46
N	86	60	50

$x^2 > .05$(n.s.)

favourable impression of the leader of the party they would vote for, as opposed to eleven who intended to vote for another party despite an unfavourable impression of its leader. These data, and the absence of any other data which might explain party switching behaviour, suggest that the perception of the national candidates offers some explanation for the voting behaviour of a very important subset of the electorate.

To summarize the findings, it appears that voters' perceptions of national candidates had a significant impact on the voting behaviour of the Hamilton sample. While this will come as no surprise to politicians, it does nevertheless introduce a note of volatility into the theories of Canadian voting. Voting theories have tended to stress the fixed factors in the electorate—regionalism, ethnic origin, religion, or class—in an effort to establish patterns of voting participation. However, these patterns apply mainly to those voters who identify themselves with a major party. This omits from the calculus the group of uncommitted voters plus party switchers, a group whose behaviour is less likely to be affected by fixed social factors and more likely to be affected by idiosyncratic factors which develop in different campaigns, such as the personality of the national party leaders. In terms of understanding the political behaviour of the majority of the electorate, a focus on the fixed social factors may be appropriate; but in terms of explaining the outcomes of particular elections, factors like candidate preference may be more important since they more heavily influence the uncommitted " "swing" voters in the election. These perceptual factors, because they are a function of the personalities of the candidates, change from election to election, and it is often difficult to establish any general theory why they develop as they do.

10

King, Meighen and Approaches to Political Leadership*

R. MacGREGOR DAWSON

The Chanak incident[1] provided an interesting contrast in Canadian political leadership, though the decisions were made under somewhat different
circumstances, inasmuch as King had to furnish an immediate answer
while Meighen could take his time—as he did—in announcing his position.
King's cautious approach satisfied Liberals of all persuasions; Meighen's
jingoistic appeal antagonized and probably alienated some of his Conservative following. Where King's policy tended to bring Progressives and
Labour closer to the Liberals, Meighen's announcement tended to widen
the existing gap between those groups and the Conservatives. King's prestige was greatly enhanced, and the country began to realize that while the
Prime Minister might lack colour, he possessed both courage and common
sense and was not to be hurried into mistaken policies on the impulse of
the moment. The alleged necessity of consulting Parliament was his way of
gaining time—to await events in Europe, to ascertain public opinion, and to
give that opinion at the same time an opportunity to take shape and
become stabilized—but it was also a policy, which Meighen's reproaches
and Lloyd George's repeated requests for assurances made abundantly
clear. If it turned out that Parliament had to be summoned (which was
always possible) the Cabinet would have to bring down a policy for parliamentary approval and it might then have to be of a more positive nature.
For the moment, however, the Cabinet considered that no case had yet
been made to justify any overt action. Some time later a Progressive member of Parliament put the matter succinctly when he suggested that the

---

* From R. MacGregor Dawson, *William Lyon Mackenzie King* (Toronto: University of Toronto Press, 1958), I, pp. 415-19, and reprinted by permission of the University of
Toronto Press. © Canada, 1958 by University of Toronto Press.
[1] This selection follows a discussion of Prime Minister King's refusal to accept the British
Government's appeal for Canadian military help in the Chanak incident until Parliament
was consulted. Arthur Meighen, former Prime Minister and leader of the Opposition,
supported the British appeal.

crisis demanded not so much a policy of "ready, aye, ready" as one of "steady, aye, steady"—certainly a fair epitome of King's policy at that time.

Mature consideration did not seem to improve Mr. Meighen's sensitivity. In 1925 he went a step further and antagonized also the right-wing Conservatives by giving a speech at Hamilton on what he felt should be done if war again threatened. The Government, he said, should decide on its policy, and not only should Parliament be called promptly, but the Government's decisions "should be submitted to the judgment of the people at a general election before troops should leave our shores." At the time he was getting ready to make this speech representative men in the Conservative party pleaded with him not to do so; but he persisted. It was followed by an immediate cry of protest, and all over the Dominion many Conservatives were incensed at his proposals. Two years later he rose in a Conservative national convention, and tried to justify what he had said; he was "as tenacious of his own opinions," wrote a commentator, "as he is indifferent to the protests of his party." The natural result was to revive the disagreement which his Hamilton speech had already caused among many Conservatives.[2]

The difference between Meighen's approach to a political issue and that of Mackenzie King was drawn by Meighen himself over a decade later at a gathering of the Conservative party which was held to bid farewell to R. B. Bennett. In the course of his remarks Meighen touched on the subject of political leadership in terms which not only provided a clue to his own ideas but also quite clearly indicated Mackenzie King as the villain of the Canadian scene:

In our Dominion where sections abound, a Dominion of races, of classes and of creeds, of many languages and many origins, there are times when no Prime Minister can be true to his trust to the nation he has sworn to serve, save at the temporary sacrifice of the party he is appointed to lead.... If anyone tells me that fidelity to party and fidelity to country are always compatible, or that the wisdom of mere numbers is the wisdom of heaven, then I tell him that he loves applause far more than he loves truth. Loyalty to the ballot box is not necessarily loyalty to the nation; it is not even loyalty to the multitude. Democracy has failed and fallen in many lands, and political captains in Canada must have courage to lead rather than servility to follow,

---

[2] Thirty-one years passed; and Mr. Meighen was still to be found at Chanak. When the unhappy Suez crisis occurred in 1956 and Canada refused to follow the lead of the British Government, Mr. Meighen was reported as follows:

"Canada, Mr. Meighen said, should have sought without delay alignment unmistakably and strongly with Britain. 'Prime Minister Anthony Eden, for whom I have the highest regard and respect, merits the support of the Commonwealth in his endeavour to maintain Britain's honor and her place in world affairs,' Mr. Meighen said.... While he refrained from any allusion to Prime Minister St. Laurent or External Affairs Minister Pearson, Mr. Meighen said it was his opinion that Canada might well have taken an example from Australia in its early and outspoken support of the British position." Toronto *Globe and Mail*, Nov. 5, 1956.

if our institutions are going to survive. There must be something better than an ambition to be re-elected, or democracy will fall, even in this Dominion.[3]

It is interesting that King and Meighen each advanced the heterogeneity of the Canadian people as a major justification of his special form of leadership. To Meighen the challenge had to be met by the formulation of some broad concept of the national interest which would transcend this diversity and in large measure obliterate it. Having formulated this concept, Meighen then invoked all the arts of rational persuasion to secure its popular acceptance. His confidence in the product of his own judgment was so profound and his advocacy so determined that the policy was open to little or no discussion, still less could it be recast or toned down in any way to meet the demands or soothe the feelings of dissenting groups or interests.

Mackenzie King also perceived in this diversity of population a challenge but a different kind of opportunity. Opposing views, as he saw it, should not be expected to undergo any rapid conversion. Such a change would come through the slow influence of sympathetic association. The emphasis should always be placed on those things which people held in common and on which they could be induced to co-operate. Shared experiences would in time lead to increased tolerance, compromise, and understanding.

> *First across the gulf we cast*
> *Kite-born threads, till lines are passed*
> *And habit builds the bridge at last!*

Nevertheless any fair appraisal would have to recognize a certain degree of truth in Meighen's criticism, and concede that King's leadership would have been improved had he been more venturesome and more willing to offer forthright guidance to the nation. King's tactics enabled him to secure and retain office—the indispensable first step. But King, too frequently, stopped right there; and because he was reluctant to press on and try to realize some independent conception of the national interest, his policies slipped into the mire of pure expediency. King was always reluctant to venture into the unknown. He avoided taking risks, and he would postpone action, if by so doing he could ensure a greater degree of safety. He dreaded unnecessary discussion which might lead to disagreement and even threaten the existing party solidarity on which the whole security of his position rested. He was not prepared to use his own power extensively in an effort to modify the character and scope of those common elements on which he sought to base his policy. He was too willing at times to yield his own judgment when confronted with opposing opinion. He was slow to admit that he had a duty as leader to exert a moderate pressure in the

---

[3] Arthur Meighen, *Unrevised and Unrepented: Debating Speeches and Others* (Toronto, 1949), p. 319.

direction in which he believed the country should move. Franklin Roosevelt, for example, was able to follow King's general course, but with a significant difference. He found it possible to maintain this precarious balance, this unending compromise and adjustment between the leader and the led. Thus in the field of foreign policy Roosevelt was usually able to keep in touch with and even follow American opinion, while at the same time his confident personality was guiding that opinion in the general direction he desired.

Meighen's excessive self-confidence inclined him to be somewhat contemptuous of and superior to public opinion. King's excessive caution and search for common ground tended to make him too acquiescent and too sensitive to that opinion. Yet King was able to accomplish infinitely more. His method was the necessary approach to office, although admittedly a stronger realization of his duty to take the initiative would have added to his effectiveness. It was, of course, King's sensitivity to existing conflicts of belief and his search for existing areas of agreement which led to Meighen's taunts of loyalty to the ballot box and servility to public opinion. King might well reply that the best hockey player in the world is no use off the ice; that a party leader who cannot get elected and stay elected cannot govern and in due course will destroy the party he is supposed to lead. A condition precedent to the exercise of power in a democracy as elsewhere is to gain a place in the seats of the mighty.

Political leadership, in short, must always meet two tests: the ability to gain and stay in power, and the ability to use power once it has been gained. King's technique in bringing conflicting groups together made him a master in passing the first ordeal, though he allowed the same talent to undermine his effectiveness after he was in office. Meighen's technique never got him over the first barrier. He showed some ability to meet the second of the requirements of democratic leadership, but he was given little opportunity to demonstrate this capacity. There is, moreover, no escaping the fact that the same difficulties which prevented him from obtaining office would have been equally operative in preventing his staying there. In point of fact, they did exactly that, for on the two occasions where Meighen attained the Prime Ministership, he was unable to secure confirmation from the electorate.

11

Pierre Trudeau on the Prime Minister's Relations with Policy-Making Institutions and with His Party

EDITED BY THOMAS A. HOCKIN

This selection of excerpts from Mr. Trudeau's responses to questions and from a key speech begins with an outline of his views of his office in policy-making. This topic is explored further in several articles in Section III of this book, and in Sections IV and V.

Two pressures for reform have affected Canada's national political parties in the last decade. One set of pressures aims for the professionalization and the technocratic transformation of parties. Other pressures move in a somewhat opposite direction towards "participatory democracy" and increased citizen involvement in the life and policy-making of the party. The professionalization and the technocratic pressures are easy to document. The increased number of full-time or almost full-time staff in party research offices, in national headquarters and in the leader's (or Prime Minister's) office, the development of a self-sustaining financial base, the use of professional pollsters, media experts and modern transport are but a few examples. (These developments are far more advanced in the U.S.[1])

The development of more participant, hospitable and open parties are real but their extent is difficult to gauge in the sense that rhetoric and self-advertisement camouflage reality. Party thinkers' conferences, policy conferences, parliamentary caucus committee consultations of outside groups and efforts by the party leader to contact people for ideas and advice outside the formal party network are examples of such developments.[2] Other

---

[1] See John S. Soloma and Frederick H. Sontag, "Development in American Party Structure: Recent Trends and Consequences for the 1970's", paper presented to the American Political Science Association, Los Angeles, California, September 8-12, 1970, pp. 4-15.

[2] See the first two articles in this volume for examples.

less obvious features of the "participant" thrust are evident when a party emphasizes the "process" of decision-making more than the substance of policy, when it emphasizes the representation of and consultation of specific groups in policy-making instead of relying on concrete policy proposals for groups, and when it establishes internal party rules to insure consultation.

The concluding three excerpts from one speech and two responses to questions by Prime Minister Pierre Trudeau show how he articulates the problems and aspirations for a more "participant" party and for responsible parliamentary performance in his party. The Prime Minister's articulation of the role of the Liberal Party in developing policy is undeniably an advocacy for a more participant party. Whether his advocacy is rhetoric or reality, utopian or practical, is for the reader to decide based on his own assessment of the argument and perhaps also by comparing it with the arguments in the Taylor and Noel selections in this volume.

THE ROLE OF PARTIES AND PARTY POLICY CONVENTION*

PRIME MINISTER TRUDEAU:
It has been quite a season for political party conferences. I think ours will be very different from the other two. I am not talking only of superficial differences—I expect that there will be less conflict than among the Conservatives and less drama than among the New Democrats.

The differences go much deeper than personalities. Our objectives are different and our means of working towards them are different. Both the other parties debated a series of resolutions and the results are intended either to bind or to guide their leaders and caucuses in the coming months. In that sense their conferences were complete in themselves. This conference is the first phase of a process which will continue over the next year.

In the second phase the papers produced for this conference and the transcripts of the discussions held here will be submitted to policy seminars organized by constituency, district and regional associations. At these seminars they will be thoroughly examined and evaluated by a broad cross section of Party members and other interested citizens in all parts of the country.

These seminars, in turn, will provide the basis for the discussions at the third phase, the National Policy Rally, to be held late next year. At that Rally we will be setting out the principles and objectives of Liberalism in the 1970's.

Our concept of a political party, which is attuned to the needs of our society, is not one which confines itself to particular employment or income groups, or which speaks for particular regions or language groups, but one which reaches out to absorb the ideas and to reflect the aspirations

* From "Notes for Remarks by Prime Minister Trudeau" at the Harrison Liberal Conference, Harrison Hot Springs, British Columbia, November 21, 1969.

of all Canadians. Consistently with this ideal, we are building into each phase of our process techniques which will encourage the widest possible participation by those interested in questions of public policy.

The list of individuals and organizations invited to contribute papers to this conference, or to attend it, was not confined to members of the Party. Over 100 national associations were invited to send representatives. We are pleased to welcome our distinguished guests who are here in that capacity.

Similarly, during phase two, voluntary associations at the regional and community levels will be invited to take part in the seminars; and we have set up a panel of non-partisan experts to advise the Party on matters within their fields of specialization.

Finally, at the National Policy Rally, the delegates will be drawn from every constituency and will be more widely representative of the people of this country than at any previous policy conference of a Canadian party.

If we view this whole process of policy formulation as a vast river drawing on many tributaries, then this conference is the fountain-head.

In the next three days we are not attempting to commit the Party or the Government to a specific course of action. Anyone who has come to the conference looking for hints about the details of upcoming legislation is likely to be disappointed.

Our time frame is not the next year, or the next session of Parliament, but the next decade. I think that is a reasonable period, and perhaps the only reasonable period, for our purposes. It would be much easier to make forecasts about the immediate future, say the next twelve months. But decisions about the goals of our society, and the means for achieving them, require a much longer perspective.

We are not asking ourselves how the country should be run during the next year. That would be an absurd result for a process which will itself take a year to complete. It would also be a role of very limited usefulness for a political party to undertake. In the short run, a party could maintain itself in power by responding to each crisis as it arose. But if it concentrated only on immediate solutions, it would be ignoring the underlying conditions which caused each crisis. It would be prescribing for the symptoms rather than the disease. Eventually the crises would accumulate and overwhelm the party.

A party's principal concern should not be how to settle a particular strike—let the Minister of Labour and the Cabinet worry about that. It should be to resolve the continuing crisis in industrial relations by working out a better system of reconciling the interests of labour, management and the public. The task is not only more difficult, it is much more important.

In a matter as familiar and as obvious as water pollution, we are paying for the decisions taken, or avoided, ten years ago. At the end of the seventies we will be living with the results of decisions taken at the beginning of the decade. Planning, whether it is by a political party or a government or a private company, must operate in a scale of time which is sufficient to permit it to alter the future.

We are like the pilots of a supersonic airplane. By the time an airport comes into the pilot's field of vision, it is too late to begin the landing procedure. Such planes must be navigated by radar. A political party, in formulating policy, can act as a society's radar. The analogy, of course, is very incomplete. As members of a political party we should be thinking not only of the type of goals we wish to achieve in our society, but of their relative importance, and of the best means of achieving them within a reasonable time.

Let us look briefly at a few of the questions which may increasingly concern us in the coming years.

The sixties have been a decade of spectacular progress in physiological engineering. The news media have been filled with accounts of the latest triumph in transplanting hearts, kidneys and other vital organs. They have created a new category of international folk hero, ranking with pop singers and shipping tycoons.

In the seventies our attention will be directed to genetic engineering. Already we have achieved marvels in improving the strain of plants and animals. Do we want these techniques to be applied to human beings? If so, have we thought about what would be desirable goals to achieve, or dangers to avoid? What controls will be needed in this field? What should be the roles of the state, the medical profession and the individual citizen? This is not science fiction fantasy. Just as Rutherford's experiments into the nature of matter led to nuclear power with all its possibilities and problems, our current experiments with high yield wheat and faster laying chickens could lead to greater control over human reproduction. . . .

Questions of such magnitude and complexity give rise to strongly held opinions, but I doubt that many people would claim to know the final answers.

I am aware of the traditional myth that a government, and certainly a Prime Minister, should know the final answers to all possible questions of future public policy. To admit to even partial fallibility, or ignorance, would be to lose the people's confidence and their votes. In the past this myth has inhibited the policy conferences of the party in power, since it is undermined by any proposal which has not been approved, in advance, by the government.

The National Policy Convention of the Liberal Federation in 1966 can be considered as a break from this tradition since the subjects for debate and the wording of resolutions were freely chosen by Party members and not subjected to any control by members of the Liberal government. However, most of the debates at that conference focused on policies which were already in force or about to come into effect. A government must be prepared to give its answers to questions which affect the country in the present and the immediate future. The Liberal government certainly accepts that responsibility.

But I think Canadians would rightly reject as incredible any government, or party, or Prime Minister, who claimed to know the answers to the large questions of public policy which we must face in the coming decade, or who pretended that lively differences of opinion on such questions could not exist between members of the same party, or even the same Cabinet. Finding the answers to such questions is a job for all party members whether they are private citizens, members of Parliament or of legislatures, or Cabinet Ministers.

The delegates to this conference who are also members of the Cabinet or of Parliament are here to take an active part in the discussions, and to express their views as individuals directly interested in the formulation of Liberal policies for the 1970's. It would be misleading to consider the conference as a test of authority over the Party or as a contest for power within it.

In fact, we should think of this conference as a "supermarket of ideas" —some brought here by experts, who are not Party members, some by representatives of national associations, and some by fellow Liberals. If there is conflict it should be between competing ideas. We welcome that kind of conflict. It can contribute to the health and vigour of our Party.

The process of policy formulation which we are inaugurating today could not only infuse new life into our Party but provide it with a whole new dimension. It may be that, in future, political parties will be distinguished from one another, not so much by the issues which they recognize as important, as by the perspective in which they view such issues and the methods which they employ in devising new policies to resolve them. A party which shows that it is capable of coming to grips with long range questions about the future of our society will have a new claim to the respect and the support of the people of Canada.

With the refinement of our techniques for forecasting and planning, we are coming to realize that the image we hold of our future is itself an important element of that future. The expectations we arouse become a strong motivating force in realizing them.

Because of Canada's size and resources, there is probably no society which has wider or more promising choices in creating the image of its future. Defining those choices is the challenge of this conference and the discussions which will follow from it. As delegates to this conference I invite you to join me in taking up that challenge.

COMMUNICATION WITHIN THE PARTY*

QUESTION:
I am personally concerned as to the relevance of a Canadian University Liberal Federation within the Liberal Party, within the government. Every year, we seem to be passing resolutions after resolutions and of course when they were passed in 1965 they are forgotten in 1965, when they are passed in 1966 they are forgotten in 1966, and so on. I am wondering if

* An answer by Prime Minister Trudeau at the Question and Answer Period, Annual Conference of the Canadian University Federation, Montreal, Quebec, February 23, 1969.

you would believe in a system of perhaps reporting back, if I may be overly presumptuous, that is of having your Ministers come down and answer to us why they have chosen to accept, reject or delay a certain resolution that we have adopted in terms of government policy. For example, if we pass a resolution on abortion, you might have your Minister of Justice down to tell us what he thought of it, during the past year that he has had time to consider it, why he accepted it, why he rejected it and so on. . . .

PRIME MINISTER TRUDEAU'S ANSWER:
Ministers would be pleased to be invited to answer questions about their policy about CULF resolutions which were or were not followed up in the government legislation. I believe that in the past that was the practice in some instances, but I believe that CULF this year let us know, as Ministers, that we were invited but it was hoped that we wouldn't sort of take any too large space of your time, and I think this is the reason why there are not many who came this year. But if you want them another year, I am sure the ministers will be able to answer more precisely than I can on the answer questions. If they are on their specific departmental field, I am sure the ministers will be able to answer more precisely than I can on the general gamut of questions. I think it's obvious that we haven't, as a party, solved the problem of communication about which many of us and perhaps myself in particular have talked a great deal. I don't know the answers to it and I think you don't either but I think we will have to find them. We have, in the sixth or eighth [sic] months since the election, I think we have [sic] tackled and perhaps solved a lot of mechanical problems and I think that as Liberals we have a right to be if not satisfied, at least not dissatisfied with the progress we've made, in new rules of Parliament, new structure of Cabinet, new structure of the cabinet committees, the enormous amount of areas of policy which we've opened for questioning and review, and so on. But we haven't solved the problem of what is a political party? Not only how do the youth participate, but how does the Caucus participate? I see Marcel Prud'homme over there, he will tell you that this is the question that we are tackling and failing to solve the most often in our caucus. How do you—and this is perhaps for ten years from now but you'll be faced with it—what is the role of the Member of Parliament in a society where data transmission, electronic machines, will take more and more place all the time. You know—when in ten years we know that any citizen will probably be able to dial a number and not get some hate propaganda but he'll get the information he's asking for, whether it concerns how does he get a passport or where does he apply for his social welfare benefit or who does he write to for information on travel in the north and so on. What will happen to the member of Parliament? How does the member—well this kind of question that Steve Otto brought into the light a couple of months ago by writing to his constituents—what does the member of Parliament do under the new committee system of Parliament? Should he have a right to change the legislation as brought in by the

Cabinet? If so, what is the role of the Cabinet in relation to caucus? How can Cabinet form its policy in consultation with caucus, and in consultation with Liberals across the land, when it's an unwritten rule of Parliament that we can't show the bill to anyone until it's tabled in the House? How do we cross that difficulty of bringing in a bill which will have been discussed across the land before showing it to Parliament and having Parliament say, you have infringed their privileges of Parliament which is to see the bill first. You know, these are very difficult problems. I'm sorry, it's a long answer to your question but I don't have the answer to the problem of communication. We're setting up regional desks in my office to try to tackle it. Senator Stanbury is experimenting with new forms of integration of our decisions through troikas or consultative mechanisms, which would be too long for me to explain to you but which are in place, and we're still tackling this. We haven't solved it, and I think it will largely fall on the caucus and on Liberal members like yourselves to think about these problems of the future. This is the kind of thing that perhaps we can get from you in terms of the future. We're dealing with everyday policies and we need to hear your feelings on that, but we also want to know how we will solve the problems of the Indians in the years to come, but how we will solve also the problem of democracy in the years to come. It's a very very difficult problem. I don't know the answer. I'm looking for it.

THE PRIME MINISTER AND THE PARLIAMENTARY CAUCUS*

MR. ROBERT: Not having first-hand knowledge of caucus, of course, which only caucus members have, I get the impression from talking to people that caucus appears much more lively this session, because perhaps of the BC members—you have six new BC members. Some have said outside the House that they have a balance of power in caucus and if it gets real tough, they're going to use that balance. Do you like that kind of an idea?

MR. TRUDEAU: I've always encouraged caucus to be as lively as possible. I even brought in a reform five years ago, at the demand of caucus, that Cabinet would not deal with substantive questions unless they had been discussed in caucus. Which means that we announce no policy, or introduce no law until caucus has had its chance to look through the whole thing with the minister. This should make caucuses lively. I think in the period of minority government, because we were so threatened from the outside, perhaps there was less occasion and desire to have strong dissent within caucus. But that has fortunately returned, and we iron out our sometimes very strong differences in caucus, and that's the way it should be.

---

* Transcript of a portion of the Prime Minister's interview with Ron Robert, Selkirk News Service, recorded November 8 for broadcast November 13, 1974.

MR. ROBERT: Have you ever had that sort of a threat in caucus, that perhaps we, say of B.C., we six members or we eight members, don't like that so therefore if you bring it up we're not going to vote for it. Have you ever had that kind of a . . . ?

MR. TRUDEAU: No, I never have. As you say as a threat, no. But that membership feels strongly about some policies and say, "if they're not modified, you know, we can't agree." But there's been never any threat of walking out of caucus, or ceasing to be Liberals.

MR. ROBERT: Where I would think the problem will come, or perhaps not a problem but where more dissension would come, would be the pipeline kind of thing, when the tankers start moving down the west coast; does the government favour the Mackenzie Valley pipeline, Panarctic favours the polar route. You get two different . . . you're riding two horses almost, it would appear. And plus of course those tankers moving down. Does that create a problem for you?

MR. TRUDEAU: No, this is a policy which has been discussed in caucus. I don't think that the caucus has been divided on it, I mean in terms of regions. There are individuals of course who feel strongly against the Mackenzie pipeline, and those who feel very strongly in favour of it. You know the government's position on it. It is one of waiting for the National Energy Board to state, well, the facts of the situation: how much energy do we have, how much it will cost, and so on. It's only after that that the government will have to give precise answers as to timing and financing and so on, and at that point, caucus will be involved.

MR. ROBERT: Mr. Trudeau, you have mentioned you would be bringing in certain parliamentary reforms. One of the areas in which there seems to be a little bit of confusion is the idea of a free vote on capital punishment and so forth where it's declared free, which implies that the other votes are not.

MR. TRUDEAU: Well, you're quite right in raising it. But I've never used the expression. I've taken exactly your point of view, that as far as I'm concerned, every vote is free in the sense that no member is forced to vote in any way. Capital punishment may be an exception because before I was Prime Minister there had been a previous government which has talked about a free vote. So it's possible that the expression was used again this time. But in my six years as Prime Minister, I've never said: well, this vote is free, implying the others are not. But you know, we're in an adversary system, and Members of Parliament realize that they're part of a team, and that if they cause a government defeat they may have to go to a general election, which may not be the best thing even for the country at a particular time. So members in their own mind—that's why we have the caucus system—make their very strong arguments, as you were putting it earlier, in caucus—try to get the government see their point of view, try to have a particular kind of policy emerge at the end of it, and then collectively say, well, we've fought and we've tried and we've got some modifications; we're not absolutely happy with the whole policy, but this is the best we can do. . . .

MR. ROBERT: You were defeated on one of these. . . . Say they could not get together, where they just could not live with that particular bill, and they did vote against your government, say on abortion, or whatever— say it wasn't declared free. Would you accept that as a vote of non-confidence or would you ask for a vote of. . . .

MR. TRUDEAU: Well, there are some precedents for that. You remember, in February '68 Mr. Pearson's government was defeated on a money bill. And he put a motion the next couple of days later to the House saying: did you mean to withdraw confidence from the government? And the Parliament said no. So I'm sure this is open. . . . certainly open to me and any prime minister, in any situation, where a vote is lost. The precedent is there—it had been used as I say before. And I don't say I wouldn't use it. But it's not. . . . you know, it would be only a very exceptional procedure. I wouldn't like to have people feel that in our system they can be. . . . in our party they can be voting against the government all the time because the next day they'll give it confidence. They would lose their own self-respect. If it were on minor matters, you'd say: well, why did you defeat the government on a minor matter, why didn't you go along? And if it were a major matter, one that went to the roots of your conscience, and you voted against your own government, people would say: why are you in that party, you know, if it goes against your conscience? They should be independents, or they should cross the floor of the House. So every member makes his own reasoning. When I was a backbencher, I voted on some measures which I didn't find to my liking. They weren't as perfect as I would want them. But by and large I felt that this is the way the team was playing it; I thought I had greater light than the majority, but the majority in the caucus felt a different way and I went along with it. And I don't feel . . . you know, there wasn't a question of conscience for me. If it were a question of conscience, something that went absolutely against all your fibres, I think the member would be duty bound to vote against the government or to stay away from the House if it were permissible to him. I've never—as a matter of fact some members have seen me in private saying: "I just can't support this one." Well, I'd say, you know your conscience is the last arbitrator; it's not the Prime Minister.

12

The Prime Minister's Role in a Consociational Democracy*

S. J. R. NOEL

The study of leadership has always been one of the central concerns of political science, whether directed to the purpose of defining the qualities of the ideal ruler, of advising actual rulers on the principles and techniques of effective statecraft, or, more recently, of identifying "political elites" by means of "community power studies". The purpose of this essay is none of these. Rather, it is to examine a theory of political leadership which purports to explain the role of elites in culturally divided, but effectively functioning, democracies and the application of that theory to Canada.

First, however, it is necessary to discuss briefly the political culture of the Canadian federation. Canada, it is often said, is a country without a strong national identity; indeed, as John Meisel has put it, Canada "is almost totally lacking in a genuinely shared set of symbols, heroes, historical incidents, enemies, or even ambitions."[1] Implicit in such a view is a comparison with the United States: what is missing north of the border is an equivalent of the American national myth. Yet this comparison, while indisputable, is also seriously misleading. For, among the countries of the world, Canada is by no means unique in its deviation from the American pattern, and moreover, excessive attention to the question of national identity obscures the fact that within Canada there are a number of strong regional and provincial identities, a recognition of which is vital to a proper understanding of the country's nature. As the historian J.M.S. Careless has pointed out, what Canadians have "sought, and to some extent achieved, is not really unification or consolidation, but the articulation of regional patterns in one transcontinental state."[2]

---

* Written for this volume.
[1] John Meisel, "Canadian Parties and Politics", in (ed.) R. H. Leach, *Contemporary Canada* (Durham, N.C., 1968), p. 135.
[2] J. M. S. Careless, "Limited Identities in Canada", *Canadian Historical Review*, L, No. 1 (March 1969), p. 3. A parallel view may be found in the field of literary criticism: "When we speak of a recognizably Canadian poet we usually mean a regional poet who uses the distinctive objects and actions of his locality as poetic materials." Milton Wilson, "Other Canadians and After", *Tamarack Review*, IX, 1958-9, p. 89.

By what means, therefore, has the Canadian federal system been able to achieve the minimum level of harmony between its regional components which, despite the lack of a strong national identity, has allowed the federal system to maintain itself by peaceful means and function with relative effectiveness for more than a century?

Perhaps the most common response of political scientists to this question is to attribute to the national political parties in Canada the same role of "consensus-building" as that performed by national parties in the United States—even though in the case of Canada the content of the alleged consensus cannot be empirically identified.[3] A non-American but possibly more promising approach is to enquire instead into the basis of political order in other economically advanced but culturally divided societies, particularly in Western Europe, where a number of countries resemble Canada in their lack of an overriding national identity, yet possess distinct, "limited" identities of region and culture. A theory which attempts to explain their operation should, therefore, be of considerable interest to the student of Canadian politics. One such theory is that of "consociational democracy" advanced by the Dutch political scientist Arend Lijphart.[4]

American pluralist theory, Lijphart points out, is unable to explain the politics of "fragmented but stable democracies" (such as the Netherlands, Austria, Belgium and Switzerland) other than by treating them as "deviant" cases. In none of these societies is there a situation of "cross-cutting cleavages", or national consensus, such as pluralist theory holds to be necessary for the successful functioning of democratic government, yet each must be regarded as a functioning and relatively effective democracy. The explanation, he suggests, is to be found in the role played by political elites in each of these countries in deliberately overcoming the effects of cultural fragmentation. Given the existence of strong limited identities or subcultures, and the absence of a national consensus on symbols and goals, it becomes the task of the political leaders of these separate subcultures to practice accommodation at the elite level in order to maintain the national political system and make it work. In other words, bargains can be made and compromises reached among political leaders which would not be possible if they required popular ratification. This type of government Lijphart refers to as "consociational democracy".[5]

For it to function successfully, those who occupy positions of political leadership must understand the perils of political fragmentation and be committed to the maintenance of the national system; they must also be able, within their respective subcultures, to accommodate divergent inter-

[3] For a more extended discussion of consensus and the role of parties, see this author's paper, "Political Parties and Elite Accommodation: Interpretations of Canadian Federalism", *Canadian Political Science Association*, Winnipeg, June, 1970.

[4] Arend Lijphart, "Consociational Democracy", *World Politics*, XXI, No. 2 (January 1969), p. 204-25.

[5] This usage follows David E. Apter, *The Political Kingdom in Uganda: A Study in Bureaucratic Nationalism* (Princeton, 1961).

ests and demands. For the masses, on the other hand, all that is required is that they be committed to their own subcultures and that they trust and support their respective elites. Since the more contact and interaction there is between the masses of the subcultures the greater the likelihood of friction between them, Lijphart suggests, "it may be desirable to keep transactions among antagonistic subcultures in a divided society . . . to a minimum."[6] In theory, there is no reason why a consociational democracy could not function satisfactorily even if among the masses of the different subcultures there was absolutely no attachment to the national political system and no sense whatever of a national identity. In actual systems, however, some degree of popular national sentiment is invariably present. The distinguishing feature of a consociational political system is the relative weakness of popular national sentiment and the overcoming of this weakness through a process of elite accommodation.

Such a skeletal account does less than justice to the scope and subtlety of Lijphart's theory, but is perhaps sufficient to suggest its applicability to the Canadian case. Firstly, and most generally, it offers a possible explanation of why the much-lamented absence of a single transcontinental identity in Canada, and the survival of strong regional subcultures, have not been inconsistent with the maintenance and relatively successful operation of federal government. Secondly, it offers an interpretation of the way in which political leaders behave in Canada, both in relation to one another and in relation to the communities (or subcultures) from which they come and which they represent. Thirdly, it offers a perspective on the office of Prime Minister which illuminates the web of inter-elite relationships which surrounds it and within which its occupant must work.

Certain adjustments must be made in the consociational model before it can be applied to Canada. The term "subculture" could be translated in a number of ways, but most usefully for present purposes as "province"; and, because of the federal constitution, a distinction should be made between federal and provincial political "elites" (defined simply as the holders of the most important offices in federal and provincial political institutions). Federal and provincial bureaucratic elites could be similarly identified. Elite accommodation in Canada takes place at several levels: in the numerous federal boards, commissions, and councils which, through convention, have provincial representation as their basis of membership; in the patterns of day-to-day communication and consultation which have developed among senior provincial civil servants; in the meetings of such interprovincial bodies as the Council of Ministers of Education; in federal-provincial conferences; and in the Federal Cabinet. All are important, but it is the latter two which are of primary concern here, for it is in these institutions that the Prime Minister is most immediately and crucially involved. They are also institutions which are central to the maintenance and operation of the Canadian federal system.

The representative character of the Canadian Cabinet, and particularly

---

[6] *Ibid.* pp. 220-1.

the emphasis placed on provincial representation is well known. What is uncertain is the practical significance of this fact in the functioning of the political system. Since constitutional convention ensures that the proceedings of Cabinet are secret, it is possible only to surmise about provincial influences on decision-making. If, however, the Cabinet is viewed in the broad framework of consociational theory, it can be seen as a mechanism of elite accommodation quite apart from the specific decisions it makes. Its importance, in other words, lies more in its function of bringing together political leaders from the provinces and maintaining their continuous involvement in the decision-making process than in the actual outputs of that process. One of the most important roles of the Prime Minister, therefore, is to maintain among cabinet members drawn from the various provinces a degree of commitment to the national political system which does not exist to nearly the same extent at the popular or mass level within the provinces themselves. One of the conditions of prime ministerial success is an ability to maintain and operate successfully not a system of "participatory democracy" (which, if ever effected, might well make the Prime Minister's task impossible), but a system of elite accommodation.

Canadian political history contains ample confirmation of such a view. Two cases may be briefly mentioned. Firstly, the inability of the Diefenbaker Government to involve a Quebec political elite in a process of accommodation at the federal level was surely one of the major factors contributing to its downfall. Its policies and decisions were not anti-Quebec; its failure to appreciate the importance of elite accommodation was. Secondly, as P. D. Stevens has shown in his study of the collapse of the Liberal party in Ontario in 1911, the failure of Laurier was not so much a failure of policy as a failure to maintain the involvement at the federal level of an Ontario political elite. After Sir Oliver Mowat's resignation in 1897 the Laurier Cabinet increasingly lacked effective representation from Ontario, a deficiency which contributed largely to its electoral defeat.[7]

Interprovincial conferences and, since 1906, federal-provincial conferences have also provided an important institutional framework for the process of elite accommodation. Even more than in the case of the Cabinet, their mere existence is more important than the agreements which they produce. Moreover, they dramatically illustrate a prime ministerial role of considerable consequence in the operation of the federal system: the presenting of a national viewpoint to provincial political leaders whose positions within the system are even more crucial than those of federal cabinet ministers. A federal-provincial conference, therefore, has a dual symbolic function: it symbolizes the vitality of the provincial fact in Canada and also the Prime Minister's unique position as the personification of inter-elite accommodation. It is politics as theatre, highlighting for a brief moment the Prime Minister's role in extracting the necessary national commitment

---

[7] See P. D. Stevens, "Laurier, Aylesworth, and the Decline of the Liberal Party in Ontario", *Historical Papers*, Canadian Historical Association, 1968, pp. 94-113.

from provincial elites (grudging and minimal though it may sometimes be) without which the federal system could not work.

This is not to suggest that the Prime Minister does not have other important executive and political roles, for he obviously does. These, however, have been dealt with elsewhere. What is suggested is that if a Prime Minister is unable or unwilling to perform what may be called his "elite accommodation role", he is unlikely to survive for long to perform the others, or to perform them well. Successful federal leadership in Canada requires an attention to provincial political elites which is matched only by the need for similar accommodation in the consociational democracies of Western Europe. Canadian political history reveals a pattern of elite accommodation which must be taken into account in any attempt to explain the longevity of the federation. From Joseph Howe, who moved from the leadership of the Nova Scotia secessionists to a seat in the Federal Cabinet, to Donald Jamieson, the present Minister of Transport who in 1948-49 was one of the leading figures in the move to keep Newfoundland out of Confederation,[8] the pattern has been the same. Time after time, provincial politicians with no more attachment to the federal system than the mass of their constituents become transformed in Ottawa into Cabinet Ministers intent on making the system work. The two cases cited are but the extreme examples of how the process of elite accommodation in Canada has provided a workable substitute for mass national integration. The measure of a Prime Minister's success is more likely to be found here than in an ability to inspire "northern visions" or "Trudeaumania", important though these may be in the altogether different enterprise of winning elections.

---

[8] See Richard Gwyn, *Smallwood: the Unlikely Revolutionary* (Toronto, 1968), pp. 102-3.

13

Political Leadership and Polarization in Canadian Politics*

CHARLES TAYLOR

[The] need to organize the constituency of reform runs against a persistent Canadian illusion that a [reform] program can be put into effect by one of the old parties with the "right" leadership. This theory is about to be put to what one might be excused for believing was a crucial test, since the Liberal Party is now supposedly under "reform" leadership. Now one of the main features of the two old parties in Canada is that they attempt to be parties for everyone, and not just for the constituency of reform. They aim to unite behind them a consensus of voters from all social classes. And, indeed, in its heyday, the Liberal Party largely succeeded, for it drew its voting strength from almost equal proportions of the voters on all income levels.

In the long run, or even in the not-so-long run, this kind of voting base is incompatible with a program of reform. For such a program is bound to cause desertion in the upper-income levels. There is no comparable mature democracy where a substantial proportion of the upper class, let alone a majority, supports anything vaguely resembling the program described above. There is no reason to believe that Canada constitutes a unique exception to this rule. Those people of progressive inclination who were dismayed to hear Pierre Elliott Trudeau in the 1968 election being studiously noncommital about reforms which could challenge corporate power—the Carter Report or the Watkins Report, to give two instances—to hear him even adopt the rhetoric of the right: "fiscal responsibility," "no more irresponsible promises," "Santa Claus is dead," had no right to be surprised. For to do otherwise would have been to lose a crucial part of the Liberal vote, and thus the election. And someone who entered the scene with the aura of newness and change had to make some effort to reassure this segment of his support.

It might be argued that Trudeau can gradually make the Liberal Party

---

* From Charles Taylor, *The Pattern of Politics* (Toronto: McClelland and Stewart, 1970), and reprinted by permission of McClelland and Stewart Limited.

responsive to important, grass-roots reforms over the coming years by seeking out greater support among the middle- and lower-income groups— to compensate for the loss of the upper classes.

Now this would mean bringing about a polarized politics and would be simply another illustration of the thesis that one cannot have meaningful reform without the political organization of its natural constituency. This point is worth making, because those who believe in reform through the old parties often confuse the two possibilities. So strong is the belief in Canada in the omnipotence of leaders that people often pass unthinkingly from the hope that a new leader will bring reform through finding a new voting base to the wild belief that sweeping changes can be made while leaving the party support essentially unchanged. This second prospect is completely impossible. Polarized politics in terms of program requires the polarization of voting as well.

But it is worth enquiring whether the first hope is well-founded— whether we can introduce polarized politics in Canada through the reform of one of the old parties. Many Canadians have believed this. But the problems involved have rarely been closely examined. It is not just the voting base of a consensus party that reflects all strata of the population. Also its personnel at all levels—through key local party people up to cabinet members—covers a wide range of the political spectrum, from the hard-line right (Thatcher) to centre-left (Marchand). Becoming a party of genuine reform means losing a big band on the right of this spectrum, either because the people concerned are unhappy the way things are going and leave, or because they constitute an obstacle and have to be removed. But this means a "purge" or, more delicately put, a radical change in personnel, right up to the cabinet level.

The common conception of prime-ministerial power among many people, including those who hope great things from the present government, would [have made] De Gaulle giddy. Having the power to dismiss recalcitrant ministers, he is thought to be able to reduce them practically to the position of office boys and make them execute his will in detail. The image given of the present cabinet by some newsmen is of a class of naughty boys cowering under the stern gaze of a new and stricter schoolmaster. Chattering in the corridors is no longer permitted. But what this conception leaves out is that a prime minister, however popular, cannot run all the ministries himself (and the fate of Daniel Johnson awaits him if he tries). He needs colleagues and, moreover, colleagues of some standing in the party which affords him his power base. The party has not elected him leader in order to be unceremoniously shunted out of the way, but in order to share power with him. And thus it is, for instance, that the present cabinet is not all that different in personnel—and certainly not in ideological orientation—from its predecessors. A prime minister can over a period of time alter the balance of power within the party, but he cannot sweep it aside, nor systematically exclude certain sections without running the risk of revolt or split.

But, in order to change the personnel of the party at the top, it is necessary to ignore certain sections. It is unlikely that these will agree to efface themselves quietly. Therefore a major change in the direction of a party—from that of a consensus party to a genuine party of the left based on the constituency of reform—is conceivable only at the expense of at least acute inner struggles. But this kind of struggle is almost always fatal to a party's electoral chances; there are few things that drive electors away more effectively than evidence of disarray and dissension within a party. And thus it is that a change of the kind we are considering is possible, but it can only be made at the cost of a long period in opposition while the party sorts itself out.

We might look for an analogous change to the transformation of the American Democratic Party in the 1920's, when it first became open at the summit to the non-WASP immigrants who had been its faithful supporters for decades. The fight revolved around the nomination of Alf Smith. The struggle was carried on when the Democrats were out of power; and necessarily—if they had been in power when it started, it would certainly have cost them office. The election of 1928 was a crushing defeat for them, but the Democrats built a more viable base for the future—which came faster than it otherwise might have because of the critical situation caused by the Crash.

But this does not exhaust the difficulties which stand in the way of transforming an old party in Canada. Both of our old parties have been traditionally élite-run—that is, they have had no significant degree of democratic government within the party. This is now changing to some degree, at least in outward appearance, but there is still no serious move towards a structure in which, say, the programs of these parties could be determined by their members. The democratization that has taken place affects the choice of local candidates and leaders (which is, of course, very intermittent, at best once every ten years).

The focus on a leader rather than on a program reflects the nature of these parties as consensus parties. What they run on is not a program but rather the value of their leadership, its ability to cope with the problems as they arise. Liberal- and Conservative-Party election programs are always hasty affairs, thrown together at the last minute, and not *meant to be taken really seriously*. The Opposition is ritualistically indignant when they are subsequently neglected, but no one is really surprised. Popular cynicism knows what to think of "election promises." What the old parties really offer is a leadership which claims the competence to extract and act on the consensus at any given time, rather than a specific view of what should be done.

This is élitist concept of government. At its worst it leads to the arrogance of a leadership which feels it has been chosen as uniquely fit to rule and need listen to none outside. The Liberals, the more successful of our two old parties, have been noted for this. But even without arrogance, the mode of government which goes with this kind of politics is that of an elite which has been chosen to run the country as it sees fit. In the absence of any mandate for change, this is usually taken as a mandate to run the country in a close and smooth working relationship with other similar élites, in particular with the business élite and the Ottawa establishment. In the case of the Liberal Party, the relationship with the Ottawa establishment is particularly intimate, since the present civil service is largely a Liberal creation. Under the Pearson administration it seemed to serve as a kind of farm team for the cabinet.

The transformation of an old party into a party of reform would, of course, mean a break in these smooth relations, and the working out of new *modus vivendi* which would have to take account of the opposition in goals. Indeed, such a transformation would raise problems between ministers and the present civil service and would make the life of *any* reform administration hard. To an old party, however, the breach in these relations would be considered intolerable by many of the party's leading figures as well.

Walter Gordon, who as Minister of Finance alienated the business world to some degree, was progressively isolated within the leadership of the Liberal Party. He was not even seriously defended by the "progressives." Any worsening of relations of this kind with other élites would, of course, be one of the things that would set off a bitter struggle within the party; and the consequences of this would be disastrous for the party.

Yet another consequence would face a reform administration that would make change very difficult for an old party. A breach in the smooth relations with the other élites would do more than merely lose support among the well-to-do who are the natural constituency of the *status quo*. There is a substantial number of voters in all classes who have a basically deferential attitude towards power in our society. One of the things they expect of a government is that it be on good terms with the leaders of the corporate system. If these relations break down, then all the pious respect and fear of retaliation which the system inspires in them makes them easily convinced that the government is wrong and must be replaced. There is no doubt that this factor had a hand in bringing down the Diefenbaker administration in 1963. Every respectable voice of power turned stridently against him, and this had a powerful effect. There is, therefore, a big potential electoral penalty on reform well outside the ranks of the well-to-do.

It may sound unfair to raise this obstacle to the transformation of an old party. Does the deference vote not stand in the way of *any* reform party, old or new? Here the important point is: The deference vote is not a fixed quantity; it is a function of the kind of politics and political movements operative in a society. Deference politics is not just a fact which old parties face, it is something that they help to create; it is their stock-in-trade. The kind of party, whose appeal to the voters is to elect a leadership with a more-or-less blank cheque to govern as it sees fit, necessarily trades on the deferential feeling that leadership knows what it is about more than anyone else and should be trusted to get on with the job. There are a number of ways that this feeling can be created. One is through the use of a cult-figure like the NYL, and we have lived through an example of this.

But the principal on-going beneficiary of deference feeling of our corpo-rate-dominated society is the business élite, and political leadership gains by being on good terms with it.

To undermine this deference towards power is, for an old party, to saw off the branch that holds it aloft. Those who believe that Pierre Elliott Trudeau can change all the rules of the game feel that charisma alone can mobilize mass support, and that a leader like Trudeau can afford to do battle with the business élite. But charisma is like lightning: it is very powerful in short bursts but it does not last very long. It is not a stable basis for power. There is every sign that Trudeau recognizes this as much as anyone else, if not more.

If an old party is going to undermine its deference support, it must do all in its power to reduce the scope of deference politics and to build up a different kind of support. And this is so for another reason as well. The kind of politics which consists in selling the electors a leadership without any real commitment to a program does not tend to generate much citizen participation. It is consequently very expensive. A charismatic leader may inspire some participation, but this is an intermittent affair, and besides, in this age of mass communications, charisma itself can be very dear. But the only source where really large amounts of money can be found in our society is big business. Thus being on bad terms with the business élite can be crippling for an old party, as the Conservatives discovered in 1963 and again in 1965.

For both these reasons, a party which breaks with the business élite must develop a new base in citizen participation. In order to break the hold of deference politics, people have to be given a sense that they do not need to rely exclusively on the élites to guide them; that they can trust their own informed judgement; that in concert they and the leadership they throw up can accomplish something. And the only way people can gain this sense is by actually participating in some collective enterprise, actually accomplish-ing something in concert with others. Deference towards élites is fed in our society less now by tradition and less and less by the gaps in education between élite and mass which are now narrowing; to a great degree it is fed by the fragmentation of groups and privatization, which makes people feel powerless, gives them a sense that power is something distant and even mysterious which only initiates can understand. The only way that this sense of powerlessness can be combatted is for people to wield power effectively, by participating in the political process and by working to-gether with others for some goal.

But citizen participation is also important for the reason that it is the only way to compensate for the lack of big money. A large number of vol-unteer workers, working over a long enough period to acquire competence and experience (one election campaign is just enough to make all the mis-takes), and a wide base of small contributors can be tremendously effective. But without this, a party is paralyzed if it attracts no large contributions.

But the only way to generate citizens' participation on a large scale and with some degree of consistency is to give the participants a voice in policy. People cannot be induced to give of their money and effort in large numbers over a period of time unless they identify with the movement concerned. Again, the personal charisma of the leader can bring this about, but not for enough people and above all not over the long haul, charisma being an intermittent thing. In an effective political movement, people must feel that it is really a vehicle for values and goals that are important to them; and for this they must at least believe that they can have a say in the politics and aims of the movement.

Three aspects of the politics of polarization seem therefore to hang inseparably together. Radical reform policies can only succeed by mobilizing the constituency of reform, basically people of middle income and less. This constituency can only be mobilized by a politics of citizen participation, which means not only fighting elections with volunteers, but also a party structure in which the members determine the policy and leadership on a regular basis. For the only way the constituency of reform can compete effectively with the constituency of the *status quo* is through a form of politics which will combat deference voting and can operate without big money. In this way the goals of reform and of democratization are, in our context, closely interwoven.

To return then to our question whether an old party can transform itself into the reform party in a polarized politics. This will now appear rather unlikely. For it will not only have to undergo a bitter and probably protracted inner struggle, but it will also have to transform completely its political mode of operation, and hence its inner structures, replacing what it loses in money and deference vote by building up a base in citizen participation. None could say that the thing is impossible, but it is hardly an easy task, and the attempts would cost the party at least a long spell in opposition. The reader can judge for himself whether a sea-change of this kind is on the cards for either of our old parties. I personally would have great difficulty believing it possible—the more so in that there is little evidence so far for any of the three changes mentioned above, in policy, in voting base, in type of politics.

In the recurrent debate on the Canadian left, between those who support the New Democratic Party and those who believe the old parties can be changed, it is usually assumed by the latter that all that is required is that the left-wingers achieve power within an old party. This is just the beginning of the process. The real task would be to transform an old party without destroying it in the process. Looked at in this way, it is very much a question whether what is billed as the short road to reform is not really the long way round.

14

Ministers' Staffs and Leadership Politics*

GERALD LENOSKI

There is no limit on the number of persons a Minister may appoint (to his personal staff) under section 37 of the Public Service Employment Act. There is a limit on the overall manpower budget allowed each Minister with which to compensate the persons he so appoints. The present limit is $130,000 per annum and it is determined by Cabinet on the recommendation of the Treasury Board.[1]

The political interface provided by ministers' staffs is a significant, although comparatively recent, innovation in Canadian Cabinet government. This relatively obscure aspect of the machinery of the political executive merits our attention, particularly because there has been minimal academic commentary to date concerning its organization and importance.[2] This select group of auxiliaries to Cabinet ministers constitutes a political network which, among other things, provides a variety of linkages with leadership politics vis-a-vis the Cabinet and party systems. Some of the roles currently performed by ministers' staffs as they relate to collective

* Written for this edition. The author currently is completing a doctoral dissertation for the Department of Government, University of Essex, England, entitled "Strengthening the Political Impulse: The Evolution and Impact of Political Staffs Supporting British Cabinet Ministers (1964-1975)". This essay is based partly on the author's firsthand experience as a Special Assistant to the Minister of Energy, Mines and Resources (1969-1970), preceded by stints as a Research and Administrative Assistant on the staffs of three Pearson and Trudeau Government Members during the period 1966-1970.

[1] House of Commons, Canada, *Sessional Papers* #300, 1st Session, 30th Parliament, p. 59 (as tabled 26 March 1975 in answer to Question No. 42, 30 September 1974, Mr. Coates).

[2] The only papers in this field published to date are: J. R. Mallory, "The Minister's Office Staff: An Unreformed Part of the Public Service", *Canadian Public Administration* X, No. 1 (March 1967); pp. 25-34; Paul M. Tellier, "Pour une réforme des cabinets de ministres fedéraux", *Administration Public du Canada*, XI, 1968; and William M. Lee, "The Executive Assistant", *Quarterly of Canadian Studies*, I, No. 1 (Spring 1971).

Cabinet responsibility will be examined in this article. It is hoped that the relationships characteristic of these activities, and especially the extent to which these contribute to prime ministerial leadership, will be identified.

The Minister's Staff—An Overview

... something like a new dimension has been added to the system with the appointment of various assistants to the Minister ... (Each) minister is supplied with various non-elected staff assistants to do a hundred tasks that he cannot possibly do himself. In recent years there has been a steady increase in the number of non-elected and non-civil service assistants of varying functions added to the offices of Cabinet Ministers ... [3]

Just as much as the cadre of personal advisers to the Prime Minister has grown increasingly over the last decade, the same is true for political staffing in the private establishments supporting his individual ministers. Indeed, the numbers and types of personal staff surrounding Cabinet members have changed substantially of late. While a typical minister in the St. Laurent Government (1948-1957) seldom had the services of more than a single political confidant (serving as a private secretary[4]), his 1975 successor is assisted in most cases by a group of reasonably well-paid politicos[5], a group quite separate from the civil service hierarchy. The typical Trudeau Government member now has an entourage of at least half a dozen assistants designated by various titles and assignments.[6] What accounts for this growth? Furthermore, through what processes have such political staffs been recruited? What qualifications must they possess? Under what conditions of appointment do they hold tenure? And what policy input can they exercise?[7]

The recent history of the minister's staff has included periods when the identities and involvements of some of its members became controversially 'front page'; usually, however, this staff has tended to maintain a

---

[3] Editorial, *The Free Press*, Winnipeg, March 13, 1965, p. 4.

[4] Along with required stenographic and clerical support. See Government of Canada, *Telephone Directory*, Ottawa, 1948-57. "In Canada, the private secretary, under whatever designation, is a personal nominee of the Minister, almost never a civil servant, and usually identified with the Minister's career and often with party politics." (J. W. Pickersgill, "Bureaucrats and Politicians", *Canadian Public Administration*, XV, No. 3 (Fall 1972), pp. 410-27.

[5] House of Commons, *Sessional Papers* #300, pp. 1-69. The salary ranges for specific staff categories at present are: Executive Assistant—up to $25 thousand per annum; Special Assistant—up to $21 thousand; Private Secretary—up to $14.5 thousand. In the absence of official Treasury Board recognition of such categories, Research, Administrative and other Assistants customarily are paid salaries equivalent to certain public service classification scales.

[6] *Ibid.* Some actually have as many as nine assistants of one kind or another.

[7] While these and many other questions on ministers' staffs warrant attention, it is not possible to study them in depth here.

discreetly low profile.[8] Staffs have evolved through trial and error and statutory legitimization. Legal status was not accorded to so-called "exempt"[9] staffs—staffs that can participate in partisan politics—until the 1961 *Civil Service Act*, passed during the Progressive Conservative Government of John Diefenbaker.[10] When the Conservatives achieved office four years earlier, greater numbers of government party adherents than during the previous twenty-two Liberal years gradually began to be placed in the inner circles of ministers' establishments, paid out of public funds.[11] Since the Diefenbaker years this trend has continued, providing ministers with "extra sets of eyes and ears"[12] for their everyday work, and for a variety of requirements. Clearly, this constitutes an admission on the part of successive ministers, together with general acceptance by the political system,[13] that the dynamics of government activity at the federal level in the latter half of the twentieth century place competing demands, and hence severe strains, on the time and energies of ministers.

To help offset the pressures faced by every minister in executing properly his multi-faceted role as departmental executive, party politician, constituency representative, parliamentarian, political executive and Cabinet colleague, political staffs have been sanctioned and consequently their availability has increased.[14] As middlemen, these staff assistants constitute the functional dividing line between politics and administration. Their chief preoccupation is to serve, and in the process to further, each minister's aims and interests according to his specific departmental responsibilities combined with his general political duties inside and outside the Cabinet as determined by regional and other representational factors. Thus, they become intimately involved with the advancement of his viewpoint—and, where possible, the enhancement of his reputation—in the department, in Parliament, throughout the party, in his constituency, in his province or region and nationally. By so doing they are in a position to complement the resources of the permanent officials. Further, they can supple-

---

[8] See Canada, *Special Public Inquiry* (Justice Frederic Dorion), 1964; and, Richard Gwyn, *The Shape of Scandal* (Toronto: 1965), regarding the Rivard Scandal, in which several ministerial assistants were implicated. See also John R. Walker, "Anonymous Elite Has Considerable Power", *The Ottawa Citizen*, 29 January 1972, p. 7.

[9] That is, exempt from the statutory impediments to participation by public servants in partisan politics.

[10] *Statutes of Canada*, 1960-61, Chapter 57, Section 71.

[11] See Government of Canada, *Telephone Directory*, Ottawa, 1957-63.

[12] In the terminology of the late Rt. Hon. R.H.S. Crossman, 1964-70 senior Labour Government Minister and advocate of ministerial support staffs in Britain, as quoted in his Fabian Tract No. 298, "Socialism and the New Despotism" (London: 1956), p. 16.

[13] The strengthening of ministers' staffs was recommended by The Royal Commission On Government Organization (see Vol. 5, p. 38.).

[14] Members of the Cabinet have not been the only beneficiaries of larger staff resources on Parliament Hill lately. Monies available for research facilities and other assistance to the Leader of the Opposition, Opposition parties' caucuses and the Government caucus were increased substantially from the late 1960s.

ment the advice of neutral civil servants with assessments and initiatives based upon political intelligence.

All members of a minister's staff, individually and collectively, have the potential for becoming a creative and constructive force, depending on several components including their own competence and commitment. Crucial is the minister himself. His willingness, along with his ability, to assert the required political leadership over that portion of the government machine under his direction, is pivotal. The size and nature of government today often permits ministers' staffs (and, in effect, sometimes the minister himself) only a peripheral impact on policy development. They can, however, exert a substantially controlling influence in the process of making policy. The degree to which they are permitted to do so depends as much on the minister's disposition as on the staff's talents, always in conjunction with civil service cooperation. Naturally, the latter seldom is easily secured, unless and until ministerial intervention is forthcoming.

The only major constraint governing a minister's choice of staff concerns salary.[16] Otherwise, by custom he is entitled to offer posts to anyone from the worlds of business, academia, the professions, or even from within the civil service itself; party stalwarts, or those with no political connections at all, theoretically can be potential nominees. The attractiveness of ministerial staff appointment is lessened of course for those legitimately concerned about insecurity of tenure.[17] As a result, it can be difficult for a minister to entice the most qualified candidates to the vicissitudes of public life. In some cases, understandably, he will endeavour to patronize from amongst his closest supporters. Nevertheless, dedication alone is hardly a sufficient criterion by which an adept minister measures the value of a would-be political assistant. No minister's staff has room for sinecures.[18]

Straightforward generalizations about specific categories of ministerial assistants are difficult to make. Every minister, according to his personality traits, socialization, political stature, portfolio, goals and so forth, really is *sui generis*. Thus, the type of staff assistance each wants and needs traditionally has been quite diverse. Despite this, certain designations have gained acceptance, and within limits the duties performed by their incumbents are uniformly recognizable.

The position of executive assistant[19] originated to provide the minister

---

[16] For years ministers have been afforded the latitude of making many staff appointments for which salaries up to ceilings established by Treasury Board have been deemed appropriate. See above notes 1 and 5. Although decent, given the long hours and pressures involved, such salary levels never have been particularly generous.

[17] All appointments from outside the civil service are at the whim of the minister concerned. The ephemeral nature of political life may have marginal appeal for serious, career-oriented individuals.

[18] Although the process of appointment and the variety of assignments do leave ample room for some ministers, on rare occasion, to stretch their budgets to include positions of negligible consequence.

[19] For a full ventilation of the duties of this senior position, see Tellier, "Pour une réforme", and Lee, "The Executive Assistant."

with a trusted manager and political organizer; someone to be his sound-
ing board and go-between, coordinator of his conflicting requirements,
synthesizer and expediter of his voluminous paper flow. In the opinion of
one former such figure:

The Ministerial Executive Assistant can be anything from an extremely powerful,
policy-influencing, unelected official to a glorified, overpaid baggage-handler . . . His
actual place in this spectrum depends upon many things; the breadth of responsibility
and authority the Minister wishes to have him assume; the background and capabili-
ties of the aide; plus such other associated matters as the nature of the Department,
the attitude of co-operation or intransigence of the Deputy Minister and other senior
civil servants; and the ability and capacity for work of other ministerial staff mem-
bers.[20]

Once the minister's sole personal aide, usually recruited through party
political channels,[21] the executive assistant's position has thrived. Its ideal
occupant is of paramount importance for the minister politically in much
the same way that his deputy minister is administratively. As chief of the
minister's political staff and as a potential unifying force providing coherence to the minister's program, he currently oversees the work of all
assistants, whatever their titles, most of whom—like him—normally origi-
nate outside the civil service.[22]

The classification "Special Assistant" gained currency especially after
it was named in the section concerning ministers' staff in the *Public Service*
Employment Act of 1967.[23] All executive, special and other like-named assistants to ministers were formally appointed by orders-in-council prior to
the promulgation of this act, and since then in accordance with Treasury
Board directives. Special assistants tend to be junior in age and experience
to the executive assistant, and are subordinate to him in the ministerial
staff hierarchy. While the executive assistant is likely to work closely and
continuously with the minister, much of the caseload of special assistants
can be dispatched adequately with less direct or frequent ministerial contact.[24] This is, of course, subject to many variables, including the minister's
style of working, the physical proximity of his department to Parliament
Hill, the kind of relationship he engenders with his staff, as well as the
type and range of problems to which different assistants must be assigned.

With rare exception ministers now appoint a minimum of two special
assistants, one each for constituency and parliamentary affairs, respec-

---

[20] Lee, "The Executive Assistant."

[21] But not exclusively. In recent times it has not been unusual for ministers to recruit from
the ranks of the civil service. In one exceptional case an individual who had been a
senior assistant to the Leader of the Opposition crossed the floor to join a Cabinet
member as his executive assistant.

[22] And he even may be delegated by his minister to take care of all necessary recruitment,
from political sources and otherwise.

[23] *Statutes of Canada*, 1966-67, Chapter 71, Section 37.

[24] During the daily grind in Ottawa, when on many days large portions of ministers'
timetables are taken up with parliamentary duties and Cabinet business anyhow. Some
special assistants frequently are intimately involved with ministerial travel in particular.

tively. In some offices these same special assistants are responsible for areas of departmental liaison too; in others, a separate legislative assistant[25] (or Special Assistant (Parliamentary Relations)) and a constituency assistant (sometimes called Special Assistant (Constituency Relations))[26] are named for those distinct purposes entirely. In these instances, additional special assistants usually are appointed to focus attention primarily on segments of departmental or other activities in which a given minister may have a personal or political interest.

The continuing diversification of responsibilities assumed by ministers in large measure has accounted for greater role specialization on the part of their bigger staffs. Whereas the executive assistant at one time could take care of virtually everything single-handedly,[27] the necessity of providing additional assistants for varying reasons has led to a fairly strict differentiation of duties amongst many ministers' staffs. Moreover, together with the executive assistant and several special assistants for designated purposes, the staff complement backing up a representative minister at the present time, will include some research,[28] administrative and/or departmental assistants.[29] Under these latter, and still other, classifications can be subsumed political operatives who concentrate on anything from press relations to speech preparation, policy analysis and a host of other requirements which must be met to help the minister fulfil his various roles.

---

[25] The occupant of which position in some instances is a civil servant on secondment from the Parliamentary Returns Division of the Department, and in others is a political outsider, given responsibility for all or some of the following: House book preparation and briefings in advance of oral questions; written answers to parliamentary enquiries; liaison with government caucus MPs, opposition party critics, standing committees; and, the legislative programme in the House and Senate. This assistant usually works in conjunction with the minister's parliamentary secretary, if one is named.

[26] Who invariably will spend the vast proportion of his time away from the national capital within the region assigned to the minister, operating out of an office convenient to the riding represented by the minister in Parliament.

[27] In close harmony with his minister's private secretary, whose position, since the emergence of the executive assistant's title and matching role, has tended to be concentrated on the provision of the minister's personal secretarial requirements, scheduling, travel arrangements, Cabinet documents, and so forth.

[28] This title has gained currency in recent years and describes a junior political functionary, probably a generalist, serving an internship as an understudy to the executive assistant and the special assistants.

[29] These titles are more or less interchangeable. More often than not a departmental or administrative assistant has been an up-and-coming permanent civil servant serving a stint as the interface between the political outsiders appointed to positions of confidence near ministers and senior departmental management. Depending on the department, this functionary might be charged by the executive assistant with nothing more than responsibility for ensuring that the paperwork flows smoothly and efficiently throughout the minister's office; or, he might be given wider scope encompassing the drafting of correspondence on one or more subjects, the supervision of projects of a technical or political theme that require co-ordination within the minister's office, between it and other ministers' staffs and/or the PMO, with branches of the same or other departments, interest groups, etc.

Ministers' Staffs and Leadership Politics in the Cabinet and Party Systems

The staff's function is to assist the executive by providing information, formulating possible courses of action, coordinating decisions, and reporting on results . . . (S) taff assistants exercise no power beyond the influence of their ideas upon the executive himself.[30]

In the Cabinet and party systems individual ministers' staffs can serve as independent sources of vitality, opinion, and, most of all, political ballast. Owing no allegiance to the civil service machine, *per se*,[31] they are in a pivotal position to help counterbalance the monopoly of professional bureaucrats on policy advice. They can affect as well as enforce the "political impulse"[32] in combination with administrative experience and continuity provided by departments; out of that blend priorities are established and decisions result. In conformity with the inclinations of the Cabinet, and subject to its concurrence, collectively the efforts of ministers' staffs can help ensure the proper synthesis of party policy with departmental policy into government policy. This becomes more of a latent than a manifest function, however, when a party enjoys longevity in power. For example, the longer the Liberal Party stays in office, the less distinguishable are differences between party and departmental policy.[33] In spite of this, and for other reasons, ministers' staffs have been known to assume an activist posture in the policy-making apparatus.[34] Fanning across the government apparatus, many of them maintain a close watch on the formulation and implementation of policy options.[35]

As mentioned earlier, the influence of political staffs hinges largely on ministers' attitudes. Indeed, a minister's interpretation of how political direction and control should be put into practice in his departments is central to the definition of his staff's manoeuvrability. Some ministers, wary of possible civil service sensitivity and cautious about challenging entrenched views, do not deploy political appointees as alternative sources of policy initiation and support. Others are prepared to risk irritating

---

[30] Peter Self, *Administrative Theories and Politics* (London, 1972), p. 122.

[31] In the majority of cases, but who, if they are shrewd or prudent enough, might be affected by the advantageous provisions of Section 37 of the *Public Service Employment Act* in their behaviour towards the career officials.

[32] That is, the momentum derived from the policy commitments undertaken during the last election campaign which, in the light of the results, mandate the Government to proceed accordingly.

[33] Many ministers' staffs operate just as much at arms length with party policy as with departmental policy, whether or not a gulf exists between the two. This kind of approach distinguishes those staffs to ministers who do not expect them to have, or who themselves do not expect or try to have, substantive policy input.

[34] Walker, "Anonymous elite."

[35] *Ibid.* Senior civil servants are not only used to bordering on political staff intrusion in some areas of the policy process; in many cases they have come to expect, if not always appreciate, it.

permanent officials by insisting upon substantive, instead of superficial, political staff participation. In the absence of empirical evidence it is fair to speculate that, in all likelihood, the approaches of as many ministers would fall midway between the two extremes as would actually resemble them.[36]

Policy and the administrative system do impose limitations on ministers' staffs in their efforts to affect the fundamentals of departmental operations. Yet in the contexts of Cabinet organization and of political leadership, conditions are different. So are the results. The valuable role of their political staffs is apparent in situations where busy ministers as leading party figures in a collegial executive headed by the prime minister are concerned. In the workings of the political network consisting of the totality of assistants to all ministers including the Prime Minister, common outlook and similar loyalties prevail. Based on these bonds relationships among members of the Cabinet are engendered and sustained constantly as a result of staff interaction. Via formal and informal contacts alike, through written and oral communications, the political staff network contributes to the reinforcement of the solidarity in which, to survive, collective ministerial responsibility has to be firmly rooted.[37]

In the abstract his staff should behave as an extension of each Cabinet member, especially regarding his instinct for political survival. The practicalities of how this is achieved (and what it can accomplish) in the Cabinet and party is revealing about some of the parameters of prime ministerial leadership. In the face of the distractions and complications of office a minister's necessary preparedness for Cabinet and Cabinet committee deliberations can be a real burden. Yet participation around the Cabinet table is the most basic criterion whereby the Prime Minister is able to judge the performance of his ministers. To lend coherence to the contributions expected of them on a wide variety of issues, many ministers rely on briefings by their assistants. Perhaps the executive assistant, or on occasion a special policy adviser,[38] prepares synopses and makes recommendations on the contents of lengthy submissions. In this way not only is a minister better equipped intellectually to deal with more topics on the Cabinet agenda, but his sense of efficacy is raised. More importantly, he is assured of greater competitive leverage in the working out of decisions, which has the added advantage of helping preserve his status and accentuating his worth in the estimation of the Prime Minister.

Ministers' staffs have become essential elements in a formalized system of country-wide information-gathering through party channels that have

---

[36] Personal experience and discussions with past and current ministerial staff members.

[37] Intermittently, meetings designed to bring together representatives of all ministers' staffs are convened for the purpose of comparing notes on strategies and tactics concerning current topics of common interest. These are organized and led by the P.M.O.

[38] Only a handful of ministers to date have identified a position so-named among their personal staffs. One former minister conceded in conversation with the author that the role of policy adviser to a minister, inasmuch as it helps short-circuit reading time when so often precious little of it is available, is the one which a minister does well to stress and depend upon.

been put together by the Prime Minister's Office (P.M.O.).[39] On the heels of losing its parliamentary majority, in late 1972 the chastened Trudeau minority government sought to improve the quality of its information base by accentuating its links with grassroots sentiment. Although regional contact always has been a notable portion of ministers' party political responsibilities[40] to the Prime Minister and Cabinet, what is called the "Umbrella Riding Concept" has counted on more of the time and public relations resources of political staffs than formerly. Structured so that the Prime Minister receives a detailed report monthly on everything from party membership to issues, complaints, and the actions of the sitting government or opposition M.P., this new system assigns each minister a territory covering from six to as many as a dozen federal constituencies. It was founded on the premise that the less regularized and comprehensive the leadership's contact with the aspirations of the party faithful (who are assumed to reflect the breadth of public opinion generally), the less secure the Prime Minister's — *ergo*, the party's—mandate becomes.[41]

Such a method of aggregating information and assuring feedback, coordinated by the P.M.O. and wholly dependent on the personal attention of ministers through their staffs, is a powerful device that reinforces the leadership of the Prime Minister especially in the Cabinet and the government caucus. Not only does it help to cushion him from the dangers of becoming estranged from party opinion, which in turn serves somewhat to protect his ministers and M.P.s against preventable electoral difficulties. It keeps the parliamentary wing in closer check by alerting it to two facts: that concerns which they must represent are reaching their leader indirectly and quite separately from their own expressions; and that the strength of the Prime Minister's popularity is a necessity which ought to be emphasized. Furthermore, it concentrates the attentions of all ministers and their staffs on the importance of maintaining a broad perspective in order to serve properly and survive politically, while reminding ministers of the dependency of their positions on prime ministerial patronage. To last, it must be nurtured through adherence to his directive to communicate in this way with the party and the country. Overall, then, the system is designed to advance unity throughout the government party generally, while bolstering the Cabinet's leadership centered on the Office of the Prime Minister.

Political Staffing By Ministers—Some Concluding Comments

If one were to delineate this newer pattern of politics by leadership, it would include the following: (1) the shift in the centre of conflict resolution and initiative from

---

[39] Personal contacts with present ministers' staffs.

[40] Arising out of the conventions that have come to be associated with Cabinet composition, such as representation from every province, and so on.

[41] According to sources currently inside ministers' offices, however, since the re-election of a majority Liberal government in July 1974, there has been a noticeable diminution in the emphasis formerly placed on the umbrella riding system.

*parliamentary bodies and economic institutions to executive leadership; (2) the prolifer-
ation of the immediate office of the chief executive from its cabinet-restricted status to a
collectivity of co-adjuting instrumentalities; (3) the tendency toward increased centralization of political parties, with the subordination of the victorious political parties as
instruments of the chief executive; (4) the calculated manipulation of irrationalities by
political leadership through the vast power potential of mass communications; (5) the
displacement of the amateur by the professional politician and civil servant; (6) the
growth of bureaucracy as a source and technique of executive power but also as a
fulcrum which all contestants for power attempt to employ.*[42]

Throughout this volume the relevance of various of these components
of modern leadership politics is demonstrated, a quarter century after they
were identified. This paper is no exception, and illustrates components 2,
3, 5 and 6 especially. The foregoing has shown that in the broadest sense
the functional value of ministers' staffs, although undeniable, defies precise description. Increased in size and scope, nowadays as before, they are
an amorphous group much of whose behaviour is subject to idiosyncratic
variables. Inasmuch as each minister is a peculiar political personality,
versatility is implicit to the staff structure that has developed to serve all
manner of his political-cum-administrative needs. On appointment and
during his period in office, within reasonable limits he is permitted to equip
himself with the necessary expertise[44] and political insulation that, compatible with his own special circumstances, can best help him respond to the
often disparate interests vying for his attention.

In spite of the differences in style and substance amongst them, the
common denominator pervading the efforts of all ministers' staffs is competitive party politics. This is derived from the inter-party contest in the
parliamentary process, the framework within which each minister's everyday existence is determined. As far as *inter*-party competition is concerned,
nonetheless, the importance of political staffs to ministers as a countervailing force cannot easily be overlooked. They are in a stategic position to
assist a minister's use of civil service expertise while providing a healthy

---

[42] Lester G. Seligman, "The Study of Political Leadership", *American Political Science Review*,
XLIV, (1950), p. 904.

[43] As such, experts have been uncommon among ministers' staffs, especially in the sense of
expertise applicable in the context of departmental areas of involvement. Lawyers would
be well in evidence among staffs to Ministers of Justice, as well as in most other
portfolios, but in general ministers have tended to recruit well-educated generalists.
Consequently, most staff members have been mobile from department to department in
much the same way as their ministers.

[44] For a provocative argument regarding the political drawbacks of ministers' succumbing
to civil service control, see Barbara Castle (at present Secretary of State for Health and
Social Security in the British Labour Government), "Mandarin Power", *Sunday Times*,
London, 10 June 1973.

balance against the enveloping influence of the bureaucracy.[45] By virtue of the exchange of information through their political network around the periphery of the entire Cabinet, they can help to preserve each minister's relative political strength vis-à-vis his colleagues. Most importantly, they may also serve as a protection against any disproportionate impact of the Prime Minister's own burgeoning political staff[46] on a minister's constitutional responsibility.

In this post-Watergate era it could not be more timely to recognize the position that ministers' staffs now occupy in the Canadian Cabinet system. In no way is this to suggest that their function is anything but justified; on the contrary, as discussed above, the roles they play are a needed adjunct to the minister's job as a political figure.

To be sure, a great deal of difference exists between the impact ministers' staffs actually have made and still make, as opposed to what the theoretical boundaries might allow. Politics and personality account for the distinction. The accretion of political staffs to ministers has taken place with the tacit acceptance of the civil service, in the absence of any expressions of concern for a rationale by any of the political parties. Initially an expedient, progressively they have accumulated a corporate identity. From time to time, especially when party competition was enlivened by the alternation of parties in power and by tenuous minority governments, minister's staffs have rallied as a highly politicized, unified and boldly supportive weapon in the Cabinet's arsenal. During periods of assured parliamentary stability the avowedly partisan tone among ministers' staffs is inclined to give way to a more technocratic bent. If this happens to any great degree, one must ask if ministers themselves are far from becoming civil servants manqués.

---

[45] For an up-to-date exposition on the workings of the Prime Minister's Office, see Thomas d'Aquino, "The Prime Minister's Office: Catalyst or Cabal?", a paper delivered at the Canada-United Kingdom Colloquium on Recent Changes in the Machinery of Government, International Political Science Association, Montréal, Québec, 19 August 1973.

SECTION III

The Prime Minister and Other Sources of Policy Influence

The following reflections by Mitchell Sharp and Jean Chrétien give their perceptions of the role and influence of the public service in policy-making.

The article by Bruce Doern defines the way in which Prime Minister Trudeau approached policy-making in the early years of his Prime Ministership through a discussion of Trudeau's philosophy of rationality, his approach to social goals, priorities and structures of policy formulation. Although modifications and deviations from his philosophy may have occurred since 1970, Mr. Pitfield's paper in Section I indicates that the rationalist ethic remains strong, at least in the P.C.O. Other features of this approach are discussed in the article by George Szablowski which includes a postscript written in late 1976. A paper by Laurent Dobuzinskis reviews the literature and practice surrounding policy-making reforms in the last 10 years. Richard Schultz questions the power of central agencies in his paper. This selection is a summary of Mr. Schultz's thoughts on the issue as the result of his Ph.D. dissertation, a case study of a policy area which involved central agency participation. This section of the book is concluded with a discussion of central agency and cabinet relations with parliament in carrying its legislative programme to and through parliament. I am grateful to Robert Jackson and M. M. Atkinson and their publisher, Macmillan of Canada, for permission to reprint from their **The Canadian Legislative Process.**

15

The Cabinet and the Public Service: Reflections of Mitchell Sharp, J. Chrétien, et al.

EDITED BY THOMAS A. HOCKIN

Remarks of Mitchell Sharp*

Let me turn to the main theme of my remarks, which is the relationship between senior civil servants and their ministers, the politicians. I served several Ministers as a civil servant for 16 years, in the end at Deputy Minister level. For over 13 years, I was a politician and Minister of several departments. In those thirty years, I gave advice, I received it.

Top public servants are powerful persons in the machinery of government at the federal level. They wield great influence. They do so because they are, in the main, professionals who have been selected for proven administrative ability and who devote their full time to government. In many cases, they have a greater influence upon the course of events than have Ministers, particularly the weaker and less competent.

This may seem somehow to be anti-democratic but it needn't be and in my experience it isn't. Government is, in fact, a specialized affair which cannot be run by amateurs without professional advice and professional execution. With rare exceptions, politicians are amateurs in any field of government administration, at least at the beginning of their political career.

They cannot be expected to be experts in fiscal and monetary policy, and in nuclear policy and in foreign policy, for example, when they offer themselves as candidates in a local constituency, yet they may find themselves having to make decisions in any or all those fields once in office. Prime Ministers are limited in their selection of Ministers to those

---

* I am grateful to Mr. Sharp for his permission to publish this address, "Reflections of a Former Minister", given before the Institute of Public Administration of Canada (Toronto Regional Group), Toronto, November 29, 1976. (Pages 6 to 19 of the 20-page text are reprinted here.)

of their party who have been elected. Sometimes, given the necessity in a federal state for geographical distribution in Cabinet, the choice may be extremely limited.

At a political meeting during the 1968 election campaign, I was asked by a brash young man what qualifications I had to be foreign minister of Canada. I replied that my principal qualification was that I had been elected to Parliament.

Politicians, particularly Ministers, require the best impartial advice that they can get if they are to make wise decisions. Sycophants who echo their boss's views are of little value; indeed they can be positively dangerous as advisers if they are not prepared from time to time to tell their bosses the painful truth that their pet idea is unworkable. That is one of the reasons why I am not in favour of the principle, which is sometimes advanced, that the top positions—the heads of departments—should be filled by those who are in sympathy with the views of the party in power and should depart with their Ministers when the government is replaced.

After some 30 years observing the process of government, I am also more convinced than I was at the beginning that there is virtue in continuity in the senior administrative jobs. Competent people are not going to be prepared to enter the public service and make a career of it if they are to be denied access to the top jobs where they can bring their talents fully to bear.

The contrary argument that senior civil servants would resist change in the event that a government with radically different views from its predecessor took office has never been very convincing to me. In the first place, knowing my own country and its political parties, I doubt that any change would be in fact very radical. The second is that it is precisely under those circumstances, were they to come about, that an experienced senior civil service would be most valuable, one that could guide a new government in the implementation of its policies and enable it to avoid the administrative pitfalls of which it might otherwise not be aware.

There is need, of course, for Ministers to have in their offices men and women to help them perform as Members of Parliament and political leaders. Such temporary appointees, however valuable they may be—and I have been fortunate in my ministerial staff over my years in office—are no substitute for permanent non-partisan senior civil servants.

From time to time, too, Governments may wish to be able to call on the services of qualified Canadians from the business or professional world who have special expertise of one kind or another. This they should be able to do and are able to do. I myself inherited a Deputy Minister appointed by the Diefenbaker administration who had not been drawn from the ranks of the permanent public service. I retained him. The test of such appointments should be the competence of the appointee and not his or her personal politics.

Do senior civil servants exert too much influence upon the government? Are Ministers puppets being manipulated by the mandarins, as is sometimes asserted or implied? These are difficult questions to answer satisfactorily because so much depends upon the way individual Ministers react to advice.

The Right Honourable Richard Crossman, according to his recently published diaries, was of the view that in Britain, the bureaucrats tried to dominate the government.

"I can't help realizing", he commented, "one has to be pretty strong-minded and curious not to be got down by this astonishing Whitehall hierarchy."[1] "One whole department is there to support the Minister. Into his in-tray come hour by hour notes with suggestions as to what he should do. Everything is done to sustain him in the line which officials think he should take. . . . There is constant debate [among the civil servants] as to how the Minister should be advised or, shall we say, directed and pushed and cajoled into the line required by the Ministry . . . I am, therefore, always on the look-out to see how far my own ideas are getting across, how far they are merely tolerated by the Ministry, and how far the Ministry policies are being imposed on my own mind."[2]

And then there is this plaintive passage. "My Minister's room is like a padded cell, and in certain ways, I am like a person who is suddenly certified a lunatic and put safely into this great vast room, cut off from real life and surrounded by male and female trained nurses and attendants. When I am in a good mood, they occasionally allow an ordinary human being to come and visit me; but they make sure that I behave right, and that the other person behaves right; and they know how to handle me. Of course, they don't behave quite like nurses because the Civil Service is profoundly deferential—'Yes, Minister! No, Minister! If you wish it, Minister!'—and combined with this there is a constant preoccupation to ensure that the Minister does what is correct."[3]

That may be so of Britain. It is my impression that the top bureaucrats there are a cohesive group who entered the public service directly from the universities and rose through the ranks, witness C.P. Snow's novels of the corridors of power. Moreover, governments in Britain tend to have shorter lives than Canadian governments with the result that their Ministers are even more dependent than ours on their permanent advisers to provide continuity of administration.

When I was a civil servant, I think it is fair to say that individual Ministers and the Cabinet as a whole depended more upon the advice of senior civil servants than they do today and they did so deliberately. When a difficult problem arose, the customary response was to refer it for study and report to a committee of senior public servants. There was also a period during the war and in the immediate post-war years when influential public servants like Clifford Clark, Norman Robertson, Graham Towers and Donald Gordon were active promoters of new ideas and

---

[1] Richard Crossman, *The Diaries of a Cabinet Minister*, Vol. 1, p. 26.
[2] *Idem*, p. 31.
[3] *Idem*, p. 21.

approaches that they persuaded their Ministers and the Cabinet to adopt. The federal mandarins then were a tightly knit group of personal friends drawn from various walks of life who had been invited to Ottawa to join the public service during both Conservative and Liberal regimes and who in turn attracted others like myself and John Deutsch and R. B. Bryce. They were not lifetime civil servants recruited at time of graduation who had risen through the ranks, as is now becoming the pattern.

Today, in the Trudeau government, when difficult problems arise, they are more often referred to Ministerial Committees than to committees of civil servants. Innovative ideas still emerge from the civil service but the process of decision-making at the Cabinet level is so complex nowadays that individual contributions are quickly submerged in the deluge of documentation. The present Ministers, I suspect, long for a return of the general rule under which as a civil servant I operated, which was that memoranda for Ministers should not exceed two pages, otherwise they might not be read.

As an illustration of the difference in procedure, then and now, let me refer to the application of price controls.

When I arrived in Ottawa at the beginning of 1942, the overall price ceiling had just come into effect and I became liaison between the then Minister of Finance, James Lorimer Ilsley and Donald Gordon, Chairman of the Wartime Prices and Trade Board. From my friends and colleagues in the public service, I heard the story of how the idea of an overall price ceiling was developed during the preceding summer and sold to the Cabinet by senior civil servants. Canada was the first allied country to adopt it.

By contrast (of course, allowance must be made for the difference between wartime and peacetime) the Cabinet took the initiative in introducing the present price and income controls. It was the Cabinet who directed the civil servants to prepare a contingency plan, many, many months ago. Later, both Ministers and senior advisers urged the Cabinet to implement controls but it was the ministers who gave the general shape and scope to the approach finally adopted.

As an aside, I sometimes thought that as Ministers we were much too zealous and that particularly under Mr. Trudeau, we worked far too hard and spent far too much time in Cabinet and Cabinet Committees discussing each other's proposals. Decisions might have taken less time, we might have had a better perspective on events and more time for politics had we delegated more to our civil service advisers and left more time for reflection.

It amuses me to read speeches and articles about the dangers posed by the activities of the Committee of 10 Deputy Ministers who have been asked to prepare reports on the future of the economy. Personally, I was relieved that the Prime Minister had asked these tough professionals to try to define the issues. It would be beneficial to the public at large if some of those on the outside who think they know the answers were to have their pet ideas subjected to equally tough analysis and dissection.

This is all very elitist and typical of a former mandarin, it may be said. I suppose it is and I make no apology. I believe a first-class non-partisan public service dedicated to the public interest is one of the bulwarks of parliamentary government. It enables the elected amateurs, gifted or otherwise, to make the political decisions and govern the country.

I can also understand the frustration of ordinary Members of Parliament on both the government and opposition benches and of the general public at not being able to gain access to the advice and information being tendered to the government by its closest and most influential advisers.

There is no easy answer to this frustration. Under our system, the Ministers have the responsibility of governing. Other Members of Parliament do not. It is their function to demand an accounting from the Ministers who must answer to them and to the public. To expose the advisers and their advice to public scrutiny is to project them into the political arena. (There is a case for subjecting senior civil servants to Parliamentary scrutiny as administrators in connection, for example, with comments by the Auditor General, although the distinction between advice and administration is difficult to draw).

What matters after all is not the advice that Ministers receive, it is the decision they make. The argument that Members of Parliament and the public cannot judge the wisdom of government decisions unless they have access to the facts and advice upon which those decisions were based has some validity (although it is sometimes an excuse for intellectual laziness) and that is why I believe that legislation placing an obligation on the government to provide access to factual documents would be a valuable instrument of public policy. However, I would not favour legislation that undermined the relationship between Ministers and their permanent advisers who, in my submission, should remain non-partisan and so far as possible anonymous, so that they can continue to fulfill their essential functions regardless of the party in power.

There are those, of course, who resent the top federal bureaucracy as such because it is part of the establishment which they associate with the Liberal establishment. There are others who accuse it of bias of one kind and another, of being socialist by those who are anti-socialist, of being reactionary by those who are socialist. There is nothing new in these attacks. They have been made against the mandarins ever since I can remember. They were made against me when I first came to Ottawa in the early 1940's. Believe it or not, to some I was a wild socialist, almost communist. To others, I was the epitome of conservatism.

I can only express the hope that these attacks will not discourage able and dedicated men and women from entering the Public Service and that governments now and in the future will resist the temptation to undermine the high standards of competence and independence that should characterize the Public Service at all levels and upon which so much depends.

Governments have a responsibility to ensure the independence and the competence of the Public Service. The Public Service itself also has a responsibility in this connection and the formation and development of this Institute is evidence that this responsibility is accepted by the upper echelons of the Service.

The mandarins cannot plead their own case; they cannot defend themselves against attack. If they do, they risk being drawn into partisan politics and thus destroying the concept of anonymity and independence which is necessary if they are to serve governments of any political persuasion.

It is not outside their mandate, however, to discuss in public, the problems and the ideals of their own profession and thus to instruct and inspire one another and promote public confidence in the institution of government itself.

Remarks of J. Chrétien, et al.*

HON. JEAN CHRETIEN [PRESIDENT OF THE TREASURY BOARD]:
Already we are dealing with six thousand submissions to the Treasury Board every year, . . . if the pre-Glassco system of control were to be in place today, we would be dealing with seventy-five thousand submissions to the Treasury Board, because the budget went from $6 billion to $42 billion for our complete total . . . what I am trying to do, and I find it is getting probably quite effective [is that] whenever a Minister comes to me with any new idea . . . I say, "Okay, find the money within your budget!" and it is amazing when the guys believe in something and they want it very badly, . . . they always manage to squeeze within their budget, their own budget, enough money to do the things. It is probably because before there was some fat around, and now I am giving them the incentive to burn the fat. We have heard stories that a lot of little things have been abandoned by departments because they needed the money. Before there was no such pressure. We are applying those brakes. . . . You speak about symbolic things; we have done some symbolic things, for example, we have said to the bureaucrats: No more first class travelling. Of course, it is not that much money, and it was just the higher echelon that could use first class travel.

SENATOR MANNING:
They took two extra along with them in economy, so the total bill is the same.

HON. MR. CHRETIEN:
We have frozen their salaries, and the MP's salaries, and the senators' salaries. You know there is no money in that really, but it is very symbolic. I think that the good senators and MP's are not very well paid. For the bad ones it is too much; for the good ones it is not

---

* From "The Senate Committee on National Finance", March 10, 1976, pages 13-14.

enough. My own deputy minister and Mr. MacDonald, I can testify that they are underpaid, very much underpaid compared with the private sector, because they are damn good and they keep me out of hot water, and it is a hell of a job. This is the kind of thing: we had to do some symbolic things like that; no new cars for this year; no new furniture for this year.

SENATOR MANNING:

Mr. Chairman, regarding what the minister has said about the departments being able to find money for new programs by, on their own, eliminating less important programs, I think that is a very commendable pressure to keep on the departments, but it does establish the point that that fat is in the department, and it is only being squeezed out when the department itself finally moves because it is told, "You cannot have any more money for new programs!" Surely, it is possible to go further than that and require these departments to catalogue all of the programs they have, and the order of priority—to say, if they have to eliminate any, which is the first one they would cut out. If that could be done, it would be a good thing. I realize the magnitude of it in a government of the size of the national government, but I think it could be done. I think you would find you could knock the bottom half dozen programs off every department and nobody would ever miss them.

HON. MR. CHRETIEN:

Yes, and we have done that. In July, because of increased costs and so on, I knew that I would not make it by the end of the year with my 16 per cent and in July I cut a billion dollars. You will remember it was announced in Mr. Turner's budget. For this present fiscal year I had, from the agreed programs, to cut off another $1.5 billion. So I did it twice in the same year, and it is not pleasant but I found that the only way to do it is on a bilateral basis: to call every department in and mostly at the ministerial level. I think that we have been able to eliminate some programs, ones that were less useful, some were seen and some were destroyed internally; some pet programs of some bureaucrats and so on have been eliminated through that process. Of course, it is very, very, very difficult to get from the department, because there is no incentive for Ministers and for bureaucrats to cut anything. I am the only one who has an incentive to do it. The rest are judged by their effectiveness to get money out of the Treasury. This is one of the problems: we have not found a system by which we give an incentive to people to do it. Now really, Senator Manning, I do not think it is very easy to get co-operation. When you go to a department and say: You know, we have to cut. I will bet you any money that the things that the bureaucrats will suggest be cut will be something that Parliament will never accept. It is very, very difficult. When I was minister responsible for Parks Canada, and I was trying to squeeze them, where there was squeezing it was always on the national parks in my area. All the time! All the time! That is the kind of thing they produce. "Oh yes, we do not have to connect the panoramic roads that exist in the park of La Mauricie. It is not a priority for us." They knew darn well it was a priority for me, but they never suggested anything else. They all do that. If you have a Minister of Agriculture who has come from Windsor, if there is an experimental farm in Windsor this is the one that we can dispense with. It is always like that. We have to say: "Come on boys". There are some games being played there, and you don't have the same priorities as others. It is amazing. I can predict —I know I cannot comment on the record, but I will tell you every department, what they will propose to do and it is always in the area of their minister that they will never cut. We have to be realistic about it for political reasons. Always they know what is hurting the political elements of the society, and if you propose to close anything it is always in the wrong place. If one place is already in trouble, they will propose to cut there, so they know very well that we will not cut in an area that is in trouble. I have sixteen per cent unemployed in my riding. Supposing I had a military base in my riding, I will bet you, Senator, that it would be the first on the agenda.

SENATOR MANNING:

I was a finance minister for ten years and I know exactly how you feel. There was one comment the minister made a few moments ago, Mr. Chairman, which was, to me at least, disturbing under the present national conditions, and yet I quite appreciate it is the case today, where you said there is not the incentive for ministers heading departments to make these economies because their performance is measured by what they spend rather than by what they save. I would suggest that in the light of the general attitude across Canada today that is a misjudgment on their part. I believe that today the performance of ministers would be measured by the Canadian people more by intelligent economies than by unnecessary expenditures.

HON. MR. CHRETIEN:

I agree entirely with you, senator. I feel more popular in the land today than I felt two years ago, and I have no doubt about it.

SENATOR CARTER:

In your own riding too?

HON. MR. CHRETIEN:

Yes.

SENATOR LANGLOIS:

There have been few cuts there.

HON. MR. CHRETIEN:

But I have to tell you, senator, that perhaps sometimes I am a bit too relaxed in testifying before committees. I have found within the ministries that when, in December, I had to cut $1.5 billion, if I can be candid here, I was asked for less than that, a little bit, because nobody thought that I could go that high, and I got in fact $1.6 billion, I think.

MR. MACDONALD:

$1.7 billion.

HON. MR. CHRETIEN:

Close to $1.7 billion. I was amazed by the, not easy, result; the kind of thing I would say to a minister was, "Let's make a deal. You cut $50 million, and if you make no deal I will suggest to the cabinet to cut you by $100 million". So I made that kind of offer. Some took the gamble to go to the cabinet and others settled, and I must say that it was settled by the cabinet in only two cases; the rest came to terms with their friend Jean! . . .

THE CHAIRMAN:

Are they any further questions for the Minister?

Well, Mr. Minister, we thank you for what I think the committee would describe as "a vintage performance." Thank you very much.

16

The Policy-Making Philosophy of Prime Minister Trudeau and His Advisers*

G. BRUCE DOERN

Prime Minister Pierre Trudeau has brought to the Prime Minister's Office a personal philosophy and advisory staff which seem to be imbued with rationalistic aspirations. Compared to previous Prime Ministers, Mr. Trudeau seems to have a much more explicit philosophy of policy-making, a fact confirmed by his public statements and by his preoccupation during the early years of his leadership with changes in policy structures. The objective of this essay is to examine the philosophical objectives and to indicate how they reflect both his own thoughts and those of other key actors in the Federal Government.

Prime Minister Trudeau, as a political leader, is difficult to stereotype and it would be foolhardy to attach labels with any absolute degree of confidence. And yet it is precisely because he has written and spoken fairly explicitly about his political theory that one can discern a philosophy of policy-making. In fact, whatever may be said about Prime Minister Trudeau's ultimate impact on Canadian society and politics, it can certainly be said that he has been a boon to the political science "industry". In the introduction to Trudeau's *Federalism and the French Canadians*, John Saywell observed that:

[H]*is work belongs in that rare catalogue of Canadians entitled 'political thought' less because of its enlightened comment on contemporary affairs than because it is based on philosophic premises about the nature of man, society and the state.*[1]

Since becoming Prime Minister in 1968, Mr. Trudeau, in his speeches and in his early political strategies, has begun to comment on "contemporary

---

* Revised from G. Bruce Doern, "Recent Changes in the Philosophy of Policy-making in Canada," *Canadian Journal of Political Science*, IV, No. 2 (June 1971), and reprinted by permission of the author and the Canadian Political Science Association.

[1] P. E. Trudeau, *Federalism and the French Canadians* (Toronto, 1968), p. vii.

affairs", especially on the topic of the nature of policy-making. I am briefly going to discuss the philosophy of Trudeau and his advisers as it is reflected in four areas: Trudeau's belief in reason and rationality; and the approach of the Prime Minister and his advisors to social goals, priorities and the structures of policy-making. The career backgrounds of Trudeau's advisory staff will also be noted.

Trudeau's most explicit pronouncement of his belief in reason and his advocacy of political rationality is to be found in his essay, "Federalism, Nationalism and Reason", written in 1964. As the title implies, his arguments were related to the broad issues of nationalism and federalism. Federalism, he argued, was to be the governmental form of the future and was inherently based on political rationality. With respect to the long-run sterility of nationalism and the future tools of politics, Trudeau wrote:

Nationalism will eventually have to be rejected as a principle of sound government. In the world of tomorrow, the expression 'banana republic' will not refer to independent fruit-growing nations but to countries where formal independence has been given priority over the cybernetic revolution. In such a world, the state—if it is not to be outdistanced by its rivals—will need political instruments which are sharper, stronger, and more finely controlled than anything based on mere emotionalism: such tools will be made up of advanced technology and scientific investigation, as applied to fields of law, economics, social psychology, international affairs and other areas of human relations, in short, if not a pure product of reason, the political tools of the future will be designed and appraised by more rational standards than anything we are currently using in Canada today.[2]

The linkage of cybernetics, science and reason in the above passage is directly related to the philosophy he has espoused as a political actor.

In his campaign for the leadership of the Liberal Party, he stressed the need for government by logic rather than by passion. In his first two years as Prime Minister, the rationalist posture has been evident in a number of policy areas. His strategy respecting the objectives and the processes of constitutional change were based on his desire to see the general goals and values of Canadian society established first in the form of a bill of rights entrenched in the constitution. Only after those goals were set should one proceed to divide up the powers of government between the federal and the provincial governments.[3] In the area of foreign policy the Prime Minister made much of the illogical relationship between foreign policy and defence policy. The latter too often determined what the former should be and he was intent on reversing that process.[4] The purpose of his foreign

---

[2] Ibid., p. 203. Quoted by permission of the publisher, University of Toronto Press, the original and controlling publisher for this selection.

[3] See Rt. Hon. P. E. Trudeau, The Constitution and the People of Canada (Ottawa, February 1969), pp. 2-6. For a critique of this strategy see D. Smiley, "The Case Against the Charter of Human Rights", Canadian Journal of Political Science, II, No. 3 (September 1969), pp. 277-291.

[4] See Transcript of Press Conference with Pierre E. Trudeau, National Press Building, Ottawa, April 7, 1968, pp. 18-19.

policy review was to discover the basic goals of our foreign policy and to base defence policy on them. In other areas, such as welfare policy, housing policy, Indian policy and foreign ownership of Canadian industry, studies and task forces were launched to gather basic data and to conduct thorough reviews of past programs and present and future goals.[5]

The above approach stands in relative contrast to the early years of the Diefenbaker and Pearson regimes, the latter launching an impulsive "60 days of decision" approach and the former developing its early policies as a direct response to the grievances of particular groups and regions which had helped put it in power.[6] While it is inaccurate to *absolutely* pigeon-hole the Diefenbaker and Pearson regimes as non-rationalists or incrementalists, and to label the Trudeau regime as rationalist, the *relative* difference does seem to be an accurate statement about their respective philosophies and models of policy-making. Trudeau's approach, and its contrast with the Pearson and Diefenbaker posture, is also a reflection of the present Prime Minister's relative distrust of the growing power of the federal bureaucracy and of the inherent conservatism of bureaucratic decision-making processes.[7] Diefenbaker also distrusted the federal bureaucracy but his early response was not to seek broad policy reviews from outside sources such as task forces, but rather to go ahead with his policies which were designed to patch up the regional and group grievances that had been festering for years. Pearson, however, had no such distrust of the bureaucracy and the Liberal's return to power, and the subsequent "60 days of decision approach" were initially viewed as a return to sound government.[8] But it was not "rational" government in the same sense as the Trudeau regime sees rationality. For the Pearson Government it tended to be

---

[5] See F. Schindler and C. M. Lanphier, "Social Science Research and Participatory Democracy in Canada", *Canadian Public Administration*, XII, No. 4 (Winter 1969), pp. 481-498.

[6] To date we must still draw our basic impressions of the decision-making approaches of the Diefenbaker and Pearson regimes from such works as Peter C. Newman's *The Distemper of Our Times* (Toronto, 1968) and *Renegade in Power: The Diefenbaker Years* (Toronto, 1963).

[7] Trudeau and his advisers frequently speak of themselves as "outsiders" both with respect to the bureaucracy and with respect even to the Liberal Party. See Press Conference, April 7, 1968, p. 7. See also Newman, *The Distemper of Our Times*, p. 447.

[8] These differences in attitude toward the bureaucracy are, in part, revealed in M. Lamontagne, "The Influence of the Politician", *Canadian Public Administration*, XI, No. 3 (1968), pp. 263-271. The different attitudes of the three Prime Ministers towards the bureaucracy are in part reflected by the use of royal commissions and task forces. Diefenbaker's distrust caused him first to ignore the civil service in implementing his early policies, but after that he launched a series of royal commissions on such major fields as transportation, government organization, and health services. This may have reflected his desire to develop information which the bureaucracy did not have, or, if it had it, with which Mr. Diefenbaker did not agree. Royal commissions were therefore, in a sense, a source of countervailing information. Prime Minister Pearson had no such distrust of the public service and tended to launch fewer royal commissions or task forces. Prime Minister Trudeau, with a more sceptical view of the power of the public service, has also launched a series of task forces.

"more of the same" based on the same post-war assumptions about the goals and development of the welfare state.

The difference (and it is clearly a *relative* difference in the sense that no government is entirely incremental in its approach to policy-making) is best reflected in Mr. Trudeau's statement at a press conference in August of 1969, a statement which reflected both his desire, and his advisers' desire, to get away from a mere incremental approach to setting priorities:

And some of the programs—it's really incredible when you begin to look at these in detail—some of the programs were started back in the 1920s—to meet a real need then. But they no longer have the same justification. And there are other needs which are greater, which we can't meet because we don't have the wherewithall without raising taxes. . . .

So, one of the purposes of these various reviews of the present government . . . is because we want to know more what we're doing, and become more efficient in it.[9]

In this area, the views of Trudeau and his advisers were strongly influenced by the developments in the bureaucracy which led to the adoption of the Planning, Programming and Budgeting system.[10] It is misleading to attribute the rationalistic tendencies of the recent period wholly to Prime Minister Trudeau. The statement quoted above, for example, both reflects and reinforces the existence of many complex factors. It reflects the broad concern that was beginning to emerge in the late 1960s regarding the general effectiveness of the welfare state apparatus that had been the main preoccupation of government and politics in most western societies since the 1930's.[11]

In the short-run, the statement reflects both the Trudeau Government's concern, and the concern of senior advisers in the bureaucracy regarding the spiralling and uncontrolled costs built in to programs created in the mid-1960's. Earlier in 1969, Prime Minister Trudeau had received long-term projections of the costs of existing programs. If *new* programs to meet *new* priorities were to be launched, it was clear that resources would be scarce unless lower level program priorities were rewarded with fewer resources or were eliminated entirely.

Many of these broader factors were apparent in the latter Pearson years. The importance of the Trudeau policy philosophy is that his own views and those of many of his senior advisers, gave intellectual support *and* reinforcement to the needs imposed by these broader policy realities. His philosophy was and is, therefore, an important and independent variable.

The emphasis on goal-setting and goal clarification has also been reflected in the changes in governmental and policy-making structures. Tru-

---

[9] Transcript of the Prime Minister's Press Conference, Ottawa, August 13, 1969, p. 10.

[10] See A. W. Johnson, "PPB and Decision-Making in the Government of Canada", a talk delivered to the 50th Anniversary Conference of the Society of Industrial Accountants, June 18, 1970.

[11] See Peter Drucker, *The Age of Discontinuity* (New York, 1968).

deau's philosophy has been reflected in his operationalism of a Cabinet Committee on Priorities and Planning, and in the addition of formal "planning units" to both the Prime Minister's Office and the Privy Council Office. Again, the importance of a philosophy is central.

The Cabinet Committee on Priorities had been technically a creation of the Pearson Government, although it never really became fully operational because it was created just as the leadership race to succeed Mr. Pearson began late in 1967 and early in 1968. Most of the senior Ministers were preoccupied. The Committee's role, moreover, seemed to be a relatively vague and quick response to the same economic and financial forces described earlier. The real conceptualization and commitments to operate the Committee began with Prime Minister Trudeau.

Similarly the addition of formal planning units in the P.M.O. and the P.C.O. reflected a formalization of roles that had been informally developing in previous years. The "political" advice of the P.M.O. and the "governmental" advice of the P.C.O. had existed before, with the P.M.O. becoming more "visible" when Tom Kent became a key adviser to Prime Minister Pearson. The P.C.O.'s role and the role of the Secretary to the Cabinet had undergone some gradual change during the Pearson years (for example, the creation of a handful of assistant secretaries to service cabinet committees, the creation of the Science Secretariat, and the special Planning Secretariat). Structures like the P.C.O. and P.M.O. therefore, had been important and critical participants in the pre-Trudeau period, but they evolved merely with the benevolent acquiescence of Prime Minister Pearson. Their increasing visibility and formalization since 1968 is a reflection of the active philosophical support of Prime Minister Trudeau.

At the Liberal Conference in Harrison Hot Springs in November of 1969, Mr. Trudeau philosophized even more broadly about the total policy process, about science and technology and about the place of governmental institutions in a cybernetic world society. He spoke of Parliament as an institution enveloped in a "Coney Island shooting gallery" approach. Problems arise, crises develop, the target is sometimes hit, but more often missed. And there is the almost inevitable expectation that even those that are hit will pop up again in a new crisis environment. He applied somewhat the same approach to the operation of political parties. If parties concentrated only on a short time frame and on immediate solutions, "it would be ignoring the underlying conditions which caused each crisis. It would be prescribing for the symptoms rather than the disease."

... A party's principal concern should not be how to settle a particular strike—let the Minister of Labour and the Cabinet worry about that. It should be to resolve the continuing crisis in industrial relations by working out a better system of reconciling the interests of labour, management and the public. That task is not only more difficult, it is much more important. [12]

---

[12] Office of the Prime Minister, "Notes for Remarks by the Prime Minister at the Harrison Liberal Conference", Harrison Hot Springs, British Columbia, November 21, 1969, p. 3.

Prime Minister Trudeau elaborated on this concept as illustrated on pages 147 and 148 of this volume.

It is by no means coincidental that terms such as "time frame" and the metaphorical conception of the party as "radar" are increasingly a part of the Prime Minister's language. The Prime Minister and his advisory staff are very sympathetic to the conceptualization of policy-making in cybernetic terms. In the Prime Minister's words:

We ... are aware that the many techniques of cybernetics, by transforming the control function and the manipulation of information, will transform our whole society. With this knowledge we are wide awake, alert, capable of action; no longer are we blind, inert, pawns of fate.[13]

That is why the Trudeau Government accepted both the substance and reason of the Task Force on Information and created Information Canada. In an earlier model of politics and policy processes, such as a structure would tend to be relatively illegitimate. For a politician with a cybernetic model of politics, such a structure becomes obvious and essential. While critics might view it as a propaganda agency, the Trudeau philosophy endorses it with great fanfare as an essential precondition to the effective development and implementation of public policy. The Trudeau shift in emphasis was symbolized, both metaphorically and structurally, by the creation of Information Canada.[14]

The expansion of the Prime Minister's Office and the collective backgrounds of the personnel he has selected to advise him have been labelled by the media and some critics as the triumph of technocrats and technocracy. In a recent parliamentary debate on overall government administration, the NDP's David Lewis offered this picturesque portrait of the Trudeau's regime's first two years:

There are certain problems that Canada has had for years. It does not require any of the long studies in which the government is engaging in order to deal at least with some of them.

But the technocrat approaches things entirely differently. He is not concerned with solving a problem which he and everyone else can see. He is concerned with finding himself a precise technocratic framework in which the particular item might fall. He is satisfied, because that is the nature of the technocrat, if he can show structures, if he can persuade you he has frameworks, that he has appointed task forces or can table white papers and reports, if he can tell you he is continuing to study the matter, because no person with that approach is as much concerned with solving a problem as with being satisfied that he has technocratically analysed it.

This is what happens every day with this government. When you have that kind of approach, if you are concerned more with style than with substance, and if you have a technocratic approach ot problems why should you pay any attention to

---

[13] *Ibid.*, p. 7.

[14] See *To Know and Be Known*, the Report of the Task Force on Government Information, Vols. I and II (especially Vol. II), pp. 15-24.

Parliament? Style is of no consequence here. The Prime Minister and his colleagues in Cabinet are not likely to persuade many members of the opposition. Style is important outside. It is important at the university, important in front of the camera. It is of no importance here.[15]

There is some truth in such a characterization, but it is too simple a generalization. The backgrounds of the Trudeau advisers in both the Prime Minister's Office and the Privy Council Office are a mixture of the legal, business and communications professions. . . .

While much of the media's attention has been rivetted on the P.M.O., it is clear that their collective philosophy has been not only supported, but, in a real sense, pre-dated, by the philosophy of several key advisers within the federal bureaucracy. Michael Pitfield, A. W. Johnson, Gordon Robertson and Simon Reisman have been among the key officials who have urged and helped bring about a change in policy machinery and policy philosophy.

There is little doubt that, as a group, the Trudeau advisers have a more rationalist conception of the way government ought to operate than any previous group of central advisers. A considerable amount of their time has been, and is being, spent in attempting to conceptualize the problems and the nature of decision-making. Their mixed backgrounds also reflect what Trudeau once viewed as the essence of his political theory, "create counterweights".

The theory of checks and balances . . . has always had my full support. It translates into practical terms the concept of equilibrium that is inseparable from freedom in the realm of ideas. It incorporates a corrective for abuses and excesses into the very functioning of political institutions.[16]

Hence, the metaphors of cybernetics are complemented by the more conventional mechanical imagery of "checks and balances" and "equilibrium".[17] They also seem to reflect Trudeau's background as a lawyer, the profession where an adversary system is most revered and institutionalized.

Thus, the presence of Prime Minister Trudeau and his advisers seems to indicate a change in the philosophy and in the conceptualization of

---

[15] Canada, House of Commons, *Debates*, 28th Parliament, March 5, 1970, pp. 4423-4.

[16] Trudeau, *Federalism and the French Canadians*, p. xxiii. This philosophy is undergoing an interesting test in the present debate about the appropriate role of that "counterweight extra-ordinaire", the Auditor General.

[17] It is worth observing at this point that political scientists tend, at times, to imply that the older "mechanistic", process-oriented models and the newer cybernetic "goal-seeking" models are polar types. Trudeau's philosophy seems to imply complementarity rather than polarity. In terms of policy-making structures, there does seem to be much complementarity. Both models seem to call for confrontation and conflict, either between structures (e.g. the Economic Council "prodding" the Department of Finance) or between kinds of information (e.g. in the P.P.B. system, one program competing against another as to which is the best way to achieve a given goal).

policy-making on several counts. Much of it seems to be congruent, on a philosophical plane, with those political scientists who have argued we ought to view the political system in cybernetic terms as a goal-seeking and error-correcting information system that will "learn how to learn".[18] Prime Minister Trudeau, in comparison with his predecessors, clearly prefers this approach. It would be a caricature of reality, however, to view the Prime Minister and his advisers as a band of super-rationalists. It is also important that we view these emphasized changes in the light of development elsewhere. The early months of the Nixon Presidency in the United States also reflect the increasing ascendancy, both in theory and practice, of the concepts of planning and program reviews. The backgrounds of the White House advisers reflect, to a greater extent than in any previous Presidency, the coming of the systems managers and planners.[19]

It is clear, however, that it is much easier to *think* metaphorically in cybernetic terms that it is to put such a concept into operation. A similar frustration undoubtedly awaits the political actor who seeks to translate his philosophy into structures and into political behaviour.

---

[18] Especially K. Deutsch, *The Nerves of Government* (London, 1966).

[19] See Andrew Hamilton, "Nixon's White House Staff: Heyday of the Planners", *Science*, CLXVII (February 27, 1970), pp. 1232-4, and "Symposium on the American Presidency," *Public Administration Review*, XXIX, No. 5 (September/October, 1969), pp. 441-500.

17

The Optimal Policy-Making System: Implications for the Canadian Political Process*

GEORGE J. SZABLOWSKI

Since the beginning of P.P.B. (Planning Programming Budgeting) under Prime Minister Lester Pearson and the development of logical extensions of it through Cabinet and Privy Council Office reforms under Prime Minister Pierre Trudeau, leadership roles at the apex of power in Ottawa are undergoing profound change. The thrust of these reforms is toward what might best be called "optimal policy-making". The effect this will have on traditional modes of elite accommodation and the consociational network outlined by Professor Noel in this volume should be acknowledged. This paper attempts to introduce these issues.

In a speech early in the seventies, A. W. Johnson, then Secretary of the Treasury Board, talked about the Planning Branch, the Programme Branch, and the P.P.B. "in the context of the broad strategy of government planning". He stressed that "to complete the description of roles in P.P.B. . . . one ought to speak of the strategic role which is played in the planning process by the Prime Minister's Office and the Privy Council Office" and of the "close liaison" that the Treasury Board Secretariat maintains with these offices. "This is essential if P.P.B. is to take account of and to reflect the broader strategy of public policy and the planning process.[1]

---

* Written for this volume and revised for this edition.
[1] A. W. Johnson, "P.P.B. and Decision-Making in the Government of Canada", an address delivered on June 18, 1970 to the 50th anniversary conference of the Society of Industrial Accountants in Toronto. Colin Campbell and George Szablowski are currently engaged in a study of central agencies in the Government of Canada. This research, supported by the Canada Council, will be published under the title *Design for Steering*.

To be sure, the optimal policy-making system in the government of Canada is still in an embryonic stage. Many will claim with justification that the new structures and decisional procedures introduced in recent years hardly constitute a system, and that in the present context neither the process of policy-making nor its outputs can be called optimal. While I would not disagree with this assessment today, it is unrealistic to disregard the systems-oriented structural groundwork which has already been laid.[2]

It is equally unrealistic to ignore linkages which are being developed and the increasing acceptance of the normative assumptions upon which the optimal model rests.[3] Once a new technology—in this instance decisional technology—has been even partially introduced and it proves to be successful, its application will be inevitably extended and in time rendered comprehensive.[4] Of course, the judgment of success is made within the same normative ethos which produced the new techniques and procedures, and significantly those making the judgment are already burdened with roles which commit them to the optimal strategy.

How does the new decisional technology affect the political process in Canada? Does it transform the leadership role and the pattern of relationships between the leader and his supporters? A preliminary attempt to answer the latter question will be made by an analysis of the changing mode of behaviour between the Canadian Prime Minister and his cabinet colleagues. The principal concern, however, is to focus attention on a broader issue: the impact of policy-making style and decisional technology on the Canadian political process.

The Optimal Model

Yehezkel Dror describes the optimal model as a "set of synergetically related changes in personnel, structure, procedure and 'organization climate' "[5] purposefully applied to the central policy-making apparatus. The model is normative and prescriptive in the sense that it tries to improve the content of public policy through a systematic, rational improvement of policy-making procedures.[6]

In general terms, optimizing is concerned with the relations among objectives. Thus, a decision-maker considering the adoption of a specific

---

[2] "A basic assumption of the Canadian P.P.B. System is that systems analysis is essential to the implementation and success of the system." Government of Canada, P.P.B. Guide (rev. ed.), September 1969, p. 14.

[3] See G. Bruce Doern, "Mr. Trudeau, The Science Council and P.P.B.: Recent Changes in the Philosophy of Policy-Making in Canada", C.P.S.A., Winnipeg 1970. Also P.P.B. Guide, pp. 8-10; and "Speech from the Throne", October 8, 1970.

[4] "The adoption of an analytic approach to governmental decision-making . . . is probably inevitable in a complex society." P.P.B. Guide, p. 6.

[5] Yehezkel Dror, "P.P.B. and the Public Policy-Making System: Some Reflections on the Papers by Bertram M. Gross and Allen Schick", Public Administration Review, XXIX (March/April 1969), p. 154.

[6] In this framework, P.P.B.S. must be viewed as a single component of a larger scheme.

policy aiming at a specific goal must take into account all the other policy goals relevant to the issue area and the resource requirements needed for their implementation. He must also examine all major alternatives. He knows that the resources available to him are limited, that the assignment of additional resources to each of the policy goals pursued is likely to have only a marginal effect, and that the relative overall performance ("probable aggregate real output")[7] is likely to decline if he yields to the incremental approach to policy-making. He concludes that more could be achieved by withdrawing some of the resources from some of the objectives and assigning them to other objectives, which promise a greater return and are likely to maximize aggregate real output. He may not give up the marginally productive policy objectives if he feels that they are still worth pursuing, but he grants them lower priority and thereby releases previously committed resources to more productive, more effective goals. His aim is to achieve the best (optimal) overall performance level for all "good" policy objectives within the issue-area in relative and relational terms.[8]

The influence of the optimal model can be illustrated by an examination of the decisional steps employed in the review of Canadian defense policy which culminated in the Prime Minister's announcement of April 3, 1969.[9] The objective of fulfilling Canada's NATO commitments was found to be excessively costly in relation to the benefits, national and international, which were being derived from it.[10] Any additional input toward that objective would have produced only a marginal return, a meager increase in the contribution to the defense of Western Europe. Moreover, continued deployment of resources to NATO at the same level would have resulted in the progressive minimization of the aggregate output in the entire defense policy area because of the size of the NATO resource allocation relative to the remaining defense policy goals. Alternative courses of action were examined and rejected. Incrementalism was also rejected. It was judged that a higher output from military resources could be gained from a better servicing of another objective, namely the surveillance of Canada's territory and coastlines. "Our first priority in our defense policy is the protection of Canadian sovereignty in all dimensions that it means," declared the Prime Minister.[11] The NATO objective was not dropped. It was ranked third in the order of priorities, and steps for a planned and phased reduction of the Canadian forces in Europe were

---

[7] Yehezkel Dror, *Public Policy-Making Reexamined* (San Francisco, 1968), p. 314.

[8] Amitai Etzioni, *The Active Society, A Theory of Societal and Political Process* (New York, 1968), p. 260. See also a summary of the phases of optimal public policy-making in Dror, *Public Policy-Making Reexamined*, Appendix B, p. 311.

[9] "A Defence Policy for Canada", a statement to the press by the Prime Minister (*External Affairs*, May 1969).

[10] "Defence Policy and Foreign Policy", a speech by the Prime Minister on April 12, 1969, to the Alberta Liberal Association in Calgary (External Affairs, June 1969). See Roddick Byers' article in the first edition of this volume; and L. Hertzman, J. W. Warnock, T. A. Hockin, *Alliances and Illusions* (Edmonton, 1969).

[11] "Defence Policy and Foreign Policy".

announced. The defence budget, however, was maintained for the next three years at the 1969 dollar level of 1.815 billion per annum with the result that a substantial manpower and material resources could be diverted from the NATO objective to the objective of protecting Canadian sovereignty.[12] The optimizing effect was also achieved in another sense: by freezing the Defense Department budget for three years, additional resources became available for other national goals which were given higher priority than peace and security.[13]

The behaviourally relevant demands that the optimal model makes on political leadership may be identified as follows:

1. High level of human energy, intellectual power, and comprehension.
2. Capacity for comprehensiveness. (To identify and examine values and goals in relation to each other and not in isolation. To look at total resources in relation to total demands.)
3. Analytic rationality.
4. Capacity for control and guidance.
5. Capacity to specialize and to use technology.
6. Readiness to grant primacy to the public 'good' and to assign to public policy-making a major role in the shaping of the future.
7. Readiness to accept larger change instead of incremental change.

Decisional Technology and the Political Process

Robert McNamara introduced the first optimal technique (Planning-Programming-Budgeting) into the United States' Department of Defense in 1961. Within a few years, it gave him unparalleled central control capability over the armed forces and reduced the level of competition for national resources among the various segments of the American military establishment.[14] "Cynics to the contrary notwithstanding, knowledge is power," wrote Charles Schultze, President Johnson's director of the Bureau of the Budget.[15] There was no surprise, therefore, when in 1965 in a public statement, Johnson extended the application of P.P.B. to all civilian agencies of the United States Federal Government, calling the new system

---

[12] Statement of the Minister of National Defence, September 19, 1969.

[13] See *Foreign Policy for Canadians* (Ottawa, 1970), p. 32.

A. W. Johnson refers to "incrementalism" as "making decisions only at the margin. . . . 'Incrementalism' does not lead to an evaluation of the many programmes which contribute to the same goal, nor does it lead to an examination of the inter-relationship between programmes which serve different goals. It does not even, in itself at least, lead to the removal of the more obvious contradictions and failures in coordination. And it certainly does not lead to the fundamental policy reviews which happily are becoming more characteristic in government today." Johnson, "P.P.B. and Decision-Making".

[14] Allen Schick, "Systems Politics and Systems Budgeting", *Public Administration Review*, XXIX, March/April 1969), p. 139. Virginia Held, "P.P.B.S. Comes to Washington", in (ed.) James W. Davis, *Politics, Programs and Budgets* (Scarborough, Ont., 1969), pp. 139-43.

[15] Charles Schultze, *The Politics and Economics of Public Spending* (Washington, D.C., 1968), p. 94.

"revolutionary".[16] It took only a little time and the issues were joined in a new debate.[17] The pluralists argue that the essence of political decision-making is "the activity by which bargains are struck and allocations negotiated"[18] between contending interests. On the assumption that no group, including the government, can claim a monopoly on wisdom, public policy must emerge as a result of the process of reconciliation of divergent values and goals and the competing groups identified with them. The final shape of a decision depends on the relative power of the participating groups and the cogency of the different arguments employed by them.[19] The pluralist critics of the optimal model fear that the newly adopted decisional technology with its emphasis on output rather than on process, with its stress on explicit identification and examination of values and goals, and with the insistence on allocating resources to preferred objectives, would tend to ignore competing groups and interests, favour the central governmental executive, and force the allocation of resources to goals on the basis of supra-policies arrived at without bargaining and negotiation.[20]

Typically however, the P.P.B. system[21] slipped quietly into the Canadian scene in 1967 and was left almost unnoticed. There was no high level public announcement[22] and no theoretical debate. Canadian political scientists appeared to be largely unaware of the issues involved, and yet these issues are substantially more critical for Canada than they are for the United States for the following reasons.

1. Unlike the United States, there is no strong national political culture in Canada which could form a basis of support for optimally generated supra-policies which may emerge in the future from the central Government.[23] (Although the possibility cannot be ruled out that some

---

[16] Held, "P.P.B.S. Comes to Washington", p. 138.

[17] See "A Symposium on P.P.B.S.", in *Public Administration Review*, XXVI (December 1966); especially Aaron Wildavsky's, "The Political Economy of Efficiency". Charles Lindblom, "The Intelligence of Democracy; 1965. A Symposium on P.P.B.S. Reexamined", in *Public Administration Review*, (March/April 1969). Two earlier works preceded the debate: Wildavsky, *The Politics of the Budgetary Process* (Boston, 1964); and D. Braybrooke and C. Lindblom, *A Strategy of Decision* (New York, 1963).

[18] Schick, "Systems Politics", p. 138.

[19] Roger Hilsman, "The Foreign Policy Consensus", in *Journal of Conflict Resolution*, III (December 1959).

[20] Schick, "Systems Politics", pp. 139-40.

[21] Bruce Doern describes the introduction of the P.P.B. System by the Treasury Board in his, "Mr. Trudeau, The Science Council, and P.P.B.", pp. 24-32. See also *P.P.B. Guide*.

[22] The Treasury Board Secretariat issued a press release on January 26, 1967, which received little attention.

[23] See S. J. R. Noel, "Political Parties and Elite Accommodation", *C.P.S.A.* (Winnipeg, 1970). John Meisel, "Canadian Parties and Politics", in (ed.) R. H. Leach, *Contemporary Canada* (1968). E. Black and A. Cairns, "A Different Perspective on Canadian Federalism", in (ed.) J. P. Meekison, *Canadian Federalism—Myth or Reality* (Toronto, 1968). J. M. S. Careless, "Limited Identities in Canada", *Canadian Historical Review*, L, No. 1, (March 1969), pp. 1-10. John Porter, "The Canadian National Character in the Twentieth Century", in *The Annals of The American Academy of Political and Social Sciences*, March 1967, p. 48. J. C. John-

types of political crises may play an increasingly important role in building layers of national consensus for major changes in policy direction this possibility should not be exaggerated. Even though it may be true that the control and guidance capacity of a government increases appreciably—even in the absence of a strong national political culture—in times of *declared* war or *declared* emergency because of the increase in its legal power and the crisis psychology of the public,[24] such emergencies are the exception not the rule in Canadian political life.)

2. The Canadian ethno-linguistic dualism is not only rooted in history and tradition, but also sanctioned territorially, institutionally and legally.[25] The often repeated argument that the federal Parliament represents (within its constitutional authority) the francophone population of Quebec to the same extent as l'Assemblée Nationale is constitutionally accurate but sociologically artificial. The "right" of the government of Quebec to bargain and negotiate with the government of Canada on issues of national policy is not quite like that of the other provinces.

3. While in the United States most policy bargains are struck in the Congressional committee rooms,[26] "the type of bargaining which is most central to the Canadian federal system takes place between federal and provincial governments".[27] The inherent tendency of the optimal model toward comprehensiveness may lead to successive conflicts between federal and provincial policy objectives and may result in a fierce competition for scarce resources. For example, the Federal Government grants the provinces 50 per cent of the operating costs of

---

stone, "Definitions of Canadian Society", in (eds.) Kruhlak, Schultz, Pobihushchy, *Canadian Political Process* (Toronto, 1970), p. 383. The Government of Canada, on the other hand, holds a contrary view of Canadian political culture. "The sense of community that exists in Canada provides the third essential reason for a federal spending power. Canadians everywhere now feel a sufficient sense of responsibility for their compatriots in other parts of the country that they are prepared to contribute to their well being." Federal-Provincial Grants and the Spending Power of Parliament, *Working Paper on the Constitution* (Government of Canada, 1969), p. 28.

[24] See Klaus Knorr, *The War Potential Among Nations* (Princeton, 1955).

[25] See Stein's definition of federalism in Michael B. Stein, "Federal Political Systems and Federal Societies", *World Politics*, XX, (July, 1968), pp. 729-731.

[26] It is worth noting that in the American Congress support staffs and analytic capabilities are already being developed and trained to review systems analyses and program budgets prepared by the President's Budget Bureau. See William M. Capron, "The Impact of Analysis on Bargaining in Government", in James W. Davis (ed.), *Politics Programs and Budgets* (Englewood Cliffs, N.J. 1969), p. 264. In spite of a "quiet revolution" in the functions of the standing committees of the House of Commons, it is most unlikely that Ottawa will endorse a similar move. See T. Hockin's discussion of House committees in the first article of this volume.

[27] See Noel, "Political Parties", p. 10. Also John Meisel, "Recent Changes in Canadian Parties", in (ed.) H. G. Thorburn, *Party Politics in Canada* (Second ed.) (Scarborough, Ont., 1967), p. 33; and R. E. B. Simeon, *Federal/Provincial Diplomacy* (Toronto, 1972).

higher education. In addition, it makes direct allocations for university research and student loans. Thus, the federal resources comprise over 50 per cent of the total national spending in this field. Theoretically, the objectives of higher education are not divisible between the federal and provincial jurisdictions, but priorities may differ widely from region to region. The optimal strategy requires that allocations be made to preferred objectives according to priority. Clearly, a conflict between federal and provincial priorities can hardly be avoided; and yet the Federal Government must adopt a comprehensive approach, if it is to adhere to optimal decision-making in this area. The Economic Council of Canada in its latest report recognized the dilemma by stating: "Although education in Canada is largely a provincial matter, it has a pervasive impact on the economy as a whole." Economic Council of Canada (Seventh Annual Review), *Patterns of Growth*, September, 1970, p. 55. In a recent article, a Treasury Board official, adopting the comprehensive approach, rejected the idea that universities can define and achieve their own goals, for example academic excellence, and concluded, "I doubt if governments can afford this when it appears based on past experience that independent and autonomous universities are reluctant to optimize the use of public funds which they are receiving."[28]

4.   Willingness to make concessions is acknowledged as a traditional trait of political leadership in Canada. "Provincial Prime Ministers look to leaders in Ottawa not for leadership but for bargaining concessions".[29] This behaviour arises directly from the strength of regional identification and the influence of regional political elites.[30] If, as Noel[31] suggests, "a key role in the working of the Canadian system must be accorded to provincial political elites and interest groups", and if the "political elites at both levels of government are primarily responsible for the accommodation of broad cultural and regional interests", then any policy-making system and its decisional technology which may either weaken or modify these consociational leadership roles strikes at the fundamental determinants of stability.[32]

Those for whom the optimal model serves as a tool of the trade, show a keen awareness of the issues. While admitting that "one must not idealize the political process" with its "deep-rooted institutional barriers to improving the policy and administrative efficiency of government", A. W. Johnson

[28] A. T. Wakabayashi, "Change and the Universities: University-Government Relations", *Canadian Public Administration*, XIII; No. 1 (Spring, 1970). See also R. Hurtubise and D. C. Rowat, *Studies on the University, Society and Government* (Ottawa, 1970).

[29] R. MacGregor Dawson, *Democratic Government in Canada* (Toronto, 1963), p. 125.

[30] Noel, *Political Parties*. Careless, "Limited Identities".

[31] Noel, *ibid.*, p. 30.

[32] For a definition of consociational behaviour, see Arend Lijphart, "Consociational Democracy", *World Politics*, XXI, No. 2, (January 1969), p. 207; and Noel, "Political Parties". See also Arend Lijphart, *The Politics of Accommodation: Pluralism and Democracy in the Netherlands* (Berkeley, 1968), pp. 197-213.

cautions that the "P.P.B. expert should not try to force the politician to substitute the rational contemplation of objectives for the intuitive perception
of the needs of the community and their solution. Rather, P.P.B. should
serve as the bridge between the intuitive perception of problems and the
rational choice of programmes" and it "should not be looked on as hostile
to the political process". (Johnson, "P.P.B. and Decision-Making".) Mr.
Johnson's distinction between "needs of the community" and "objectives"
is not clear. The latter, he maintains, should be contemplated rationally by
the P.P.B. experts, while the former should be perceived intuitively by the
politician. It is not difficult to imagine who would hold the upper hand in
such a "division of labour."[33]

The Leadership Role and the Optimal Model

What is the effect of the optimal policy-making model on Canadian political leadership? I will attempt to examine here only one aspect of the
leadership role: the relationship between the leader and his team of immediate colleagues and supporters.[34] Professor F. G. Bailey in a stimulating
work entitled *Stratagems and Spoils*[35] distinguishes three ideal types of relationships between the leader and his supporters: the transactional, the
bureaucratic, and the moral. These relationships are undeniably relevant to
Canadian political leadership at the apex. Individuals who contract out
their support to the leader in return for profit or expected profit (whether
money, influence, power or prestige) form part of a transactional team.
They are committed to the extent of their investments and not more, and
the leader's control over them is dependent on the relative size of each
capital investment. The leader can hardly issue commands to those who
have committed only a small portion of their total resources to him. If he
needs their support, he must use other tactics to maintain it. A transactional supporter is free to withdraw some of his investment and receive a
smaller dividend or to increase the investment and to demand more in
return. He is also free to bargain with the leader either for himself or on
behalf of others, usually his own supporters. He can retain separate loyalties and represent *within the team* outside interests. As a member of the

---

33 Johnson, "P.P.B. and Decision-Making".

34 This approach expressly neglects other aspects of political leadership. Seligman suggests
that the study of political leadership should concern itself with generalizations concerning four types of relations: (1) the relations of leaders to led within particular political
structures, (2) the relationship between leaders of political structures, (3) the relationship
between leaders of one structure and the followers of another, and (4) the relationship
between leaders and the "unorganized" or nonaffiliated. Lester G. Seligman, "The Study
of Political Leadership", *American Political Science Review*, XLIV, (December 1950), pp. 904-
15.

35 F. G. Bailey, *Stratagems and Spoils* (Oxford, 1969).

team, he will accept and observe any rules of conduct provided they maintain his position and make his investment secure (for example, the rules of cabinet solidarity and cabinet secrecy). The transactional supporters continue their commitment as long as they believe in the leader's ability to deliver the goods, i.e. the dividend expected from their investments. The leader thus must spare no efforts in order to perpetuate this belief. His relationship with the transactional colleagues is pragmatic and businesslike and he is well aware that some of them are his potential rivals.

The traditional relationship between the Canadian Prime Minister and his cabinet colleagues has been transactional. It permits the Ministers to retain regional loyalties and to represent regional interests within the Cabinet.[36] It does not demand from them a moral commitment to the leader. It leaves them free to bargain and to consolidate their own influence while attending to the business of governing as political heads of their departments. It would appear now, however, that this traditional transactional relationship is undergoing a transformation. Through the means of the cabinet committee system, the Prime Minister divides his leadership role into specialized functions which he then distributes as committee chairmanships to some of his transactional colleagues. For himself, he retains the overall competency: priorities and planning. Each cabinet committee, receiving staff support either from PCO or from the Treasury Board Secretariat, acts as a socializing and educating agency, providing common experiences in the on-going decisional process. In this way, the transactional ties are modified and new relationships emerge characterized by specialization and inspired by the optimal ethic. The committee system cuts across the departmental portfolio divisions and assigns to each committee chairman a specific, functional policy area: economic; social; external and defense; science, culture, and information.[37] A small high-level personal "bureaucracy" is thus created, which no longer adheres to the purely pragmatic, businesslike attitudes toward the leader, but becomes increasingly burdened with normative considerations. Its members tend to discard regional loyalties and to refrain from bargaining on behalf of regional interests; they are no longer prepared to play with ease the accommodation roles.[38]

Bailey argues that what applies to personal bureaucracies "can also be said about any group which is held together by a shared ethic . . . Support is

---

[36] See for examples some of the interpretations in F. W. Gibson (ed.) *Cabinet Formation and Bicultural Relations*, Studies of the Royal Commission on Bilingualism and Biculturalism (Ottawa, 1970).

[37] It is worth noting that the P.P.B. System administered by the Treasury Board Secretariat also contains a functional classification of programmes which cuts across the traditional departmental lines. See *P.P.B. Guide*, Appendix A, p. 58. See also Press Release, Prime Minister's Office, February 16, 1971.

[38] All hypothetical statements contained in this part of the essay are logical deductions from Bailey's ideal type constructs (transactional-bureaucratic-moral). These statements obviously require empirical verification.

gained ... at the price of renouncing any tactic which could offend the normative values of the group. ... Moral leadership" becomes "a matter of manipulating symbols. ... Control of these symbols and of the means of counteracting them constitute political capital."[39] We tend to think of political symbols as relating only to traditional and extrarational manifestations of power and authority. This view is unnecessarily limited. In a post-industrial society, the optimal rhetoric replaces the symbols, signs and cults of the past.[40] In Wolin's own words, "its use serves to overcome distance, to communicate a common set of meanings, and to evoke the presence of authority".[41] It also legitimizes political leadership of the cybernetic age.

Yehezkel Dror is frank about the normative weight of this transformation: "Insofar as knowledge that is relevant to human action becomes available, it is our moral duty, as well as our best bet, to use it as much as possible. ... Put in these terms, it seems to me that careful but determined and purposeful redesigning of the public policy-making system must be our best strategy."[42] In the course of a talk before a group of federal officials assembled recently in an Ottawa library auditorium, Dror repeated his belief in the moral duty of governmental elites to strive toward the optimal model. No one showed surprise or attempted to question him on this point.[43] Clearly, the optimal policy-making model is highly congruent with the concept of moral or neg-entropic leadership, characterized by courage, clarity of purpose, high level of energy and a sense of superior public values. Such leadership would not shirk determined action. It would not be afraid of tension between various segments of society. It would see conflict and polarization as a means for building public consensus. It would welcome a high load input into the decision-making apparatus, and it would refrain from engaging in an "overarching cooperation".[44] It bases its position on the belief in an inherently entropic condition[45] of a post-industrial society in which tendencies toward disorder, chaos and violence

[39] Bailey, *Strategems and Spoils*, pp. 83-3.
[40] Sheldon S. Wolin, *Politics and Vision* (Boston, 1960), pp. 76-7. M. Edelman, *The Symbolic Uses of Politics* (Illinois, 1964), pp. 44-73 and Leon Dion, "The Concept of Political Leadership", *Canadian Journal of Political Science*, (June 1969).
[41] *Ibid.*, p. 76. Wolin defines modern elite as "a group whose superiority rests on its excellence in manipulation." *Ibid.*, p. 420.
[42] Dror, *Public Policy Making Reexamined*, p. 301.
[43] From personal experience.
[44] See Lijphart, "Consociational Democracy". Lijphart, whose model has been applied to the Canadian political process with insight and considerable success by Noel, maintains that "overarching cooperation" among representative elites in a consociational system is greatly facilitated by low-load input on the decision-making apparatus.
[45] Entropy is defined as "absence of form, pattern, hierarchy or differentiation; a general trend of the universe toward death and disorder". *Webster's Third New International Dictionary*, 1969. Negative entropy refers to action aimed to countervail this tendency. See Dror, *Public Policy Making and Reexamination*, p. 18. Marion J. Levy, " 'Does It Matter If He's Naked?' Bawled the Child", in (eds.) K. Knorr and J. Rosenau, *Contending Approaches to International Politics* (Princeton, 1969), p. 90.

cannot be controlled or contained by consociational techniques.[46]

In summary, my principal theoretical contention is as follows: Under the impact of the optimal decisional technology, the political leadership role and the relationships between the leader and his supporters are being transformed from transactional to bureaucratic to moral. If this hypothesis can be empirically confirmed, its implications with regard to the political process in Canada are far reaching.

It is hoped that the issues raised in this article will provoke among Canadian political scientists an already overdue debate and will stimulate research in this neglected area of linkage between systems of decisional technology and political process.

Postscript

I wrote the preceding pages in January 1971 shortly after my departure from the Treasury Board. I chose the term "optimal model" in order to capture the main thrust and meaning of the normative underpinnings of the structural reforms introduced in Ottawa since 1968 and intended to improve the effectiveness of the federal policy-making process. I argued that new knowledge—which I called decisional technology—gave rise to two beliefs:

1. that it is desirable to design a new set of structural arrangements for governmental policy-making; and
2. that when such a design is implemented, or grafted upon the existing pattern of institutions and executive/bureaucratic relationships, the quality of policy and program outputs will significantly improve.

The optimal model, then, reflects the objectives[47] which the designer wants to realize, and the degree to which he intends to modify the existing pattern of institutions and executive/bureaucratic arrangements. His success in reaching these aims is uncertain. Moreover, the design may produce unintended and unanticipated consequences. I argued that such con-

---

[46] See "Speech From The Throne", October 8, 1970, House of Commons *Debates*. "Because, of the clash between these new values and the old, because of the quest by the young and the disillusioned for some resolution of attitudes, we live in a period of tenseness and unease. It is an age frequented by violence as desperate men seek ill-defined goals; an age of frustration as gentle men question impatiently old assumptions. It is an age in which the life-support systems of the biosphere may collapse unless man reverses his present course and begins again to live in harmony, rather than in competition, with his environment. It is an age in which the forces of science and technology now in motion are so massive, so swift, and so comprehensive that man may be facing his last opportunity to control his own destiny rather than be subject to it. ... Man can no longer afford the luxury of reacting to events. He must anticipate and plan." See also Victor C. Ferkiss, *Technological Man* (New York, 1969), pp. 245-73.

[47] I have identified the core objectives sought in the federal design as follows: systemic integration of structure; analytic rigour in process; comprehensive rationality of actors; and measurable effectiveness of output. See my "Decisional Technology and Political Process in Canada", Ph.D. dissertation, McGill University, forthcoming.

sequences—which often become apparent only after some passage of time —may be serious; they may lead to a significant change in the relationships among political elites; they may influence the political process; they may even threaten the stability of the country. I hold the same opinions to-day.

This is not the place for an examination of the evidence about the relative success or failure of the optimal design at the federal level.[48] Literature on this controversial subject is rapidly growing.[49] It will be useful, however, to offer one illustration which comes in the form of two charts recently developed and made available by the Treasury Board Secretariat. These charts do not depict reality; rather, they portray schematically how the decision-making process and the cabinet committee system ought to look and function. They disclose the Treasury Board's simplified version of the optimal design. The "official" definitions of policy and program are equally revealing.

JULY 1976

Definitions

POLICY
A government policy is a statement by the government of a principle or set of principles it wishes to see followed, in pursuit of particular objectives, which may be stated in such a way as to suggest possible courses of action (programs) and as to indicate how success of the policy may be measured (criteria).

PROGRAM
A course of action or instrument to implement a policy (or policies), sometimes involving legislative mandates and usually, public expenditures. (A program also has objectives, which will in general be more operational than those of a policy, and be suggestive of possible criteria against which accomplishments of the objectives may be measured).

Source: Treasury Board Secretariat, November 1975.

---

[48] For a preliminary assessment of a similar design in Ontario, see my "Policy-Making and Cabinet: Recent Organizational Engineering at Queen's Park" in D. C. MacDonald (ed.) *Government and Politics of Ontario*, (Toronto, 1975).
[49] In addition to the well known work of Bruce Doern and the articles by Marc Lalonde, Gordon Robertson, and A. W. Johnson published in 1971 in CPA and CJPS, one should single out the following: Donald Gow, *The Progress of the Budgetary Process in the Government of Canada*, Special Study No. 17, Economic Council of Canada, Ottawa, 1973; Peter Aucoin and Richard French, *Knowledge, Power and Public Policy*, Background Study No. 31, Science Council of Canada, Ottawa, 1974; C. M. Drury, "Quantitative Analysis and Public Policy Making", *Canadian Public Policy*, I, (Winter 1975), p. 89; Michael Pitfield, "The shape of government in the 1980s: techniques and instruments for policy formulation at the federal level", *Canadian Public Administration*, XIX, (Spring 1976), p. 8; D. G. Hartle, "Techniques and processes of administration", *Canadian Public Administration*, XIX, (Spring 1976), p. 21; T. A. Hockin, *Government in Canada* (Toronto, 1976), pp. 145-157; W. A. Matheson, *The Prime Minister and the Cabinet*, (Toronto, 1976), pp. 87-99.

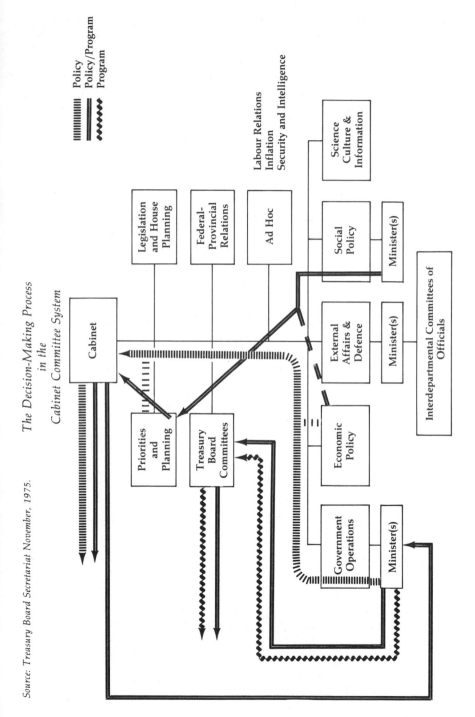

Source: Treasury Board Secretariat November, 1975.

The Decision-Making Process
in the
Cabinet Committee System

Source: *Treasury Board Secretariat November 1975.*   *The Decision-Making Process*

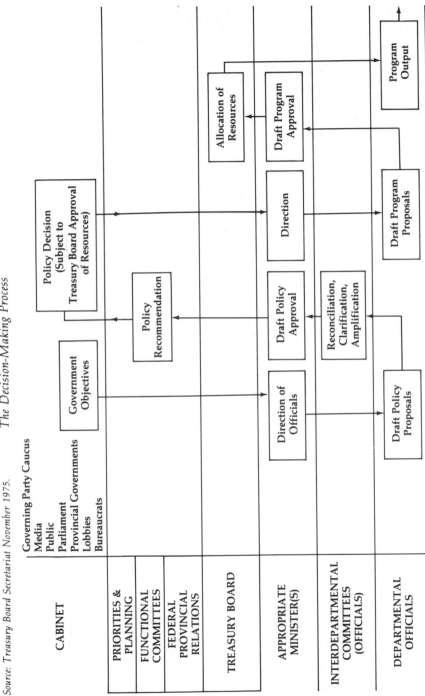

18

Rational Policy-Making: Policy, Politics, and Political Science

LAURENT DOBUZINSKIS

We are aware that the many techniques of cybernetics, by transforming the control function and the manipulation of information, will transform our whole society. With this knowledge we are wide awake, alert, capable of action; no longer are we blind, inert pawns of fate.[1]

Is cybernetics to Prime Minister Trudeau what eighteenth century reason was to Frederick II? In fact, for Mr. Trudeau and for many students of public policy, the two notions are linked. It has been commonly expected from the implementation of various decisional techniques (more or less directly inferred from cybernetics) that public policy-making will become more rational. To what extent have these expectations been met? More generally, how rational is the process of "rationalization" which we have seen at work at the federal level for a little more than a decade?

Our purpose here is to assess critically how the literature in the field has provided us with an answer to this question, or, at least with propositions of a logical nature which still need to be empirically tested.

What is meant by rationality in this context? P. Aucoin states that:

... rationalist models have suggested that policies are formulated through a series of sequential steps where the policy-makers
1) recognize a policy problem exists, 2) identify the nature of the problem through

---

[1] Quoted from Prime Minister Trudeau's speech at the Harrison Liberal Conference (1969) in: G. Bruce Doern, "The Development of Policy Organizations in the Executive Arena", in G. Bruce Doern, and Peter Aucoin (eds.), *The Structure of Policy-Making in Canada*, (Toronto, 1971), p. 65.

investigations, 3) call for the presentation of alternatives, 4) rank their priorities, 5) make predictions on the risks and consequences of the various alternatives, and finally, 6) come to a decision by combining the qualitative and quantitative values they have considered.[2]

Let us remember that central to Mr. Trudeau's philosophy and to contemporary management theory is the necessity to clarify goals before deciding upon alternative courses of action. "[F]or a policy to be rational it must have goals" notes J. P. Roos in a laconic, but forceful manner.[3] The decisional techniques alluded to above enter mainly at the stage where alternative programs are being prepared for final selection.

Rationality, however, can be analyzed at a higher level; Max Weber's well-known distinction between "formal" and "substantive" rationality applies here. Whatever the goals, a formally rational decision-maker will try to achieve them to a maximal degree or with minimal effort; the emphasis is on calculability. By contrast, substantive rationality is associated with a primary concern for the nature of the goals themselves.[4] It seems almost certain that policy-making in Ottawa has become more formally rational, but to what extent is the question to which we will first address ourselves. Then we will ask whether the transformations carried out in the name of efficiency and effectiveness are also substantively rational given the logic of the Canadian political system, particularly from the point of view of governmental responsiveness; conversely, we will not try to pass judgement on specific policy outcomes for this would be too contentious.

Toward Rational Government?

Rationalization in policy-making can take two forms: improving the efficiency or the effectiveness of government operations. The former refers to a concern for the optimal use of resources in implementing a given program, which may or may not fulfill its supposed objectives; the latter refers

---

[2] P. Aucoin, "Theory and Research in the Study of Policy-making", in G. Bruce Doern and Peter Aucoin (eds.), *The Structures of Policy-Making in Canada*, p. 15.

[3] J. R. Roos, *Welfare Theory and Social Policy—A Study in Policy Science* (Helsinki, 1973), p. 19.

[4] Which is not to say that in the rationalist model no attention is paid to the validity and consistency of policy objectives—it is quite the contrary if we bear in mind that it stands as an antithesis to the incrementalist model—nor to suggest that techniques such as cost-effectiveness analysis are only concerned with the choice of optimal means of achieving arbitrarily set up objectives. But substantive rationality entails a re-examination of a society's political choices on a scale which tends to outstep the boundaries of routine policy-making. This nuance is sometimes expressed in the literature by differentiating between "goals" and "objectives": the former are quantifiable and interchangeable (e.g. improve the quality of first-aid services to reduce the number of deaths by traffic accidents by x percent, or alternatively reduce the number of accidents by y percent); the latter are qualitative and incommensurable (e.g. improve the general health of the population, or achieve equity in income distribution). The rationalist model helps only to evaluate "objectives", not "goals".

to a concern for the optimal design of the program itself so as to maximize a measure of goal achievement. In practice, efficiency gains are obtained through more or less extensive transformations of the bureaucratic structure; a concern for effectiveness results in more profound changes in both values and methods.

The work of the Glassco Commission has often been criticized for its narrow and exclusive preoccupation with efficient management.[5] C. Guruprassad has observed that

... the influence of Glassco, with his emphasis on improved financial and personal management, squeezed planning to a lower level.[6]

Under Prime Minister Trudeau, planning has become a dominant concern and the criterion of efficiency subservient to that of effectiveness, at least in principle, if not in practice. As a result, "fused, personalized and passive" relationships within the policy structures have given way to "differentiated, bureaucratized and active" ones.[7] These changes entailed i) a few but significant reforms at the Cabinet level, ii) the implementation of a series of managerial techniques.

As far as reforms at the apex are concerned, the most important one has been the development of a more complex and permanent Cabinet committee system, dominated by the Committee on Priorities and Planning. But one should not neglect other reforms such as the creation of new departments. The Departments of Regional Economic Expansion, and Industry, Trade and Commerce were established in 1969 to provide a more integrated and systematic response to the demands of an increasingly complex economy;[8] the Departments of Supply and Services, and the Ministries of State for Urban Affairs and for Science and Technology were established to perform coordinative function, and, in the case of the latter two, to inject

[5] The Royal Commission on Government Organization, or Glassco Commission, was established in September 1960; its mandate directed it to "recommend changes ... [which] would promote efficiency, economy and improved services in the dispatch of the public business [by the Government of Canada]" quoted from the Commission report in W. L. White and J. C. Strick, Policy, Politics and the Treasury Board in Canadian Government, (Don Mills, Ont., 1971), p. 89; for an evaluation of the task accomplished by this Royal Commission, see R. S. Ritchie, A. D. P. Heeney et al, "The Glassco Commission Report: A Panel Discussion", Canadian Public Administration, V (1962), No. 4, pp. 385-401, A. W. Johnson, "Efficiency in Government and Business", Canadian Public Administration, VI (1963), No. 3, pp. 245-260, and T. H. McLeod, "Glassco Commission Report", Canadian Public Administration, VI (1963), No. 4, pp. 385-406.
[6] C. Guruprassad, "Planning for Tax Administration in Canada", Canadian Public Administration, XVI (1973), p. 418
[7] Doern, pp. 41-42.
[8] But here the Trudeau Government is merely following in the footsteps of the Pearson Government which had established the Departments of Manpower and Immigration (1966), Consumer and Corporate Affairs (1967), see R. W. Phidd and O. P. Dwivedi, "Bureaucracy, Politics and Public Policy-Making in Canada: An Appraisal", Conference paper, C.P.S.A. Annual Meeting, Quebec City, June 1976, pp. 15-21.

new policy alternatives in the overall planning process.[9] The consequences of these reforms have not been entirely positive, as it will be argued, but they have at least provided a favourable context for the implementation of managerial techniques rendering policy-making more formally rational. They have proved favourable insofar as they help to replace the outcomes of the latter within a broader political perspective. For instance, Donald Gow has suggested that the Committee on Priorities and Planning provides a forum for the "processing of values" (using Dror's expression) thereby making explicit what could be merely implicit, or even altogether neglected, in technical studies.[10]

As far as the managerial reforms are concerned, the Planning-Programming-Budgeting System (PPBS) needs to be analyzed first. Since PPB was first implemented in the U.S. Department of Defence in 1961 under Robert McNamara and introduced in Canada in 1967, too much has been written about it to be summarized and analyzed here.[11] Let us simply recall that the purpose of PPBS is to make the budget reflect the cost of achieving most effectively a set of preferred long term objectives.

Now, D. Hartle has recently pronounced PPBS dead in Ottawa.[12] A. Wildavsky is even more categorical when he states that "PPBS has failed everywhere [in all countries] and at all times."[13] *A posteriori* it appears that PPB's major weakness is that it has been conceived as a rigid system. Besides, the choice made in Ottawa (and incidentally also in Washington earlier) to follow a top down strategy for implementing PPBS has reinforced its built-in rigidity and provoked negative reactions at all levels. It is easier to insist upon the necessity of developing elaborate structures of objectives, as the Treasury Board Secretariat did, than to relate actual policy decisions to such abstract categories. We will come back to this point later. Despite the hopes it generated some years ago, PPBS has

---

[9] Following the recommendations of the Committee on Government Productivity, the Government of Ontario has made very similar reform by establishing a Policy and Priorities Board of Cabinet and three functional policy committees chaired by "policy ministers" (officially called Provincial Secretaries), see James D. Fleck, "Restructuring the Ontario Government", *Canadian Public Administration*, XVI (1973), No. 1, pp. 69-72, and G. Szablowski, "Policy-Making and Cabinet", in D. C. MacDonald, (ed) *Government and Politics of Ontario*, (Toronto, 1975), pp. 114-135.

[10] Donald Gow, *The Progress of Budgetary Reform in the Government of Canada*, Special Study No. 17, Economic Council of Canada, 1973, p. 58.

[11] See Government of Canada, *Planning Programming Budgeting Guide*, revised edition, (Ottawa, 1969); G. Bruce Doern, "The Budgetary Process and the Policy Role of the Federal Bureaucracy", in Doern and Aucoin, pp. 79-112; Gow, *Progress of Budgetary Reform*; A. W. Johnson, "Planning, Programming, and Budgeting in Canada", *Public Administration Review*, XXXIII, No. 1 (January 1973), pp. 23-31.

[12] See D. G. Hartle, "Techniques and Processes of Administration", *Canadian Public Administration*, XIX, No. 1 (Spring 1976), pp. 21-34.

[13] Aaron Wildavsky, *The Politics of the Budgetary Process*, 2nd ed., (Boston, 1974), p. 205; on the situation in the United States, see A. Schick, "A Death in the Bureaucracy: The Demise of Federal PPB", *Public Administration Review*, XXXIII (March 1973), pp. 146-156.

become little more than a cumbersome ritual. However, there is room for disagreement about the extent of the failure. At least one element of the system, i.e., the functional classification of expenditures, represents an improvement over previous practices. Moreover the fate of PPBS does not mean that the planning approach in general has been abandoned. Are there more convincing applications of the latter?

At present, the most attractive alternative, at least in the view of the believers in the rationalist approach, seems to be Management by Objectives (MBO), introduced in the federal government in December 1971. A department using MBO must first define its overall policy objectives; then, at each level of the organization, officials are assigned sub-objectives (the definition of which they participate in, at least in principle), and their performance is evaluated in relation to these objectives.[14] This is made possible by the data produced by yet another managerial system, namely Operational Performance Measurement System (OPMS).[15] In contrast with PPBS which brings about rigid procedures directing information flows from top to bottom, the advocates of MBO stress that the opposite is true with the latter.

However, are these developments compatible with the notion of accountability upon which the Canadian political system is based? The Glassco Commission advised: "Let the managers manage". The rationale for this at the time was a concern for efficiency, i.e., avoiding costly duplication of tasks. MBO constitutes a more ambitious project; it "represents an attempt to create a managerial environment in which imagination, innovation and risk-taking are encouraged".[16]

Yet who is to control the "risk-taking" civil servant? D. Hartle's comments on this question are instructive:

Now, in my view, the idea that public servants are managers is fallacious. In a well-run system public servants are not managers: they are policy advisers and/or . . . negotiators, and/or administrators . . . the term "manager" implies a substantial degree of discretion. In a parliamentary system the bureaucrat should have little decision-making discretion.[17]

Even if it could be established that in the present context a public official must have some degree of discretion, we still need to redefine administrative accountability. Considering the extent of their involvement in policy-making, A. R. Cahoon, for instance, proposes to make public servants accountable to the public-at-large and to eliminate the present security-tenure system:

---

[14] On MBO, see J. S. Hodgson, "Management by Objectives—The Experience of a Federal Government Department", Canadian Public Administration, XVI (1973), No. 3, pp. 422-431.

[15] On OPMS, see D. G. Hartle, "Operational Performance Measurement in the Federal Government", Optimum, III, (1972), No. 4, pp. 5-18, and Treasury Board, Operational Performance Measurement, Vol. I, Ottawa, January 1974.

[16] Treasury Board, Operational Performance Measurement, p. 19.

[17] Hartle, "Operational Performance Measurement", p. 22.

The new role behaviour for public administrators ... would mean that they would now be held accountable for the power they presently possess. The role changes from one of neutral advocacy ... to one of client advocacy and the promotion of greater social sensitivity in government administration.[18]

We have here two apparently contradictory answers to a problem that MBO worsens rather than solves.

Eventually, as another illustration of a shift from a procedural approach to a more informal one emphasizing analysis rather than structures, one could mention the development of various kinds of social indicators research projects.[19] The impact of social indicators on policy-making is still limited. Serious methodological obstacles (e.g., how to define the concept of "quality of life") and attitudinal resistance from some segments of the bureaucracy (e.g., there is strong opposition from senior statisticians to the development of "subjective" or "perceptual" indicators of well-being) impede progress in this field. Moreover, social indicators still do not amount to relevant political indicators in the eyes of politicians.[20] Yet inertia at the political level cannot be taken as an insuperable obstacle. D. G. Hartle, for instance, has elaborated a theoretical framework for translating politicians' concerns into operational terms (e.g., "diversity and intensity of the voters wants", "the frequency with which the same losers have lost in the past and are likely to lose again in the future", etc ...).[21]

It seems also reasonable to assume that social indicators will soon play a more important role in the context of "the ongoing extension of public

---

[18] Allan R. Cahoon, "The Need for a New Definition of Administrative Responsibility for Public Policy Makers", paper presented at the 1976 meeting of the CPSA, Quebec City, 1976, pp. 16-17.

[19] The nature and functions of social indicators have been given several definitions which are not always convergent; basically, a social indicator is a quantitative measure of some relevant aspect of a social condition such as health, education, housing etc ... An indicator is said to be "objective" if it is expressed in physical or monetary units, or "subjective" if it describes the level of satisfaction with some social condition expressed by individuals. On social indicators research in Canada, see The Canadian Council on Social Development, *Social Indicators*, Proceedings of a Seminar, Ottawa: 13-14 January 1972; the Economic Council of Canada has been for many years an active supporter of that kind of research: in its VIIIth annual review, the Council advocated the elaboration of 'goal indicators' which would help to " ... monitor the changing conditions of our society over a broad spectrum of concerns" (*Design for Decision-Making*, Ottawa, 1971, p. 71), the IXth and Xth reviews were more specifically concerned with economic indicators, but in the XIth review (*Economic Targets and Social Indicators*, Ottawa, 1974) one finds again a strong case for broader considerations. See also D. W. Henderson, *Social Indicators: A Rationale and Research Framework*, Economic Council of Canada 1974, and the review of this work by A. C. Michalos in *Canadian Public Policy*, I, No. 2, pp. 263-265.

[20] See Rose, "The Market for Policy Indicators", in A. Shonfield and S. Shaw (eds.), *Social Indicators and Social Policy* (London, 1972), pp. 119-141.

[21] See Douglas G. Hartle, "Objectives of Government Objectives", mimeo, Ottawa, 1972, and "A Proposed System for Program and Policy Evaluation", *Canadian Public Administration*, XVI (Summer 1973), pp. 243-266; the fact that this author has more recently expressed his skepticism about the desirability of such an approach, does not necessarily reflect upon its feasibility.

authorities in matters formerly social", and of the "swallowing of the social by the political".[22] The likely development of some form of guaranteed income system in the wake of the 1973-75 Social Security Review is a case in point. Under these conditions, it is premature to warn about the dangers of an imminent and deliberate attempt by the public authorities (federal or provincial) to "monitor social change" on a large scale;[23] but if the precedent of the very consequential changes brought about by the development of economic national accounting some thirty years ago is to be taken seriously, social indicators represent the most far reaching techniques of all those mentioned hereto.

Now all these techniques (with the possible exception of social indicators which have potentially broader applications) are instrumental in what Bruce Doern calls "expenditure decision-making", as opposed to regulatory activities; the distinctiveness of the latter being that " . . . the regulatory arena of political activity does not go through a process of assessment analogous to the budgetary process."[24] Until the recent "rediscovery" of this "other half" of policy-making, "Virtually all the attention being given to new approaches has been concentrated on expenditure decision-making rather than on regulative activity and the relationship between the two."[25] Because of this relative neglect, there is less to be said about the subject of regulatory reforms. Nevertheless, we can observe here also a tendency to favour a rationalist approach, in the sense that there is some attempt to set priorities and to account for the costs and benefits involved. It remains that the complexity of the issues at stake and the fact that regulatory policy entails clearly identifiable winners and losers, hence high political costs, make these attempts rather frustrating. As examples of regulatory reforms in the past few years, one could mention the creation of the Health Protection Branch within the Department of National Health and Welfare,[26] the transformation of the Department of Transport into a Ministry of Transport,[27] and, of course, more recently the establishment of the Anti-Inflation Board.

---

[22] D. V. Smiley, "The Managed Mosaic", *Canadian Forum*, April 1972, p. 39.

[23] On the implications of social indicators research see Michael Springer, "Social Indicators, Reports and Accounts: Towards the Management of Society", *The Annals of the American Academy of Political and Social Science*, March 1970, pp. 1-13.

[24] G. Bruce Doern, "The Concept of Regulation and Regulatory Reform", in G. B. Doern, and V. S. Wilson (eds.), *Issues in Canadian Public Policy*, (Toronto, 1974), p. 8.

[25] G. Bruce Doern, *Political Policy-Making: A Commentary on the Economic Council's Eighth Annual Review and the Ritchie Report*, (Montreal, 1972), p. 16.

[26] Which has been rather positively appraised by P. Aucoin, see P. Aucoin, "Federal Health Care Policy", in G. B. Doern and V. S. Wilson (eds.), *Issues in Canadian Public Policy*, pp. 55-84.

[27] J. W. Langford has described the Transportation Council set up at the apex of MOT as a well organized forum for the comprehensive review of policy proposals, but asks whether this form of corporate planning is adaptable to the political problems MOT has to deal with. See J. W. Langford, "The Ministry of Transport as a Policy-Making Institution", in K. W. Studnicki-Gizbert (ed.), *Issues in Canadian Transport Policy*, (Toronto, 1974), pp. 408-443.

218 APEX OF POWER

In summary, the transformation of the machinery of government and the implementation of the new planning techniques outlined above leave the impression that some steps toward rational government have been made. Certainly more attention is being paid to the determination of long term priorities, if only in a few policy areas; indeed, one is hard pressed to give more than two or three examples of the application of the rationalist approach to strategically important questions (e.g., the Defence Policy Review, 1968-69, the Social Security Review 1973-75). The failure of PPBS has made it very difficult to convert these policy decisions into specific programs in a manner that would be qualitatively different from previous practices. MBO and OPMS could lead to more "rational" decision-making, but presumably with a reduction of political control and administrative coordination. Now we have also suggested that a more extensive use of politically relevant social indicators by, for instance, Cabinet committees could result in far reaching changes, but, as has been emphasized, such a proposition still remains purely hypothetical. Under these conditions, we concur with Jackson and Atkinson when they remark: "In Canada we have created the structures of rational policy-making, but incrementalism predominates within them".[28]

Why did all this happen in Ottawa since Trudeau? Clearly the mushrooming of government spending has something to do with it. There seems to be a perceptible correlation between the growth of personal incomes and the growth of governmental expenditures.[29] Under these conditions, problems of resources allocation have become very acute in Canada, at the federal as well as at the provincial level. Hence a growing concern for effectiveness has emerged in Ottawa. Development in Washington of new methods for public management also served as an incentive for their adoption in Canada. It has been repeatedly shown that the success or failure of sophisticated planning methods, elaborated by experts, depends largely on the support, or lack thereof, given to their implementation by decision-makers at the apex. There is ample evidence that Prime Minister Trudeau is committed to the rationalist approach, and this is also true of a few Cabinet members, past and present, although certainly not of all of them.[30] However, PPBS was introduced in Canada before Mr. Trudeau became Prime Minister, and the role played by senior civil servants (men like A. W. Johnson, former Secretary of the Treasury Board) cannot be ignored.

---

[28] R. J. Jackson and M. M. Atkinson, *The Canadian Legislative System*, (Toronto, 1974), p. 61.

[29] R. Bird has reviewed several theoretical interpretations of this observation which he criticizes for neglecting political factors. See Richard M. Bird, *The Growth of Government Spending in Canada*, (Toronto, 1970).

[30] See G. Bruce Doern, "Recent Changes in the Philosophy of Policy-Making in Canada", *Canadian Journal of Political Science*, IV (1971), No. 2, pp. 243-264; Doern regrets that political scientists " . . . have not zeroed in on the more explicit structures and philosophy which have been associated with the immediate environment of the executive-bureaucratic levels (*ibid.* p. 243).

Little is known about the motivation underlying proposals for reform such as those outlined previously, but D. G. Hartle goes so far as to suggest that

Those who advocate changes in techniques and processes are, for the most part, . . . [seeking] changes in the existing power structure. They are responding, in large part, to their own interests.[31]

If, as we have seen, the reforms accomplished in the name of effectiveness are more symbolic than real, the rituals through which these symbols are exchanged have serious implication for the Canadian political system. The next section should make this clear.

Rationalization in Perspective

a) RATIONALITY REVISITED. Should the determination of overall priorities, which implies an ability to anticipate the issues and to alter perceptions of the common good, be the primary role of politicians; or, on the contrary, should their role be more passive, if not even one of limiting the involvement of the public authorities in societal processes?[32] And is it realistic to expect rational long term planning from the federal government and from the Canadian political system in general? Critics answering negatively to the last question, that is to say, pointing to the methodological difficulties, political constraints etc., lying in the way of a planning approach tend also, more or less implicitly, to answer negatively to the first one, thereby making an important value judgement.

Bruce Doern maintains that when dealing with both political life as a whole and the interactions within Cabinet or the bureaucratic structure,

. . . the management of legitimate coercion—the securing of acceptance and compliance —is an essential ingredient if we are to understand and improve the process and the substance of policy-making.[33]

The "securing of acceptance and compliance" entails a computation of political costs and benefits that technical studies too often fail to consider. Yet to emphasize respect for the importance of these political factors may be to implicitly emphasize respect for the status quo as well. If so, it is necessary to draw a line between, on the one hand, the criticisms of the simplistic assumptions found in the rationalist model of policy-making— particularly the illusion that effectiveness is a necessary and sufficient criterion to evaluate political choices—and, on the other hand, the endorsement of the incrementalist model. The weakness of the latter is twofold. In the first place it posits that marginal policy changes are adequate political

---

[31] "Objectives of Government Objectives", p. 24.

[32] For a defence of the first alternative, see A. Etzioni, *The Active Society*, (New York, 1968).

[33] G. Bruce Doern, *Political Policy-Making: A Commentary on the Economic Council's Eighth Annual Review and the Ritchie Report*, p. 12.

220 APEX OF POWER

responses to societal demands. It may be in many cases—as a matter of fact the rationalist model goes too far in the opposite direction—but should it be a rule? More importantly, it de-emphasizes the significance of external effects which, on the contrary, appear to be the main source of social and political conflicts in "post-industrial" societies like Canada. The following analysis of the inadequacies in the rationalist model is not meant to invalidate the planning approach in general. Although we do not intend to prove it, one could argue, on the contrary, that the inadequacies in the rationalist model reflect a misunderstanding of the logic of a truly cybernetic approach to policy-making.

The deficiencies of the particular techniques derived from the rationalist model have been discussed, but it is also necessary to deal with the inherent flaws of the model itself. Many observers have noted that the determination of policy objectives is in many cases an almost impossible task and that no technique, no matter how sophisticated, can solve this problem. Most policies, or programs, serve several interdependent and partially contradictory objectives. As Rittel and Webber suggest, planning problems are "wicked" ones for which " . . . there is no definitive formulation".[34] Moreover, "wicked problems do not have an enumerable (or an exhaustively describable) set of potential solutions."[35] This is obviously a very serious methodological limitation. Unfortunately, economic rationality has, in practice, inspired the rationalist reformers. The technical consequence of this evolution is that microeconomics has superseded systems analysis, and with microeconomics comes the notion of optimality.[36] It is all the more unfortunate because, as G. Szablowski hypothesizes, Cabinet members now tend to reason in terms of optimal solution, even if their conversion to this new standard may not be total.[37] Moreover, Szablowski suggests that

Under the impact of the optimal decisional technology, the political leadership role and the relationship between the leader and his supporters are being transformed from transactional to bureaucratic to moral.[38]

---

[34] H. W. Rittel and M. M. Webber, "Dilemmas in a General Theory of Planning", *Policy-Sciences*, IV (1973), p. 161.

[35] *Ibid.*, p. 164.

[36] Microeconomic thinking allows the reduction of functionally distinct parameters to monetary evaluations which can then be used for the formulation of a *single* optimal solution. Systems analysis, on the contrary, posits that such a reduction is not permissible: there is no such thing as a single optimum in complex systems. See Medow, Paul, "The Place of Budgeting by Systems in Policy-Making", mimeo, Systems Planning Group, York University, October 1969. For a theoretical critique of the idea of optimality by systems theorists see also Stafford Beer, *Designing Freedom*, (Toronto, 1974), and E. Jantsch, *Design for Evolution*, (New York, 1975).

[37] See George Szablowski, "The Optimal Policy-Making System: Implications for the Canadian Political Process", Chapter 17 in this volume.

[38] "Transactional" here refers to the traditional accommodation of regional or special interests by Cabinet members, "bureaucratic" to the new functional division of labour within Cabinet, and "moral" to the normative implications of the commitment to ration-

But is it rational—from a substantive point of view—to expect that decisions made by Cabinet will always correspond to the (optimal) common good, and that, consequently, Cabinet members should be morally committed to the priorities proposed by the Prime Minister and his policy advisors? The political irrationality of an optimization paradigm seems obvious in view of the various cleavages characteristic of the Canadian society.

Another weakness of the rationalist philosophy is the assumption that "knowledge is power." (Knowledge is taken here in a rather restrictive sense, namely the outcome of in-depth policy analyses). As already mentioned, the two Ministries of State for Science and Technology (MOSST), and for Urban Affairs (MSUA) are the institutional expressions of this dogma insofar as they do not operate programs but are only concerned with policy development and coordination on the basis of extensive research.[39] Aucoin and French have found that both in the executive and bureaucratic arenas (in the latter context MSUA fares better) MOSST and MSUA play a minor role: "they are hostages to the power of the line departments."[40]

However, if the control of policy analysis sources does not confer power to those who have no other means of exchange, it seems that it can greatly enhance the power of those who, like the Prime Minister, already command important political resources, as we shall discuss hereafter.

b) CAN WE AFFORD RATIONAL GOVERNMENT? Could it be that what seems to be rational to the Prime Minister, Cabinet, or the federal government as a whole, appears dysfunctional from another point of view? To approach this

---

ality the Prime Minister expects from his colleagues; see Szablowski, "'Optimal Policy-Making System"; on the contrary, F. Stark argues that "transactional" relationships also entail some form of moral commitment (namely to national unity) as the elite accommodation theory posits: it is likely, according to this author, that "... planning techniques alone [do not] dictate social and political interactions in the Cabinet or eliminate the federal symbolic functions of the Prime Minister's Office." Szablowski's answer to that argument implies that the validity of the elite accommodation theory is questionable as far as Canada is concerned. See F. Stark, "The Prime Minister as Symbol: Unifier or Optimizer?", *Canadian Journal of Political Science*, XVI (1973) No. 3, pp. 516-517.

[39] However, the Central Mortgage and Housing Corporation and the National Capital Commission have been transfered to MSUA.

[40] P. Aucoin and R. French, *Knowledge, Power and Public Policy*, Science Council of Canada, Background Study No. 31, Ottawa, 1974, p. 79. D. Cameron has also concluded that MSUA represents the "triumph of form over substance", see D. Cameron, "Urban Policy", in G. Bruce Doern and V. Seymour Wilson (eds.), *Issues in Canadian Public Policy*, p. 247. It is very instructive to compare this evolution with the fate of the three Provincial Secretaries in the Ontario government; in a few years these "superministers" have been relegated to a secondary position, because, as with the federal Ministries of State, the fact that they are not responsible for actual programs, and therefore lack political exposure or the direct support of a clientele, makes them powerless; see G. Szablowski, "Policy-Making and Cabinet", in D. Macdonald (ed.), *Government and Politics of Ontario*, (Toronto, 1975), pp. 114-135.

global concern the discussion now centres on the concepts of centralization and responsiveness.

A wide dispersion of resources allows different units (individual and/ or agencies) to make decisions independently of each other, even if in principle they are hierarchically related; whereas centralization establishes clear lines of command. Centralization, as understood here, is a concentration of resources (administrative, political, financial, etc.) and information (organizational intelligence, technical data etc.) at a certain level of governmental structure.

Responsiveness refers to the capacity of the political system to meet the demands of individual members of collectivities and of society as a whole.[41]

A low degree of centralization increases the responsiveness of the political system to particularistic demands, but presumably at the cost of incoherence. A high degree of centralization increases the responsiveness of the political system to society as a whole, but presumably by alienating large sectors of society. There is, of course, no proper balance between the two, but the hypothesis proposed here is that in Canada responsiveness is a crucial variable, and that centralization can rapidly become dysfunctional. How does the present policy-making system affect the responsiveness of the Canadian political system?

In the first place, one can look at its effects on the executive-bureaucratic structure. There is conclusive evidence to support the view that the Prime Minister, the Prime Minister's Office (P.M.O.), and the central agencies [Privy Council Office (P.C.O.), and Treasury Board Secretariat] have attained greater leverage. As Gordon Robertson argues (quoting Arnold Heeney) "under the pressure of events and in response to actual need", since 1940 the development of the Cabinet committee system brought "substantial" growth to the P.C.O., both in the size of its staff and in the extent of its activities.[42] The revamped committee system established in 1968, however, coupled with Prime Minister Trudeau's determination to counterbalance the policy advisory role of the bureaucracy (i.e., line departments),[43] has further strengthened the role of the P.C.O. as well as that of the P.M.O.[44] The function of the latter is to provide the Prime Minister with political advice, but Marc Lalonde once admitted that, because of the new role that this office has assumed," . . . there do exist certain gray areas where the advisory role of the P.M.O. and the public service (P.C.O. and

[41] See A. Etzioni, *The Active Society*, pp. 503-526.

[42] (Appointed in 1940 by Prime Minister Mackenzie King, A. Heeney became the first secretary to the Cabinet.) See Gordon Robertson, "The Changing Role of the Privy Council Office", in O. Kruhlak, *et al.* (eds.), *The Canadian Political Process*, 2nd edition (Toronto, 1973), pp. 438-457.

[43] On this point, see the interview with Lord Chalfont in this volume, p. 262.

[44] Recently the Federal-Provincial Relations Division of the P.C.O. has been transformed into a Federal-Provincial Relations Office whose secretary reports directly to the Prime Minister.

other) overlap".[45] One can argue that the new planning functions of the P.M.O. and P.C.O. have been worked out as the result of a gradual adaptation to changing circumstances:

The support and coordination of the process whereby Ministers set priorities for government and decide the content and means of implementing programs . . . have been evolved over time as part of the larger effort to meet the requirements of governing a modern state in accordance with the principles of parliamentary and Cabinet government.[46]

It is clear from its evolution that decision-making in Cabinet no longer corresponds to the conventional image of ministerial collegiality. As F. Schindeler has suggested" . . . [power has passed] from Parliament to Cabinet; from Cabinet to public service; and now, from public service to Prime Minister".[47] At first sight it could be said that the requirements of the Cabinet committee system force ministers to be more knowledgeable about their own and other departments; and the PCO helps them in this regard. Indeed, the old days of ministerial fiefdoms are past, and in this sense ministerial collegiality has been strengthened. However, interactions among ministers are now structured along strictly functional lines (re: Cabinet committees)[48] thus enabling the Prime Minister—and the members of an admittedly ill-defined "inner Cabinet"—to reserve, more than ever before, the prerogative of deciding the more exclusively political aspects of governmental policy. In other words, politics is a global concern which cannot be divided into so many policy fields. We would like to argue that the reallocation of political arbitration to the Prime Minister's Office provides us with a better explanation of the development of the PMO and PCO than platitudes about the " . . . requirements of governing a modern state".

This being granted, speculations regarding the alleged emergence of a quasi-presidential system in Canada are taking the argument a little too

---

[45] Marc Lalonde, "The Changing Role of the Prime Minister's Office", *Canadian Public Administration*, XIV (1971), No. 4, p. 523, see also Thomas D'Aquino, "The Prime Minister's Office: Catalyst or Cabal?", *Canadian Public Administration*, XVII, (1974), No. 1, pp. 55-79; and D. Smith, "Comments on the Prime Minister's Office: Catalyst or Cabal? *Ibid.*, pp. 80-84. The P.M.O. has experienced some setbacks in its development: as a result of the 1972 elections and of the political attacks directed toward the technocratic character of the first Trudeau Government the two organizational innovations which had furthered the rule of the P.M.O. were disallowed: a Program Secretary was not reappointed and the four regional desks that had been set up to" . . . provide the Prime Minister with an additional view of social and political developments in each region" (Lalonde, p. 265) have been officially disbanded (however, some less visible functional equivalents have been established).

[46] Privy Council Office, "Policy Planning . . . ", Chapter 3 in this volume.

[47] F. Schindeler, "The Prime Minister and the Cabinet", Chapter 2 in this volume.

[48] Cf. Szablowski's characterization of these interactions as being "bureaucratic", see G. Szablowski, "The Optimal Policy-Making System."

far.[49] This charge can be dismissed on several grounds; however profound the impact of organizational reforms may be, the traditional and constitutional constraints a Prime Minister must reckon with are still of primary importance to him: there is a limit beyond which he cannot go in exercising his leadership over Cabinet and his parliamentary majority.[50]

The new budgetary process also illustrates the centralizing influence of the rationalist model. According to A. W. Johnson, the Treasury Board is less entangled in the day-to-day routine of departmental decision-making than it used to be. It focuses its attention on the relationships existing between " . . . the broad policy directions that have been decided upon" by Cabinet and the programs submitted by the departments. But does not this approach impose more severe constraints on the activities of the line departments than this author implies? Indeed, Jacques Benjamin has observed that " . . . [PPBS] seems to have strengthened the interference of the Treasury Board with decision-making in each department."[51] Similarly Van Loon and Whittington suggest that " . . . the power of the individual departments has been decreased through the placing of new power in the hands of the more centralized Treasury Board secretariat".[52] As the same authors comment, the more significant role played by the Treasury Board secretariat enhances the power of the bureaucracy to the extent that the former is a part of the latter; alternatively, Treasury Board being formally a Cabinet committee, such an evolution can be viewed as an instance of greater political control over bureaucratic decision-making.[53] In either case, however, the strict standards set by the Treasury Board secretariat, because they place a heavy emphasis on "objective" analysis, make bargaining more difficult. Under these conditions, there is probably a greater need for and a greater reliance upon the power of arbitration as exercised by the Prime Minister and the Minister of Finance.[54]

See Denis Smith, "President and Parliament: The Transformation of Parliamentary Government in Canada", Chapter 25 in this volume; for a more controversial statement of a similar argument, see W. Stewart, *Shrug: Trudeau in Power* (Toronto, 1971).

[50] See Joseph Wearing, "President or Prime Minister", Chapter 26 in this volume.

[51] Jacques Benjamin, "La rationalisation des choix budgétaires: les cas québécois et canadien", *Canadian Journal of Political Science*, V (1972), No. 3, p. 361 (my translation).

[52] R. J. Van Loon and M. S. Whittington, *The Canadian Political System*, 2nd ed., (Toronto, 1976), pp. 405-406.

[53] *Ibid.*

[54] Because of the secrecy surrounding Cabinet discussions, documentation of this point is difficult to obtain. However, some indirect evidence is available. Mr. G. Osbolderton, Secretary of the Treasury Board, has recently articulated one of the most serious weaknesses of PPBS: the lack of criteria for comparing equally effective programs (communication to a seminar, York University, 1976). Taking this into account, we would like to argue that the Treasury Board secretariat tends to generate high expectations from departments or agencies able to present a good case more convincingly, by encouraging a more extensive use of policy analysis, yet these efforts are thwarted by the inescapable finiteness of budgetary resources, and tough political choices have to be made more or less arbitrarily.

It seems reasonable to asume that the consequences of these converging trends are a progressive clogging of the channels of communication at all levels of the executive-bureaucratic system and a resulting decrease in governmental responsiveness.

Another obvious deficiency of the rationalist model is that it almost totally ignores Parliament. To be sure, the establishment of a standing committee system in 1969 can be viewed as an attempt to adapt parliamentary procedures to the requirements of a planning approach. Yet, in retrospect

... the executive has been able to preserve its virtual monopoly over the formulation and initiation of policy—a situation which has resulted in a deterioration in members' interest in committee work. This has ensured that the unequal distribution of power between the executive and legislative branches remain intact.[55]

But most authors would argue that the supremacy of the executive antedated the implementation of the rationalist model; why lament Parliament's inability to match the power of the Cabinet and the expertise of the bureaucracy when its role now and for decades has been primarily to serve as a forum for adversary politics?[56] There are two reasons why this argument, although valid, does not altogether resolve existing questions about the alleged decrease in Parliament's importance within the Canadian political system. In the first place, to implement a truly rational planning approach which would not cause an information overload at the apex nor contradict Canadian political pluralism, requires the active involvement of the MP's in the formulation of strategic priorities.[57] But if this point sounds a little utopian, it remains true that in the long run even the adversary function of Parliament could be affected by a further development of present practices. The more comprehensive and "scientific" (in appearance) the information provided by policy analysts to Cabinet, the more difficult it becomes for " ... the opposition ... to re-interpret the Government's performance, in a way different from the Government's interpretation".[58]

Finally, any new policy-making system in Canada must be related to

---

[55] J. R. Happy, "Optimal Policy-Making and the Independence of Members of Parliament: A Proposal for Fixing the Election Date at the Federal Level in Canada", Paper presented to the Annual Meeting of the Canadian Political Science Association, Quebec City, 1976.

[56] See Thomas A. Hockin, "Adversary Politics and the Functions of Canada's House of Commons", in Kruhlak, O. et al. (eds), The Canadian Political Process pp. 361-381.

[57] This point is made by J. R. Happy who also proposes to establish a fixed election date so as to enable MP's " ... to assume a more independent policy-oriented role" ("Optimal Policy-Making" p. 3). D. V. Smiley points to the dangers inherent to that sort of "partnership" ("The Managed Mosaic" p. 39), but, precisely, more independent members, both in the opposition and the majority, could play an "obstructionist" role and still actively participate in the formulation and selection of policy priorities.

[58] T. A. Hockin, "Adversary Politics and the Functions of Canada's House of Commons", in Kruhlak, O. et al. (eds), op. cit. p. 378.

federal-provincial relations. It is generally accepted that we have entered an era of "cooperative" or "executive" federalism in Canada. Cooperation may at times appear lacking (cf. the inconclusiveness of the federal-provincial conferences on energy in the recent past), but the federal and provincial governments have to coordinate their policies in a great many cases, by virtue of necessity.

The reforms discussed previously may not have a direct impact on negotiations carried out at the first ministers' level because there the issues at stake are so obviously political that technical arguments, or even appeals to global rationality, cannot usually sway the decision in a specific direction if the political cost of doing so appears too high.[59] On the contrary, it is generally accepted that

... the more limited the focus of [the] interactions [within the federal-provincial organization] the more likely there is to be agreement—agreement based on the norms of such experts as engineers, correctional officers, public health specialists, professional foresters etc . . . [60]

Because the formal rationality of new planning techniques helps to make these norms more explicit and more "objective" (e.g. better indicators of the effectiveness of a shared cost program), one is tempted to conclude that it should improve the performance of intergovernmental machinery. However, the very premises of such a hypothesis are questionable: it is doubtful whether experts are more likely to agree than politicians. Experts belong to bureaucratic organizations which have their own—not necessarily compatible—goals, and within these organizations they pursue personal interests. Hence divisive conflicts are to be found at this level too.[61] In fact, the growing concern for long-term planning and effectiveness may even make matters worse. For instance, if the two levels of government happen to have their own analytic models and these produce divergent forecasts leading to the choice of divergent priorities, each side will defend its position all the more arduously because it is almost impossible for them to retreat. And what guarantees that, in each case, the selected statistics are relevant to the situation under review, that the criteria used are not biased, etc.?[62]

Such clashes are by no means limited to technical issues. In a broader context, rationalization and federalism, while not incompatible principles, can be difficult to conciliate. As D. V. Smiley observes,

---

[59] Nevertheless these arguments can be used as technical weapons, see R. Simeon, *Federal-Provincial Diplomacy* (Toronto, 1972), Chapter 2.

[60] D. V. Smiley, *Canada in Question: Federalism in the Seventies*, (Toronto, 1972), p. 60.

[61] See Chapter 19 in this volume.

[62] Manitoba, Ontario and Quebec have already adopted PPBS; Saskatchewan has more recently developed a variant of it which is supposed to be more in tune with the needs of the line managers. See D. M. Wallace, "Budget Reform in Saskatchewan: A New Approach to Program Based Management", *Canadian Public Administration*, XVII (1974), No. 4, pp. 586-99.

The new organizational strategies have important consequences for federal-provincial relations. To the extent that governments proceed in terms of comprehensive and precisely-formulated goals there are more incentives than otherwise to reduce the uncertainties of their external environments, including of course the actions of other governments in the federal system.[63]

Indirectly contradicting his earlier statement discussed previously, but not without reasons, the author adds in a forceful manner:

Thus despite the vast amount of incantation both from Canadian scholars and Canadian officials about the need for federal-provincial coordination and the alleged association between such coordination and rationality, the increased sophistication of these governments leads directly to conflicts of a somewhat intractable kind.[64]

That is to say that rationality does not mean the same thing to everyone. Of course, the first ministers can overcome some technical obstacles on an *ad hoc* basis, but in the long run they cannot altogether avoid these "intractable" conflicts.

Conclusion

To clarify goals, to determine alternative courses of action (presumably choosing "optimal" ones among them) by relying on quantitative information and sophisticated analytical techniques, and to assign responsibilities for their achievement are, as we have seen, the principles which have inspired the reforms discussed in this paper. There is no doubt that they were needed in some degree to adapt the policy-making process to a changing environment, notwithstanding their conceptual limitations (e.g. the fallacy of the optimum) and the triumph of form over substance (e.g. the performance of the Ministries of State). But if necessary, they were not, as we have suggested, sufficient cause to rationalize the political process as a whole. It appears that the primary motivation for some, if not all, of these reforms is not so much to make policy-making more rational as to deliberately redirect the flows of information and thus to alter the power structure. Yet the logic of the political system is often that the "medium is the message": the means ought to be more sacrosanct than the ends. The relative decline of Cabinet as a collective decision-making body is a case in point here—another being the failure to reduce the imbalance between Parliament and the executive. Yet if the ultimate purpose of politics is to satisfy some, if not all, of society's expectations, then administrative or political reforms decreasing governmental responsiveness (e.g. centralization at the prime ministerial level, or the creation of yet more causes for federal-provincial conflicts) should be regarded as substantively irrational. Nevertheless, governmental responsiveness does not have to be understood as a pas-

---

[63] D. V. Smiley, "Federal-Provincial Conflict in Canada", *Publius*, Summer 1974, p. 19-20.

[64] *Ibid*, p. 20.

sive and *a posteriori* reaction to societal demands; what is needed is a more global planning approach in the development of which political scientists should play a major part. Unfortunately the political science community in Canada has devoted relatively less attention to policy-making than to the "input" side of the political process, although this is now changing.[65] It is crucial to reestablish the primacy of the political dimension in policy analysis, without negating the contributions made by other disciplines and approaches. One would hope that such efforts will help policy-makers stay clear of the pitfalls of excessive faith in technocratic solutions on the one hand, and of confusing political constraints with value judgements, on the other hand.

[65] This point is well argued by Peter Aucoin and Dale Poel ("A Political Science Perspective on Public Policy Analysis", paper presented to the Annual Meeting of the Canadian Political Science Association, Quebec City, 1976)

19

Prime Ministerial Government, Central Agencies, and Operating Departments: Towards a More Realistic Analysis*

RICHARD SCHULTZ

There is almost universal agreement that the last decade has seen a continuing effort to make the Prime Minister a more effective "chief executive". One major result of the quest for greater effectiveness at the centre has been a debate over the consequences of increased power at the centre on other actors in the parliamentary system. Critics have argued that Prime Minister Trudeau's initiatives with respect to his office and the Privy Council Office have fundamentally transformed the nature of the Canadian parliamentary system. The thesis of strong central control associated with "prime ministerial government" has also emerged in studies of federal-provincial negotiations where it has been argued that the fundamental characteristic of contemporary intergovernmental relations is the dominance of central agencies and the exclusion of other participants except in a strictly supportive role.[1]

In an effort to test this latter hypothesis, the author's research on a particular case of protracted federal-provincial negotiations focussed on the role of central agencies in that conflict. Federal officials in both operating departments and central agencies were interviewed to ascertain their roles in the conflict but were, in addition, questioned at length about their general perceptions about the relative roles and resources of different actors and the nature of relationships between such actors within the federal government. The results of this research, although admittedly based on but

---

* Adapted for this volume from the Conclusion of the author's "Federalism, Bureaucrats and Public Policy: A Study of the Making of Transportation Policy", Unpublished Ph.D. York University, 1976.
[1] Richard Simeon, *Federal-Provincial Diplomacy*, (Toronto, 1972) esp. pp. 35-39.

one case, may have broader significance in that they suggest the centralization thesis has been exaggerated and indicate the need for more realistic
assumptions about the role of central co-ordination. It would appear that
analysis of the role of central agencies needs to be far more subtle than is
suggested by the term "strong central control". Indeed, Bruce Doern's
conclusion that "the Treasury Board is caricatured too much as the bogey-
man of the present structure, and . . . deserves a more thoughtful analysis"[2]
appears to be equally appropriate for other central agencies such as the
P.M.O. and P.C.O.

The case study from which this article is derived was on the protracted
negotiations surrounding the question of implementation of Part III of the
National Transportation Act of 1967. The federal government, by means of
this section, sought to assume the power to regulate the extra-provincial
motor carrier industry which had been delegated to the provinces by
means of the Motor Vehicle Transport Act of 1954 as a result of the
Winner decision of the Privy Council. Part III was considered by its
defenders to be a fundamental component of the N.T.A. because the extra-
provincial trucking industry was the main competitor for the railways and,
in fact, its growth has been credited with setting in motion "the process
which culminated in passage of the National Transportation Act."[3] As a
result, regulation of the industry was crucial if the Canadian Transport
Commission was to fulfill its basic mandate to "co-ordinate and harmonize" the operations of all carriers under federal jurisdiction.

The negotiations on Part III were conducted at both the ministerial and
official level over a period of five years from 1967 to 1972. At the end of
the negotiations, Part III had still not been implemented and the federal
objective had been frustrated. The purpose of the study was to explain the
failure to implement Part III. The answer was found in the conflict, not
between the two levels of government in Canada but within the federal
government. The provinces were victors in this particular round of intergovernmental conflict because they were able to exploit the conflict that
existed between the Canadian Transport Commission and the Ministry of
Transport to further their own objectives.

Although no claim is made that this particular issue was necessarily a
typical example, the conflict on Part III did provide an excellent opportunity to test Richard Simeon's argument that senior Cabinet ministers and
central agencies now dominate the intergovernmental bargaining process.
In contrast to Simeon's findings, the study found that no actor or group of
actors was able to dominate the other principal federal actors. Far from
unity and single-minded purpose within the federal government, which are
supposed to result from central control, there was endemic and pervasive
conflict on values, goals, strategies and tactics. In the intergovernmental
negotiations, the federal government seldom spoke with one voice; when it

[2] Bruce Doern, *Science & Politics in Canada*, (Montreal, 1971) p. 205.
[3] Hon. E. J. Benson, President of the Canadian Transport Commission, Speech to the
M.O.T. Senior Management Training Course, October 26, 1973, p. 5.

did the voice was muted. On other occasions, the federal government spoke with multiple, conflicting voices. Insofar as actors from the central agencies were concerned, they played a distinctly secondary role, that of ally for one or the other of the principal factions. In the end, far from being able to dominate the other actors and dictate an agreement or even force the combatants to resolve their differences the major impact of central agencies was to cause a stalemate. The federal government was never able to resolve its internal disputes with the result that the intergovernmental negotiations went into limbo. This analysis of the intergovernmental bargaining process and the impact of bargaining within one government on that process has prompted the following speculations which suggest that much more research is required on the role of central agencies within the federal government. The comments that follow are not presented as conclusions but rather are intended to suggest some of the variables that should be considered in any such research.

In the following discussion the focus will be on the relationship between central agencies and operating departments and through this relationship, between the Prime Minister and his Cabinet colleagues. Although no "hard" evidence is provided in this paper to support the arguments, my Ph.D. thesis research upon which this discussion is based would suggest that the growth of power and effectiveness at the centre is a question of relativity that involves not only a comparison with circumstances prior to the changes introduced under Trudeau but also reflects obstacles that still exist. There seems to have been a general acceptance at face value of the claims of some of the critics of such changes as if they represent reality rather than at best the hopes of the architects. In truth, departmental actors are not easily excluded or dominated by actors from central agencies. In fact, central agencies may be in a far weaker position than is commonly assumed. The following discussion outlines some of the reasons why this may be the case.

In the first place while much has been made of the growth in the size of the central agencies, the disproportionate distribution of manpower resources between central agencies and the operating departments must be recognized. A brief examination of the Government of Canada telephone directory will suffice to demonstrate this fact. Within the Ministry of Transport's Ottawa headquarters, for example, there are more officials at the Director level and above than there are total staff in the newly-created Federal-Provincial Relations Office.[4] Notwithstanding popular tales of the topsy-like growth, the staff within central agencies are over-burdened and over-extended with responsibilities. In the Federal-Provincial Relations Office, for example, an officer will be responsible for monitoring not only two or three departments but several provinces as well. Much the same

[4] When P. M. Pitfield was appointed Clerk of the Privy Council and Secretary to the Cabinet, the Federal-Provincial Relations Office was created with R. G. Robertson, the former Clerk, appointed Secretary to the Cabinet for Federal-Provincial Relations. The new office was created by statute, Bill C-38, in December, 1974. See the statement by the Prime Minister and subsequent debate in the House of Commons, December 18, 1974.

situation applies in the case of the Privy Council Office and the Prime Minister's Office. Given what is in fact a situation of limited manpower and the scope of programs and policies that such personnel must monitor, central agencies face serious handicaps such that their capabilities are stretched if they are required to participate intensively in more than a few issue areas at any one time.

The problems central agencies face, however, are not simply those of numbers of either men or issues. The more critical problems relate to the nature of the individuals and issues. The complexity of most issues requires reliance upon specialists. Such specialists are primarily found in the operating departments and such departmental specialization is an important resource in the intra-governmental policy formation process. For their part, central agency officials are normally not familiar to any great degree with the substance of any issue. What must be remembered is that central agencies are staffed by individuals who, while they may indeed be specialists in the "machinery of government" or in intergovernmental relations, are essentially amateurs and generalists when specific policy issues are involved. Furthermore, policies usually emerge in response to specific problems rather than from the application of any "grand strategy". In the intergovernmental policy arena, although some central agency officials may wax enthusiastic over the development of "common policies of all federal-provincial relationships"[5], thereby strengthening the role of such officials, agreement on such common policies or a "grand strategy" is likely to be either so elusive or else at such a level of generality as to be virtually useless as a guide on a specific issue. Similarly, the Trudeau Government's recent "priorities exercise" encountered such fundamental roadblocks that the results were ignored and the exercise was ultimately abandoned.[6]

It is in the interactions between central agencies and operating departments that such variables as manpower resources and expertise become significant. In such interactions, contrary to the assumptions of "strong executive authority" made by the critics of "prime ministerial government", it can be argued that the process is in fact tilted in favour of departments and not central agencies. Departments are normally the initiators of the policy process. Simply because problem and issue definition are crucial aspects of this process and because such tasks are initially and principally departmental responsibilities the departments gain enormous leverage over the process. Departments are also the primary sources of policy alternatives and because they ultimately must implement any program that emerges, these functions further ensure that departmental preferences will be accorded due respect. Moreover, some departments for a number of reasons such as their prestige, their mandate, their expertise, their minister of the day, may be extremely aggressive in asserting their

---

[5] This was the comment of a senior Ontario official quoted in Simeon, *Federal-Provincial Diplomacy*, p. 37.

[6] See the report on the "priorities exercise" in the *Toronto Star*, Nov. 7, 1975.

prerogative to perform their responsibilities with only minimal policy guidance or co-ordination from central agencies. Indeed, such departments may not fully accept the coordinating role assigned to central agencies, particularly insofar as the P.M.O. is concerned as this office is looked upon with suspicion and a not insignificant degree of apprehension over its legitimacy.

Another important consideration in the interactive process between central agencies and departments is the question of timing. Departments, while they may indeed concede that at some point in the process central agencies will have to be involved, may work to ensure that at that point their position is favoured. Departments, for example, may attempt to mobilize sufficient support among other principal actors such that by the time central agencies become involved they may be faced with a virtual "fait accompli" endorsed by all other relevant actors. Central agencies, under such circumstances, face severe constraints in choosing among competing options. Another departmental tactic may be to bide one's time and not go to central agencies until the last moment when a decision is imperative and there is little opportunity to canvass seriously alternative proposals.

When central agencies are major participants in the policy process it must be recognized that departments may not necessarily defer to them in cases of conflict and, if forced "to do battle", possess significant resources. One such resource, already mentioned, is information control which if exploited imaginatively can influence any outcome. Departments may flood central agencies with information which they have neither the expertise nor time to digest. Alternatively, departments may provide only the barest minimum of information with central agencies unable to generate additional information. Another tactic, apparently a common one, is to provide biased information with central agencies again facing severe constraints in their ability to assess such information.

In doing battle with central agencies departments may exploit certain bargaining tactics such as the mobilization of necessary support, mentioned earlier, and/or dividing the opposition. Departments may attempt to play off actors within central agencies against one another and this may be easiest in terms of the partisan-bureaucratic divide between the P.M.O. and P.C.O. Within the bureaucratic "non-partisan" central agencies, this tactic may also be possible with the "hiving off" of the Federal-Provincial Relations Office from the Privy Council Office. Furthermore, if it thinks its cabinet submission can get a more favourable reception, a department may try to have it referred to the more receptive Cabinet Committee. A department may, for example, seek to have the Cabinet's Social Policy Committee rather than the Federal-Provincial Relations Committee consider an issue or, alternatively if this does not succeed, at least have a joint committee meeting in order to offset the role of federal-provincial relations officials.

Another aspect of the interactive process is that some senior officials may hold the view that the role of central agencies is not to adopt, or lobby for, a specific course of action but to ensure that all the actors within the government who should be, are, in fact, consulted. If departments respect this principle, even in the most perfunctory manner, then central agencies may have little alternative but to go along with a department's proposals. On other occasions, central agency actors may in fact have no particular viewpoint on an issue with the result they may be reduced to playing the role of spectator or perhaps passive ally of those who are advocating acceptance of a specific course of action. The efficacy of central agencies may also be affected if they adopt a less restrictive or passive role. In the intergovernmental arena, for instance, in some circumstances actors from central agencies may bring to bear on an issue a perspective that emphasizes a desire to establish or maintain a harmonious relationship with provincial governments, a perspective which may well lead to conflict with a departmental concern for the implementation of a specific program regardless of provincial wishes. In this context, it may be accurate to suggest that at times central agency actors responsible for federal-provincial relations regard the provinces as their clientele or constituency with the result that far from being impartial umpires or coordinators, they may act, or be perceived, as partisans or advocates in a dispute. This may diminish the legitimacy of any claim to be co-ordinators in the eyes of the various actors involved. Furthermore, it is a plausible hypothesis that central agencies have reached the pinnacle of their influence in the area of intergovernmental relations and now may face somewhat of a decline. During the 1960's, as intergovernmental relations became increasingly complex, officials in the Privy Council Office responsible for such relations gained pre-eminence because, while they were generalists in a policy sense, they became in fact specialists in the process of intergovernmental relations. It was the complexity of intergovernmental relations in the 1960's that helped to establish the influence of such intergovernmental specialists. This influence may be being attenuated, however, as operating departments respond to this complexity by establishing their own specialized intergovernmental relations units.[7] Such specialists within departments may challenge the competence of, and compete for influence with, the central agency process specialists.

The purpose of this discussion is not to deny the influential role played by central agencies but to pose a challenge to some of the more exaggerated claims about such a role. Nor is the argument that all actors within the government are equal for such an argument misrepresents "both constitutional and political reality".[8] The basic weakness of the argument concerning the contemporary role of central agencies, vis à vis operating departments and consequently, the relationship between the Prime Minister and his Cabinet is its extreme generality. There is simply not enough known about the scope for autonomy of operating depart-

---

[7] As of December 1975, there are ten departments with units specializing in intergovernmental relations.

[8] Keohane & Nye, "Transgovernmental Relations and International Organizations", World Politics XXVII (Oct. 1974), p. 43.

ments or about the role of central agencies in the policy process. Central agencies may indeed dominate other actors within the government but we need to know at what cost, by what means and for how long. The basic questions are under what conditions do they attempt to dominate and why and how do they succeed.

Rather than assuming that central agencies dominate other actors, much more attention should be played to the complex nature of the roles played by central agencies. Such an analysis should not stress "hierarchical controls" at the disposal of central agencies for it is debatable whether, in fact, such agencies possess such controls *vis à vis* operating departments. Power in a parliamentary system would appear to be much more diffused than is suggested by either the term "hierarchical controls" or the emphasis on "prime ministerial" power. Although it is conceded that some Cabinet portfolios possess more power than others[9] and that is an unequal power relationship that consequently exists between members of the Cabinet, it is not strictly a hierarchical relationship between the Prime Minister and his colleagues because it must be emphasized, they are his colleagues and not his unquestioning subordinates. One major reason for this has been recognized by the editor of this volume: "Ministers, in fact, are institutionally responsible to the Cabinet, not to the Prime Minister. If a "presidential" system was to be installed in the place of present cabinet-prime ministerial relations, Ministers would be made responsible to the Prime Minister alone and not to the Cabinet at all. Deputy Ministers could report to the Prime Minister alone and not to the Cabinet at all".[10] It is because of the relationship that exists between Cabinet, Ministers and Prime Minister that operating departments are not the subordinates of the central agencies although they may, like their ministers, on occasion be dominated by them. If this perspective is a valid one, central agencies should be viewed as providing but one set of actors among many within the government who rather than being in a position to dictate to others, must "influence, bargain with and persuade" their colleagues. According to this perspective central agencies play a variety of roles such as co-ordinator "knocking heads together", "watch-dog" or "gate-keeper", evaluator, goal-setter, monitor and advocate or partisan. The influence of central agencies, it is suggested, will vary according to which one of these roles, or combination thereof, these agencies play in specific instances. An analysis of the variety and complexity of the roles played by central agencies could add significantly to an understanding of the dynamics of the policy process both within and between governments in Canada.

The basic argument of this discussion of the relations between central agencies and operating departments is that power, in fact, is far more

---

[9] G. Bruce Doern, "Horizontal and Vertical Portfolios in Government," in Doern & Wilson (eds.), *Issues in Canadian Public Policy*.

[10] T. A. Hockin, "The Prime Minister and Political Leadership: An Introduction to Some Restraints and Imperatives", Chapter 1 in this volume. See also Joseph Wearing's "President or Prime Minister", Chapter 26 in this volume.

dispersed and diffused than is suggested by some of the commentaries on the impact of the changes introduced by Prime Minister Trudeau in an attempt to increase his effectiveness as "chief executive". As a result of this diffusion of power there are many actors contending to influence and shape the direction the government takes on any issue. Equally important is the fact that issues are seldom clear-cut but rather are multi-faceted. Different actors and units within a government, for a variety of reasons, will disagree on the nature of an issue and will consequently disagree on the nature of the objectives to be pursued or the means for attaining those objectives. Many actors may have a stake in the decision and because the process of arriving at a governmental decision on an issue will involve the shared prerogatives of a number of individuals and organizations, with perhaps no actor in a position, or willing, to impose a decision on the others involved, there will need to be bargaining, competition, negotiations and compromise.

This bargaining is usually behind the scenes in a parliamentary system rather than public, as it is to a large extent, in a presidential system like that of the United States.[11] In large part because of the non-public nature of this bargaining process, supported as it is by the canons of collective responsibility and the entrenched high regard for secrecy, there simply has not been adequate attention paid to the importance of intra-governmental conflict in the policy process. An additional consequence has been that, for want of evidence, some of the more exaggerated claims about the impact of Trudeau's changes have gone largely unchallenged. We need to recognize the potential for competition and conflict and consequently need to know much more about such competition and conflict and the battles and bargains within the government. We need to determine what resources the various actors possess and to examine how they exploit such resources to influence the outcome of the policy-making process. A basic justification for such studies is that the process of determining a position on an issue is recognized to be a serious determinant of the substance of that position. A further justification is that such studies should lead to a more realistic appraisal of the nature and extent of "prime ministerial" government in Canada.

---

[11] For an excellent study of the bargaining process within the British Government, between Treasury and the "spending departments", see Hugh Heclo and Aaron Wildavsky, *The Private Government of Public Money*. For an "insider's" view of "Whitehall politics" see Richard Crossman, *The Myths of Cabinet Government*, esp. pp. 41-76.

20

The Government's Legislative Programme and Its Linkage to Parliament*

R. J. JACKSON AND M. M. ATKINSON

The first operation in the development of a legislative program occurs when the Clerk of the Privy Council writes to heads of departments and agencies to request their list of proposed legislation and details about the availability and urgency of each item. This preparatory step normally occurs approximately one year before the parliamentary session for which these items are intended. When they arrive in the PCO, the legislative proposals are classified according to government goals and priorities. The initial analysis of the proposals is made by an ad hoc committee of officials from PCO, PMO, the Department of Justice and, more recently, the Office of the President of the Privy Council. Departments which submit proposals may prefer to believe that they are in a constant state of readiness to pursue them, but it is intended that this committee should review departmental proposals in terms of practical impediments such as drafting deadlines, administrative requirements and parliamentary feasibility. Although the committee does not meet again to review this list, its participants advise the leading political actors in the policy prism about the progress of each item in both parts of the legislative system.

The reformulated list of legislative proposals is forwarded to the Prime Minister and the Cabinet Committee on Priorities and Planning. Together they establish the political criteria on the basis of which items are chosen from the list. Either the Cabinet Committee on Legislation and House Planning or an ad hoc committee selects the specific items which will be developed by departments. The process of these cabinet committee meetings is somewhat similar to that suggested by the mixed scanning model in

* Acknowledgment for use of this selection is extended to Macmillan of Canada for permission to reprint pages 62-73 of R. J. Jackson and M. M. Atkinson, *The Canadian Legislative System* (Toronto: Macmillan, 1974).

that politicians examine some of the proposals in detail while other proposals receive only a brief mention. Relatively minor bills and departmental housekeeping items are of almost no interest to ministers. On occasion some of these bills have been included on future legislative programs even though literally no one outside the department knew anything about them. The selection process may become so undisciplined that in some circumstances a legislative item could be chosen even though it had a low ministerial or departmental priority. When cabinet finally settles on the content of the program, the PCO employs the decision to prod departments into bringing forward legislation, and the PMO uses it to write the first draft of the Speech from the Throne.

The development of this list of legislative proposals provides, in practical terms, the most important occasion for significant political contribution to the whole program. The list instructs departments and agencies about overall cabinet preferences and in the year prior to an election it also becomes part of the government's total campaign strategy. Since at least a year is required from the construction of this program to the writing of policy memos, the drafting of bills and, finally, the introduction of legislation in Parliament, there is little scope for the addition of items except for emergencies. The constraints of time make it extremely important, therefore, that when the cabinet's decision on the content of the program is circulated to departments, the government's political thrust be at the heart of it. Such emphasis on the government's philosophy is often missing in the face of the demands on the program emanating from items carried over from earlier sessions of Parliament, statutory requirements, departmental aspirations, and recommendations and reports of task forces and royal commissions. As we have pointed out, the presence of a political thrust in the legislative program requires ministers, or the Prime Minister, to have a clear conception of what the government wishes to achieve. If there is no commitment to espoused goals, then ministers will be forced to negotiate, on an individual basis, with groups in the legislative system and may find they are unable to withstand special interests or the conservative forces in the public service.

In addition to the difficulties inherent in relating the legislative program to the government's predetermined goals, the central coordinating agencies have not devised adequate means of forcing individual departments to respond to the legislative program, nor have they succeeded in coordinating the multitude of stages involved in both parts of the legislative system. On occasion, the government has even run out of legislation to place before the House of Commons and at other times there have been so few draft bills available that cabinet has been unable to enjoy the luxury of a selection.

The development of the legislative program imposes a framework and a timetable on departmental formulation of pieces of legislation. The sources of legislation are numerous. Political parties, interest groups, and occasionally members of Parliament suggest legislative initiatives, but it is the administration and evaluation of existing programs which usually provides the inspiration for ministerial and bureaucratic measures.

If a minister merely wishes to make minor administrative amendments to the law, he is likely to submit a legislative proposal which may be channelled quickly through the system. If, on the other hand, he intends to change government policy or emphasis he will be required to follow a more difficult route. He must first submit a policy memorandum to cabinet. The Prime Minister through the PCO will determine which subject-matter committee will receive the memorandum and when it will be placed on their agenda. Prior to the original submission it is likely that interdepartmental committees will have attempted to ensure that the new policy is coherent and consistent with other government activities. It is also their task to anticipate and resolve ministerial conflict which could emerge in cabinet. At the cabinet committee meeting, two perspectives will be brought to bear on the policy memorandum. It will be placed in its widest possible setting and discussed in terms of its political impact. Discussion will also concentrate on the details and technical requirements of the policy. Policies are usually so long in the developmental stages, often being returned to departments for reconsideration, that experienced ministers have been thoroughly briefed by their own officials, been approached by interest groups, and been engaged in lengthy discussions with caucus and individual members of Parliament.

When the complex process of achieving a cabinet decision on the policy memorandum is completed, different governmental structures become involved.[1] Cabinet first approves the legislative proposal for drafting. At this stage the sponsoring department is supposed to provide a comprehensive set of instructions to the drafting office of the Department of Justice so that drafting in both official languages may begin. Usually, however, the original policy memorandum serves as the basis for drafting and because of its general nature draftsmen often encounter inconsistencies and situations in which policy details have not been related to existing Canadian statutes. In the discussion between drafting officials and the sponsoring department, minor policy is made in the resolution of these difficulties. Some officials consider that the final policy impact is influenced almost as much by these details as by the original policy memorandum. "You can have the policy, leave the details to me," has been the philosophy of at least some senior administrators. Moreover, in their quest to provide unity to Canadian law the draftsmen also make what might be called "legal policy inputs." If drafting considerations were made an integral part of policy formation, perhaps some of the practical difficulties could be anticipated and the legal details could be made to serve the general policy intention. In the United Kingdom preliminary drafts of bills are circulated to all departments to provide extensive opportunities for senior officials to comment on the legal and administrative ramifications.

When the sponsoring minister accepts the draft legislation, it is returned to cabinet via the Committee on Legislation and House Planning. This committee, chaired by the President of the Privy Council, attempts to

---

[1] E. A. Driedger, "Legislative Drafting," *Canadian Bar Review*, XXVII, No. 3 (March 1949), pp. 291-317.

examine the draft bill clause by clause to ascertain if it accords with the policy memorandum, and to determine the reception it is likely to receive in the House of Commons. In the minority situation following the 1972 election, cabinet ministers used this setting to inform their colleagues of discussions they had held with opposition spokesmen about the passage of their bills. Nevertheless, this committee tends to be preoccupied with the legal expression of government policy. In recent years departments have appended an explanatory memorandum to the draft bill to aid ministers in the discussion of its technical and legal aspects. The chairman is briefed by officials in his own office and by the Legislation and House Planning Secretariat of the Privy Council Office. Draftsmen are always in attendance and lawyers on the committee furnish much of the debate.

If the committee is generally dissatisfied with the draft legislation, it is returned to a subject-matter committee. Normally, however, the committee makes only minor changes, approves the bill, and relays it to cabinet for inclusion on the agenda for items requiring only perfunctory approval. The draft bill is then submitted to the Prime Minister for his signature. The formal transmittal to Parliament occurs when the draft bill, signed by the Prime Minister, is sent to the Clerk of the appropriate House for introduction. At this stage, parliamentary strategy and tactics become paramount and the structures which link the pre-parliamentary and the parliamentary stages of the system go into operation. This does not end cabinet's legislative role either in Parliament or after the successful passage of the bill. Most statutes require the government to develop detailed regulations for the administration of the general provisions and these are given legal authority by orders-in-council, of which cabinet passes approximately six thousand annually.

Coordination of the legislative system has occasionally suffered from inadequate attention to the time required to complete the various stages of the process. On some occasions the government may be without sufficient parliamentary time to handle its available legislation and on others it over-taxes institutions in the pre-parliamentary stages in order to obtain a minimum number of bills. The difficulties may be illustrated by an incident related among members of the Department of Justice. In replying to a command for the immediate production of a very difficult bill, a senior official told the Prime Minister that it reminded him of a story. A young child, after having been promised a baby brother by Christmas, was told by his mother that there was no longer enough time available. Somewhat dejected, he suggested that his mother do what his father would do—"Hire more men!" When cabinet shifts priorities to cope with emergencies or to introduce new ideas, the time difficulties are understandable. But when the government runs out of legislation or demands that Parliament work over-time, it is often due to a lack of coordination in the legislative system which could be corrected by an overhaul of some of the structures.

Linkages with Parliament

In a parliamentary form of government it is necessary to remember that the executive and the legislature in combination form the legislative system. In chapter 2 we treated conceptually the links between the executive and the legislature and outlined the functions this system performs. The structures that actually link the institutions in the inner circle with Parliament have often been underestimated in descriptions of the organization of Canadian government. The crucial factor in this linkage is the requirement that members of cabinet hold a position in the House of Commons or the Senate. This simple requirement structures the activities of virtually every institution and the behaviour of every actor in both parts of the legislative system. Neither the legislature nor the executive could operate democratically if ministers did not have to defend in Parliament their legislative proposals and account for the actions of their departments before their parliamentary peers. Bagehot's classic description of cabinet as "a hyphen which joins, a buckle which fastens" may fail to appreciate the contemporary role of the Prime Minister, but it remains the most appropriate metaphor to describe the nature of the executive-parliamentary link.

In addition to the pervasive influence of overlapping membership, several devices exist to bridge activities in both parts of the legislative system. The results of these linkages are reminiscent of open convenants, secretly arrived at. The Throne Speech, which is read by the Governor General in the Senate chambers at the beginning of every session, outlines what has been prepared in the inner circle for presentation to Parliament. It is considered by cabinet to be the most important public statement of its political intentions. It forms the basis for all parliamentary business and as such should be used in evaluating cabinet's performance in governing the country. The Throne Speech consists of a rather vague statement of government goals and the legislative program which the government will place before Parliament. Ideally, the goals and priorities would be the same as those which had been used by the Cabinet Committee on Priorities and Planning to determine departmental priorities and new policy directions. The Throne Speech, which includes a summary of the legislative program discussed earlier, is drafted by the PMO or PCO and, like any important document, is discussed in cabinet. Unfortunately, the utility of this link is diminished by the weakness already present in the relation between goals and legislative proposals.

In 1968 the British practice of attaching a list of all the legislative proposals was included in the Canadian Speech from the Throne. In this fashion the government informed the House of its entire program and thereby encouraged both public servants and parliamentarians to focus on the relationship among the policies and bills. Despite this, and the fact that the cabinet considers it a significant political document, the government was reluctant to have the public judge its accomplishments against the promises in the Throne Speech. In fact, governments often depart from the original list of legislative items and sometimes introduce trial balloon bills merely to ascertain the reactions of Parliament and the public. In light of this, the government must be prepared to accept that a degree of cynicism will accompany the introduction of any legislation.

Once the Throne Speech has been delivered, the government deposits with Parliament its bills, estimates, regulations, white papers, the reports of royal commissions and advisory committees, and those departmental and agency reports required by statute. The avalanche of documents is accompanied by ministerial answers to thousands of written and oral questions both on the floor of the House of Commons and in its committees. Such activities are organized for the government by the Prime Minister, the Government House Leader and their advisors. Negotiation on substantive issues is required with government followers in the House and on the scheduling of government business with the leaders of other parliamentary parties. Coordination with the government caucus is facilitated by the fact that it always meets the day after Priorities and Planning and the day before full cabinet. The four parliamentary house leaders meet at the beginning of each week to plan the sequence of parliamentary activities.

The task of linking the executive to Parliament falls most heavily on the caucus of the governing party. The government caucus is composed of all party members who support the government. An elected chairman presides over meetings and maintains continuous contact with backbenchers and the House Leader. Cabinet ministers attend caucus and provide information about pending government policy which serves as a foundation for caucus debate. Much of this information is given before caucus committees whose terms of reference parallel, to some extent, cabinet's subject-matter committees and the standing committees of the House of Commons.

This open forum affords opportunities to discuss and reconcile divergent opinions. Backbenchers occasionally use caucus to demonstrate to the Prime Minister that divisions exist in the cabinet, and individual ministers may employ it to illustrate that support exists for their pet projects. Caucus is able to amend, stall and even stop legislation when it is cohesive and has the support of at least some provinces or some interest groups. In recent sessions of Parliament the Liberal caucus has, for example, succeeded in delaying parliamentary consideration of the Young Offenders bill and in halting a minor amendment to the British North America Act which would have increased the size of Parliament. Most of the time, however, the government can obtain, at minimum, acquiescence in its policies and in its schedule of business for the House. The preeminence of the Prime Minister and cabinet exerts unarticulated psychological pressures on caucus members, even within their own jurisdiction. In addition, there are some organizational advantages available to the Prime Minister, particularly his traditional prerogative to review the substance of the entire meeting immediately before adjournment. When Prime Minister Trudeau was openly criticized by an outspoken member of caucus over the government's foreign ownership bill, he utilized this prerogative to reply that all viewpoints had been heard, compromises made and that no new major amendments could be entertained. Frequently, as in this case, outspoken caucus members will encounter opprobrium from their colleagues and feel conscious of the need to refrain from such open confrontations in the future.

Every party in Parliament can claim a direct link with the executive through the consultation among House leaders which takes place each week in the office of the Government House Leader. While each minister conducts a defence of his department in the House, it is the Government House Leader who represents the interests of the entire cabinet in its parliamentary interface. He is in charge of his party's whip and manages the flow of business and the innumerable personal matters which are so important to individual members of Parliament. The House Leader's meeting has become the forum where all parties are told of the manner in which the government intends to use parliamentary resources and the place for negotiation over the scheduling of parliamentary and committee activities. The amount of time devoted to a legislative item and the procedures to be adopted during its passage exert considerable influence on the likelihood of its success. Since Prime Minister Trudeau came to office in 1968, and especially since the 1972 election, the responsibility for negotiating solutions to parliamentary problems has rested heavily on the four House leaders because of their sensitivity to the mood and the sometimes cumbersome mechanisms of the House of Commons.

If we juxtapose the personal influence which the Government House Leader exercises over the parliamentary timetable with the fragmentation of responsibility in the pre-parliamentary part of the legislative system, it can be appreciated that a certain incoherence in policy formation and legislative action may occasionally emerge. It is somewhat incongruous that the government should erect a complex set of institutions for the development of legislation without considering how it might strengthen all the linkages in the legislative system. When the government introduced its monumental tax bill in the fall of 1971, parliamentary advisors soon realized that the bill had been drafted with so few clauses and so many sections that a united opposition could stall the bill by forcing a debate on what sections required a vote, or by debating and voting on almost every sentence. This and other procedural questions required renewed cabinet deliberation and set in motion a series of private meetings between representatives from the Departments of Finance and Revenue, the PCO, the PMO, and the Office of the President of the Privy Council. The issue was finally resolved, with the aid of an all-night parliamentary sitting, but if more foresight and concern for parliamentary procedures had been demonstrated at the drafting stage, some of the obstacles could have been avoided.

There has been a general unwillingness among both parliamentarians and public servants to accept that they share a responsibility for the entire legislative system. The first requirement in the reform of the Canadian legislative system is to improve these inchoate links between the executive and Parliament. If the inner circle is to supply the guns and ammunition for what Trudeau has called Canada's parliamentary "Coney Island shooting gallery" then actors in the inner circle will be obliged to become more aware of the procedures, activities and functions of Parliament.

SELECTED BIBLIOGRAPHY

Since the first edition of this book was published a considerable number of articles, reports and books dealing with policy-making in the federal government have appeared. The following is a selected bibliography for those interested in pursuing issues raised in this section of *Apex of Power*.

AQUINO, THOMAS D', "The Prime Minister's Office: Catalyst or Cabal?", *Canadian Public Administration*, Vol. XVII (1974), no. 1, pp. 55-79.

AUCOIN, PETER, and R. FRENCH., *Knowledge, Power and Public Policy*, Science Council of Canada, Background Study no. 31, Ottawa, 1974.

BENJAMIN, JACQUES, "La rationalisation des choix budgétaires: les cas québécois et canadien", *Canadian Journal of Political Science*, Vol. V (1972), no. 3, pp. 348-64.

BIRD, RICHARD, *The Growth of Government Spending in Canada*, Toronto: Canadian Tax Foundation, 1970.

CANADIAN COUNCIL ON SOCIAL DEVELOPMENT, *Social Indicators*, Proceedings of a Seminar, Ottawa, January 13-14, 1972.

DOERN, G. BRUCE, "Recent Changes in the Philosophy of Policy-Making in Canada", *Canadian Journal of Political Science*, Vol. IV (1971), no. 2, pp. 243-264.

————, *Political Policy-Making: A Commentary on the Economic Council's Eighth Annual Review and the Ritchie Report*, Montreal: The Private Planning Association of Canada, 1972.

DOERN, G. BRUCE and PETER AUCOIN, eds., *The Structures of Policy-Making in Canada*, Toronto: Macmillan of Canada, 1971. In this volume, see especially Aucoin, Peter, "Theory and Research in the Study of Policy-Making" (pp. 10-38); Doern, G. Bruce, "The Development of Policy Organizations in the Executive Arena" (pp. 39-78) and "The Budgetary Process and the Policy Role of the Federal Bureaucracy" (pp. 79-112).

DOERN, G. BRUCE and V. SEYMOUR WILSON, eds., *Issues in Canadian Public Policy*, Toronto: Macmillan of Canada, 1974. See especially two articles by G. Bruce Doern: "Horizontal and Vertical Portfolios in Government" (pp. 310-336), and "The Concept of Regulation and Regulatory Reform" (pp. 408-443).

ECONOMIC COUNCIL OF CANADA, *Design for Decision-Making*, Eighth Annual Review, Ottawa, 1971.

————, *Economic Targets and Social Indicators*, Eleventh Annual Review, Ottawa, 1974.

GOVERNMENT OF CANADA, *Planning Programming Budgeting Guide*, revised ed., Ottawa: Queen's Printer, 1969.

GOW, DONALD, *The Process of Budgetary Reforms in the Government of Canada*, Ottawa: Economic Council of Canada, Special Study no. 17, 1973.

GURUPRASSAD, C., "Planning for Tax Administration in Canada", *Canadian Public Administration*, Vol. XVI (1973), no. 3, pp. 399-421.

HARTLE, D. G., "Operational Performance Measurement in the Federal Government", *Optimum*, Vol. 3 (1972), no. 4, pp. 5-18.

————, *The Objectives of Government Objectives*, mimeo, Ottawa, 1972.

————, *Techniques and Processes of Administration*, A paper presented to the Annual Meeting of the Canadian Institute of Public Administration, September 1975.

HENDERSON, D. W., *Social Indicators: A Rationale and Research Framework*, Ottawa: Economic Council of Canada, 1974.

HODGSON, J. S., "Management by Objectives: The Experience of a Federal Government Department", *Canadian Public Administration*, Vol. XVI (1973), no. 3, pp. 422-31.

JOHNSON, A. W., "Planning, Programming, and Budgeting in Canada", *Public Administration Review*, January 1973, pp. 23-31.

KRUHLAK, OREST M., et al., eds., *The Canadian Political Process*, 2nd ed., Toronto: Holt, Rinehart and Winston, 1973. Particularly relevant are Johnson, A. W., "The Treasury Board of Canada and the Machinery of Government in the 1970's" (pp. 416-437), and Robertson, G., "The Changing Role of the Privy Council Office" (pp. 438-457).

LALONDE, MARC, "The Changing Role of the Prime Minister's Office", *Canadian Public Administration*, Vol. XIV (1971), no. 4, pp. 509-537.

LANGFORD, J. W., "The Ministry of Transport as a Policy-Making Institution", in Studnicki-Gizbert, ed., *Issues in Canadian Transport Policy*, Toronto: Macmillan, pp. 408-443.

MALLORY, J. R., "The Five Faces of Federalism", in Meekison, J. Peter, ed., *Canadian Federalism: Myth or Reality*, 2d ed., Toronto: Methuen, 1971, pp. 55-65.

PRIVY COUNCIL OFFICE, *Policy Planning and Support for Ministerial Decision-Making*, mimeo, Ottawa, 1975.

RITCHIE, RONALD S., "Policy-Making for the Long Term: The Need to Do More", *Canadian Public Administration*, Vol. XVI (1973), no. 1, pp. 73-82.

SIMEON, R., *Federal-Provincial Diplomacy*, Toronto: University of Toronto Press, 1972.

SMILEY, D. V., *Canada in Question: Federalism in the Seventies*, Toronto: McGraw Hill, 1972.

————, "Federal-Provincial Conflict in Canada", *Publius*, Summer 1974, pp. 7-24.

SMITH, D., "Comments on The Prime Minister's Office: Catalyst or Cabal?", *Canadian Public Administration*, Vol. XVII (1974), pp. 80-84.

STARK, F., "The Prime Minister as a Symbol: Unifier or Optimizer?", *Canadian Journal of Political Science*, Vol. VI (1973), no. 3, pp. 516-17.

SZABLOWSKI, GEORGE, "The Optimal Policy-Making System: Implications for the Canadian Political Process", in Hockin, Thomas A, ed., *Apex of Power*, 2nd ed., Toronto: Prentice-Hall, 1977, Chapter 17.

_____ "The Prime Minister as a Symbol: A Rejoinder", *Canadian Journal of Political Science*,Vol. VI (1973), no. 3, pp. 517.

TREASURY BOARD, *Operational Performance Measurement*, Ottawa, 1974.

WHITE, W. L., and J. C. STRICK, *Policy, Politics and the Treasury Board in Canadian Government*, Don Mills, Ont.: Science Research Associates, 1971.

Reflections and Case Studies on the Uses of Prime Ministerial Power

In contrast to the other parts of this book which emphasize the general context of the office, this section by the use of case studies focuses directly on the Prime Minister's exercise of power and influence.

The first selection in this section is composed of the remarks of two Canadian Prime Ministers on dimensions of the office. Mr. Diefenbaker emphasizes the unavoidability of the responsibilities of the office; Mr. Pearson discusses political leadership. Mr. Trudeau's comments taken from various interviews discuss various elements of prime ministerial influence and power. This is followed by comments on similar subjects by Joe Clark, then MP for Rocky Mountain, and elected Leader of the Official Opposition in February 1976; Stanley Knowles, spokesman for the New Democratic Party; and John Reid, spokesman for the governing Liberal party.

In his article, Gerald Wright discusses the general question of Mackenzie King's exercise of power to accomplish his objectives. Peyton Lyon's study centers on a unique event of crisis decision-making.

21

Three Canadian Prime Ministers Discuss the Office

EDITED BY THOMAS A. HOCKIN

Interview with The Right Honourable
John G. Diefenbaker
(Prime Minister of Canada 1957-1963)*

The Prime Minister and Parliament

MR. HOCKIN:

How did your many years of experience in Parliament help you personally as Prime Minister?

MR. DIEFENBAKER:

He who doesn't know Parliament cannot be a good Prime Minister. You say that we've got such a Prime Minister now. We have! And look what has happened to Parliament! The House of Commons today is the most preposterous caricature of Parliament I have ever seen.

MR. HOCKIN:

What disturbs you especially?

MR. DIEFENBAKER:

Were you in the gallery yesterday?

MR. HOCKIN:

Yes.

MR. DIEFENBAKER:

Well, did you learn anything?

MR. WRIGHT:

I don't think you can learn much about the substance of policy.

MR. DIEFENBAKER:

Well I'm not talking about policy. I'm talking about Parliament. 90 per

---

* Interview conducted in Ottawa, Canada, May 7, 1970, by Thomas A. Hockin and Gerald C. V. Wright.

cent of the questions asked in Parliament are as innocuous as it is possible for them to be. Do you read British *Hansard*?

MR. WRIGHT:

Hansard on the British question time?

MR. DIEFENBAKER:

Do you read it?

MR. WRIGHT:

No, I don't.

MR. DIEFENBAKER:

If you do read it you will see what I am speaking of. Here in our Parliament the Speaker now says you must not be opinionative or controversial or argumentative. Read British *Hansard*. There they tear Ministers apart on supplementary questions.

MR. HOCKIN:

Are they allowed more supplementaries; is that why?

MR. DIEFENBAKER:

They are allowed supplementaries that are devastating. Such are not allowed here. The restriction of questions has made a mockery of Parliament. Apparently you people are enamoured with what you see.

MR. HOCKIN:

Oh, I'm not so sure.

MR. DIEFENBAKER:

You are. It's obvious even though you tell me otherwise. Read British *Hansard* for a period of three months. I'm not speaking about the general debate. I'm speaking about the question period because that's where governments are unmade. You don't ask for information. If a member doesn't know the answer before he asks a question he shouldn't ask. Otherwise indiscriminate questions provide an opportunity for the Government to disseminate its propaganda in Canada's House of Commons. The question period now is, for all practical purposes, ineffective.

The Prime Minister and Decision-Making

MR. HOCKIN:

How did you use your Ministers on difficult decisions? Could you delegate many decisions?

MR. DIEFENBAKER:

The responsibility finally rests on the Prime Minister. No one else. He takes the best advice he can get. But decision on all vital matters must finally receive his approval. The Cabinet Minister who heads the portfolio directly concerned with the decision made by the Cabinet often speaks about what he had done with a tone of subdued personal adulation. But when things turned out badly "the old man", they said, "was always responsible."

MR. HOCKIN:

Can you think of some decisions where you in effect had to make a major policy decision alone?

MR. DIEFENBAKER:

To use the words of Harry Truman, over each Prime Minister's desk there is an imaginary plaque. It carries the message, "The buck stops here." Take for example the Avro Arrow decision and the devaluation decision. The Cabinet took the decision on ending production of the Avro Arrow. That decision should have been taken before the Liberals left office. Indeed, St. Laurent and Howe decided they would close it out in 1956 but decided not to do so before an election. That was a very hard decision to make for my colleagues and me. The responsibility for the decision finally rested on the Prime Minister. I came to the conclusion that the day of the bomber was virtually over, that the Intercontinental Ballistic Missile would become in the immediate future the Russian threat to Canada and North America. That being so there was no reason why Canada should spend $7,700,000 for each individual aircraft which could only travel at a very limited outward distance at full speed. What defence would that assure for Canada? Virtually nothing.

MR. HOCKIN:

It certainly was expensive.

MR. DIEFENBAKER:

We substituted an aircraft from the United States that was not as attractive in appearance but we got it for much, much less. That decision had to be made even though I realized there would be the strongest opposition. When hard decisions conscientiously arrived at have to be made, leaders must make them.

MR. HOCKIN:

Did you refer a moment ago to opposition in the country as a whole or in the Cabinet or in the party?

MR. DIEFENBAKER:

Naturally the attack on the decision was concentrated in the area particularly affected and then across the country.

MR. WRIGHT:

You lost the seat most affected by the cancellation in the next election.

MR. DIEFENBAKER:

Very obvious. But you will remember that in President Nixon's message in 1970 to the nation on defense of the United States, he said that the day of the bomber was over. I took that stand in 1961. Devaluation of the dollar was another decision that had to be made. The devaluation of the dollar would have been made after the election but then President Kennedy stepped in during the election campaign and was able to undermine confidence in the Canadian dollar. The decision made during the election campaign rested on the shoulders of the Prime Minister. It was a frightening decision to make. Across Canada on the border the people said the dollar was down and out. The Liberals said they would reverse the devaluation immediately even though it brought to Canada the greatest increase in trade in its history. Once elected, the Liberals maintained the peg until the spring of 1970. I don't understand that type of political chicanery.

A responsible sense of integrity is to me as essential to leadership as advice of experts. To secure an opinion on this extremely complex problem I consulted economists or had them consulted and there was a variety of uncertainty expressed by them. Harry Truman, I think, was one of the greatest Presidents the United States has had in 75 years, far above Franklin Roosevelt. Truman had terrible decisions to make such as that which resulted in the use of the atomic bomb.

The Public Service and Mr. Diefenbaker

MR. HOCKIN:

As Prime Minister did you ever feel that the public service dragged their heels a bit on helping you?

MR. DIEFENBAKER:

I can give you an example. Over the years I had advocated the need for loans on farm-stored wheat because of the pile-up of wheat in Western Canada. They (the public service) said, "It couldn't be done". Knowing the collective view of the experts I stated to one of them that "the only difference between impossibility and improbability is that one takes a little longer than the other", and requested that a bill be drawn up to provide for such loans. Some of them feared a large loss to the Treasury if action was taken. Actually, the loss to the Treasury was an infinitesimal fraction of the total amount loaned. But they had contended, "We can't do it."

MR. HOCKIN:

Why would they say that?

MR. DIEFENBAKER:

It is not for me to understand the vagaries of other minds. But they get set in their ways. Some public servants get quite concerned about anything new, about something that hasn't been done. But I never found (except for two individuals both of whom will be identified when I write memoirs), I have never found that the advice given me as Prime Minister was politically orientated in any partisan way or by the fact that the civil servants had been for years under Liberal Prime Ministers. Now you take one, for whom I have a tremendous respect, Bob Bryce, (then Secretary of the Privy Council). There was no limit to the time he would work. He is Deputy Minister of Finance today [1970]. I know some of these ideas now being pressed by Benson (Minister of Finance), they were in assorted areas of the Bryce mind of my day. I recall that some of Benson's views now were Bryce's then. But Mr. Bryce was dependable to the utmost degree. As I stated, there were one or two senior civil servants who were not helpful to me, but by and large I found that the civil service gave me the kind of advice that, in my opinion, was free from partisan considerations.

Public Opinion and the Role of the Prime Minister and the Prime Minister's Office

MR. HOCKIN:

Sir, another question I submitted to you was how you went about identifying that elusive phenomenon "public opinion"?

MR. DIEFENBAKER:

It is not well understood. I immediately say this: The only person who *can* find it out *is* the Prime Minister for there is a wide spectrum of communication with him.

MR. HOCKIN:

How did you go about it though? What do you think of public opinion polls for example?

MR. DIEFENBAKER:

Not much! As far as polls are concerned, I would never have been Prime Minister if polls had had anything to do with the result. I just said last evening when I was speaking at a press conference, they asked, "What do you think of a bill to eliminate polls during an election?" My reply was that polls (or poles) are for dogs.

MR. HOCKIN:

Polls are no good, then?

MR. DIEFENBAKER:

Be careful. I am not saying that polls have no *effect*. If a particular item of policy is asked for polls can give a generally accurate opinion. Polls *cannot* determine what psychological or other influences finally determine the ballot right up to the second when the voter marks his ballot. (The polls for example were far wrong in the United States presidential election in 1948. I was in Philadelphia the night the Republicans chose Dewey and that night some Republican said to me, "Well, we've chosen a President of the United States." I said, "If you have, I'll be very surprised. Any person who has been described as being able to strut sitting down will have tremendous difficulties.")

But polls can have a serious *effect* on the outcome of an election. In 1963 I was defeated because of President Kennedy moving in his minions. They poured money into the funds of the Liberal Party. Kennedy sent Harris [a pollster] to Toronto under an assumed name to help in the Liberal campaign for the last couple weeks. It was the same in the 1965 general election when only a few thousand votes would have spelt victory. Those polls had a very detrimental effect.

MR. WRIGHT:

Did you ever think in terms of progressively educating public opinion for a particular policy that you wanted?

MR. DIEFENBAKER:

Well, we did not have a Louis Gagnon, the new head of "Information Canada". He'll educate the public opinion all right! Canadians ought to get fairly firm political direction from Information Canada. But, in general public thinking is very uncertain. Generally, you have to rely on certain informants. If I want to go over to that wall, if I proceed directly I'll have to climb over the desk and possibly fall over the telephone wire. I'll get over but with unnecessary difficulty. If on the other hand I go around the longer way eventually I'll get to the destination I have in mind.

MR. HOCKIN:

Can you give an example of doing that yourself?

MR. DIEFENBAKER:

I will mention that only as an example of the need of gradually taking a stand where public opinion has not yet quite fully understood the implications of the potential objective you have in mind.

MR. WRIGHT:

Did you ever feel the need, as Prime Minister, to have a large office of people to help you in gauging public opinion and organizing your time and decisions?

MR. DIEFENBAKER:

The growth of the Prime Minister's Office under Prime Minister Trudeau is the biggest hoax that has ever been created. It indicates first a complete lack of knowledge of Parliament and of the Prime Minister's responsibilities. The multiplication of positions in the Prime Minister's Office is becoming so numerous around here that they will soon have to get badges to assure that they will not be consulting each other. I operated the Prime Minister's Office on $50,000 a year; now it costs almost a million. [Over two million by 1976. Ed. note.]

MR. HOCKIN:

Would you do more of this work personally or as Prime Minister would you use Parliament more? What is your complaint?

MR. DIEFENBAKER:

Parliament today is becoming a rubber stamp to validate the legislation that is brewed by the public service and there is little effective debate. Too many speeches are read—and the clash of divergent opinion is lost. Under the Trudeau Government, Parliament is virtually inoperative in any normal sense. Now some civil servants, who sit in their gilded towers have all the solutions for all problems of Canada.

All this is dangerous. Let me give an example of what I mean. Legend has it that a United States Senator became chairman of one of the major committees of the Senate and by conjunction of time and seniority he rose to a position of importance. All observers were quite surprised when he did so well in his first two speeches, after becoming chairman. The speeches were good because he had hired a costly speech writer. The Senator became rather overwhelmed by the degree of eulogy that was heaped on him, and he wrote to his ghost writer and said, "Those are two damn good speeches, but I wish from now on you would write in a little simpler language so I would understand what the hell I'm talking about." So the next speech he got from the ghost writer (who decided he was through with him but didn't tell the Senator) was read by the Senator and he droned on and on until he came to the top of page 8. It read, "From now on, you old buzzard, you're on your own."

Interview with The Right Honourable
Lester B. Pearson
(Prime Minister of Canada 1963-1968)*

The Prime Minister and Federal—Provincial Conferences

MR. HOCKIN:

The first question deals with only a part of the Prime Minister's job, but it was an important part of your tenure as Prime Minister: How do you define the Prime Minister's role in federal-provincial conferences at the premier-prime ministerial level as distinguished from the role of other officials. Can one make a general statement about that?

MR. PEARSON:

In a way you can. The prime ministerial-premier conference is a summit conference. I've always felt that summit conferences in international affairs cannot usefully be held until the ground work has been done at a lower level, where the answers to problems are sought, if not found. Therefore, the top level conference should be more for ratification and confirmation than for negotiation. While the analogy to international affairs is, of course, not exact in the case of federal-provincial conferences, there is some resemblance, in my mind, between the two. This means that the chairman, who is the Federal Prime Minister, should often act more in a diplomatic capacity than in a political negotiating capacity.

Because the main work really should have been done before, on the various items on the agenda. His job as chairman, as I visualized it, was to keep out contentious politics as much as possible. It wasn't always possible; indeed when one is talking about tax-sharing and things like that, it often became quite impossible. But I thought it was wise to act as a chairman, rather than a political negotiator, when that was possible. In most situations, this was the easier in my case, I suppose, because of my view that the Federal Ministers themselves should discharge their own responsibilities to the greatest possible extent. Therefore I would have the Federal Ministers concerned with me, at the Conference especially the Minister of Finance, (and in the case of one conference, you remember, the Minister of Justice, Mr. Trudeau); and I encouraged them to give the federal point of view on the particular items on the agenda that fell within their responsibility. This meant, for instance that the Minister of Finance would sometimes be even more active in discussion than I would be. That's how I interpreted my role as Prime Minister.

MR. HOCKIN:

Well, you seem to see it more as a diplomatic role, and not a negotiating one. However, it is clear that the provincial premiers in these

---

* Interview conducted in Toronto, Ontario, February 28, 1970, by Thomas A. Hockin and subsequently edited and added to by Mr. Pearson.

conferences are in there to heighten the awareness of the items on the agenda as being a redistribution against them and sometimes even to make them politically controversial. In reaction, it seems that since 1945 Canadian Prime Ministers in these conferences are always trying to say, "now listen everybody, not only the Federal Government but all the provinces will benefit from the federal proposals" and the Canadian Prime Minister tries to portray a quite different point of view, and therefore he is doing something more than acting as a diplomat.

MR. PEARSON:

Yes, and I was going on to that point. The chairman, who is the Federal Prime Minister, is always directly involved in the matter under discussion even if he has also this diplomatic role. His position also tends to make him at times defensive because the Federal Government is often one against ten. There is no doubt about that. It is not true in every respect, of course, but normally the provinces tend to line up against the Federal Government. They come to Ottawa to get something out of the Federal Government which in its turn has to protect its own interests, and not give up too much, either in terms of money, or in terms of jurisdiction. After all, it has the responsibility of looking at all problems from the national point of view and as you have just said, of reconciling these regional and provincial demands with responsibility for the whole country. Discharging that general responsibility may, I agree, end up being the most important part of the chairman's job.

MR. HOCKIN:

If that was so, why did you televise these conferences? After all you were only one voice among eleven.

MR. PEARSON:

We televised it, in my view, for two reasons. One was that the pressure had been growing for open conferences and it seemed desirable to try them out. Also we thought then—at least I thought so, and some of the others did—that if the press and public opinion were exposed to the disadvantages as well as the advantages of public conferences, it might be that in the future—as indeed happened at the last conference —it would be easier to continue to have most of the meetings in executive session and only occasionally have a public conference.

The other reason, I think, (apart from the pressure from provinces who felt it was to their advantage to get publicity. After all they were the "attackers") was the feeling that this constitutional conference was the beginning of what was going to be a long and difficult process. So it seemed desirable to have a public conference with the provinces so that more people in the country could get a feeling, an impression of what the process of constitutional revision would be like; how important it was and how difficult. We were not getting down to negotiating details at that first conference. I thought that this particular televised conference worked out very well. But it brought out the old argument: "How can you negotiate in public?" It also became quite clear that some of the participants spoke to the television camera rather than to the meeting in the hope of getting national and provincial prestige and publicity from the impression they created. I was not conscious of this myself; no doubt because I was getting toward the end of my term anyway, and was going to leave politics.

This tendency to speak to the country, and not to the conference, is a disadvantage but not as great as it may seem; because even when our conferences were confidential the delegations customarily distributed their statements to the press. Also after the secret meetings, the leaders would get in front of the camera, and say what they wished. So it can be argued that it is just as well to have them do it openly, publicly, and officially at the meetings, in front of the camera and the press, as to have them do it afterwards in the corridors.

I think that this open conference worked out very well but I would hate to see every federal-provincial conference held in public.

MR. HOCKIN:

Although you emphasize the Prime Minister's presiding role and not his negotiating role, were there occasions when you would meet with a Premier and really settle a substantive matter because only you as Prime Minister could do so?

MR. PEARSON:

Yes, indeed there were occasions when my role had to become a negotiating one. I don't want to give the impression all I had to do was keep order! I think particularly of the conference in Quebec about the national pension scheme, when everything nearly broke down. I had to discuss matters privately with Jean Lesage directly to see whether Quebec would come into the scheme or not; and on what terms. I pointed out to him that we couldn't settle this matter finally at this conference. We were going from bad to worse in discussions of our differences. At the meetings, my position was "You've got to appreciate our point of view. I will try to appreciate yours. Let's not go any further at this time and run the risk of widening these differences. As soon as the conference is over we'll get together and see if we can work out an agreement based on certain changes made by both sides which will enable you to come into a national pension scheme, which remains acceptable to us federally."

I wouldn't want to give the impression the Prime Minister just sits there and presides. But there is such a presiding role, keeping a friendly atmosphere in which to do the negotiating, the discussing, in the best possible conditions.

MR. HOCKIN:

And you did this "negotiating" personally?

MR. PEARSON:

I did it personally. I've also had many unofficial personal talks with the provincial leaders on particular problems; tax sharing, constitutional amendment and things like that. At every conference—I suppose it is still the practise—I would have the premiers around the first evening to the house (24 Sussex, the Prime Minister's residence). We would sit down, meet in a friendly, social atmosphere and discuss things informally. These meetings were very useful. And I'm sure they still are.

MR. HOCKIN:

I suppose there are many examples, but can you think of serious examples when you ran into some *unexpected* provincial proposals at these meetings? I am certain your soundings before the meetings enabled you to have a good idea of what each province would say, but were you ever thrown off guard with some provincial proposals?

MR. PEARSON:

Oh, yes, this happened occasionally, more because of the tactics and personality of a provincial premier than because the subject was a new one. You would never really know what Premier X would come up with. He might knock us off base at times because of the suddenness or impracticality of a proposal, often stated with complete assurance and confidence.

MR. HOCKIN:

But you generally think your prior intelligence on provincial positions is pretty good?

MR. PEARSON:

Oh yes, for example in regard to the first constitutional conference, which was a very important one, federal representatives, went across the country, as you remember, beforehand; to every capital, to discuss matters with their provincial opposite numbers.

The Prime Minister and Political Leadership

MR. HOCKIN:

To shift from federal-provincial relations. Can I ask you some questions on how you would characterize the different kind of leadership required from you to set the tone and the direction of your administration in the parliamentary party, in Parliament, before the public and in Cabinet?

MR. PEARSON:

Well, I can say something about this, though it is not easy to go into detail. There are different kinds of leadership involved, as the nature of your question indicates. Leadership in the party has to be established first with party members; and in the parliamentary caucus. I used to take caucus meetings very seriously and I was always available to members of the caucus for discussion. I never missed a caucus meeting if it was possible to be there. Not all of my predecessors or all my colleagues felt that way.

MR. HOCKIN:

Did you ever chair caucus as Prime Minister?

MR. PEARSON:

No, a private member is chairman of the caucus, but I was always there and I used to subject myself—as my colleagues did—to every kind of examination. I used to encourage the frankest kind of questioning, however critical. That helped, I hope, to establish and maintain a leaders' position with his parliamentary colleagues. I tried to do this in the country by travelling and meetings. I did more travelling than most previous leaders, I think; that is travelling on party affairs and having party leaders come to Ottawa to discuss matters with me.

As for Parliament, you can't really establish leadership there as Prime Minister unless—I don't want to be too dogmatic about this—you have a deep and genuine feeling for Parliamentary institutions. For this, it is a great help to have had a long parliamentary experience; to have risen from the ranks in Parliament where you can acquire, if you have not had it instinctively, a feeling for Parliament, of its importance and its traditions. I always had a feeling of deep respect for Parliament (after all I had been a constitutional historian!), but I entered at the top, on the front benches. I had been in civil service for many years before being elected and I had never done any Parliament apprenticeship. And I confess I never had any great love for parliamentary battles and rows. I could get worried up about issues as much as anybody else, as a competitive human being, but I always thought debates which were repetitive and prolonged and too violent wasted too much time. I used to get impatient because you couldn't get things done quickly enough because of those struggles in Parliament that other people may have loved. I was anxious to improve parliamentary procedure; make it more effective by improving its rules. I was very keen about this. I hope I gave some leadership in that sense. I could have done much more if I had had a majority of, say, 30; I think then I would have been able to do a lot more about parliamentary reform, without destroying or weakening the reality of parliamentary work, and the importance of parliamentary opposition.

As for leadership in the country at large, you do this primarily by the impression you create, and by the action you take, the measures you put through Parliament. This requires speeches and appearances across the country, as well as speeches and, more important, action in Parliament.

A television image seems now to be very important—too much so I think. One can appear to be a leader on television if he is a good performer, a good actor. I always found this very difficult. I had no liking or aptitude for this kind of performance and always found it difficult to pretend that I was somebody else on television; or act a part. Indeed, I found it very difficult to be other than myself in my public appearances; too bad. I have been told I was only effective on television when I got excited about something—the flag resolution for example—that I could be forceful on such occasions and effective on television or in speaking. But generally I think you have to be a good "performer" even if you are not all worked up about the subject of the performance, if you are to impress masses of people as a political leader.

MR. HOCKIN:

Could you begin to predict what the media would feature, say on the 11 o'clock news, about what you had said? Could you, after a while, predict what parts of your speeches they would seize on and what they would not?

MR. PEARSON:

I've never ceased to be amazed at the frequent failure of reporters and commentators to get what I thought was the most important part of a message that I was delivering. They so often seemed to pick out some aside, or some off-hand comment, or something more newsy than important; and miss what I, at least, considered to be the important point.

I have a tendency to make quips just for the fun of it. My wife used to say that quips would be the death of me. Certainly they seemed at times to blanket the substance of what I was trying to say. This was a mistake, I suppose, but I'm afraid I didn't worry about it as much as I should. I let the quips fall where they may!

The Prime Minister and Meetings with Other Heads of Government

MR. HOCKIN:

A key leadership role only a Prime Minister can exercise is in meetings of heads of governments in international affairs. For example, when you were Prime Minister, you visited the President of the United States, and the Prime Ministers and Presidents of other countries. What were you perceptions of the use of these gatherings? Often the press seems to give the impression—by recording a rather empty communiqué—that meetings of heads of government are more symbolic activities than anything else, that they do not have a great deal of importance for solid policy.

MR. PEARSON:

Well, I think to some extent that's true. I can give you one example. Right after I became Prime Minister I visited London. I don't remember anything very important being settled or even discussed there, but I felt the trip was of symbolic and political importance because some people were saying that we were dominated by the United States in everything; that I, especially, was too pro-American. So I thought it was wise to try to off-set that impression by not making my first trip as Prime Minister to the United States but to the U.K.; which I preferred to do in any event.

I won't name names but there are leaders of governments who, quite frankly, seem to use many of their trips abroad mostly for domestic political purposes, in order to receive publicity and attention with political benefit back home.

Of course I don't think these visits are always merely symbolic. They can be very useful, and important, in putting to your opposite number a point of view which you wish him to have on certain policy matters that are being considered—by your government or his.

I remember that when I went to see Lyndon Johnson, that although it was difficult on occasion to discuss many things in depth and in detail (he was rather a busy man!—with interruptions even in the midst of meals or conversations) I was able to give him a Canadian viewpoint on issues, that were not directly Canadian, but which might be of help to him even if it did not always harmonize with his own. It might give him a different perspective.

MR. HOCKIN:

What do you mean "different perspective"? For example—with the U.S.—when you talked to the President did you talk about tough continental problems like oil imports or energy problems?

MR. PEARSON:

Well, that's a good example. On discussing oil for example, when Washington was thinking of cutting back on the import of oil from our country, I could give the Canadian point of view first hand to the leader of the U.S. Government. I could point out, for instance, that if they cut down on imports of Canadian oil, the Government of Canada would quickly be forced for economic and political reasons to build a pipeline to the East and this could mean the end of shipments of Venezuelan oil into the eastern part of Canada. I could tell the President. "You know who owns the Venezuelan oil companies?—your own people." Mr. Johnson might be struck by this argument so I would be able to bring him a "different point of view" than that which might have been put to him by those lobbying on behalf of the U.S. independent oil producers.

The Prime Minister, His Cabinet and the Public Service

MR. HOCKIN:

Could you characterize the style of your operation with the Cabinet compared with Mackenzie King or St. Laurent?

MR. PEARSON:

It is my impression that Mackenzie King was a better listener and analyser of points of view than a reader of documents beforehand. He operated more on intuition and impressions received from listening and discussing rather than by conclusions from examining briefs. Mr. St. Laurent's operation of Cabinet—I had first hand experience of this —was very businesslike; he always had read his documents very carefully. He was well briefed as a lawyer would want to be. As for me, I am a reader and examiner of briefs and memos dealing with points coming up. So I was well informed on the subjects under discussion. But I always encouraged Cabinet Ministers to speak up, argue their case to their colleagues, who were also encouraged to speak. My philosophy was to let a Cabinet Minister, as far as possible, run his own show and that it was not my job to be interfering in details. I felt that I should, in most cases, let Cabinet Ministers take the initiative in policy discussions in their areas and defend their initiatives in Cabinet. I would then have to make the decision if there was a division of opinion. I often met with cabinet members individually to talk to them about policies in their fields and give them advice when necessary; but basically, I tried to let them run their own departments. My style of conducting cabinet meetings was relaxed, and informal; more so, I believe than was the case with my predecessors. Mackenzie King, you know, never allowed anyone to smoke in Cabinet or have a coffee or any other kind of break. He was the headmaster! Mr. St. Laurent's Cabinet was more formal than mine, but he was always a very considerate and courteous chairman, and anxious to encourage the widest participation in discussions.

MR. HOCKIN:

As far as your control over policy generally, did you find that often policies were firmed up at the middle to deputy minister level and that often decisions were taken that at that level left the Prime Minister surprisingly little control?

MR. PEARSON:

I must say in the case of the budget I often felt this. The budget—as was customary—would come to my desk about a week or so before it was to be brought before the full Cabinet and, really, that is pretty late for even a Prime Minister to have much influence on it, though I may have had talks previously with the Minister of Finance on general policy matters underlying the budget. Other members of the Cabinet had even less time to examine the budget. I could, of course, have major influence on the broad lines of policy in a budget; but in accord with parliamentary practice, the other Cabinet Ministers really had little or nothing to do with the budget itself.

MR. HOCKIN:

This might be more of an American than a Canadian question but there is a great problem American Presidents have of getting Government departments to respond to their wishes. Did you ever feel the public service did not respond to your wishes or the wishes of the Cabinet?

MR. PEARSON:

Oh, I don't think this is a real problem in our system. Mr. Diefenbaker complained, I've heard, about what he called the "Pearsonalities" in the Department of External Affairs, when he was Prime Minister. But I've found that public servants are loyal to the government of the day as they should be. For example on unification of the armed forces, nearly all of the top military men were against it or doubtful about its wisdom but they got in line when the Cabinet laid down the policy; with only one or two exceptions.

I was a civil servant myself for many years. I admit that I can remember when the minister would decide (for instance) to open an Embassy somewhere and we in External thought we knew better than the minister on the subject; we might try to delay action, hoping to convince the Minister that he should change his mind. But that would really be the extent of it and even that wasn't frequent. He made the decision, and if he didn't change it, we carried it out. I served both Mr. Bennet's and Mr. King's government and tried to be 100 per cent loyal to both. Our civil service maintains and is proud of that tradition.

MR. HOCKIN:

What about your control over Ministers on policy? Did you always leave general initiatives to Cabinet or to individual Ministers?

MR. PEARSON:

There were occasions, of course, when I took initiatives of my own, aside from what other Ministers might wish to do, or not to do. For example in Medicare, as to carrying out our electoral commitments at a particular time. The same with the Canadian flag. The caucus and the cabinet were divided on both issues. I heard arguments on both sides and then decided. There was also the nuclear weapons issue, though this was when we were in opposition. I talked to one or two of my senior colleagues about the matter, but I knew that if I talked to too many and we had too much discussion, any decision would leak out prematurely and I didn't want that. I had been agonizing over the question for months myself and I found it difficult to come to a conclusion that was satisfactory. I was finally driven to the conclusion that we had to do something, largely by the Cuban crisis, when we were completely impotent to use, in time, certain weapons we had acquired, if there had been war. And yet we had accepted these weapons as a member of N.A.T.O. knowing that they could not be of any value if they did not have nuclear warheads for them; knowing that in an emergency the decision for use of such weapons might have to be made at once, and knowing finally that the other members of the alliance, especially the U.S.A., assumed that we had accepted the weapons on this understanding. So I decided that since there was going to be an election, and I would have to take a stand in the election, I'd better take it before the campaign and I did. I just didn't do this off the top of my head. I made what I thought was the right decision having regard to all that had gone before.

Pierre Trudeau on Policy-Making and the Growth of the Prime Minister's Office since 1968*

LORD CHALFONT:

There is one development that seems to be taking place during your prime ministership which is very relevant to this idea of how you exercise influence and power. I am referring to the tendency there seems to be for you to aggregate more power into your own entourage

---

* Transcript of Prime Minister's interview with Lord Chalfont for the BBC, taped February 13, 1975, for broadcast March 11, 1975.

into the Prime Minister's office. This is a criticism which I'm not making myself but reflecting. People say that you are eroding the power of departments to make policies and of your individual ministers by second guessing, to use the American expression, with a powerful and highly articulated Prime Minister's office. What is your reaction to that?

MR. TRUDEAU:

I guess it's really a matter of personal style, of intellectual approach. A counterpart to that accusation is that I run my Cabinet too much like a seminar or with platonian methods of asking questions to advance the discussion. And in order to do that I have to be informed myself. I have to be able to challenge the minister and say, look this may be good in your particular department but have you thought of the effects of it on agriculture, on transport, or on the Treasury. In order to do this, in a very complex society, obviously I need staff to inform me about the decisions which are being requested of Cabinet. I don't believe that my role is merely one of chairman of the board, in waiting for a consensus to develop, and in calling out that consensus. I do believe in counter-weights. I do like to be challenged in my own ideas and I do like to challenge others. That's what Cabinet is for me. It's a forum where certain questions which transcend the needs of a particular minister or department are discussed collectively. You know, a minister's job I suppose in 99% of what he does is within his department. But there's that one per cent that affects other departments or affects other regions of the country. For instance, the Minister of Agriculture may be from the East, and may be thinking of policies which are good for his constituents in the East but which are very bad for the West. It's important that his ideas in that respect be challenged by me or by some Minister sitting in the West who may not be the Minister of Agriculture.

LORD CHALFONT:

Yes, but of course, as you know Prime Minister, in Britain, for example, I merely cite it as an example of another Parliamentary democracy, that kind of judgment of departmental issues against each other is done at the official level; at a series of committees, a series of discussions between officials sometimes involving what we call the permanent under-secretary, what you call the deputy minister, so that when an item comes to Cabinet, all those issues—the inter-departmental issues—have been allegedly ironed out. It's then a matter for Cabinet to arrive at a decision by discussion in committee.

MR. TRUDEAU:

What if there is a conflict between the officials of two departments? Who resolves that conflict? Cabinet obviously. We have inter-departmental committees too. I sometimes feel that they should work more than less because perhaps too many questions do come to Cabinet. We have not enough time for other things. But this is a matter of degree. We have inter-departmental committees. I encourage them to produce not policy decisions, but policy alternatives. Because I think it's the job of the elected representatives, the ministers, to make the policy choices.

LORD CHALFONT:

I'm sorry, could I interrupt please. What you're saying is that you encourage the officials in departments to present their ministers with policy options.

MR. TRUDEAU:

Right.

LORD CHALFONT:

And then when the ministers come to Cabinet, the elected representatives make the decisions, but you are furnishing yourself with independent advice about the issues. Advice totally independent of that which is given to the ministers by their own officials.

MR. TRUDEAU:

I try to get what you call the political input. I must think in terms of the regions of the country—or of the French-English balance, or of the new Canadians' approach to any particular problem. A minister will present a departmental point of view. He will present options to Cabinet and generally say, well, I think this is the option which is best and I recommend it. Other ministers will challenge those recommendations on a basis of their departmental interests. Some may challenge the recommendation on the basis of geographical interests. But the role of the Prime Minister's Office as I see it, is to inform me of the political data, to make sure that I am aware of how people are thinking on particular problems in political terms.

LORD CHALFONT:

Now, there are some people who would suggest, and probably have suggested, I imagine, that this has a certain flavour of presidential government about it. It is, as I'm sure you'll agree, a very different matter from the United States where there is a separation of powers, and where the powers of the president are very much kept under control by the Senate and House of Representatives. Where we don't have separation of powers, as in Canada and in Britain, people have always been wary of the Prime Minister who adopts presidential styles or tools of government. Do you find that criticism in Canada?

MR. TRUDEAU:

Yes I do find that criticism in Canada. I think it's based on a misapprehension of how our system works. The Prime Minister must be as informed as any one of his ministers. That's all I ask. I have a department of civil servants who inform me of the bureaucratic or technical aspects of a problem. I have a staff—so-called an exempt staff—which informs me of the political data. But every minister does too. Every minister has his. He has got something like $120,000 a year to hire people outside of the civil service to advise him on the policies of his constituents, both in the geographical sense and a substantive sense. And the only difference with a prime minister, is that I have a bit more. But the theory is absolutely the same. If ministers had only their departments and no political advisers, then I would be in a special case. But every minister, and it's true in Great Britain, has his political advisers.

LORD CHALFONT:

Oh, it is absolutely true. I think the point that I was making, I expect some Canadians would make, is that your Prime Minister's office seems to have grown very considerably recently and become very much larger. This seems to indicate either that you felt that the previous system was inadequate and inefficient, or as I say, you are moving imperceptibly or even perceptibly towards a presidential style of government.

MR. TRUDEAU:

Well, I would say that the alternative is the former. And that's a matter of judgment. But if you look through the sixties, in a period where minority governments held sway, and where the provinces were led by strong premiers and strong political parties, I think the central government was gradually becoming or appearing to become ineffective. We were having minority governments. There were elections—several of them in a short period of years—and Ottawa did not appear to have a strong central government. No doubt that I've tried to build a strong central government in Ottawa. I believe that a federation can only survive if it has a strong central government and strong provincial governments. And that's why it's not right to campaign for a minority government. But the effects of a majority government are that the national government has real power to exercise, and I think this is indispensable in a country which has so many centrifugal forces as in Canada. So there's no apologies. I just say that we couldn't evolve towards a presidential system. I think the accusation is either misinformed or malicious. You can't have a presidential system when the Prime Minister himself has to be elected by his constituency, where he is only first amongst a series of colleagues. If too many of them resign, or too many of the back-benchers are dissatisfied, the Prime Minister ceases to be Prime Minister, not like the President who can go on till the end of his term. So, obviously, if you are Prime Minister you have to take into account the system and make sure that you have a cohesive party and a cohesive cabinet. You can't fire too many ministers without destroying your own basis.

Government and Policy-Making*

MR. CLARK:

A few months after you first took office a reporter asked you what had struck you most about being Prime Minister. I think you said that what surprised you most was the limited influence a Prime Minister

---

* Transcript of Prime Minister's interview with Gerald Clark of the *Montreal Star* on September 13, 1974, for a feature article published in the *New York Times Magazine* for Sunday, November 3, 1974.

really had... maybe 10 per cent impact on the governing of the nation, while the permanent machinery, the bureaucracy, held the rest. Would you say the same today after 6 years or revise your percentages? Or what kind of evaluation would you put on it?

MR. TRUDEAU:

Gosh, I don't remember that quote quite honestly. My impression is that if I said that it would have been wrong to say the rest was held by the bureaucracy. Surely what I meant, and I think I remember the image I was using, I said that the ship of state is a big thing to turn around to give another direction to. And this isn't just the bureaucracy you know, these are the whole structures of a society which is as large as ours, with such different regions where consensus is difficult to obtain. So, a society isn't a plastic thing that you mould after the particular image of a government of the day, that's what I wanted to convey, and I think I would still say the same today. I think the important point is that over a period of time, even if you are only acting at the margin as it were, you can choose your priorities and objectives in a way which do give a different direction to the society. But it's not the Prime Minister alone, it's the Prime Minister and the Cabinet and Parliament and the party and everything else; it's a heavy apparatus. But if you choose certain priorities they will be achieved, perhaps longer than in the time span you had planned for.

MR. CLARK:

Well, in looking for priorities can you see a change in your own evolution, your own political thinking, your own philosophy, in the time you have had this very important, powerful job? Any major changes in your philosophy, any minor changes?

MR. TRUDEAU:

I would think that the priorities are still basically the same. It is a search for greater justice in the distribution of the wealth of society between regions, between language groups, between ethnic communities, between men and women and so on between the different age groups. I think this is essentially what a government must do; and in our case, well we've created not only a Department of Regional Economic Expansion, but I think we have given a thrust over the past few years which certainly has reduced the disparities, the inequities. If you look at half a dozen years ago and compare it to the figures today, you will see that the spread from the national average of say provincial revenue in the have-provinces, per capita, as opposed the per capita revenue in the have-not-provinces, it is closer to the mean now. We've I think begun to reverse the trend of out-migration from the poor regions of Canada and people are beginning to return there. And so in that area I think we still have the same philosophy, the same objectives. But we have moved in the right direction—say the philosophy we had to give better equity between French and English. I can't remember the exact date but I think it's since we had that other interview that we passed the Official Languages Act, that we've implemented it and

that more and more French-speaking Canadians are beginning to recognize that Ottawa is also their capital, not only the capital of the
English-speaking Canadians. And I think this is borne out by the
several recent federal and provincial elections where people basically
have opted for federalism in Quebec.

MR. CLARK:

I think you anticipated the oil crisis through one of the study groups in
your own office or the Privy Council Office. Initially you started out
with this very elaborate thought of studying a great number of problems, because, I think, you believed you can't run a government on an
ad hoc basis. Now there's been some change hasn't there? I'm just
wondering, in other words, whether you learn to fly more by the seat
of the pants after a while.

MR. TRUDEAU:

In practical terms, in political terms, yes, you have to fly very often by
the seat of your pants. And I guess particularly in the last Parliament,
when we did not have a majority and we needed the support of other,
opposition, parties for various things, we were much more in a tactical
situation where we were, as you put it, adjusting and flying by the seat
of our pants. But the other half of the answer is that because of these
long-term studies, and because we had, way back in '68, decided to try
and look ahead and understand in advance the kind of big problems
which would be facing our society, we accumulated a lot of intellectual
capital and technical data which we've been drawing on, in the minority Parliament where we didn't have time to sit down and at the last
election, which as you know was thrust upon us and therefore we
didn't plan that one ahead. But the big decisions we took in the last
Parliament, where we were so uncertain of our future and so unstable
in a sense, were taken on oil and energy because we had this accumulated wealth of studies. The decisions we took on minerals and the
study we published on that had begun years before. The position that
we took on social security and the whole new approach to it, including
the guaranteed annual income for those who can't work, was the fruit
of several years of study, our position on the Law of the Seas which is
beginning to bear fruit in the councils of the world. . . .

MR. CLARK:

Can you contrast that with something you might have decided almost
by instinct? Is there anything that comes to mind that after 5 or 6 years
you decided had to be done without any heavy study?

MR. TRUDEAU:

Let me try and find some examples. . . . I guess within the broad areas
I'm outlining, the broad strategies that are referred to, you're taking
tactical decisions all the time and you're shooting from the hip. But I'd
be hard pressed to give you any great important example of something
major.

MR. CLARK:

But even day to day tactical things that do come up more prevalently
now perhaps than 6 years ago . . .

MR. TRUDEAU:

Yes, although you know in those days when we'd be discussing a budget, the Minister of Finance and myself, or income tax reform and so on, after weeks and months and sometimes years of study at some point you have to say: 'OK this is what we're going to say.' But I can't think of very major re-directions given to our society which haven't been well thought out. The changes sometimes indicate that we hadn't thought about them enough in contemporary or in changing times. I guess our approach to Indian policy was a good example of that. When we spelt out our Indian policy almost 5 years ago, I think it was in '69 that we published our paper on Indian policy, it was, I think, a good rational paper and it threw the options at the Indians. We said: 'You are at the crossroads, you either have to become integrated, not assimilated, but integrated into the rest of society, and we will abolish the Indian act and the reservations and so on, or you can continue going down the road of being special people within our society and having different rights than the rest of them'. You know, it was a kind of a good logical approach, but since then we've realized that you don't solve this problem just with logic and this kind of choice that we were asking them and the rest of the Canadians to make is not an easy choice in emotional terms. That's why we've adjusted and discussed and said time and time again that we were prepared to modify our policy according to the directions that they and we together could . . . so these are examples of changes, but I can't think of any big example of what you suggest. . . .

MR. CLARK:

You're the only leader in the West I think with a majority government or clear mandate from the people in terms of, say the United States where the President has no direct mandate. Maybe Giscard would be an exception, but I think, generally, you are the only one with a majority government. Does this give you any special feeling? Is it perhaps a reflection of the more secure mood we now seem to enjoy in Canada compared, say, with 1970? Another part of the question might be: Do you think the trend in the world is going to continue towards minority governments, governments of the centre. Another part of that: Who among the big western countries do you see now in a position of leadership?

MR. TRUDEAU:

Well, I can't talk about the rest of the world, but talking about Canada I think this is a reflection of a mature reaction of a mature society. We're still young as a nation, but I think Canadians were looking for the stability which you refer to. I think even those who voted against us and those who voted notably for the Tories were kind of hoping there would be a Tory majority. They were making a choice, and I think the drift away from the third parties, NDP and the Social Crediters, the example of Canadians saying: 'Well, you know, we have a pretty good society here, let's not blow it, let's make sure there is someone in charge'. That's why votes polarized against the Conservatives and the Liberals. In the event, more judged that the Liberals were able to give stability than the Tories, but I would say that even those who voted Tory were trying to express their desire for stability. The fact that a majority was determined, a clear majority in terms of seats, I say reflects something of which Canadians should be reasonably proud, particularly since for years pundits have been saying that Canada would no longer find majorities, it was just exceptional flashes in the pan, that our society was split by nature. So I think this was a good answer of Canadian desire for stable growth, both economic and social. Now, I can't judge other societies too much. Perhaps the people themselves, perhaps the institutions, are not so geared as to permit the expression of this kind of majority.

MR. CLARK:

Can you anticipate governments of the centre now increasing generally?

MR. TRUDEAU:

Governments of the centre?

Mr. CLARK:

Well, yes, tending toward the centre rather than representing one party or another, one ideology or another. . . .

MR. TRUDEAU:

Oh, I suppose everyone who exercises some form of democratic power tends to move to the centre after he has been elected. If he's been elected on the right he tries to occupy some of the centre while protecting. . . .

MR. CLARK:

Is this what the voters will be inclined to expect now more and more, or is it just a temporary phase we are going through?

MR. TRUDEAU:

Well, I'd be inclined to think they will tend to expect more and more for a reason which I would volunteer. I think the electorates everywhere, certainly in Canada, are becoming more sophisticated. They are better informed, they know more about the problems, and I think they are rejecting simplistic answers, easy answers.

MR. CLARK:

. . . May I ask one final, very general question? I think I heard you say, or I read, that you would be quite content if your greatest contribution to Canada would be the retention of integrity of government. Is that too simple a way of putting it? Let me phrase it again: What would you be content with as your contribution?

MR. TRUDEAU:

I can't remember saying that in so many words, but it's certainly a preoccupation that I've had and which I put very high. And I don't mean integrity purely in a moralistic sense, I think by integrity I mean the wholeness of government. I think that governments in complex societies have to be flexible, they have to be accepted by most of the people but at the same time they can't run around trying to please everybody, everywhere, all the time about everything. In that sense they must retain their authority, their ability to act and their integrity in a metaphysical sense. They must be whole, the governments must continue to find ways in which people will continue to want to obey them. The basis of law is not the army or the machine guns, it's the acceptance by the people of one basic principle that the law should be obeyed by and large. What has worried me in my time, not only about the Canadian society, but about many others, is that obviously the psychological inclination to obey the law has been eroded. And I am not making a moral judgment. Perhaps a lot of the laws haven't kept up to the times, perhaps they should have been changed earlier and had they been changed they would have been more obeyed.

MR. CLARK:

Eroded, what by people, by governments? . . .

MR. TRUDEAU:

By the people, by the psychological inclinations to obey governments, authority, laws which have not kept up to the changing times. . . . This applies as much to the churches and to the universities as it does to the governments. That period in which we were living in the 60s was a good example of it. You know, the word revolution was on everyone's lips. It didn't mean armed revolution and barricades, though it came to that in some instances, but it meant a revolutionary change in the values of the society. And there was for a while, I feared, a danger of governments not being able to govern. I guess we saw that in October of 1970 in Quebec. We saw that in universities, where the faculty and executive of the university would just sort of lay down their arms. We see that in industrial strife these very weeks, where labor unions and workers have refused to obey not only the general law, which is the contract which they signed, but the law of the legislature which says you go back to work, and they didn't go back to work. We see that in many many aspects of our society. . . .

22

A Parliamentary Exchange on the Powers, Prerogatives and Privileges of the Office of Prime Minister— Joe Clark, Stanley Knowles John Reid*

EDITED BY THOMAS A. HOCKIN

Private Members' Motions

Suggested Committee Study of Powers, Prerogatives and Privileges of Office of Prime Minister

MR. JOE CLARK (ROCKY MOUNTAIN) moved:

> *That, in the opinion of this House, a committee should be selected to consider the powers, prerogatives and privileges attaching to the office of Prime Minister and to report what safeguards are desirable or necessary to secure the constitutional principles of the sovereignty of parliament and the supremacy of the law.*

He said: Mr. Speaker, I should point out to the House that the language of this resolution was drawn from a resolution introduced to the British House of Commons on precisely this topic several years ago. I can say, in a certain hopeful sense, that the resolution was accepted at that time in that House. I hope it will receive similar treatment here today.

In the past ten years there have been a great many deliberate changes in our political institutions. New departments of government have been introduced and a range of new procedures developed from impact studies to local initiative government spending designed to bring governments and

---

* Taken in slightly abridged form from the *House of Commons Debates* (December 9, 1974), pp. 2071-77.

citizens into closer harmony. Last year parliament passed the Election Expenses Act which will end the secrecy of political party financing and encourage all parties to become more active and more broadly based. The rules of parliament have been dramatically changed, and the Speech from the Throne suggested that more radical changes will be proposed. Those changes have been made deliberately, usually after extensive study and public debate.

In that period the office of Prime Minister has also changed dramatically, and it is one of the curiosities of our system that so little serious attention has been paid to the extent or significance of the power of that office. In the United States, books and theories and countless columns are written about the power of the presidency. In Canada, with rare exceptions, we focus for a moment on a sudden growth in staff or an expenditure on suede sofas, and then largely leave the question alone. However, it is too important a question to leave alone and the purpose of this resolution is to allow an examination of the role that should be played by the office of Prime Minister in a modern, federal parliamentary state.

I underline and emphasize the fact that what is sought in this resolution is an opportunity for a committee of this parliament to examine the role of the office of Prime Minister. The resolution makes no assumptions about that role except the assumption that the powers of the Prime Minister, like the powers of parliament, should be discussed and decided in public and in the context of the requirements and the traditions of the whole country.

Let me say a word about those traditions. In my view there is no tradition in Canada of a weak Prime Minister. We are told, in parliamentary theory, that the Prime Minister is merely the "first among equals" in parliament, with the assumption that Her Majesty can quite easily choose another of us equals to be first. That is the theory. In fact, the Prime Minister has always been a strong figure in Canada, with his parliamentary leadership buttressed by his party leadership and with official responsibilities and an official reputation far beyond those of his peers and at least equal to those of Her Majesty.

Therefore, the tradition is not the theoretical tradition of being merely the first among equals, answerable to the Queen but, rather, the practical tradition of exercising leadership in a federal state with a parliamentary system which requires the governors to be responsible to the governed through this parliament. Nobody is suggesting that we go back to a weakness that never was. However, throughout our history there has been another tradition to balance the necessary strength of the office of Prime Minister; that is, that the powers of the Prime Minister should not be developed or exercised in isolation but must be set in a federal parliamentary context and be subject to detailed and regular parliamentary scrutiny. There is no such scrutiny today.

The Prime Minister comes to the question period on most days, but the questions are usually about his judgment, seldom about his powers; and anyway there is no requirement that he answer. After the so-called

Pearson precedent of 1968 there is a real question whether parliament can defeat a Prime Minister by vote in this House, except on matters of obvious confidence, like a budget. If our capacity to defeat a Prime Minister is so limited, so is our capacity limited to control him by the threat of defeat. As the chief minister, he is less bound by Treasury Board than any of his colleagues, and appointments to or by his office can be made without recourse to the Public Service Commission. His estimates are brought before the miscellaneous estimates committee. However, they are not dealt with there by him, but by a parliamentary secretary to another minister.

The Prime Minister reports to no standing committee and there is no statute to define his responsibilities. Ironically, parliament probably has less real control over the Prime Minister than we have over the president of Air Canada or the president of CNR, because a Crown corporation is established by statute while the Prime Minister's office is not, and its officials must appear regularly before standing committees while the Prime Minister's officials do not. No matter how loosely you define "responsible" government, parliament should have some direct control over the actions of its Prime Minister beyond his mere appearance for questions in the House. If that has been important in the past, I suggest it will be even more critical in the future, for reasons I will enumerate.

First, whatever the theory, the fact is that our system of government in Canada is a system of cabinet government, not parliamentary government. Occasionally, initiatives by private members are adopted by the government and from time to time members can amend a bill in committee or a committee of the whole House. However, the bulk of the power of initiative lies with the cabinet. It is the same in Britain, and one distinguished participant in and observer of the British system, the late Richard Crossman, suggested that in the system of the Mother of Parliaments, the process of a concentration of power has gone even further. Writing a decade ago in the introduction to Bagehot's "The English Constitution", Crossman said:

In Bagehot's day, collective cabinet responsibility meant the responsibility of a group of equal colleagues for decisions taken collectively, after full, free and secret discussion in which all could participate. It now means collective obedience by the whole administration, from the foreign secretary and the chancellor downwards, to the will of the man at the apex of power.

We have no expert testimony on this trend in Canada, but it is safe to assume—and certainly it is the public assumption—that the Prime Minister controls his cabinet and that it is the Prime Minister, not the cabinet, and certainly not parliament, who regularly makes the final and the important decisions.

Second, the power of the Prime Minister grows as government grows. We have increasingly an interventionist state which controls or strongly influences more and more of the processes of our society. The merits of that development can be argued another time. The simple point I want to make is that as the government becomes more powerful in the nation, so does the leader of the government become more powerful. The present Prime Minister, by virtue of his office, has much power in Canada than did Louis St. Laurent, John Diefenbaker, Lester Pearson or any of his predecessors. The state might have got out of the bedrooms of the nation, but it has more than made up for that everywhere else, and the one office that has grown most in power is the office, in Mr. Crossman's words, "at the apex of power".

Third, the same active agenda which has increased the role of government has decreased the power of parliament to control government. Parliament once had a virtually unlimited power to scrutinize and delay. While parties might disagree about the nature of specific reforms, all of us recognize that the old, easy rules would not have let the business to be done. But we have paid a price for that reform, and the price has been that at the same time as the powers of the executive have increased, the powers of parliament have decreased; so we have less control on bigger government.

The fourth factor in the growing power of the Prime Minister is television. Today, every head of government has become a star personality whose advisers cultivate the talent to manipulate opinion and whose office has the permanent opportunity to command attention. Professor Denis Smith, in his article "President and Parliament" argues, and I quote:

Canadian Prime Ministers have always made their primary appeal for support not in the House of Commons, but outside, to the electorate.

That is much easier now, with mass media. All of us here, if we are realists, know that the most effective place for a Prime Minister to get his message across is on television, not in this House. That is a fact of life which adds immensely to the power of the Prime Minister and diminishes, again, the capacity of this parliament to control an official whose whole authority is presumed in theory to arise from this chamber.

Fifth, the present Prime Minister has, in effect, established for the first time a new "Department of the Prime Minister" in the privy council office and the office of the Prime Minister. His purpose was to provide a means by which he, as head of government, could keep track of and co-ordinate the various initiatives of a mammoth government. I understand that purpose and, speaking personally, approve of it as the only means to ensure that there is, in fact, some over-all control of the direction of government by the elected politicians whom the Prime Minister commands. However, this new department was created in the absence of authority from, or discussion in, parliament. It operates beyond our scrutiny and, having the ear of the Prime Minister, it has the capacity virtually to change any direction or challenge any initiative that arises either in parliament or in the public service.

Without dwelling on them too long, I would suggest that certain other forces which traditionally have restrained a Prime Minister have been weakening recently. For example, we accept the notion, without much evidence, that Canadian political parties control their leaders and, in particular, prevent them from the excesses we associate with Watergate. But when did that last happen? Did the Liberal Party in Newfoundland ever restrain Joey Smallwood? Did the Union Nationale restrain Maurice Duplessis? Parties do not behave in that way because they know that in attacking their leader they attack themselves. This is particularly true now that campaigns are so heavily influenced by national media and voting is more often for the personality of the leader than it is for the local candidate or a specific issue.

Again, we have assumed that a Prime Minister can be controlled by the public which, at each election, has the chance to "throw the rascals out." However, public control of the Prime Minister depends upon a competitive electoral system. In Canada, the electoral system is, unfortunately, not competitive in Quebec, which means, as it did in 1972, that a Prime Minister can be rejected by most of the country and still survive.

Finally, there is the argument that the professional public service can provide a counterbalance to a powerful Prime Minister. That capacity also is being weakened first by the deliberate establishment of a "Department of the Prime Minister" precisely to confront such a capability in the public service and second, by the increasingly frequent appointment to public service positions of individuals who have personal or partisan loyalties to the Prime Minister.

Hon. members can disagree about the extent or significance of any of the factors I have discussed today, but I think we must surely all agree that two main trends are occurring. The first is a trend toward the concentration of formal and informal power in the office and person of the Prime Minister. Second is the weakening of any effective means to control that power. In a modern state, it may well be impossible or even undesirable to reverse the first trend. But surely we cannot let that power grow unscrutinized and uncontrolled.

I think it is safe to say that if we saw a corporation, a union or any other private agency accumulating the power that is developing now around the office of the Prime Minister, we would want to develop some assurances that the public interest was being served. It is particularly important that we apply that same standard of scrutiny and control to an office whose original authority was as a creature of this House.

The resolution before us suggests simply that this is a matter which we cannot ignore. It does not propose a particular remedy or imply that anything improper has been done. It simply asserts that the tradition of parliamentary control requires at least a formal consideration of the powers which now attach, and the restraints which should apply, to the most powerful office in our political system. There is a danger, of course, that this discussion will be seen as simply one more step in a struggle for power between members on one side of the House and those on the other, or between the executive and the legislature. However, that is not the case, as I hope my arguments have shown. There is another dimension to the problem; it is the very real harm that can be done to a country like Canada by any concentration of power.

Our federal parliamentary system was not developed by accident or by simple, blind importation from elsewhere. We are a diverse country and we need institutions which both reflect and accommodate that diversity. The best institution for that purpose has been parliament, because it draws its membership from truly every corner of the country and has traditionally encouraged its members to express the views of their locale. But parliament was never designed to be simply a talking shop; the assumption was that the Prime Minister and the cabinet, who came from parliament, would heed the views of the various locales. If they didn't, in theory, parliament would bring them down.

But parliament, the forum of diversity, has lost this control over the executive, and the Prime Minister is increasingly able to construct a government which reflects his own views better than it reflects the diversity of the country. If that double trend continues—the weakening of the forum of diversity and the empowering of a particular group—those regions and attitudes which lack power will naturally tire of the system. That is the special Canadian danger of this kind of concentration of power, and it must be on our minds as we consider the powers and prerogatives of the office of the modern Prime Minister. Mr. Speaker, I thank the House for its attention and hope that this resolution will commend itself to the support of hon. members.

SOME HON. MEMBERS: Hear, hear!

MR. JOHN M. REID (PARLIAMENTARY SECRETARY TO PRESIDENT OF PRIVY COUNCIL: Mr. Speaker, I congratulate the hon. member for Rocky Mountain (Mr. Clark) for bringing this subject to our attention and also on the excellent speech he has just made in favour of his proposition. I agree with him it is important for us to examine the institutions of government from time to time, to analyse changes which concern us and question the direction government seems to be taking, especially if it is one about which we do not feel comfortable.

The hon. member would not expect me to agree with him in all regards, but I do share his concern about the way in which various government institutions are developing in an attempt to cope with the questions which confront them—questions to which there are no easy answers. The point I am making is that government develops in response to stimuli from outside. It is no accident that within the last 15 or 20 years the power, as well as the expenditure, of government has expanded to a remarkable degree. The government has acquired a whole series of new powers, not because of any particular attempt on its part to do so but largely in response to developments within Canadian society which have forced it to act, to legislate, to transfer authority in order to carry out detailed programs approved by parliament.

It is true that today, as when this country came into being in 1867, the Prime Minister is the first of equals. It is true now, as it was then, that the Prime Minister is called to his office by the Governor General. And it is true now, as it was then, that the Prime Minister calls upon colleagues of his in the House of Commons to sit with him and form a government which is responsible to the House of Commons. All this still applies.

Nothing has changed. The Prime Minister is subject to parliament. The way in which parliament organizes itself is a significant factor in the success which it can expect in controlling the executive, of which the Prime Minister is the head—not the whole, not the heart and not the soul.

I think it is important to realize that the powers of the Prime Minister today are really no different from what they were 100 years ago; it is the scope of government that has widened. The powers of the government have increased, and with that increase and greater scope so also have the powers of the Prime Minister increased in keeping with the expansion in government in general. I think it is important to realize that the powers of the Prime Minister are totally dependent upon the powers that this parliament gives to the government.

Having said that, I think it is important to look at the development of the Prime Minister's office as it stands today. As hon. members know, it was the Liberal government in the days of Louis St. Laurent that brought in the concept of the executive assistant. It was the government of the right hon. member for Prince Albert (Mr. Diefenbaker) that brought in the concept of the special assistant—in other words, staff designed to serve the minister as minister.

What we have in the Prime Minister's office is the same kind of staff, except that the constituency of the Prime Minister is not a region in a province, in some cases in one of the smaller provinces, but the whole of Canada. For it is the whole of Canada which the government and the Prime Minister seek to govern, and to govern in tune with what they feel is going on. For example, half of the staff of the Prime Minister's office today works in the correspondence section. The Prime Minister received an unparalleled number of letters. I cannot recall the exact number, but I remember that one year when I appeared before the Standing Committee on Miscellaneous Estimates it turned out that the number one subject about which the Prime Minister had received letters on that particular day was on the question of robins in New Brunswick and the campaign to save them, and the letters numbered some 11,000. All of these letters have to be answered, and so do inquiries, thus, a good 50 per cent of the bodies in the Prime Minister's office are engaged in correspondence.

The Privy Council office is an office of long standing. Even 25 years ago the Privy Council office comprised no more than a handful of officials who acted as a secretariat to the cabinet so as to ensure that decisions taken in cabinet were truly communicated to the departments concerned, and enforced. Under the changes that have taken place in the government, basically those same functions are being carried on. Because the Prime Minister is chairman of the cabinet, it is he who has the ultimate responsibility for ensuring that the collective decisions taken in cabinet are communicated to the departments and enforced by those departments. You will understand, of course, Mr. Speaker, that many departments put their own interpretation on what should be done, and because many of them have grown in response to the legislative demands we have made upon them, often they are not in harmony with the decisions taken by cabinet and they resist them. Those who are ministers and those who have criticized ministries know this to be the fact.

As for the responsibilities of the Prime Minister, he attends the question period daily. In point of fact, I think that if hon. members will check the record they will find that the present Prime Minister probably has one of the best records over the last 20 years for appearing in the House of Commons to answer the criticisms of his government made by members of the opposition, whose right and duty it is to put these criticism to him. I think it is quite clear that the Prime Minister is not isolated; he is in the House in the question period and answers questions daily. These questions apply not only to his own operation but to the operations of the government as a whole.

There is no way that the Prime Minister can escape the barrage of questioning that comes from hon. members opposite. He is here in the House, he responds to those questions, and he is accountable on the floor of the House of Commons for any criticisms made by members of the opposition. That, I think, is absolutely clear. In point of fact, if one looks at the volume of questions it would be crystal clear in all our minds that it is the Prime Minister who responds to most of the questions. There is no question that he is the target of the opposition and number one spokesman for his government.

The hon. member for Rocky Mountain raised a very interesting point about the nature of our politics. He complained that this parliament is not necessarily the vehicle for holding the Prime Minister in check or for defeating the Prime Minister. I tend to agree with that interpretation. I myself regret that most of the important politicking in this country is not carried on in this chamber but, instead, takes place outside the chamber. I think there are two reasons for this. First of all, we tend to use this chamber not as a political forum. I think we waste our time doing too much with other things rather than concentrating on political issues. We also waste our time with antiquated procedures. We do not have the time to debate the issues that the Canadian public wants debated in public. I think that because the House of Commons has not taken action to deal with this reality, it has lost, and is losing, a great deal of respect on the part of Canadians.

About two years ago a Gallup poll that was published showed that the respect the people had for members of parliament and for parliament as an institution was declining. I feel that we are not making it our responsibility to check the government and to forcibly bring it to account. I think parliament can do a great deal more to bring its procedures into tune with the times. It can appropriate powers unto itself and become a much more effective forum.

This would mean that many members of this House would have to give up a lot of things which they regard as important and vital to the way in which they as individuals carry on their business. I submit, Mr. Speaker, that it would be an extraordinarily painful experience for many members of parliament if the House were to change its procedures, but I hope that program of parliamentary reform upon which the House leader has embarked will be the vehicle for making parliament more germane, more important, more the centre of political activity in Canada.

I do not agree with the former leader of the Social Credit party, Bob Thompson, who once complained to the Speaker that a terrible thing was happening in the House of Commons—it was becoming a political body and political debate was being introduced. I think that is the spice of this institution. It is important that we consider the way we behave and do business in this House, with a view to dealing expeditiously with those matters about which there is a great deal of agreement. We must put the important issues before the Canadian people, debate them and then find a mechanism for bringing them to a conclusion after meaningful debate, instead of the one-sided monologues that we have in this house at the present time. Because for debate to be meaningful there must be contributions from both sides. Under our existing rules and practices in the House, this does not take place, consequently, in many respects we are responsible for lulling the Canadian people to sleep instead of taking advantage of their natural instinct for things political in Canada.

I should also like to make the point that when the Prime Minister and ministers of the government find themselves going outside the House, over the head of parliament, as the hon. member for Rocky Mountain expressed it, there are two good reasons. First of all, it is helpful and healthful for both the Prime Minister and his ministers to get out of the House of Commons, out of the stultifying atmosphere that is Ottawa, to where the "real" people are, so they can become continually reinforced in their awareness that Canada is a land of diversity. If the Prime Minister, ministers and backbenchers were to stay in Ottawa all the time, there would be a tendency for them to get sucked into the kind of mentality that pervades this place. This is why members of parliament are able to come back here from their constituencies in all regions of Canada and contribute an input into the civil service during the question period, in committee hearings and by making speeches on various subjects in the House of Commons. This could bring back the administration of the country to the House of Commons. My main point is that prime ministers and ministers go outside, into the country, for this helpful reason, and because it is an important form of communication with the electorate. Governments, prime ministers, ministers and backbenchers from all sides like to be re-elected. Any prime minister, minister or backbencher who finds himself losing contact with his constituency is not going to last very long around here. So it is healthful to go back and speak to your people and have them speak to you.

The Prime Minister (Mr. Trudeau) and other ministers have large constituencies. The hon. member for Winnipeg North Centre (Mr. Knowles) has a large constituency for which he speaks. He speaks for the old age pensioners and is recognized as one of their spokesmen, so it is a national constituency for which he speaks. The Prime Minister also has a national constituency, so it is very important for him to travel nationally, making a point of being seen and being available.

The fact that it is interpreted that he is going over the head of this House is an indication that this House is not in tune with what is going on, because if the House of Commons were in tune with what is going on, that charge naturally would not be made.

It is my hope that when we have the opportunity to deal with the placing of television cameras in the House of Commons, and making available the televised record of this House to those who wish to see it, this will mark a change in the approach we as politicians have taken toward the use of television in Canada. I think the existing scrum that takes place after the question period is a disgrace. It would be far better if cameras recorded what goes on in the House of Commons and transmitted it to the people in their homes, so that they could see what takes place in this place as well as anybody else.

AN HON. MEMBER: You better be careful because they will see the Cabinet.

MR. REID: Cabinet ministers often say to me that they never get on television. I think most Cabinet ministers would look with a great deal of anticipation to the opportunity of becoming television stars.

AN HON. MEMBER: I would rather watch Lassie.

MR. REID: It may well be that the Cabinet ministers and their families would be the only ones who watched, but at least the opportunity would be given Canadians to see the performance not only of Cabinet ministers but also of members opposite. That is also an important consideration.

The hon. member made reference to the fact that one of the ways in which the government could be kept in check is if we had what he called a competitive electoral system. I tend to disagree with the interpretation he places upon the situation, in that he said we did not have a balanced system. He referred to the province of Quebec and to the fact that his party has difficulty in getting seats there. My party has difficulty getting seats in the west. If you take a look at the total of all seats you will find that the two tend to balance off, except that I think we do much better in the west than the hon. member's party does in Quebec.

Surely the reasons for the situation are historical and have to do with the position that political parties have taken on the great issues of our time. They have to do with the way in which these parties are seen as the defenders of their interests. It may very well be that, in a country like Canada with such diversities, it is impossible for any political party to be popular simultaneously in all parts of the country. My feeling would be that if indeed a party could ever be simultaneously popular in all parts of the country either there would be something the matter with the political party or something wrong with the Canadian population. I do not believe it is possible, or that it would be particularly healthful.

I would reiterate the point I made in reply to the hon. member a few minutes ago. I think parties get their strength from the decisions they have taken while in government and in opposition. This is the result of the decisions taken by parties on public issues of the day. We have to take responsibility for the stands and decisions we take, and I think that is the only fair way to go about it.

I do not think the hon. member should say the political system is unbalanced. His party came far too close to winning in 1972, and if the party opposite had fought us as hard as it fought itself during the last federal election its hon. members might well have won and be sitting in these seats. That party did not win. Consequently justice prevailed, and truth is in its chair.

I want to deal with the constitutional relationship raised by the hon. member, and the concept of parliamentary democracy versus Cabinet government. It is quite true that we have a system of Cabinet government. It is also true that we have a system of parliamentary legislature. There is a distinction between the two. The job of the government is to govern. It is not our job as legislators to govern but to legislate.

If you were to take a look at the amount of legislation passed through the House of Commons over the last 15 or 20 years you would find quite clearly that the productivity of the Canadian parliament has been declining. This decline in the ability of parliament to cope with changing social situations and the necessity to legislate old legislation into conformity with new situations is one of the reasons why the Canadian parliament has not been highly regarded by the Canadian people in recent years.

The point I want to make is that there is no disharmony between the concepts of Cabinet government and parliamentary democracy. The Cabinet is drawn from the legislature and it is accountable every single day of the week in the House of Commons. The Prime Minister and the ministers are in their seats and questions are asked. In addition there is an unparalleled opportunity, I think unique to a parliamentary system, whereby parliamentary committees have the opportunity to question officials about the administration of legislation.

No longer must we be satisfied with the bland explanations we used to get in the good old days when estimates were dealt with by the House in committee of supply, when ministers would sit there with two officials in front of them providing information. That information did not flow to members of parliament, and members of parliament had very little input in the administration of programs. We now have the opportunity, under the existing system, to influence not only the policy but also the administration of the policy. It seems to me this is a significant thing we have acquired, obtained or won, depending on your position.

What seems clear is that the government feels it is not receiving sufficient scrutiny in the House of Commons. I think the government feels that the calibre of the opposition in examining policies and programs is not as good as it should be. I think the government feels the need for that kind of hardnosed opposition, because it is that kind of opposition which keeps the government and civil servants on their toes. This is a vital part of the way in which the government comports itself inside and outside the House of Commons.

When the opposition is digging in on various government policies it is not surprising to see changes made in their administration, and hon. members opposite, as well as backbenchers on this side, have a significant input into the way in which governing is carried on here in Canada. This seems to me to be the role of the politician. It is not part of his political role, but is part of his role as a legislator.

If we are to talk in terms of bringing the Cabinet to heel and being subject to closer examination, it seems that members opposite have to ask themselves if the opportunities now available to them are being fully exploited. If you look at those opportunities in an objective way I am sure you will find that, in fact, the existing opportunities have gone by the wayside and are not being exploited. Parliament is the master of its own fate. It has the power to effect change, and the power if required to institute different procedures in order to redress an unbalance.

I think one would find that backbenchers on this side of the House and the government itself would be prepared to co-operate in bringing such an undesirable thing to a happy end because we feel that the basis of the democratic system in Canada is a Parliament which is respected and looked up to, Mr. Speaker. We feel this is not now the case. We feel the prestige of the government, of the Prime Minister—

MR. DEPUTY SPEAKER: Order, please. I regret to interrupt the hon. member, but his time has expired.

MR. STANLEY KNOWLES (WINNIPEG NORTH CENTRE): Mr. Speaker, this is an extremely interesting subject that the hon. member for Rocky Mountain (Mr. Clark) has introduced. I suspect that many of us agree that it is unfortunate that there is only an hour for this debate. Of course that could be corrected if the motion of the hon. member passed and the matter were dealt with by a committee.

I believe one might also say there is more common ground between the hon. member for Rocky Mountain and the Parliamentary Secretary to the President of the Privy Council (Mr. Reid) than one might have anticipated. Both, and I agree with them, feel that we should avoid having a one-man dictatorship, an all-powerful prime minister as the one and only person running this country. I agree with the view expressed by both preceding members that perhaps the best way to make sure that we do not have a master as a prime minister of this country is to strengthen parliament itself. I regard this motion as useful in that it encourages us to think of ways in which this institution might be strengthened.

I have a number of ideas but I shall not have an opportunity to get them all across because one must not speak for too long in this hour. First, however, I want to say there are ways in which parliament is a stronger institution today more than it was in the so-called good old days. I was here in the days of Mackenzie King. Let me tell members on all sides of this House that the word of Mackenzie King was law with respect to every last detail in the operation of this House. He did not have to ask for unanimous consent in respect of things cabinet ministers ask for such consent today. He just said that was it, and that was it!

I remember an occasion in the 1940's when I had my first experience as a member of a committee on procedure. The committee had produced what I thought was a pretty good report. It was presented, debated for a day, and then it stood for some time on the order paper. In my naiveté as a young member, I wondered what was wrong. Brazenly one day I went over to Mr. King—I knew he was the boss; he was the one to see—and asked him if he could not do something about having this report brought back for further debate. His answer to me was no, that the report proposed that the House adjourn at 10:30 at night and that we could not possibly do that. He said that we had been sitting until 11 o'clock for years, and that the report was no good. Mackenzie King did not like the suggestion that the House adjourn at 10.30, and so the report was denied.

I remember later when I dared challenge him on something he had said which was out of order. I just about got put out of the place. Here was I, a young man in my thirties, criticizing the Prime Minister! Mind you, that was a day when children were more respectful of their parents, and a day when teachers and principals ran the schools. Society has changed. Today backbenchers have a voice, and cabinet ministers and prime ministers do not rule the roost in terms of superficial details, if I may call them that.

One other factor in those days was that we did not have the sound amplification system, and many members of the House of Commons in the fourth or fifth rows did not speak during a whole session because their voices were timid and they could not be heard. Some of us who could shout and be heard thought that the introduction of the sound system was unfair because it gave an opportunity to the timid souls to be heard. Times have changed, and participation by members in all parts of the House is much more the case now than it was in the forties.

There was a similar situation in respect of the French-speaking members in those days because it was an English-speaking House, with the translation of the French appearing at the end of *Hansard*. Many times a translation did not appear at the end of *Hansard* because the French-speaking members saw no point in speaking because they were not understood. A change came about in that regard.

When I first came here, at the beginning of a session a first meeting would be called, in one room, of the 20 or 25 committees for the purpose of electing the chairmen of these various committees. I remember that one day at that mass meeting I asked if there was a quorum present of the particular committee of which I was a member and for which a chairman was being named. I was told by the government whip of that day that it always had been done in this manner and that the chairmen were elected in this way. I was put in my place.

Most of the committees did not hold meetings. I would say there were a good dozen committees that would go through a whole parliament without meeting, or meeting perhaps only once, such as the Committee on Printing to agree not to print certain documents, and the Committee on the Restaurant to approve raising the price of meals in the dining room from 50 cents to 75 cents, or something like that.

There is now far more participation by individual members of all parties than was the case when I first came here. I say this with some regret because in those days we, as members of a small party, were the prima donnas and we produced the action. Now there are prima donnas in all parties; there is the electronic system and everybody gets in. There is, as I said, more participation by private members, and this is good.

I think there is a good deal of merit to what the last speaker said about the question of respect for parliament today. I also agree. I think one reason is that we do not make the best use of our time. We spend the same amount of time on unimportant as on important issues.

SOME HON. MEMBERS: Hear, hear!

MR. KNOWLES (WINNIPEG NORTH CENTRE): I hope we will adopt a system—I may put it in as precise terms as I see it—whereby we decide every session that there are three categories of bills, routine and quite unimportant things, things that have a reasonable measure of importance, and then the crucial ones.

In respect of the routine housekeeping measures let us not spend any time on them at all, but ship them to the committees.

SOME HON. MEMBERS: Hear, hear!

MR. KNOWLES (WINNIPEG NORTH CENTRE): As for the medium group I suggest we should have an agreement that there would be a certain number of hours for debate on any one of those bills.

SOME HON. MEMBERS: Hear, hear!

MR. KNOWLES (WINNIPEG NORTH CENTRE): My next suggestion should receive applause from this side of the House. I say that the opposition should have the right in every parliament to say that there are five or six bills which we regard as crucial, and that these must be before the House without a time limit. The result is that we would spend most of the available days on five or six crucial bills, but let the routine and medium class bills be dealt with in a routine way. I think then we would have sharper debate and would increase the respect held by this country for parliament.

I feel the same way about estimates, the study of which is another major function around here. I think the way we spread ourselves over the whole gambit of billions of dollars, and do not do a very good job on any, is wrong. I would rather see us handle half a dozen departments a year so that we would do the whole job in the course of a four-year parliament. I would also like to see us bring back to the floor—I realize what the member said about the value of doing things in committee—three or four departments a year at the choice of the opposition—and I think an element of surprise would have a salutary effect—so that when we study the estimates we would do a really thorough job.

I have lots of other ideas, but that is enough time for me to take today. I agree completely with my friend, the hon. member for Rocky Mountain, that we do not want a master prime minister; we want parliament to be supreme. I agree with the hon. member for Kenora-Rainy River that the way to do that is to look at our procedures and try to strengthen them. I believe we can do so, and I hope we can get at this very soon.

23

Mackenzie King: Power over the Political Executive*

GERALD C. V. WRIGHT

How does a Prime Minister get what he wants? How, in particular, does he do this when it requires the cooperation of the men with whom he shares executive authority over both the governmental machine and the parliamentary party—the cabinet members and senior bureaucrats?

This approach to the study of political leadership is taken in Richard Neustadt's incisive analysis of presidential power.[1] He compares the exercise of power with a process of bargaining between the President and other office-holders, each of whom possesses certain bargaining advantages. The analogy of a bargaining process has only limited application to the dealings between a Canadian Prime Minister and his colleagues, for the distinction between their selfish and their shared motivations is often very difficult to discern. It also fails to capture very accurately the psychological elements of fear and respect, of loyalty and suspicion, of decisiveness and command, which must govern many of the actions and reactions around the cabinet table. It is even less adequate where the outcome desired by the leader is often contrived to emerge of its own accord rather than as a direct result of pressure or persuasion.

Yet while the conceptual framework may be inadequate, the fundamental problem remains—the problem of the man at the centre, with the whole population as his "constituency" and a set of constraints and imperatives that are national in scope, trying to impose his will on another, formally subordinate and more restricted, constituency (in this case, a regional group, interest group, or concerned segment of opinion), which may have different priorities and possibly divergent ambitions. Power, in this context is the ability to achieve one's desired objectives through the agency of others whose cooperation is indispensable but whose acquiescence is by no means automatic. It is measured by the frequency with which these objectives are attained.

---

* Written for this volume.
[1] Richard E. Neustadt, *Presidential Power* (New York, 1962).

Mackenzie King's Objectives

It is natural that an essay on prime ministerial power in Canadian politics should draw on the career of William Lyon Mackenzie King. His success in obtaining his own way established a pattern of political leadership in Canada that has not yet lost its influence. He sometimes miscalculated and he was often merely lucky, yet he sought actively after power and, like Roosevelt, he had a "feel" for it. Of all Canadian political leaders, there was probably none who weighed so carefully the implications for his own position of every policy decision, appointment and pronouncement that he made as Prime Minister.

An appreciation of Mackenzie King's control over the political executive will naturally depend on an assessment of what his objectives were. He had, I believe, two fundamental aims. Firstly, he wanted to maintain the allegiance of French Canada to the Liberal Party and a sense of full membership in the nation among French Canadians; secondly, he wanted to make his party and his Government as broadly representative as possible of the diverse groups which made up the country. It is the measure of King's insight into Canadian politics of the twenties, thirties and forties that his personal ambition of continuance in office and his prime political aim of warding off divisive and disruptive movements in the nation were so inextricably intertwined. As his diary reveals, even in his own conscience, Mackenzie King could battle the enemies of his tenure and call them the enemies of national unity.[2]

The Cabinet was the most significant theatre in which King pursued his objectives. In its most important members reposed the trust of their constituencies; their presence in the Cabinet provided the guarantee of policies that would not be biased against any group. Keeping them in harness together was a practical necessity for King, for during a prolonged period of apparent amity in the Cabinet, sectional rifts might be palliated and his leadership strengthened.

The Sources of his Power

To achieve his goals, he drew influence over his colleagues from the formal powers of his office, his political reputation, and his political strategy.

HIS FORMAL POWERS.
Neustadt has pointed out that a leader's formal powers are his "bargaining advantages" or "vantage points" in dealing with his colleagues.[3] Standing alone, however, the Prime Minister's powers—such as chairing cabinet meetings, appointing and dismissing Ministers, advising dissolution of Parliament, and making senior appointments in the public service—are much less impressive than those of the American presidency. It is the way the

---

[2] See J. W. Pickersgill, *The Mackenzie King Record*, Vol. I: 1939-1944 and (with D. F. Forster) Vol. II: 1944-1945 (Toronto, 1960 and 1968).
[3] Neustadt, *Presidential Power*, p. 31.

Prime Minister can tie them to the achievement of some end much greater than their technical purpose which gives the Prime Minister influence in the Government.

Part of the Prime Minister's political strategy is the manner in which he structures the discussion of important issues. His control of the cabinet agenda and of cabinet meetings enable him to do this. Intent on preventing a split in his Cabinet, King acquired an early mastery of the strategy of delay. He deliberately drew out the battles of the twenties over a freight rate structure that would be equitable and economically rational, and would provide a fair return to the railways, in order to bring both sides to terms. In those same years, he struggled to keep the fight between high- and low-tariff Ministers within the confines of the council chamber. In each case, the extended clash of opinions simply made the case for compromise.

King also tried to define the issues and set the priorities for cabinet discussions. In the conscription crisis, this meant trying to get his Defence Minister to turn his attention from military commitments and recruitment figures to the broader picture that was painted, albeit in extravagant tones, by the Prime Minister. It was a picture filled with portends of likely national disunity following the imposition of conscription for overseas service—a prophecy of civil strife, a repetition of the destruction of the Liberals in 1917, an upsurge of the Left, encouragement to Hitler, and even a mortal blow to the British Empire.[4]

King needed Ralston, who had become, in Bruce Hutchison's words, "the custodian of the Canadian soldiers' faith in the Government and the nation's personal guarantee that the war would be fought and won".[5] Yet the differing experiences of the two men and their differing vantage points in government gave them radically different perspectives on the problem. In the end, King's strategy succeeded, not in keeping Ralston in the Government or preventing conscription, but in warding off the two catastrophic eventualities that would have resulted from deciding the issue on Ralston's narrower terms—the departure of the conscriptionist Ministers including Ilsley or a fatal blow to both the influence and the confidence of the French Canadians including St. Laurent. By keeping the broader picture constantly in front of their eyes, King maintained the adherence of the former group to the breaking point, by which time he had sufficiently proven his sincerity to the latter and to most of their followers.[6]

The powers of appointment and promotion can also be used to strengthen the likelihood of the Prime Minister obtaining his own way in the Cabinet. At the beginning, in 1921, King's major weakness derived from the poor balance of cabinet representation. He was overshadowed by

---

[4] See especially Pickersgill and Forster, *Mackenzie King Record*, II, p. 122.

[5] Bruce Hutchison, *The Incredible Canadian* (Toronto, 1952), p. 311.

[6] C. G. Power, Air Minister and a Quebec M.P., did resign from the Cabinet. Two-thirds of the Quebec members voted for a resolution opposing conscription, but the province voted overwhelmingly Liberal in the general election of 1945.

the presence of his close rival for the Liberal leadership, W. S. Fielding, who had been Premier of Nova Scotia for 12 years and Laurier's Minister of Finance for 15. In discussion of the 1923 Budget, in which Fielding left tariffs untouched and aroused furious protests from the low-tariff western-ers, King was hard put to prevent increases proposed by the strong contin-gent of protectionists—Sir Lomer Gouin, an ex-premier of Quebec with close connections on St. James Street, Henri Béland, T. A. Low and James Robb. The agrarian representatives, Motherwell and Stewart, were no match for them.[7]

The Prime Minister's own policy of national unity required a balanced ministry. Significantly, King's first important tariff reduction—on the im-plements of production in the primary industries—did not come until 1924 when Fielding and Gouin had both retired from the Cabinet. By giving increased prominence to Ernest Lapointe, leader of the left wing of younger Quebec Liberals, as Gouin's replacement, King was making it easier for the Liberal Party to fulfill its promises of tariff reduction, and prevent the West from falling completely to the Progressives. Later he was able to find stronger cabinet representation for that region.

The more effectively a Prime Minister can govern the political careers of his colleagues the better he can employ them to enhance rather than impinge on his own authority. Again, the policy of national unity served King's personal ambition well. This surely explains why he would seek to include in his Cabinet men like Charles Dunning of Saskatchewan, men whose power and ambition appeared likely to make them contenders for his job. Permitting them to be effective regional or interest-group spokes-men enhanced his own role as peacemaker and may well have helped to disqualify them from consideration for the national leadership.

After 1939, the size and complexity of the Government's activities made it inevitable that a substantial degree of influence over policy would descend below the cabinet level. King attempted to associate the public service with the achievement of his own ends by giving close attention to the most sensitive appointments—for example, the appointment of General MacNaughton as commander of the expeditionary force and of Donald Gordon as chairman of the Wartime Prices and Trade Board. Both superin-tended government policies which he had hoped to avoid and which were fraught with political hazard—military participation in a European war and active intervention in the economy; yet both were his personal choice. The diary shows that he established continuing personal links with some of the higher officials, particularly Clifford Clark, the Deputy Minister of Fi-nance.[8] The cooperation—indeed, the active advocacy—of Clark and his de-

---

[7] See R. MacGregor Dawson, *William Lyon Mackenzie King*, Vol. I: 1874-1923 (Toronto, 1958), pp. 441-5.

[8] Clark attended a number of cabinet meetings in some of which he was the instrument, in others the object, of Mackenzie King's persuasion. On occasion he would sound out Ilsley, the Minister, through Clark, the Deputy. The Prime Minister even tried to per-suade Clark of the importance of his political strategy of undercutting the Left. See especially Pickersgill and Forster, *Mackenzie King Record*, II, 31.

partment was essential in developing the social programmes, including family allowances and universal old-age pensions, with which King hoped to deflect the growing challenge of the C.C.F.

HIS POLITICAL REPUTATION.

A politician can only gauge the significance of a Prime Minister's threats and promises in terms of what he knows of the man. The likelihood that he will go against the Prime Minister may be governed by how much he needs the latter to keep his job, to give him credibility as a formulator and spokesman of government policy, or to support him in intra-cabinet squabbles. He may mentally weigh the Prime Minister's prestige against the strength of his hold over his own constituency of support; though only a few Ministers in each Cabinet actually have constituencies of any size. Alternatively, the respect and loyalty he gives the Prime Minister may follow automatically from the quality of the relationship that the leader's past actions will have established between them. The Minister may have been permanently cowed into submission, or encouraged to feel that he could afford to act independently. One of the assumptions in his calculation of bargaining advantages, therefore, as well as a psychological factor of first importance in dealings between Minister and Prime Minister, is the latter's political reputation.

Mackenzie King built his reputation largely on a string of remarkable political successes. It is true that in only one of his seven elections as Liberal leader did he achieve a majority of the popular vote; yet in four of those elections the Liberals finished over ten percentage points ahead of the Conservatives. The election victories showed King's ability for gauging the mood of the people and for choosing issues that undercut his opponents with their simplicity and directness—like economy in Government and low taxation in the 1920's, and an end to "dictatorship" and government interference in the economy in the 1930's. It was this ability which impressed the men around him—the technocrats like Howe who wanted to get on with the management of the economy, the pro-consuls like Gardiner who sought safeguards and benefits for the West, and the political strategists like Power whose eye was forever on elections yet to come.

The politics of war-time demanded a somewhat different style of national leadership from that of King's premiership in the twenties and thirties. He went to great trouble to give the impression of a close relationship with both of the war-time leaders, Roosevelt and Churchill. He coveted invitations to visit them, and to perform public acts that identified him as a world leader, such as addressing a joint session of Parliament in London. Within the Cabinet, he sought to associate their prestige with his own political aims. During the conscription crisis, for example, he tried, without success, to get a telegram from Churchill indicating that the opinion of the British Government was that the war would soon be over (and continued Canadian reinforcements would thus no longer be necessary).[9]

Yet the keystone of his political reputation was the calculated identification of himself and his party with the cause of national unity. Other

[9] Pickersgill and Forster, *Mackenzie King Record*, III, especially p. 167.

290 APEX OF POWER

Canadian political leaders, Macdonald and Laurier for example, have realized the importance of unity and attempted to build a lasting union by positive action. Still others, like Diefenbaker who framed his political strategy in disregard of Quebec, have found themselves subject to the fundamental exigencies of federal politics in their cabinet appointments and policy decisions. But King was unique in this respect; he convinced his Cabinet, Parliament, and many of the electorate, as he convinced himself, that in him alone lay the chance to escape internal strife. He sought successfully to be acknowledged in a dual role—both the essential peacemaker and the protector of group interests. His own continuance in office was his positive policy for national unity and the sense of this policy was accepted by many other than himself.

Mackenzie King applied this facet of his authority with telling effect in the Cabinet. One particular technique of re-establishing his control of a situation, which he used several times in the conscription crisis, was to offer or suggest his own resignation.[10] On at least one occasion, he polled the Cabinet in pretended search for an alternative leader. No one was bold enough to volunteer.

Equipped with this unique, self-made instrument of power, Mackenzie King operated with supreme self-confidence, his most powerful personal support, and many of the Ottawa community, and of the population at large too, judged him to be the indispensable man. At the end of his career, one of his bitterest critics was to say that of all political leaders of his generation King alone really understood that "the essential task of Canadian statesmanship is to discover the terms on which as many as possible of the significant interest groups of our country can be induced to work together in a common policy".[11] Nowadays we might be less inclined to accept this as one of the eternal verities of Canadian politics, but it is nonetheless impressive evidence of the reputation of the man.

The Consequence of Mr. King

How did King's active use of prime ministerial power stretch the power potential of his office? In some respects, it is true, he appears closer to Walter Bagehot than Pierre Trudeau. Potential opposition from the Cabinet held him back on occasion, and individual Ministers were often a significant restraint upon his freedom of action. Lapointe's utility as French Canadian lieutenant would have been seriously endangered if the Govern-

---

[10] King's diary reveals how clearly he understood the potency of the resignation weapon. "I had never seen a look of greater concern on the faces of my colleagues. For a moment, they seemed to be struck dumb. They were face to face with the future of the Party without myself as its leader. Howe spoke out quite emphatically on this as did one or two of the others. That there would be no one who could save the after-war situation if I were defeated." From Pickersgill and Forster, *Mackenzie King Record*, II, p. 201. Reprinted here by permission of the University of Toronto Press and Mr. Pickersgill.

[11] F. H. Underhill, *In Search of Canadian Liberalism* (Toronto, 1960), p. 126.

ment had brought forward programmes of social legislation against La-pointe's will. Ralston and Ilsley both carried such prestige in the war-time administration, that King probably felt that his Government could not stand the resignation of either.[12]

Furthermore, if he were to invite powerful men to his Cabinet, he could not infringe on their control of their departments. From his arrival in Ottawa in 1935, James Gardiner held sole power over western agriculture; under his aegis, agricultural policy was revolutionized to incorporate the principle of commodity prices guaranteed by the state. Nor was King well equipped to align the rest of the Government with his own purposes when these involved administrative detail. A personal staff capable of under-standing troop wastage rates could have alerted him to the impending reinforcement gap in 1944, and given him more time to avert the crisis which followed.

There were, thus, traditional limits to his power that he could not ignore; others he was able to overstep. A largely unwritten constitution, such as Canada's, permits an unusual confusion of principles as to the derivation of power and the degree of autonomy with which it can be exercised. Mackenzie King expanded the powers of the Prime Minister by exploiting the flexibility afforded him by the unwritten rules. He left it a more powerful position because he had demonstrated the potential man-oeuvrability available to its incumbent. He had shown that the Prime Minister possessed a surprising degree of freedom to locate critical issues in his chosen area of the governmental system or to move them to a more favourable location, depending on his needs of the moment. Two examples are his conduct of Canadian foreign policy and his handling of the con-scription crisis.

As head of the fledgeling External Affairs Department and as chair-man of the Cabinet, King seldom permitted the subject of foreign policy to be raised in cabinet at all in the years prior to World War II. That subject was likely to arouse sectional sensitivities in the Cabinet which he was determined to prevent. Such important decisions as the repudiation of Riddell's proposal of more severe sanctions against Italy in 1935 and the acceptance of President Roosevelt's suggestion of a joint board on defence were taken without reference to his Ministers.[13]

The traumatic issue of conscription, on the other hand, was precipi-tated by a Minister, Colonel Ralston. It caused a major cabinet crisis in

---

[12] Ralston's eventual replacement was made possible only by the availability of General MacNaughton who possessed the same kind of popular appeal. Ralston was the only important Minister ever dismissed by King. The Prime Minister's need of a balanced ministry made the threat of dismissal almost a nullity, as it has been since.

[13] Lapointe, alone of the Cabinet, was involved in the former decision. The Ogdensburg Agreement setting up the Permanent Joint Board on Defence was approved by cabinet minute on August 20, 1940, two days after the agreement had been made public. On the subject of King's conduct of foreign policy between the wars, see James Eayrs, *In Defence of Canada*, (Toronto, 1965), Vol. II.

1941-42 and almost brought about the collapse of the Government in 1944. The first crisis was eased by the Prime Minister's decision to hold a plebiscite requesting release from the Government's commitment not to impose conscription for overseas service. The second, and much more serious one, was contained in the Cabinet until the final decision to draft men overseas. During the critical days of October and November of 1944, however, Mackenzie King several times threatened the calling of Parliament and then an election. When his *volte-face* occurred, he was about to ask the House of Commons for a vote of confidence.

In the first example, King was actually exploiting what Harry Eckstein has called "the myth of the fusion of authority" in cabinet government, to present as government policy decisions which his colleagues had no hand in making. Such autonomous action is often possible in the case of new programmes or new governmental responsibilities. The Prime Minister's connection with the project or policy is more intimate, and policy-making procedures have not yet been institutionalized so that Ministers and departments could rightfully claim a part in them.

Translating the conscription issue to a wider theatre—as King did, in effect, by the 1942 plebiscite—could not have been done a second time without possibly fatal cost to the Prime Minister. But the immediate problem was one of authority over the conscriptionist Ministers, and the more mindful he could keep them of the wider democratic processes, the greater was his authority. In Parliament and *a fortiori* in a general election—as was the case in the 1942 plebiscite—Ministers would have had to line up behind the leader or else join forces with their political enemies. That is the real potency of the weapon of dissolution. As King noted in relation to the earlier crisis, "Seeing the position as King or Meighen, puts everyone on the spot in regard to their support."[14]

There were convenient rationalizations at hand to support King's strategic moves and make credible his threats. The old "grit" principle that all power resides in the people could be used to justify his request of a dissolution of Parliament in 1926, which precipitated a constitutional crisis, and his sudden dissolution in 1940. If Parliament were the chosen theatre of action, King would proclaim the standard liberal tenets of the supremacy of that body and the responsibility of Ministers to it. If the Cabinet were to legislate by order-in-council, then it could be argued that the Government had been "mandated" by the electorate. Even in his time, the leader's pre-eminence in election campaigns was such that he was in good position to impose his own interpretation of the party's "mandate" on his Ministers,[15] or forcefully remind them of their obligation to the party.[16]

Naturally the Prime Minister's manoeuvrability was often circumscribed by the type of issue confronting him and by other political forces. Nor was it always sufficient to attain his goals. It was, however, the most

---

[14] Pickersgill, *Mackenzie King Record*, I, 336.

[15] *Ibid.*

[16] Pickersgill and Forster, *Mackenzie King Record*, II, 146.

distinctive element of his political strategy, and extended the formal powers of his office beyond what had theretofore been considered their constitutional meaning and significance. It was this newly tested ability to manoeuvre and manipulate issues that was Mackenzie King's chief legacy to his successors. Its significance lay not so much in its use, as in the demonstrated potential of the prime-ministerial office. It is this potential which today underlies the power relationships of Prime Minister and political executive.

24

Prime Minister Diefenbaker and the Cuban Missile Crisis*

PEYTON V. LYON

Before the exposure of the Soviet missile bases, Canadians had shown little sympathy for the American preoccupation with Cuba, and they were disturbed by bellicose oratory in the congressional election campaign. They had not forgotten, moreover, the misleading reports put out by Washington at the time of the disastrous landing at the Bay of Pigs. The government had some apprehensions about Soviet activity in Cuba, but was not informed on October 14 that the American reconnaissance aircraft had discovered the missile bases. Mr. Diefenbaker told the House on October 16 that "there appears to be no justification to associate or link together the questions of Cuba and Berlin." Concerning Berlin, he warned, "there have been some indications that the Soviet Union may shortly precipitate a new, if not a grave, crisis in that city." The Prime Minister appeared to be much less worried about Cuba, and said the United Nations was providing "an opportunity to ensure that all possible steps are taken to arrive at a peaceful solution."[1] Canada, like the other NATO allies, was not taken fully into American confidence during the week of October 14-20 when the quarantine action was being planned; the Prime Minister learned through intelligence channels about the missile build-up on Sunday, October 21,[2] but the government did not receive its first information concerning

---

* Revised and abridged from Peyton V. Lyon, *Canada in World Affairs 1961-63* (Toronto: Oxford University Press, 1968), pp. 32-54, by permission of the Oxford University Press.

[1] Canada, House of Commons, *Debates*, 16 October 1962, p. 567.

[2] There are reports, that I have not been able to verify, that the government had received some information even earlier than 21 October through NORAD channels. One of Mr. Diefenbaker's grievances may well have been that such vital information reached him through military channels rather than more directly from the President. Five years later, Mr. Diefenbaker complained to the Canadian Press that the President had phoned about 2 p.m. on the day the American counter-measures were announced to request that all Canadian forces be placed on alert. "I interpreted that to mean a national emergency", Mr. Diefenbaker explained. "There was no consultation whatever. He thought that what he wanted Canada to do we would do." (*The Globe and Mail*, 28 October 1967, "Canada

the proposed counter-action until approximately two and a half hours before the President's television address on October 22. Canada, as Mr. Diefenbaker subsequently stressed, had been "informed", not "consulted".

Mr. Livingston Merchant, the President's emissary, met with Messrs. Diefenbaker, Harkness, and Green at about 4:30 p.m. Mr. Merchant was accompanied by Mr. Ivan White, the American Chargé d'Affaires, and two U.S. intelligence officers. On Mr. Diefenbaker's insistence, no Canadian officers or civil servants were present. Mr. Merchant, who was received coolly by the Prime Minister, showed the Canadian ministers photographs of the missile sites and informed them of the proposed counter-measures. He also read the text of the statement prepared for delivery by the President. He bore no request for specific Canadian action, and was unable to say what steps NORAD was being asked to implement. (NORAD, in fact, did not receive instructions to go on alert status until after the President had spoken on radio and television.) In response to a request by Mr. Diefenbaker, Mr Merchant phoned Washington and obtained the deletion of one sentence from the text. The Prime Minister went home without attempting to meet with the rest of his cabinet. There, after watching the President on television at 7 p.m., he received a phone call from Mr. Pearson requesting that he return to the House to make a statement as soon as possible. This he did shortly after 8 p.m., briefly summarizing the President's pronouncement and urging Canadians "not to panic". Although he asserted that "the existence of these bases or launching pads is not defensive but offensive", he neglected conspicuously to endorse the President's proposed action, or to offer support. "The determination of Canadians", he said, "will be that the United Nations should be charged at the earliest possible moment with this serious problem." He made one specific proposal:

What people all over the world want tonight and will want is a full and complete understanding of what is taking place in Cuba. . . . I suggest that if there is a desire on the part of the U.S.S.R. to have the facts, if a group of nations, perhaps the eight nations comprising the unaligned members of the 18-nation disarmament committee, be given the opportunity of making an on-site inspection in Cuba to ascertain what the facts are. . . . it would provide an objective answer to what is going on in Cuba. As

---

emergency state asked without talks, Diefenbaker says".) If Mr. Diefenbaker really received such a call, it would of course detract from his claim that Canada was badly treated; apart from Prime Minister Macmillan, the leader of no other U.S. ally appears to have been favoured by a presidential call. It would also be more difficult to understand Mr. Diefenbaker's relative inactivity during the remainder of the day. None of his associates, however, appears to have been told about this phone message at the time, and it seems probable that in 1967 Mr. Diefenbaker's memory is at fault. The same Canadian Press report quoted an official as saying that Canada had learned three weeks earlier, through its own sources, of the Russian missiles. This appears very doubtful; although the Canadian Embassy in Havana had confirmed the presence of missiles, they had probably not been identified as IRBM's capable of striking at continental cities. Mr. Diefenbaker was almost certainly correct when he denied that he had been informed of the IRBM three weeks before the President's proclamation. (*Ibid.*)

late as a week ago, the U.S.S.R. contended that its activities in Cuba were entirely of a defensive nature. . . . the only sure way that the world can secure the facts would be through an independent inspection.

The Prime Minister then invited the views of Mr. Pearson and the other party leaders, stressing the need for unity and for suggestions to alleviate "the obvious tensions that must grip men and women all over the world tonight". "My prayer", he concluded, "is that those who have the responsibility of statesmanship will always have in mind the need for doing everything that can be done to assure peace."[3]

Mr. Pearson was also hesitant about the American counter-measures. He welcomed the reference of the matter to the United Nations and the OAS, and agreed that "these international organizations should be used for the purpose of verifying what is going on." "Perhaps", he suggested,

it would be possible for Canada to take part in the discussions that will be held before the Organization of American States because the President referred to them as western hemisphere discussions. While we are not a member . . . this would be a suitable occasion for Canada to participate in this particular meeting.

Mr. Pearson feared that the situation might deteriorate into "the indescribable horror of nuclear war" and pledged the government his party's full co-operation in seeking "peace and freedom in this crisis".[4] For the Socreds, Mr. Robert Thompson stressed the importance of doing "what is morally right", and urged Canada to make its influence felt within the OAS. He thought the current serious assault of Chinese troops against India was probably "a convenient smoke screen for the situation in Cuba". He too avoided any specific endorsement of the American counter-action.[5]

The shortest contribution was by Mr. Herridge, the House leader of the NDP, who committed his party to co-operate with the government and expressed relief that the United States had referred the issue to the United Nations and the OAS; his major concern was to find out if Canada had been "consulted or informed".[6] Mr. T. C. Douglas, the national leader of the NDP (who had that very day won re-entry to Parliament in a byelection), expressed skepticism in Vancouver about President Kennedy's

---

[3] *Debates*, 22 October 1962, pp. 805-6. It appears that Mr. Diefenbaker's proposal was one that had been prepared by some of his advisors who knew that there were reports of offensive missiles on Cuba, but not that their presence had been fully established, or that Mr. Diefenbaker, along with three other allied leaders—de Gaulle, Adenauer, and Macmillan—had been shown the photographic proof in advance of the President's public statement. In other words, it was a proposal designed to be helpful in a different situation. The Prime Minister may have been anxious to say something constructive and, in view of the time element, could not have had time to consult about the appropriateness of using the suggestion for a UN inspection team after the Americans had shown him their photographic evidence.

[4] *Ibid.*, pp. 806-7.

[5] *Ibid.*, p. 807.

[6] *Ibid.*, pp. 807-8.

charges—"we have only the statements of the Americans"—and considerable sympathy for the Russian case—"before we get too excited we should
remember that for fifteen years the Western powers have been ringing the
Soviet Union with missile and air bases."[7]

Later that evening the government learned that the American units in
NORAD had been placed on an alert technically described as "Defcon 3".
(This indicated serious international tension but not that war was imminent.) Mr. Harkness and his senior advisors assumed that the Canadian
forces would immediately follow suit. At that time, however, the Minister lacked the authority to implement on his own the Canadian alert equivalent to Defcon 3, and consequently Mr. Harkness sought clearance from
the Prime Minister. Mr. Green, who was also present, raised no objections,
but Mr. Diefenbaker insisted that the decision be put off until the cabinet
could meet the following morning.[8]

The same evening, Mr. Green let it be known outside the House that
Canada had withdrawn permission for Russian planes to fly over Canadian
territory, or to land at Canadian bases, on their way to Cuba; aircraft
from other Communist countries landing in Canada en route to Cuba were
to be searched for warlike materials.[9] (Although Washington obtained
similar co-operation from other countries, including neutral African states
such as Guinea and Senegal,[10] the government later contended that this
action demonstrated the promptness of its support for the American response to the Soviet challenge.)

Most members of the cabinet met the following morning (Tuesday) in
the expectation that the placing of Canada's forces on an advanced state of
alert would be a formality. None of the ex-ministers whom I consulted
appeared to have a clear recollection of the discussion that ensued, and
their reports differ in important respects. However, one ex-minister told
me explicitly,[11] and several others implicitly, that Mr. Diefenbaker alone

[7] *Canadian Annual Review 1962*, p. 128.

[8] According to Peter Newman, Mr. Diefenbaker, after giving tentative approval for the
alert, asked for delay until it could be co-ordinated with the announcement of an
increased state of readiness in the federal civil defence organization. *Renegade in Power: the
Diefenbaker Years* (Toronto, 1963), p. 337.

[9] In September, Senator Kenneth Keating of New York had criticized the Canadian practice of providing RCAF courtesy crews for Soviet planes crossing Canadian territory.
(See *The Globe and Mail*, 12 September 1962, "RCAF Courtesy Crews Aid Red Flights to
Cuba".) In fact, the Canadian purpose was less to be courteous than to be able to keep a
check on these Russian flights. One of the reasons the Soviet flights were stopped, and
the aircraft of other Communist countries thoroughly searched, was the possibility that
they might be transporting nuclear warheads f·r the missiles being installed on Cuba.

[10] Elie Abel, *The Missile Crisis* (Philadelphia, 1966), pp. 136-8.

[11] In conversation with the author. After he had resigned from the cabinet, M. Pierre
Sévigny told reporters that he had first considered resignation as a protest against "the
vacillating attitude" of the cabinet during the Cuban crisis. (*Toronto Daily Star*, 11 February 1963, "Sévigny Raps PM on Cuba"). Mr. Diefenbaker does not appear to have
informed most of his cabinet colleagues about the Merchant briefing until after the crisis
had passed.

had argued strongly for delay. Subsequently Mr. Green gave him some support, but the Prime Minister's attitude was decisive. Had he favoured immediate action, the cabinet would certainly have gone along.

Why did Mr. Diefenbaker hesitate? During 1962-3 he found it especially difficult to make decisions of any sort, and for several of his close associates this in itself provides an adequate explanation. One of them told me that the Prime Minister had also been convinced by his mail that Canadian opinion would be greatly upset if he took a firm position in favour of the American action. Subsequently Mr. Diefenbaker complained publicly that the Americans had failed to consult Canada properly and that his government had insufficient information upon which to act.... Irritation with the short notice given the government by Washington was probably an important factor in the Prime Minister's thinking. One of his colleagues informed me that the cabinet knew the Americans had not yet placed their forces on the maximum alert; they calculated, therefore, that it would be safe to delay Canadian action in order to register dissatisfaction with Washington's failure to consult earlier with Ottawa. Another minister gave me a somewhat contradictory explanation: he said that the decisive factor was a telephone conversation between Mr. Diefenbaker and Prime Minister Macmillan of Great Britain. According to this account, the British leader, hearing that the world was poised on the brink of nuclear war, had implored the Canadian government to avoid any action that might appear provocative to the Kremlin. This message, however, appears not to have been conveyed to the entire cabinet, and several of the ex-ministers more directly concerned with international affairs could not recall hearing anything about it. My informant himself questioned the accuracy of Mr. Diefenbaker's report of the content of this transatlantic conversation; Mr. Macmillan's government had already taken a firm public position in favour of the American quarantine, and he remained in very close touch with President Kennedy during the crisis.[12]

Another account of the same phone call suggests that Mr. Macmillan, instead of adopting an alarmist tone, may have confirmed Mr. Diefenbaker's conviction that the Americans were exaggerating the significance of the Soviet threat and the possibility of war. This informant said he was struck by the sharp contrast between Mr. Diefenbaker's attitude during the Berlin crisis of 1961 and his attitude during the Cuban crisis of a year later; the Prime Minister, he told me, had been deeply worried that war over Berlin was imminent, but had refused to believe that either the Russians or the Americans were prepared to fight over Cuba. Almost all authorities now concur that the world came closer to nuclear war in October 1962 than in the fall of 1961. If Mr. Diefenbaker held the contrary view, his judgement must be considered faulty. On the other hand, it is not difficult

---

[12] "President Kennedy spoke on our special telephone every day—sometimes two or three times a day...." Harold Macmillan, *Winds of Change* (New York, 1966), p. 26. Mr. Green is one of the ministers who says he cannot recall a mesage from Mr. Macmillan.

to understand how he might have come to adopt the minority position. Washington's alarmist attitude towards Cuba, and the Bay of Pigs fiasco, had given genuine cause for skepticism, and Mr Diefenbaker had become convinced that Mr. Kennedy intended to push him, and Canada, around.[13]

Whatever the reason for his attitude, the Prime Minister's will prevailed. The Tuesday-morning cabinet meeting disbanded without any decision being taken to alert the Canadian armed forces. After this meeting, Mr. Harkness, acting on his own, authorized the forces quietly to take all the steps planned for an alert apart from the recall of men on leave, an action that would certainly have attracted attention. Among other measures, Canadian naval units based in Halifax put to sea and RCAF stations were provisioned for the expected arrival of American squadrons. Mr. Harkness and his senior officers, however, and their American associates, continued to be disturbed by the Prime Minister's refusal to proclaim an alert and implement the measures that they had assumed, on the basis of the NORAD agreement, and exercises staged under NORAD, would be routine in the event of a serious threat to North America.

The Americans were shocked and dismayed by Ottawa's response to the revelation of Soviet missiles on Cuba. However, the precise requests that they made, and the channels employed to convey them, remain matters of dispute. The Americans certainly expected that the Canadian forces under NORAD would be brought to an advanced state of alert, and that this would be proclaimed immediately to strengthen the appearance of allied solidarity. They probably also assumed that they would be able to equip their interceptors already on Canadian bases with nuclear ammunition, and to disperse other nuclear-armed squadrons northwards. The level at which any such requests were made is less clear. They do not appear to have been presented formally to the Canadian government, probably because informal inquiries indicated they would be turned down. . . . [there is no validity whatever of the reports that Washington requested, and Ottawa declined, permission to increase greatly the number of over-flights of Canadian territory by U.S. bombers carrying nuclear bombs.]

When the House met on Tuesday at 2:30 p.m., the Prime Minister informed the members that there had as yet been no confrontations at sea or Soviet counter-measures in other parts of the world. The Security Council was to meet at 4 p.m., and he anticipated that the U.S.S.R. would veto the American resolution calling for a stop to the conversion of Cuba into a base for offensive nuclear missiles. He appeared to have been made aware of American displeasure with his hasty proposal for a neutral inspection commission, which had implied reservations about the accuracy of the President's facts, and he was anxious to correct this impression:

I was not, of course, casting any doubts on the facts of the situation as outlined by the President. . . . The government had been informed of and it believes that there is ample evidence that bases and equipment for the launching of offensive weapons have been constructed . . . in sufficient quantities to threaten the security of this hemisphere.

---

[13] See P. V. Lyon, *Canada and World Affairs 1961-1963* (Toronto), p. 496-7.

The purpose I had in mind ... was to be ready to put in motion steps which could be taken in the ... general assembly in the event of a Soviet veto, or if the Soviet union denies the existence in Cuba of offensive ballistic missile bases.[14]

In response to a question from Mr. Pearson, he said the United States had not requested Canadian assistance in implementing the quarantine. Mr. Herridge repeated his question as to whether Canada had been "consulted" or "informed". "Mr. Speaker," replied the Prime Minister, "the government of Canada was informed."[15] Mr. Hellyer asked if emergency steps, such as the alerting of Canadian units in NORAD or of naval units in the North Atlantic, had been taken. Mr. Harkness replied: "By and large the answer ... is no. Naturally we have been reviewing plans to meet all possible contingencies.[16]

Later that day, during a discussion of general economic policy, a Conservative back-bencher from Edmonton, Mr. Terry Nugent, delivered a blistering attack upon the legality of the American quarantine; as a sovereign nation like Canada, Cuba had "the right to arm itself with whatever arms it can get ... [and] to make any alliance that it wishes". He could see in the United States action "no legal right, other than might", and contended that firing on ships which refused to stop "would constitute an act of war". He feared that "the other side will not back down ... and where it stops, no one knows." The United States should be told that "we cannot, as a nation with a national conscience, permit ourselves to be associated in an action which constitutes unprovoked aggression."[17] Eventually, the Committee Chairman, Mr. Gordon Chown, questioned "whether it is in the best taste to be dealing with a subject that is so highly sensitive", and expressed fear that opinions expressed in ignorance of the full facts "might have a most embarrassing effect on our beloved neighbour to the south". After being scolded for disputing from the chair the content of Mr. Nugent's case, Mr. Chown succeeded, with the help of Works Minister Fulton and Veterans Affairs Minister Churchill, in stifling further debate on the delicate Cuban situation.[18]

International tension reached its peak the following morning, Wednesday, when the naval quarantine went into effect. The cabinet met again to

---

[14] *Debates*, 23 October 1962, p. 821.

[15] *Ibid.*

[16] *Ibid.*, p. 822. In view of the steps the RCAF and the RCN were taking, this answer was misleading. The movement of RCN ships out of Halifax freed ships of the U.S. Navy to take up positions further south in the quarantine area. It was not until 1 January 1963 that the NORAD headquarters announced that the Canadian elements in NORAD had been on an increased alert from the beginning of the Cuban crisis. *The Globe and Mail*, 2 January 1963, "RCAF Alerted at Crisis Start, NORAD Asserts". *The Globe and Mail* had reported on 10 November 1962 ("RCAF Took Initiative in Crisis Preparation") that the RCAF had initiated its alert two days before receiving cabinet permission, and had moved its Voodoo aircraft to forward bases. Mr. Harkness was quoted as describing a similar report in *Time* as full of inaccuracies and mis-statements.

[17] *Debates*, 23 October 1962, p. 852-3.

[18] *Ibid.*, pp. 853-6.

301 DIEFENBAKER AND CUBAN MISSILE CRISIS

discuss the crisis. In spite of an earnest plea by Mr. Harkness, who felt that Canada was in default on its NORAD obligations, the Prime Minister remained adamant, and the meeting broke up without any new decision. In the House that afternoon, the ministers doggedly frustrated opposition attempts to draw them into a detailed discussion of the crisis. The Prime Minister, in reply to Mr. Pearson, said Canada had not been represented at Tuesday's session of the OAS and he declined to associate Canada with the resolution that the OAS had passed voicing support for the United States. Mr. Martin's repeated suggestion that the External Affairs Minister, or at least his parliamentary secretary, should be in New York brought from Mr. Green the retort: "I really do not need any prompting from him as to what is my duty." The Minister told Mr. Lewis that Canada could not appropriately submit a resolution to the Security Council requesting both major powers to withdraw their ships from the impending confrontation, but, he continued, "the suggestion made by the Prime Minister the other evening [presumably the proposal for a neutral inspection team] is being very helpful." He confirmed that a Cuban aircraft landing in Canada that day had been searched for warlike material before being allowed to proceed. Mr. Harkness reiterated that Canada was taking "no part . . . whatever" in the American quarantine. "Certain precautionary military measures", he announced, had been taken, but he refused to go into details or to confirm that the United States had requested an improvement in Canada's state of readiness. The Prime Minister replied to a query about the degree of civil defence preparedness by voicing an appeal to withhold questions "which at this time might be considered as provocative or fear-producing." Mr. Hellyer asked for confirmation or denial of a report that Canada had "defaulted on its solemn obligation in respect of the NORAD treaty, in time of crisis, by refusing to accede to the request of the United States air force to arm Canadian Bomarc squadrons with atomic warheads and to permit United States airplanes to use Canadian air bases". "Emphatically no", replied Mr. Harkness, "we have not defaulted." He also denied that NATO headquarters had requested an increase in Canada's forces in Europe. He reported, however, that the planned rotation of about one-third of the brigade in Germany had been postponed. Mr. Hees told the House there had been no change in Canada's policy on trading with Cuba. The Prime Minister, after some pressing, agreed to give a comprehensive statement on the crisis when and if it became "helpful both to the House and also to Canada's security'.[19]

Messrs. Pearson and Herridge had hoped to get the views of their parties on the parliamentary record in the course of the customary statements in commemoration of October 24 as United Nations Day. When Mr. Diefenbaker forestalled this move by issuing his statement outside the House, the two opposition leaders gave their views in statements to the press. Mr. Pearson urged sympathy for the position adopted by the United States: "We should also give that position, as the Latin American republics

---

[19] *Debates*, 24 October 1962, pp. 882-8.

have given it, all the support that is possible as well as the constructive and considered counsel that can mean so much from a friend but has no value from a satellite."[20] Mr. Herridge criticized both the Soviet Union for installing missile bases in Cuba, and the United States for establishing its blockade.[21]

As this was the day when the world seemed closer to all-out nuclear war than at any other moment in history, the impatience of the House for more information was understandable. The morale of the members, however, and that of the nation, was not helped that evening when Mr. Green allowed himself to be interviewed for half an hour on CBC television. Appearing tired and confused, the Minister repeatedly evaded questions as to whether or not Canada agreed with the American counter-measures in the Caribbean; he strongly implied a negative reply by stressing that "Canada always has stood by her friends and of course Americans are our friends". "We are trying", he explained, "to keep the Canadian people and the people of Ottawa from getting all excited about this business and from panicking." "The situation is extremely grave", he conceded, but "it wouldn't help the Canadian people very much if we were to start telling things that would only make trouble and probably make for more danger." He referred to the situation as one "which may turn out to be the worst crisis the world has ever known", and concluded "that we could be heading for a nuclear war but that the Canadian Government will do everything it possibly can to avoid that. . . . I think we can do quite a bit." During the interview, Mr. Green also confessed that he did not know what went on in Russian minds; expressed an almost desperate faith in the willingness of Russians and Cubans to respond to world opinion; and denied that the crisis was the concern of NORAD.[22]

That same evening, Mr. Harkness, who had learned that the Americans had increased their state of alert, again tackled the Prime Minister. This time he succeeded in persuading him to authorize the Canadian alert without waiting for a further cabinet meeting. Mr. Diefenbaker insisted, however, that there be no announcement until he could make one in the House the following afternoon. Canada's forces thus went formally on alert two days after their American counterparts in NORAD. For Mr. Harkness and his advisors, it had been a long two days.

The next morning, Thursday, Mr. Pearson was invited to be present during a briefing of the cabinet defence committee by the Chiefs of Staff. Tension had eased since it had become clear that Soviet ships were being diverted away from the bockade zone to avoid contact with the American patrols. In the House, at 2:30 p.m. the Prime Minister responded to the demand for a comprehensive statement, and belatedly declared Canada's solidarity with the United States. The bases, he contended, "are a direct

---

[20] The *Globe and Mail*, 25 October 1962, "Pearson Urges Canada Support Action by U.S."

[21] *Ibid.*

[22] From a text provided by the CBC. One of Mr. Green's cabinet colleagues described this interview to me as "disastrous".

and immediate menace to Canada ... [and] a serious menace to the deterrent strategic strength of the whole western alliance". "We intend", he affirmed, "to support the United States and our other allies in this situation." At the same time, Canada's "purpose will be to do everything to reduce tension".[23] Even before the President's address on Monday, Mr. Diefenbaker reminded the House, the government had "acted to ensure that Canadian air space and ... facilities were not being used to carry arms to the Soviet bases in Cuba". He reported that the Canadian forces in NORAD had been brought to the same state of readiness as the American component and that the civilian departments had been requested to bring up to date their plans to meet emergencies. Although he was encouraged by the "restraint being exercised at the moment" by the Russians and the Americans, he warned that it "would be dangerously premature" to assume that the critical phase had passed. He commended the proposals of the Acting UN Secretary-General, U Thant, for a standstill in the Caribbean to permit time for the negotiation of a solution.[24]

Mr. Diefenbaker dealt vigorously with the critics of the American quarantine; the complaints about illegality he described as "largely sterile and irrelevant. ... Legalistic arguments ... cannot erase the fact that the Soviet Union has posed a new and immediate threat." Noting the contention that the Soviet bases in Cuba were no more objectionable than American bases on the periphery of the Soviet Union, he countered:

The United States bases abroad have been installed only in response to the threatening pressures from the Soviet Union, and have never been concealed from the public. The west, moreover, has refrained in recent years from any move to upset the world balance.

Western countries including Canada had deliberately decided not to acquire nuclear arms "in order to avoid the proliferation of these dangerous weapons throughout the world".[25] "In this light", he reasoned, "the call for the dismantling of these new, threatening facilities in Cuba is not unreasonable. It is the Soviet Union itself which has disturbed the balance, and it is for it and Cuba to restore that balance." The Prime Minister closed by expressing the hope that the dismantling of the bases "would represent a first practical step on the road to disarmament", and by guardedly reaffirming his suggestion for international inspection of the bases in Cuba.[26] It was a balanced, reassuring statement that would have been effective had it been delivered two or three days earlier. Compared to the statements being made by the leaders of the other allies of the United States, it was still conspicuously lacking in expressions of confidence in President Kennedy's leadership.

---

[23] *Debates*, 25 October 1962, pp. 911-12.
[24] *Ibid.*
[25] This was a clear indication that the government had decided not to use the crisis as the justification for accepting nuclear warheads.
[26] *Debates*, 25 October 1962, p. 913.

Mr. Pearson's contribution closely paralleled that of the Prime Minister. Although concluding that "it is good to know that the Canadian government is right behind our friend and neighbour", he did not necessarily mean that he "approved without qualification" all the details of the American action. . . .

The crisis, as we have noted, was effectively ended the next day (Saturday, October 27) by a remarkable exchange of messages between Messrs Kennedy and Khrushchev. The outcome was nevertheless shrouded in doubt until Sunday, when it became completely clear that the Kremlin had capitulated. (Three months later, Mr. Green told the House: "On the Saturday night after the Cuban crisis arose, I believed, and I have no doubt many other people did, that before morning Ottawa might be demolished, as well as Montreal, Toronto, and my home city of Vancouver.")[27] On Sunday evening the Prime Minister told reporters that the role played by the United Nations, and the "high degree of unity, understanding, and co-operation among the Western Allies", in which Canada had "played its full part", were responsible for the satisfactory outcome of the Caribbean confrontation.[28] Most other observers and participants were skeptical about the impact of the well-intentioned efforts of U Thant, and inclined to give the lion's share of the credit to President Kennedy's cool diplomacy. Mr. Diefenbaker had even less support for his claim that Canada had "played its full part".[29]

For a brief moment it appeared possible that Canada would have a role in winding up the crisis, and that Mr. Diefenbaker's proposal for a UN inspection team would receive partial fulfilment. The U.S.S.R. had agreed to the inspection of the sites on Cuba, and the American administration hoped to persuade U Thant to institute the necessary arrangements on his own authority. U.S. aircraft were ordered to stand by on the Sunday that the crisis eased, and instructions were issued to paint them white with UN markings. According to Elie Abel, Canada agreed to supply experienced pilots.[30] Unfortunately, these plans came to nothing. The Cuban Ambassador in Ottawa had already indicated on October 25 that his government would regard any UN inspection as a violation of Cuban sovereignty. In this he correctly anticipated the reaction of Premier Castro, who was in no mood to be persuaded either by the Secretary-General or by Moscow. Since U Thant declined to act without the concurrence of Cuba, the proposals for UN or Red Cross inspection were not implemented.

At the beginning of the crisis, many Canadian newspapers reflected the uncertainty of the politicians and also their resentment of the failure of the United States to consult before acting. On the whole, however, the editorial writers were much quicker than the political leaders to give voice to the ground swell of Canadian support for the leadership of President Kennedy. Conservative papers were especially prompt and enthusiastic in

[27] *Debates*, 24 January 1963, p. 3068.
[28] *Canadian Annual Review, 1962*, p. 113.
[29] *Ibid.*
[30] *Ibid.*, p. 208.

endorsing the United States action. The *Vancouver Province*, for example, commented at once: "Not only does the United States have no alternative, but their fateful decision is right. . . . There comes a time when individuals and nations must take a stand against those things that threaten them." "Free nations can be pushed a long way", observed the *Ottawa Journal*, "but in 1962 as in 1939 an aggressor would be wise to remember the adage: 'Beware of the fury of a patient man.' " The *Regina Leader Post* wrote that "the President won himself new stature", and the *Hamilton Spectator* contended that "Canadians have no other reasonable course than to support President Kennedy's forthright program". The *London Free Press* praised the President's restraint, and the *St. John's News* believed that "the action taken by the President is the least he could take in the circumstances."[31]

Some papers, however, reflected the Canadian instinct to turn to the United Nations in time of crisis. The *Globe and Mail*, for example, was severely critical of Mr. Kennedy for not going first to the Security Council and said that Mr. Diefenbaker "deserves the fullest credit for his statesmanlike attitude when he spoke in the Commons immediately after the President's broadcast".[32] The *Ottawa Citizen* went so far as to brand the American action "wrong", and also praised Mr. Diefenbaker's proposal for a neutral inspection team.[33] Fernand Bourret, writing in *Le Devoir*, strongly censured the Conservatives, Liberals, and Socreds for blindly supporting American imperialism.[34]

Most Canadians appeared to have supported President Kennedy's action. A sampling taken during the first two weeks of November by the Canadian Peace Research Institute indicated that the American conteraction had the endorsement of 79.3 per cent of the Canadian public, while only 12.7 per cent disapproved.[35] By December even Mr. Green was praising "the firmness yet moderation shown in the Cuban crisis" by the Americans, and he credited the outcome with improving considerably "the diplomatic position of the alliance" thus enabling the free world to achieve the initiative in East-West dealings. At the December ministerial meeting of NATO, he reported, "no real complaint was made against the United States for the manner in which the allies were consulted or informed. . . . [36]

---

[31] Quoted in the *Globe and Mail*, 24 October 1962, "Canada Press Views U.S. Move", and 26 October 1962, "Press Views on U.S. Action".

[32] The *Globe and Mail*, 24 October 1962, "Canada and the Crisis".

[33] Quoted in the *Globe and Mail*, 24 October 1962, "Canada Press Views U.S. Move".

[34] *Le Devoir*, 27 October 1962, "Le Canada a la remorque de l'imperialisme americain".

[35] *Ibid.*, 23 November 1962, "Poll Finds Canadians Back U.S. Cuban Stand."

[36] *Debates*, 17 December 1962, p. 2699: Mr. Green had already said in his television interview of 24 October that, although all the allies had wanted to be consulted, there had been no opportunity, "That was impossible . . . The fact is that we were informed . . . before the speech was made." Later he told me in conversation that Canada had no complaint to make regarding the consultation that had taken place. And in a letter dated 31 October 1967, he wrote: "As I have explained to you previously, External Affairs and State Department worked together closely throughout the whole affair." Mr. Diefenbaker's recollection is rather different.

A week after the crisis, Prime Minister Diefenbaker baldly asserted that there had been no doubt about Canada's position: "We supported the stand of the United States clearly and unequivocally."[37] By December 28, he sounded less certain. Speaking in Nassau, he explained: "There was no delay on our part. There was, however, an extension of a day or so in order to prepare our defences. . . . " He also asserted that neither Canada nor Britain were "consulted in advance",[38] and in subsequent statements contended that this was the reason for the delay.[39] The delay, however, was only in proclaiming the alert. The relevant military action, as we have seen, had already been taken without the knowledge of the Prime Minister or his cabinet. The Canadian response to the missile crisis thus demonstrated the ability of the Prime Minister to delay for two critical days a decision strongly desired by Canada's principal ally, and by a large majority in the Cabinet, Parliament, civil service, press and public. It also suggests the probability that, at the moment of any nuclear confrontation, the authority of the Prime Minister of Canada will count for little. If he, or Canada for that matter, is to have any part in the management of a supreme crisis, it will almost certainly need to come at the stage of contingency planning.

---

[37] *Canadian Annual Review 1962*, p. 134.
[38] The *Globe and Mail*, 5 January 1963, "Recollections over Cuba".
[39] *Debates*, 25 January 1963, p. 3127.

SECTION V

Comparative National Leadership

The following four selections are meant to encourage a comparative perspective on the role of the Prime Minister of Canada in the political system and of Prime Minister Trudeau in particular, by comparing the office, and Trudeau's approach to it, with the office of the U.S. President and the British Prime Minister.

Denis Smith identifies some "presidential" assumptions about Prime Minister Trudeau's approach to Parliament and Joseph Wearing pursues some of the themes introduced in Section I of this volume by closely delineating some of the differences between the office of Canadian Prime Minister and the office of President of the United States. Richard Neustadt's famous comparison between Whitehall and White House discusses similarities and differences which should encourage some reflections about the Canadian Prime Minister in Neustadt's terms of reference. A brief example of such a reflection is the editor's concluding note.

25

President and Parliament: The Transformation of Parliamentary Government in Canada*

DENIS SMITH

In the last five years, the Canadian House of Commons has gone through the first thorough and comprehensive reform of its procedures since 1867. The process of reform that was begun in 1964 came to a stormy climax last July with the adoption under closure of the Government's proposal for a regular time-limitation (or guillotine) rule. Though the Government has agreed that there should be a review this autumn of the House's experience under the new rules, and though certain adjustments and refinements are likely, the body of the reformed rules will probably stand for a few sessions at least, while the House learns new habits and absorbs the effects of the changes that have occurred. These changes have been substantial ones, and it will take some time before their full implications become clear. What I would like to do in this paper is to try to make some assessment of the forces that led to the transformation of the House; to consider precisely what kinds of changes have taken place; and to speculate about where these changes may be leading us, whether we want to go that way, and what, if anything, might be done about it. This study will extend beyond the contemplation of House of Commons procedure in the narrow sense.

The Breakdown of Orderly Procedure

Members of the Canadian House of Commons have intermittently criticized aspects of the House's rules and practices since Confederation; and there have been desultory attempts to alter the rules in this century, espe-

* A paper presented to the Priorities for Canada Conference, Niagara Falls, Ontario, October 10, 1969, and reprinted by permission of the author.

The author is grateful to the Canada Council for a grant to assist research on the condition of parliamentary government in Canada, of which this paper is a reflection.

cially in 1906, 1913, 1927, 1947, and 1955.[1] The rules adopted in 1867, which were taken over from the Legislative Assembly of the Province of Canada, followed the loose British parliamentary tradition of the period, allowing great latitude for free expression in the House, and giving the Government no special advantages.[2]

For nearly forty years the House carried on unchecked. The period up to 1906 was marked by lengthy speeches, obstruction by the Opposition, and a total lack of efficiency in the conduct of business by the House.[3]

Government legislative programmes were small, much of the business of the House was in the form of private members' bills encouraging national development; there was not much need for a sense of order or urgency in the House. While the British House of Commons abandoned this generous tradition of unrestricted debate under the pressure of brisk obstruction in the 1880's, the Canadian House was faithful to the tradition for decades longer.

The measures of reform adopted from time to time in this century have all tended to restrict unlimited debate in the House, by limiting acceptable motions and debatable motions (1906, 1913); by providing for the possibility of closure (1913); by limiting the length of speeches (1927, 1955, 1960); and by restricting the number of days devoted to major general debates on the Speech from the Throne, the Budget, and Supply (1955).[4] But the most severe restrictive measure, the closure, has rarely been used, because of its clumsiness and the likelihood of public criticism; and the other measures have done little to make the House's operations more orderly or more subject to the efficient leadership of the Government. As late as 1966, one observer commented:

The trend of these and other formal rules has been decidedly against the Opposition and the private member. But, in fact, these reforms have not materially restricted their right to speak. Nor have these reforms been significantly helpful to the Government's attempts to achieve efficient dispatch of Government business. The whole House is still a scene of protracted discussions on both generalities and details. The committees of the House have seldom been used to good effect. The question period has lengthened, sometimes to over one hour. In the wake of heated political rivalry and expansion of Government business in the last decade rules not dissimilar from those of 1867 when the budget was $25 million are not equal to the task of the 1960s when the budget approaches $9 billion. Five elections in twelve years have increased the tendency of the

---

[1] See W. F. Dawson, *Procedure in the Canadian House of Commons* (Toronto, 1962), Chap. ii; Thomas A. Hockin, "Reforming Canada's Parliament: The 1965 Reforms and Beyond", *The University of Toronto Law Journal*, XVI, no. 2 (1966), 326-45, esp. 329-30; Donald Page, "Streamlining the Procedures of the Canadian House of Commons, 1963-1966", *Canadian Journal of Economics and Political Science*, XXXIII, no. 1 (February 1967), pp. 27-49.

[2] Dawson, *Procedure*, p. 21.

[3] *Ibid.*, p. 21.

[4] *Ibid.*, pp. 20-8; Hockin, *Reforming Canada's Parliament*, pp. 329-30.

opposition to linger in Supply, to prolong other debates and to sharpen and prolong the question period.[5]

Since the mid-1950's, every Government has hurled charges of obstruction at the Opposition. These charges, when seen through the eyes of governments, both Conservative and Liberal, have frequently seemed to be fair ones. But seen from the other side, the charges were only half fair. It was the *rules* that created disorder; the Opposition only had to use them. Naturally, it could seldom avoid the temptation, because its political instincts teach it to undermine the Government's good reputation in whatever (mostly legitimate) ways it can. By 1960, the rules of the House of Commons, in the hands of a determined Opposition, had become the chief source of frustration for governments. Lester Pearson's four horsemen used them against the Government of John Diefenbaker, and John Diefenbaker, in his turn, used them easily against Lester Pearson after 1963.

The House of Commons was slow to appreciate what had happened. Until about 1963, Canadian Governments and most Members of Parliament generally tolerated the casualness of the rules. While Governments repeatedly expressed their frustration at the processes of the House, familiar habits were valued, and there was no urgent pressure for reform in the House of Commons. The Clerk of the Privy Council, Gordon Robertson, said in 1967:

I think the public generally and perhaps we ourselves [in the federal administration] fail to realize fully the extent to which the nature, scope and complication of government have changed in the last few years. . . . Indeed I think it is only in the last ten years that the cumulative effects of the change in the nature of government have been fully felt.[6]

He went on to offer evidence that "the sheer mass of legislation for Parliament to deal with, and the mass of material on which the Federal Cabinet must decide, are enormously greater than ever before in our history."

I found that, in the five year period from 1957-1962, the greatest number of days per Parliamentary session was 174: in the last five years we have had sessions of 248 and 250 days. Between 1957 and 1962 the largest number of bills passed in any session was 64; at the last session of 1967 the number was 97. Our largest printed volume of statutes in the first five year period had 583 pages of legal text; in 1964-65, Parliament passed 751 pages of statutes, and in 1966-67, 1,273 pages. By every one of these indices we have an increase from one five year period to the next of something between 40 and 100 percent.[7]

---

[5] Hockin, *Reforming Canada's Parliament*, p. 331.
[6] R. G. Robertson, "The Canadian Parliament and Cabinet in the Face of Modern Demands", unpublished paper, 1967, pp. 6, 7.
[7] *Ibid.*, pp. 7, 8. Donald Page, in his article cited above, uses a different set of comparisons in coming to the same conclusion about the overburdened House of Commons. He mentions that before 1963, only six sessions of Parliament produced more than 1,000 questions on the order paper; but the short 1963 session produced a record 1,906 questions, and the 1964-65 session, 3,078. He reports that in the two sessions of 1963

On the side of the Cabinet, Robertson found that from 1957 to 1959, an average of 382 documents per year were placed before Cabinet; from 1964 to 1966, the average had grown to 656, and in 1967 the volume was still mounting.[8] The capacity of the House and the Cabinet to deal in a rational and orderly way with the measures before them was being severely tested by the volume and technical complexity of government business.

It has been clear in the last ten years that the House of Commons has not been the only bottleneck and source of frustration in the system. While the Commons, up to December 1968, had done relatively little to quicken its pace and give order to its proceedings to match the potential mass of business that faced it each session, there were occasions, nevertheless, when the Cabinet's disorganization meant that for short periods it had no new business to place before the House. When this could be made evident by the Opposition, it was a source of embarrassment to the Government, because it suggested that the House, by comparison with the Cabinet, was not so badly organized after all.

Big government had overtaken both Cabinet and Parliament. In Canada as elsewhere in the industrialized world over the last half century, the size, responsibilities and opportunities for initiative of the permanent administration have expanded enormously. While departments have multiplied and divided, while independent agencies and crown corporations have been born and grown prematurely into monsters, the instruments of Cabinet and parliamentary control of the leviathan have remained negligible. By 1964, the orderly system of cabinet leadership and parliamentary scrutiny had broken down under the load, and members in all parties had recognized it. The Pearson Government took the initiative in encouraging parliamentary reform, with support of the other parties, and five years of innovation began. But before considering the effects of these reforms, I think it is important to put them into a broader perspective.

Parliamentary Government: Myth and Reality

What may be equally as important as the growing burdens of government is the mythology of parliamentary government. The mythology has disguised the reality. We are still bemused by the classic models of parliamentary government presented with such grace and clarity by Walter Bagehot and John Stuart Mill to an English audience in the mid-nineteenth century. They were describing, and prescribing for, the British Parliament of that time; but their influence on *our* perception of our institutions

---

and 1964-65, the average number of appeals against speaker's rulings was more than double the number in any previous year. Questions of privilege increased from an average of 32 per session in 1957-60 to 85 in 1963 and 111 in 1964-65. The two sets of statistics perhaps illustrate that the growth in the House's "obstructive" consumption of time on questions, appeals and questions of privilege parallels consistently, and probably reflects, the burdens placed upon the House by the Government.

[8] Robertson, *The Canadian Parliament*, pp. 8, 9.

has been profound. A century later, the major works on Canadian parliamentary institutions still take for granted as fundamental the framework of the liberal parliamentary constitution which Bagehot and Mill established in describing Westminster.[9] We have, we are told, a system of responsible parliamentary government, in which the public elects individual Members to the House of Commons and the House of Commons, in turn, chooses a government. Thereafter, while the Cabinet governs, the House holds it responsible for all the actions of the administration, and in the event of parliamentary disapproval, can overthrow the ministry, or force it to seek a fresh mandate from the electorate. The Prime Minister is chairman of the Cabinet, the public service is the loyal and anonymous servant of the Cabinet; the Cabinet is the servant of the House of Commons and only indirectly of the electorate. The theory puts the House of Commons close to the centre of the system, where it is meant to act as "the grand inquest of the nation", influencing, supervising and controlling the actions of the executive.

While the Canadian literature of politics points out that parliamentary control may not be quite up to the theory, the theory is maintained as the ideal. As a result, many of the real forces at work in Canadian politics are under-rated or ignored. The tendency is, when describing forces and practices which contradict the model, to see them as aberrations pulling the system away from the Victorian ideal, but rarely as primary forces in their own right which may be basically shaping the system.

In describing a political system, one must start from *some* sort of model, and in Canada the starting point has been natural and obvious.[10] But a point may come, in adding up the distortions and aberrations from the norm, when it becomes more comprehensible to abandon the original description and try to put together another one which accommodates the evidence more completely and satisfactorily. I think this point has been reached in understanding how the Canadian system works.

---

[9] See, for instance, J. A. Corry, *Democratic Government and Politics* (2nd ed.) (Toronto, 1955), Chaps. vi, vii, xi; R. M. Dawson, *The Government of Canada* (4th ed., rev. by Norman Ward) (Toronto, 1963), Chaps. ix, xviii, xix; Alexander Brady, *Democracy in the Dominions* (3rd ed.) (Toronto, 1960), Chap. iv. C. B. Macpherson's *Democracy in Alberta* (Toronto, 1955) takes a more independent position on the Canadian political tradition, arguing that it is plebiscitary rather than parliamentary. M. S. Donnelly, *The Government of Manitoba* (Toronto, 1963) and F. F. Schindeler, *Responsible Government in Ontario* (Toronto, 1969) are also free from the dominating influence of the traditional model. It may be significant that these studies all deal with provincial institutions and politics, where the legislative tradition has been weak. Westminster and the textbooks have been less referred to, and thus the means of escape from the classical model has been easier than it has been in Ottawa.

[10] W. F. Dawson, remarking on the absence of major American influences in the form and style of procedure in the Canadian House of Commons, says that "the United States, which contributed much to the federal form of the country, has had only a slight influence [in the House] which may be seen in the provision of desks for members, page boys to run errands, and roll-call votes. These are relatively insignificant borrowings." Dawson, *The Government of Canada*, p. 14.

To say this is hardly to say anything revolutionary about parliamentary government. Observers of the British parliamentary system began as long ago as 1902 to take apart the classical model as it applied to Westminster. The work of demolition has increased in volume and intensity since the 1920's, and especially in the last twenty years.[11] As in the Canadian approach to parliamentary reform, so in our comprehension of the parliamentary system, Canadians have stuck relatively uncritically for much longer to the classical model than have Britons.[12]

The best short reassessment of the British model—and now a familiar one—is Richard Crossman's introduction to the 1964 edition of Bagehot's *The English Constitution*. Here, Crossman argues that Bagehot's description of the Cabinet in Parliament was falsified soon after publication of *The English Constitution*. The emergence of highly disciplined mass parties took independent power from individual Members of Parliament. The immense new administrative bureaucracy took much ordinary decision-making power away from Ministers; and an organized secretariat for the Cabinet, and especially for the Prime Minister gave the Prime Minister the effective powers of a President.[13]

Even in Bagehot's time it was probably a misnomer to describe the Premier as chairman, and primus inter pares. *His right to select his own Cabinet and dismiss them at will; his power to decide the Cabinet's agenda and announce the decisions reached without taking a vote; his control . . . over patronage—all this had already before 1867 given him near-Presidential powers. Since then his powers have been steadily increased. . . . [Each Minister] owes his allegiance not to the Cabinet collec-*

---

[11] See, for example, M. Ostrogorski, *Democracy and the Organization of Political Parties* (London, 1902); L. S. Amery, *Thoughts on the Constitution* (London, 1947); John P. Mackintosh, *The British Cabinet* (London, 1962); Andrew Hill and Anthony Whichelow, *What's Wrong With Parliament?* (London, 1964); R. H. S. Crossman, "Introduction to Walter Bagehot, *The English Constitution*" (London, 1964); Max Nicholson, *The System* (London, 1967); W. J. Stankiewicz ed., *Crisis in British Government* (London, 1967); Humphry Berkeley, *The Power of the Prime Minister* (London, 1968); Bernard Crick, *The Reform of Parliament* (2nd ed., London, 1968); Lord Fulton, *The Civil Service*, Vol. I, *Report of the Committee, 1966-68* (Cmd. 3638, London, 1968); Robert J. Jackson, *Rebels and Whips* (London, 1968); Hugh Thomas, ed., *Crisis in the Civil Service* (London, 1968); Ian Gilmour, *The Body Politic* (London, 1969). Two more traditionalist responses to the presidentialist literature in the United Kingdom are Ronald Butt, *The Power of Parliament* (London, 1967) and Henry Fairlie, *The Life of Politics* (London, 1968).

[12] Besides the exceptions previously mentioned, another is the *Toronto Star* columnist Anthony Westell, who wrote in the *Star* on June 21, 1969: "To the extent that anyone expects Parliament to make significant changes in government policies and programs, it is a myth. Prime Ministers and Cabinets tend to hold themselves accountable to the country at election time rather than to the opposition in Parliament. They are not much interested, therefore, in hearing the views of the opposition, and most debates in the Commons are conducted in an almost empty chamber. . . . It is the basic structure of the parliamentary system which seems to be at fault. The Prime Minister and the Cabinet are not accountable to the legislature, in any meaningful way, and the parliamentary process is mostly play-acting—a farce which has become increasingly transparent to the public."

[13] Crossman, "Introduction to *The English Constitution*", pp. 40-53.

tively but to the Prime Minister who gave him his job, and who may well have dictated the policy he must adopt. In so far as the ministers feel themselves to be agents of the Premier, the British Cabinet has now come to resemble the American Cabinet.[14]

Crossman sees that the doctrine of collective cabinet responsibility has been turned inside out.

In Bagehot's day, collective Cabinet responsibility meant the responsibility of a group of equal colleagues for decisions taken collectively, after full, free and secret discussion in which all could participate. It now means collective obedience by the whole administration, from the Foreign Secretary and the Chancellor downwards, to the will of the man at the apex of power.[15]

The constitutional purists, says Crossman, insist that the essential distinction between presidential and prime ministerial government remains: "A President, we are told, cannot be removed before the end of his term of office; a Prime Minister can be."[16] Crossman admits the distinction, but notes that the Prime Minister is so powerful that "he can never be removed in real life by public constitutional procedure. The method employed must always be that of undercover intrigue and sudden unpredicted *coup d'etat.*"[17] The British system of government is not cabinet government, nor parliamentary government, but thinly disguised presidential government, in which the Prime Minister possesses some powers of discipline and direction unavailable even to an American President.[18]

Does the story sound familiar in Canada? It does. The Canadian Prime Minister, indeed, may be further along the road to being a presidential leader than the British, for distinct Canadian reasons.

For one thing, the Canadian House of Commons has never possessed the reserve of aristocratic prestige which once gave the British House of Commons some leverage alongside or against the Prime Minister. For most of its life, the Canadian House has been a popular chamber, based on wide popular suffrage; Canadian Prime Ministers have always made their primary appeal for support not *in* the House of Commons, but outside, to the electorate. Humphry Berkeley notes the effect on the new party managers

---

[14] *Ibid.,* pp. 51, 52.

[15] *Ibid.,* p. 53.

[16] *Ibid.,* p. 54.

[17] *Ibid.*

[18] Crossman suggests that this secret of the modern constitution has been successfully kept from the public, just as, in Bagehot's time, the secret of Cabinet government was hidden by the camouflage of the monarchy. He illustrates the reality of the Prime Minister's power by noting that the decision to manufacture the British atomic bomb was taken by Prime Minister Attlee without any discussion in Cabinet or Parliament, and that the Anglo-French decision to attack Egypt in 1956 was made by Prime Minister Eden without Cabinet discussion, and in the knowledge of only a few ministers and civil servants. *Ibid.,* pp. 55, 56. Humphry Berkeley, in his recent book *The Power of the Prime Minister,* asserts more strongly than Crossman that Parliament has been overridden by a system of presidential rule, and proposes a number of reforms to restore balance to the system.

of this focus on the electorate after the extension of the franchise in the United Kingdom. They soon realized the relevance of "Macaulay's maxim" that since the electorate had to be appealed directly

it was easier to project a personality than an idea. And so from the moment the electorate achieved any significant size, one man came in the mind of the nation to represent an entire government and that man had of course to be the Prime Minister.[19]

The House of Commons is diminished in importance, as compared to the British House in the period from 1832 to 1867, because it is the electorate, not the House of Commons, which chooses and deposes Prime Ministers. The essential influence upon government is the sovereign public, not a sovereign Parliament. Prime Ministers keep their eyes upon the Gallup Polls, and not normally upon readings of the House of Commons' temperature. And the public sees the Government as one man's Government. This public assumption gives the Prime Minister great power over his colleagues.

The fact is a commonplace in Canadian understanding, and yet it is not satisfactorily integrated into the normal liberal model of the parliamentary constitution. We know that general elections are competitions between party leaders for the Prime Minister's office; we concentrate our attention upon the leaders, and the parties encourage us to do so; once in office, we see that Prime Ministers exercise almost tyrannical power over their Ministers and backbenchers; Prime Ministers frequently ignore the House of Commons, or treat it with disdain, unless they perceive that the public is watching (which it only occasionally is); and our Prime Ministers freely admit their own predominance over the House of Commons and the necessity of it. When they fail to exercise the power the system gives them, as Louis St. Laurent failed in the last year of his administration, or Lester Pearson sometimes did in his, the House of Commons falls apart, and we blame the leaders personally. Yet we still cling to the "constitutional purist's" belief that the governing party in the House of Commons, or the House of Commons as a whole, can routinely control or depose the Prime Minister and replace him with a person more acceptable to it.

Two occasions in the twentieth century are cited to illustrate the ultimate power of the House of Commons over the Prime Minister: the replacement of Mackenzie King as Prime Minister by Arthur Meighen in 1926, and the defeat of the Diefenbaker Government in the House in 1963. Each is a bad example, and better illustrates the power of the Prime Minister over the House of Commons than the opposite.

The result of the constitutional confusion of 1926 was to give Mackenzie King an electoral victory with a clear majority, and probably to guarantee that no subsequent Governor General would refuse to grant the request of a Prime Minister for a dissolution of Parliament. A Prime Minister has two basic sources of authority over his followers and the House, one retrospective and one prospective: the former is the respect, gratitude and

---

[19] Berkeley, *ibid.*, p. 38.

control of patronage he gains from bringing a party to power in the previous general election; the latter is the discomfort he can create among M.P.s by threatening to call the next general election at a time of *his* choosing. The lesson for opposition leaders of Arthur Meighen's defeat in 1926 is that one should not accept the prime ministership when the previous Prime Minister has asked for and been refused a dissolution: he will convince the public that you acted wrongly, and you will soon be out of office. 1926 reinforced the usefulness of the power of dissolution as a weapon in the hands of the Prime Minister. The Constitutional niceties and the quiet life in the House of Commons were not important.

In 1963, John Diefenbaker accepted defeat in the House, dissolved, and lost power as the result of the general election that followed. The superficial lesson seems to be that the House can, in the extreme, overthrow a Prime Minister. The classical theory of the Constitution seems to be sustained. The real lesson is different. The defeat and dissolution appear to have been the result of a miscalculation, based upon the outmoded view that the House could defeat a Prime Minister and replace him with a more acceptable leader without facing the inconvenience of a general election. According to the account of Patrick Nicholson,[20] Robert Thompson and his Social Crediters were only persuaded to vote against Mr. Diefenbaker (they provided the margin of defeat) on the clear understanding that following the defeat in the House and before Mr. Diefenbaker could request a dissolution, he would be deposed in a Cabinet *coup* and be replaced by the Hon. George Nowlan. Nowlan would ask the House for a vote of confidence, Social Credit would swing back to support the Government, and the session would continue. Had it occurred, this chain of events would have sustained the theory of the House of Commons' power to make and unmake governments. But it did not occur, for, as Mr. Diefenbaker has said, the plan failed to take account of one person: the Prime Minister. What happened is familiar to all. John Diefenbaker was *not* deposed, he received his dissolution, and most of the innocent Social Crediters lost their seats forever. If they had had a more realistic view of where power in the parliamentary constitution really lies, they would probably have voted to save their seats and keep Mr. Diefenbaker in power.[21]

These events illustrate Richard Crossman's claim that a Prime Minister can no longer be replaced by public and constitutional means if he does not wish to go. They illustrate more than that. Given an alert Prime Minister, it is virtually impossible to replace him even by "undercover intrigue and sudden unpredicted *coup d'etat*". He has too many weapons of influ-

---

[20] In his *Vision and Indecision* (Toronto, 1968), pp. 255-6.

[21] The situation was perhaps volatile enough that the Government might have been defeated on some other occasion soon after. But the point stands; in that event, too, defeat would have resulted in a dissolution, not in the replacement of the Prime Minister.

ence and patronage in his hands, and his adversaries have too few.[22] He is virtually as immovable as an American President during his term of office. The five years of minority government under Mr. Pearson emphasized the same point. Even without a majority in Parliament, a Canadian Prime Minister is normally secure in office, and scarcely faces the danger of defeat in the House, because one or another of the opposition parties is almost certain to vote with the Government on any division to assure its own survival. The Parliament of 1963-1965 could probably have run to a full term of four or five years, as could the Parliament of 1965-1968; each one was dissolved on the decision of the Prime Minister when he sensed the possibility of an electoral victory.[23] When the Government was defeated in the House by its own carelessness in February 1968, the Prime Minister simply chose not to treat the defeat as a matter of confidence, whipped in his followers and gained Creditiste support the next week to show that he could still manage the House as he wished (even as a lame duck Prime Minister just about to give up his leadership to a successor). Against the power of the Prime Minister, the House of Commons has little of its own to match.

In both the United Kingdom and Canada, the Prime Minister gains his predominance over his colleagues and the House of Commons by winning general elections and exercising the power of dissolution at his own discretion. But in Canada the Prime Minister possesses still more authority granted him from outside Parliament which brings him closer to the American President. He is chosen by a popular convention. The Canadian conventions have increasingly come to duplicate the effects of the American presidential conventions. Under the open embrace of gavel-to-gavel television, the conventions have become as central a part of national political life as the campaigns, and perhaps more central, because of their concentrated drama and intense TV coverage. In the conventions the political process is almost entirely personalized, issues fade away, and the winner is the only one to walk away alive. (A year and a half after Mr. Trudeau's accession to the Liberal leadership, his two leading rivals have disappeared from politics. In the Conservative Party, too, the runner-up was left without a politi-

---

[22] Four of the last five British Prime Ministers have faced substantial dissatisfaction within their parties and Cabinets, but no attempts to overthrow them have been successful. Winston Churchill, Anthony Eden and Harold Macmillan retired in ill health, on their own decisions; and Harold Wilson, who is healthy, has not been budged. The illnesses may have been related to the party pressures being experienced by these Prime Ministers; and they may have become more vulnerable during their illnesses, as Henry Fairlie suggests was true of Anthony Eden in 1957 (Fairlie, *The Life of Politics*, p. 61). But in no case did a *coup* actually occur.

[23] Apparently on the theory that the king can do no wrong, the Hon. Walter Gordon unselfishly sacrificed himself to the conventions of prime ministerial power by resigning his portfolio after the 1965 election because he had recommended the dissolution and yet the party had failed to win the majority of seats he predicted.

cal career.)[24] If anything has accelerated the trend to presidential politics in Canada, it has been the enthusiastic adoption of televised national leadership conventions. Given the available technical means and the example next door every four years, the practice could scarcely be resisted.

Reforming the House

Set against the overwhelming power and public prestige of the Prime Minister are the traditional duties of the legislature. Even if one admits that the power of overthrowing governments has been surrendered, the House of Commons is supposed to retain the power and responsibility to provide a public forum of discussion on national issues, to scrutinize spending and legislation, and to safeguard the rights and freedoms of citizens by its vigilant criticism. These are worthy goals; but even *they* fade on closer examination. In certain crucial instances, such as the defence production debate of 1955, the pipeline debate of 1956, the nuclear arms debate of 1963, the Rivard revelations of 1964, the flag debate of 1964, and the rules debate of December, 1968, the House does occupy a central place in public consciousness and does serve as a restraining and moderating influence upon the Government. But these occasions are rare ones. In its less spectacular day-to-day performances, the House of Commons normally, if grudgingly, does the work the Government directs it to do, and does so without making much critical impression on government measures or on the public. This is so because the Government wishes it to be so, and because, until the December 1968 reforms, the House was the victim of its own diffuse rules, which did not lend themselves to sharp, critical investigation of government measures.

Students of Parliament have agreed for years that the House's scrutiny of financial measures was inadequate.[25] Members were given little opportunity to influence the form of other legislation, except occasionally, because the Government used its majority to enforce conformity upon its backbenchers. The question period, emergency debates, and the general debates, while sometimes spectacular, bring little information to the public about the Government's rationale for policy or about the processes of administration because the habit and preference in Ottawa is one of strict administrative secrecy.[26] On balance, the House of Commons was not

---

[24] On the leadership conventions, see D. V. Smiley, "The National Party Leadership Convention in Canada: A Preliminary Analysis", *Canadian Journal of Political Science*, I, no. 4 (December 1968), 373-97; Joseph Wearing, "A Convention for Professionals: The PCs in Toronto", *Journal of Canadian Studies*, II, no. 4 (November, 1967), 3-16; and Joseph Wearing, "The Liberal Choice", *Journal of Canadian Studies*, III, no. 2, (May, 1968), 3-20.

[25] See especially Norman Ward, *The Public Purse* (Toronto, 1962).

[26] See Donald C. Rowat, "How Much Administrative Secrecy?" *Canadian Journal of Economics and Political Science*, XXXI, November, 1965, 479-98: House of Commons, *Debates*, February 17, 1969, pp. 5631-2; *Report of the Royal Commission on Security*, June, 1969, especially pp. 79-81, "Administrative Secrecy". The tendency of the *Report* is illustrated by the following comments it makes on the possibility of general access to government

performing even a modest job as the watchdog of the public interest, and by 1963 many Members knew it. Government backbenchers, especially, frequently expressed their frustration at the apparent fact that they served no purpose in Parliament except to vote blindly for government measures they had had no hand in producing.

The growing frustration of individual Members over the inconsequence of their role in the House, and the frustration of the Government at the cumbersome and obstructive procedures of the House, combined at last to produce a widespread interest in the House in parliamentary reform. But this interest in reform had two sources and two—not always compatible—objectives. The wish of the Government was primarily to organize the proceedings of the House in an orderly way—to "programme" the business of the House—so that it could expect as a matter of course to get its large agenda of business through the House with a minimum of delay and confusion each session. Government backbenchers and opposition Members admitted the legitimacy of the Government's wish, but their chief interest was to give themselves a more satisfying and informed role in the control and assessment of government policy. While the Government's major objective was to streamline proceedings to serve the needs of the Prime Minister and his administration, the House's major objective was to give itself more of the powers it was supposed to possess according to the classical model of Parliament.

In the two Pearson Parliaments (of 1963-1965 and 1965-1968) some notable reforms were achieved which served both purposes to a limited degree. Stricter time limitations were imposed on the question period and the discussion of supply; the hours of sitting were extended; dilatory appeals against the speaker's rulings and frivolous questions of privilege were eliminated; parliamentary committees were modified to reduce their size and to bring their areas of concern roughly parallel to those of the

---

documents: "We are not required to make general recommendations about these problems, but, as far as Canada is concerned, we would view suggestions for increased publicity with some alarm. We think the knowledge that memoranda might be made public would have a seriously inhibiting effect on the transaction of public business. We believe that the process of policy-making implies a need for wide-ranging and tentative consideration of options, many of which would be silly or undesirable to expose to the public gaze. To insist that all such communications must be made public would appear to us likely to impede the discussive [sic] deliberation that is necessary for wise administration. In Canada, the bureaucracy is not vast, and the numbers of serious enquiries quite small. It seems to us that there is no reason why controlled access to specific administrative files or documents cannot be permitted and arranged on an ad hoc basis when a genuine requirement can be established." (pp. 80-81) This section, and the *Report* in general, assumes that the Canadian system is a closed, not an open one; it further fails to distinguish between what are the legitimate concerns of state security, and what are, rather, the political concerns of the party in office to protect its own convenience. The *Report* takes for granted that it should be the administration, not the legislature, which determines what documents it would be "silly or undesirable to expose to the public gaze." Opposition Members of Parliament might not always share a Minister's or a civil servant's judgment in such matters.

Government departments; a weak guillotine procedure was provided for, which soon proved unusable. The reforms cautiously balanced the interests of Government and Parliament. While they began to give the Government the order it claimed in the House's business, they also began to encourage Members of Parliament to act with greater independence.[27]

But there was no doubt who intended to remain in control. When, in the spring of 1965, the Special Committee on Procedure and Organization grew too radical in its proposals for the Cabinet's liking, the Prime Minister conveniently let the Committee die at the end of a session, and declined to present to the House some of the Committee's more thorough proposals for change.[28] Instead, the Prime Minister introduced the Cabinet's own selection of proposals.

The work of reform was tentative and unfinished. The House recognized this by making the changes in the rules adopted in June 1965, provisional ones, subject to review and confirmation. They were extended into the 27th Parliament and again into the first session of the 28th Parliament in the fall of 1968. Further committees on procedure continued to work, and in September 1968, the House directed the latest committee to present permanent proposals for reform by December 1968.[29] The committee did so, and following an extended debate December, 1968, all but one of the committee's proposals were accepted unanimously by the House.[30]

The reforms of December 1968, while extending some of the principles first outlined in 1965, were notably more radical. They reorganized and simplified the manner of passing legislation in the House; they diverted detailed debate on all estimates and virtually all legislation from the floor of the House to the specialised committees; they established an annual time-table for the consideration of spending estimates; they created a Special Committee on Statutory Instruments; and they reduced to 28 the number of days in an annual session controlled by the Opposition for debate on topics of its choice. Again, the nice balancing of concessions to the House against concessions to the Government brought the agreement

---

[27] See Donald Page, *"Streamlining the Precedures"*; Thomas Hockin, "Reforming Canada's Parliament"; Pauline Jewett, "The Reform of Parliament", *Journal of Canadian Studies*, I, no. 3 (November, 1966), 11-16.

[28] All the Committee's *Reports* were unanimous ones, including the support of the Liberal members of the Committee, among whom was the government whip, James Walker, M.P. The major recommendation of the Committee in the spring of 1965 was that of Stanley Knowles, M.P., for regular adjournments of the House to permit parliamentary committees to concentrate on their work, and to allow Members regular periodic visits to their constituencies. Both reforms may have been seen by the Government as too likely to enhance the prestige and critical knowledge of individual M.P.s.

[29] Canada, House of Commons, *Debates*, September 24, 1968, pp. 394-437.

[30] *Ibid.*, December 10—December 20, 1968.

of all parties to the proposals.[31] (In addition, in November 1968, the Prime Minister had announced that the estimates would contain annual grants to the leaders of the opposition parties to finance research offices.)[32] But on the other side of the balance, the Prime Minister also introduced a rota system for Ministers during the question period, which freed Ministers from attendance in the House for two days of each week.[33] Besides limiting the opportunities for Members to question Ministers, the change had the further (perhaps intended) effect of concentrating more attention upon the Prime Minister, who continued to attend the question period daily, and who was inclined to substitute his own replies for those of his absent Ministers.

The reform measure that was held by the Government House leader and by the Prime Minister to be the most important of all, was the only measure unacceptable to the opposition parties (as it has been unacceptable to them in the committee). This was Rule 16A, which provided for the allocation of time in advance for debate on legislation, and in the absence of agreement among the parties, permitted the Government to impose its own timetable (or guillotine) on the House by majority vote. The role was extraordinarily carelessly drawn, and was bound to arouse the suspicion and distaste of the Opposition: it allowed the Government House leader alone to constitute a quorum of the Proceedings Committee, and it gave him authority to propose time-tabling orders which might theoretically cover all the legislation of a session, before its introduction, under a single time allocation motion. During eight days of debate, the Government fell back on the old accusation of filibustering against the will of the majority.[34] But in the meantime, with its presidential antennae out to the electorate, the Government concluded that the public—including the Liberal public—understood and sympathized with the Opposition's case to an unusual extent.[35] Finally, the government withdrew its request for the approval of Rule 16A and the remaining package of reforms was adopted by the House.

But in December, the Prime Minister warned that the guillotine was still dear to him, and would appear again reincarnate at a moment appro-

---

[31] It is useful to note that this careful balancing of interests was accomplished by an all-party committee, not by the Government, which merely endorsed the committee's unanimous recommendations. In the heat of debate in July, 1969, the Prime Minister claimed that all the concessions to the House's interest were granted by a generous Government out of its own good will. He was reminded forcefully by David Lewis, M.P., that his memory was inaccurate. (House of Commons, *Debates*, July 24, 1969, pp. 11571, 11574.)

[32] *Ibid.*, November 15, 1968, pp. 2790-2820.

[33] *Ibid.*, September 25, 1968, pp. 446-9.

[34] House of Commons, *Debates*, December 10, 1968, p. 3787.

[35] The newspapers were almost unanimous in condemning the proposal, and the results of a private telephone poll of Liberal party supporters confirmed this reaction.

priate to the Government.[36] The new Procedure Committee went to work
again in 1970 and the Government brought its revised guillotine proposal,
Rule 75, to the House in July. The Opposition—and the Government—had
worked conscientiously to make the rule less objectionable to the House
than 16A, and it *was* less objectionable. But it still contained too much
sting for the combined Opposition, in section 75C, which gave the Government, in the absence of agreement by the other parties, the power to
timetable discussion on the stages of individual bills by Government resolution, following notice and a short debate.[37] The provision meant that if
necessary a determined Government could guide a piece of controversial
legislation through the House in a minimum of four days of debate over a
period of ten sitting days, against the protests of the minority.

The persistence of the Trudeau Government in pressing for the guillotine made its impression on the Opposition and the press, and during July
negotiations went on among the parties to compromise on a measure
which would grant the Government's wish but extend the minimum period
of ten days to something longer. When the Opposition seemed hopeful of
reaching agreement with the Government, the Cabinet suddenly broke off
discussion, closure was imposed, and the measure was adopted on division
in its original form.[38]

The sudden reversal by the Government was curious: it can probably
be explained by the Prime Minister's unerring presidential instincts. As in
December, the Prime Minister was watching public reaction to the debate
more closely than the House's reaction. He apparently found that the
public, this time, was not unduly concerned. In mid-July, he commented
on the debate that it was a "stupid filibuster", and said that no one outside
Parliament cared what was going on in the House.[39] In his speech before
the closure, he remarked:

*In a democracy the ballot box, not the filibuster, is the ultimate and appropriate
technique of assessment.*[40]

And in the adjournment debate the next day, he let fall his testy comments
about the inconsequence of parliamentary debate to the public that elects
Prime Ministers:

*The opposition seems to think it has nothing else to do but talk. . . . That is all they
have to do. They do not have to govern, they have only to talk. The best place in
which to talk, if they want a forum, is, of course parliament. When they get home,
when they get out of parliament, when they are 50 yards from Parliament Hill, they
are no longer hon. members—they are just nobodys, Mr. Speaker.*[41]

[36] Toronto *Globe and Mail*, December 24, 1968.
[37] *Votes and Proceedings of the House of Commons of Canada*, July 2, 1969, No. 180, pp. 1, 2.
[38] House of Commons, *Debates*, July 22, 1969, pp. 11470-78; July 23, 1969, p. 11504; July 24, 1969, pp. 11534, 11544-11550.
[39] *Toronto Star*, July 21, 1969.
[40] House of Commons *Debates*, July 24, 1969, p. 11572.
[41] *Ibid.*, July 25, 1969, p. 11635.

Judging that Members of Parliament are political nobodies, the Prime Minister felt it prudent to ignore the real possibility of agreement within the House on a compromise rule acceptable to the other parliamentary parties, turned his back on the discussions, and imposed his will on the House in a matter of its own procedure. This was as clear an indication as there has ever been that the Canadian Prime Minister is inclined to think of himself as a crypto-president, responsible directly to the people and not to the House of Commons. But Lyndon Johnson would never have spoken this way of Everett Dirksen!

Where Are We and Where Do We Go From Here?

We seem to have created in Canada a presidential system without its congressional advantages. Before the accession of Pierre Trudeau, our presidential system, however, was diffuse and ill-organized. But Pierre Trudeau is extraordinarily clear-headed and realistic about the sources of political power in Canada. On the one hand, he has recognized the immense power of initiative and guidance that exists in the federal bureaucracy; and he has seen that this great instrument of power lacked effective centralized political leadership. He has created that coordinated leadership by organizing around him a presidential office, and by bringing order and discipline to the Cabinet's operations. He has made brilliant use of the public opportunities of a party leader, in convention, in the general election, and in his continuing encounters outside Parliament. He has recognized that the public responds first to personalities, not to issues, and so he campaigns for the most generalised mandate. And now, finally, he has successfully altered the procedures of the House of Commons so that it may serve the legislative purpose of an efficient presidential administration.

In doing all these things he has taken advantage of trends and opportunities that already existed. All Prime Ministers have been moving—under pressure—in the same direction, but none so determinedly as Prime Minister Trudeau; he has taken the system further, faster, more self-consciously, than it would otherwise have gone. Are we now to be left with this completed edifice of presidential-parliamentary government, in which the House serves the minor purpose of making presidential programs law without much fuss?

Probably not, because the system still contains some fundamental inconsistencies. How clearly the Prime Minister and Members of Parliament see these inconsistencies, I cannot be sure; but they exist, and they will create difficulties. As we have seen, the changes in the rules and practices of the House have not only served the Government' s purposes; they have also, in many ways, benefited individual Members and the opposition parties.

In the course of achieving rules of procedure much more tractable for the Government's purposes, the reforms and the reforming atmosphere have also created a more intractable membership of the House, with new and potentially powerful instruments of leverage against the Government in their hands. The opposition parties are better equipped by their research funds and their role in legislative committees to criticize the administration from a basis of knowledge. The restrictions of time allocation in the House give these parties an incentive to organize their attacks with more precision and directness than before. Government backbenchers, long silent and frustrated by party discipline, permitted only to express their opinions freely in secret caucus, have been given the taste of greater freedom in the new committees of the House. (Already the paradox has been recognized by Steve Otto, M.P., who has publicly asked his House leader why Government backbenchers should not feel free to propose substantive amendments to Government legislation in committee.) For the moment, the Government may hold the reins tightly, but the pressures in the House are likely to mount.

One result may be that the Government will find itself more frequently embarrassed by independent backbenchers. They will probably continue to demand their own research assistance, and increasingly the rights to speak critically and to vote against Government measures; first in committee, and then, by extension, in the House. But always more and more in public, where they can be heard. The party discipline of the majority will be put under increasing strain, and the Opposition will take every chance to encourage the tension. If we have a President, they will be saying, in effect, then why shouldn't we also have an independent Congress?

The Government, in response to such pressures, may put on the screws in private, but it will have difficulty withdrawing the public machinery of criticism that it has now acquiesced in. The House will never agree to return to its fumbling and disorganized pattern of pre-1965. With the taste of influence, and facing a more efficient executive, it will be more inclined, not less, to be independent and sometimes intransigent. If we believe, as the parliamentary myth leads us to believe, in the virtues of *public* policy-making and strong *public* criticism of Government, this will surely be a salutary development. The Prime Minister will be challenged by the kind of countervailing force that he believes in.

The other possible response of Governments may be to accept the logic of these parliamentary pressures, and to move more surely to a system of congressional checks and balances. This would involve the granting of independent powers to parliamentary committees to choose their own chairman, hire their own substantial staffs, pursue their own independent investigations, initiate their own legislative proposals, and freely amend and reject the Government's measures. It would involve the provision of administrative assistance for M.P.s comparable to that available to Senators and Congressmen, and salaries matching their new responsibilities. It would involve, undoubtedly, the admission of television cameras to committees and to the House floor in order to bring the House closer to the public. It would involve, finally, and probably gradually, the abandonment of the convention of confidence, so that Governments could expect to stay in office for full terms in spite of regular defeats in the House. Gordon Robertson saw the possibilities with more prescience than most observers in 1967:

The American system may be better suited in some respects to these times than the British. It may be that we will have to accept compromises to make the principle of Ministerial responsibility flexible enough to work today.[42]

Who is there, I wonder, to play Senator Fulbright to Pierre Trudeau's Lyndon Johnson?

---

[42] Robertson, *The Canadian Parliament*, p. 12.

26

President or Prime Minister*

JOSEPH WEARING

Why is it that there has been book after book written on that fascinating institution, the presidency of the United States, whereas virtually no attention has been given to an office that is as central to our politics as the Canadian prime ministership? Thankfully such analysis has been begun by my colleague, Professor Denis Smith, in an excellent and provocative paper. Focusing on the Prime Minister's relationship with Parliament, his thesis is that parliamentary government in Canada has been transformed into a presidential system.[1] He concludes that his term of office is virtually as secure as an American President's[2] and that Parliament has, except under rare circumstances, little influence on the Government. The most vivid indication of that came in the 1969 debate on the Guillotine rule (75C), when the Government invoked closure because, as the Prime Minister said, "No one outside Parliament cared what was going on in the House".[3] Any comparison, however, can be overdone. By way of providing an alternative analysis, this paper seeks to concentrate on the dissimilarities between the American presidency and the Canadian prime ministership and, if it in turn goes too far, perhaps it can be taken as a "counterweight" to Professor Smith's "presidentialism".

First of all, the so-called "classical" period of parliamentary supremacy in Britain, when governments were really made and unmade by the House of Commons, was of quite short duration. Before 1832 and for some time afterwards, an English ministry had various ways of controlling the House of Commons through the Crown and the House of Lords. Both the Monarch and the Lords were able to exert a considerable influence at elections and in the House itself. Pocket boroughs, secret service money, "government constituencies", deference and all the other forms of influence were

---

* Written for this volume.
[1] Denis Smith, "President and Parliament: The Transformation of Parliamentary Government in Canada", a paper presented to the Priorities for Canada Conference, Niagara Falls, Ontario, October 10, 1969, and appearing in this volume.
[2] *Ibid.*, p. 325 in this volume.
[3] *Ibid.*, p. 322 in this volume.

so successfully employed that no government clearly lost an election from 1717 until 1830.[4] In this way, the House was kept subservient and one historian has commented that "executive influence in the Commons was a necessary feature of eighteenth century Government".[5] As these influences declined and the Tories split over the repeal of the Corn Laws, there came a period of about 20 years when the lives of governments were ended by defeats in the House of Commons on six occasions. However, by the 1870's, the House was becoming subject to the restraints of party discipline in place of the earlier influences of which governments had availed themselves; in the hundred years since 1870, only four governments' lives have been ended by defeats in the House.[6] It is rather odd then that a short period of parliamentary supremacy, amounting to about 20-odd years, should be called a "classical" period.

Even if a high degree of government control over Parliament is in fact more traditional than the "classical" model, this control should not be exaggerated. Professor Smith points out that a Prime Minister has "two basic sources of authority over his followers and the House: . . . [the] control of patronage he gains from bringing a party to power in the previous general election; and the discomfort he can create among M.P.s by threatening to call the next general election at a time of his choosing".[7] But does this make him "virtually as immovable as an American President during his term of office"?[8]

The threat to dissolve is not always an appropriate deterrent. Under minority government, the threat will work if there are enough opposition M.P.'s who fear an election to give Government a *de facto* majority. On the other hand, if opposition members comprising an overall majority of the House membership think their parties' (and their own) prospects are promising, the threat falls flat. The first case fits the period immediately following the 1965 federal election when the public was tired of elections and would conceivably have punished any party which provoked one. However, the second category seems to best describe the mood of the opposition parties in the first two or three months of 1968, when it appeared probable that the Liberal Party would not be able to find an appealing leader to succeed Mr. Pearson.

---

[4] I. Jennings, *Party Politics*, Vol. I: *Appeal to the People* (Cambridge, 1960), p. xxiii.

[5] A. Briggs, *Age of Improvement* (London, 1959), p. 93.

[6] I. Jennings, *Cabinet Government* (3rd ed.) (Cambridge, 1959), pp. 512-33. A defeat and resignation which has followed a general election that went against the Government has not been counted, since defeat then becomes almost a formality.

[7] Smith, "President and Parliament", p. 315 in this volume. In Britain, a third power would be added, that of threatening to remove official party endorsement at the next election. This is probably less of a threat in Canada since central control over the constituencies is not as great as it is in Britain, particularly in the Labour Party. Secondly, independents have a slightly better chance of getting elected here than in Britain. However, in 1968, renegade Liberal Ralph Cowan was not able to get himself re-elected after being denied his party's nomination.

[8] *Ibid.*, p. 317 in this volume.

A Prime Minister may also threaten to dissolve, so the argument runs, if his backbenchers are in revolt against him. But such a threat is a two-edged weapon. To carry through with the threat and to call an election when the Cabinet and parliamentary party are deeply split is tantamount to collective hara-kiri. The party is sure to lose seats and the Prime Minister his job. Conceivably, there is the Prime Minister who prefers a *Götterdämmerung* to submission, but the real point is that under a parliamentary system a Prime Minister cannot dissolve against his own backbenchers and win re-election. His tenure of office is dependent on how many M.P.s his party elects. Nevertheless, a Canadian Cabinet Minister has noted that "some Prime Ministers . . . [have used] regularly the threat of dissolution as a disciplinary measure against ministerial and parliamentary colleagues"[9] and, interestingly enough, his Prime Minister agrees that the power is a potent weapon.[10] But when Cabinet Ministers or M.P.s fall into line under this threat, they are really deciding, consciously or unconsciously, not to "rock the boat" and the validity of the threat remains questioned.

Professor Smith discusses the fall of the Diefenbaker Government in 1963 and argues that, rather than demonstrating the "ultimate power of the House of Commons over the Prime Minister", it better illustrates the opposite. He supports the proposition that the Diefenbaker Government fell because of a Social Credit miscalculation and points out that, in spite of his parliamentary defeat, Mr. Diefenbaker was neither deposed nor deprived of his dissolution.[11] Several comments should be made. Firstly, Mr. Diefenbaker was able to resist the cabinet revolt partly because he retained the loyal support of the Conservative caucus and partly because the attempted Cabinet *coup* was mismanaged.[12] Sixty-seven years before, a successful cabinet revolt against Sir Mackenzie Bowell *was* successful.[13] Bowell was much less inclined to fight back than Mr. Diefenbaker had been in 1963 and this brings in the question of personality—in many ways, one of the most critical variables in the changing dynamics of prime ministerial power. Other examples of differences in individual behaviour come to mind. When King's Government got fewer seats than the Conservative Opposition in the election of 1925, he clung to power by courting the Progressives.[14] St. Laurent in 1957, when the election results were almost identical to those of 1925, resigned without hesitation even though there were suggestions from members of his Cabinet that he attempt to carry on

[9] Hon. R. A. Bell, "Ministerial Responsibility in Modern Parliamentary Government", notes for an address given at the Third Commonwealth and Empire Law Conference, Sydney, Australia, n.d.

[10] C.T.V. television broadcast, "Our World: John Diefenbaker's Parliament Hill", June 30, 1970.

[11] Smith, "President and Parliament", pp. 316 in this volume.

[12] P. C. Newman, *Renegade in Power: The Diefenbaker Years* (Toronto, 1963), pp. 355-82.

[13] J. T. Saywell, ed., *The Canadian Journal of Lady Aberdeen 1893-1898* (Toronto, 1960), pp. 298-341.

[14] H. B. Neatby, *William Lyon Mackenzie King*, Vol. II: *The Lonely Heights* (Toronto: 1963), pp. 77-129.

with CCF support.[15] In the same way, not every Prime Minister faced with cabinet resignations would be equally determined to stay in office. A thick-skinned Prime Minister will admittedly be more difficult to remove, but accordingly the Opposition to him will have to be more determined and more widespread in both Cabinet and caucus.[16]

Secondly, Mr. Diefenbaker's dissolution was certainly not obtained under ideal circumstances. He was forced into an election with his Government in disarray and electoral defeat a certainty. It may be that the Social Crediters miscalculated the effect of a vote of non-confidence carried against the Government, but this was not the first miscalculation in Canadian parliamentary history that had led to the fall of a government; an American President does not have to worry about such miscalculations bringing his term of office abruptly to an end.

This raises the question as to whether it would always be constitutionally proper for a Governor General to grant a request for a dissolution coming from a Prime Minister whose Cabinet and party were clearly opposed to his continuing as Prime Minister and leader. In such circumstances, not only is the right to ask for dissolution an empty one because the Government's chances of winning are slim, but an election would also be quite meaningless since the process of leadership change would have been interrupted only temporarily and the electorate's opportunity to choose beteen competing party leaders frustrated. An important feature of democracy in most western countries is that the electorate has the right to choose between prospective heads of government nominated by their respective parties. The electorate's rights, then, are abused if an election is allowed to take place while one of the participating parties is in revolt against its leadership.

According to cabinet minutes, the recommending of dissolution is the special prerogative of the Prime Minister,[17] but there is some difference of opinion as to whether this means that the Prime Minister makes his recommendation to Cabinet or whether it is made to the Governor-General without prior cabinet approval.[18] In Britain, from having been a well-established rule that the Prime Minister could not ask for a dissolution without the agreement of his Cabinet, the practice changed suddenly in 1918 to being one in which the Prime Minister takes the decision *without*

---

[15] D. C. Thomson, *Louis St. Laurent: Canadian* (Toronto, 1967), p. 519.

[16] The choosing of party leaders by conventions rather than by parliamentary party caucuses adds a presidential feature to our system. It is significant, however, that when the Liberals and Conservatives recently provided for leadership reassessment by convention, they excluded the period when a leader might be Prime Minister. The exception implies that the leader, when he is Prime Minister, is responsible to Parliament and not to the party convention which elected him leader.

[17] A. D. P. Heeney, "Functions of the Prime Minister", in P. Fox, *Politics: Canada* (2nd ed.) (Toronto, 1966), p. 213.

[18] See, for example, R. MacG. Dawson, *The Government of Canada* (4th ed., rev. by N. Ward) (Toronto, 1963), pp. 222, 363; N. Mansergh, *Survey of British Commonwealth Affairs*, Vol. I: *Problems of External Policy 1931-1939* (London: 1952), p. 396.

referring it to Cabinet.[19] In Canada, the evidence is conflicting. In 1925, for instance, King consulted with his Cabinet on the date of the election, but in the end, it was his decision.[20] In 1926, however, not only was the question of dissolution discussed and agreed to by the Cabinet, but King left his Ministers to set the date while he went to request a dissolution from the Governor General.[21] In 1965, Mr. Pearson had difficulty making up his mind. According to Peter Newman, the Cabinet was polled (17 in favour, 4 against, and 1 undecided); but in the end, Newman says it was Mr. Pearson who had to make the final decision and he did so with several advisers (most of whom were not Cabinet Ministers) two days later.[22]

Although there is no clear Canadian case of a Prime Minister request-ing a dissolution against the views of his Cabinet, the South African crisis of 1939 is instructive. The Prime Minister, Herzog, asked for a dissolution when it appeared that a majority of his Cabinet did not support the request and that he had lost his majority in Parliament to Smuts.[23] The Governor General refused to grant the dissolution and at least two constitutional authorities agree that he was right to do so because the dissolution "was advised only by a minority of the Cabinet". Eugene Forsey comments: "To allow the Prime Minister alone to advise dissolution would certainly be contrary to the general trend of constitutional tradition, both in Britain and overseas; it would also be objectionable on grounds of public policy as tending to increase unduly the Prime Minister's personal power."[24]

One might ask whether the Governor General was right in 1963 to accede to Mr. Diefenbaker's request for a dissolution. The case is not clear cut because, although Newman claims that rebels outnumbered loyalists in the Cabinet following the Government's defeat in the House, Mr. Diefen-baker was able to cow them into submission in the famous caucus that met prior to the Cabinet.[25] While the Governor General's prerogative powers have not exactly flourished since Byng exercised them rather clumsily in 1926, one can question whether a Canadian Prime Minister really has the constitutional power to discipline his colleagues by threatening dissolution —whether, in fact, the two-edged weapon exists.

According to Professor Smith's analysis, Parliament's inability to act as a check on prime ministerial power has been furthered by the recent reforms whose primary aim has been the efficient conduct of government business rather than the effectiveness of Parliament as a check on govern-ment.[26] Spokesmen for the Government, on the other hand, tend to feel

---

[19] Jennings, *Cabinet Government*, pp. 417-19.

[20] Neatby, *Mackenzie King*, pp. 61-2.

[21] *Ibid.*, p. 145.

[22] P. C. Newman, *The Distemper of Our Times* (Toronto, 1968), pp. 337-44.

[23] Mansergh, *Survey of British Affairs*, pp. 381-400.

[24] E. A. Forsey, *The Royal Power of Dissolution of Parliament in the British Commonwealth* (Toronto, 1943), pp. 251-6.

[25] Newman, *Renegade in Power*, pp. 375-7.

[26] Smith, "President and Parliament", pp. 314-23 in this volume.

that the most significant change in procedure has been the much greater opportunities given to the committees. The automatic referral to Committee of Estimates and Bills after second reading and requests for committee studies appear to have kept M.P.s busier so that time spent on committee work may now be second only to constituency matters. Committees have even made minor amendments to government legislation and had the amendments accepted. However, it is too early to tell whether invigorated committees will provide an effective check on the Prime Minister and his Cabinet or whether they are just an attempt to keep Government M.P.s amused and out of trouble. One has the impression that, at the present time, M.P.s and the Prime Minister tend to go their own separate ways. Basically, the situation is explained by two factors which have more to do with the present political situation than any more fundamental change in Parliament's power and influence. Firstly, government backbenchers on the whole are pleased with a government which has carefully avoided the sort of missteps that plagued the previous administration. There has been no *cause célèbre* to test the independence of the committees or the Liberal caucus. It is not that the Prime Minister so completely awes Liberal M.P.s, as that they have been happy to leave him to his work and get on with theirs. (As further amplification of this point, one Liberal M.P. made the observation that caucus is chiefly an occasion for the M.P. to embarrass a Cabinet Minister in front of the P.M.; in other words that the backbencher *uses* the Prime Minister to win an argument against a Minister.)

The second factor in the present situation is that, as members of all parties will freely admit, the Conservative Opposition was very weak following the defeat of so many of its key figures in the 1968 election. Parliamentary opposition had a crucial role in gradually wearing down the Diefenbaker Government and continually harassing the Pearson Government. Mr. Pearson was always on edge when facing Parliament, partially because he never knew what to expect from his arch antagonist, Mr. Diefenbaker. The constitutional separation of powers that puts Congress a comfortable mile down Pennsylvania Avenue from the White House was not for Mr. Pearson. Throughout the course of Canadian parliamentary history, the pairing of Prime Minister and opposition leader has usually been no less colourful or combative: Brown and Blake versus MacDonald; Meighen and Bennett versus King; and Drew versus St. Laurent. Mr. Stanfield's style of opposition is very different from Mr. Diefenbaker's and many of his predecessors. The closest parallel, and one that might make Liberals uneasy, can be found in another Nova Scotian's mostly low-key opposition to another French-Canadian's Government which eventually defeated itself in 1911—but Borden had to endure two election defeats first. If Mr. Trudeau can afford to be somewhat remote from Parliament and bored with its debates (his appearances are generally restricted to "question period"), his aloofness is more like that of a President of the Fifth Republic than of the United States. But in reality there have been no institutional changes, only a particular set of circumstances—in a world that does not remain set for long.

A whole new perspective is provided if attention is focused on the Prime Minister's relationship to his Cabinet and through them to his party. In Canada, the office begins to look quite unpresidential—at least when the system is working well.

The secrecy that surrounds the operation of the Canadian Cabinet makes it a difficult body to write about. The operation of power probably ebbs and flows in many different ways; but the student of politics can never observe the institution in operation. We can glean tidbits on the workings of earlier Cabinets chiefly from the growing number of fine biographies on the Prime Ministers, but there is little on Cabinets as such. The biographies may not be very helpful in determining how the present Cabinet operates, because such a small and intimate institution changes as its membership changes and especially when administrations and Prime Ministers change. The leaks that came from the Pearson Administration were a boon to journalists and political scientists as is Judy LaMarsh's personal account of her years in Ottawa.[27] (Why is it that, on the whole, Canada's public men are such an unliterary lot? The dearth of political memoirs is a national deprivation.) Welcome as these are, however, they have to be treated circumspectly because such sources tend to provide us only with highly individual apologies. But even the suspect wells have dried up in the arid desert of the Trudeau Administration. That in itself affects the operation of the Cabinet, because under Pearson, if a Minister's policy was subjected to criticism that became public, the attack was taken as a personal one, especially since a more or less open campaign for the leadership was being waged by several Ministers almost for the duration of Mr. Pearson's prime ministership.[28] Now that the Cabinet once more has its discussions under heavy wraps, we are assured that there have been terrific rows which, however, because they are in confidence, ar less personal and acrimonious. However, we don't know for certain.

With these caveats, then, let us plunge into the largely uncharted waters of the Prime Minister and his Cabinet. We do have a goodly number of cases of prime ministerial autocracy: Laurier reintroducing separate school rights for the new provinces of Alberta and Saskatchewan while Sifton was out of the country;[29] R. B. Bennett giving his famous "New Deal" radio addresses without having discussed them with his Cabinet;[30] Mr. Pearson engineering secret meetings that led to the great compromise with Quebec officials on the pension plan—done without the knowledge of the Minister responsible[31]—or his about-face on allowing an inquiry into the dismissal of civil servant, George Victor Spencer,—done without consulting his Cabinet.[32] The Prime Minister's unrestricted power to hire and fire is even more spectacular: Laurier getting rid of Israel Tarte,

---

[27] Judy LaMarsh, *Memoirs of a Bird in a Gilded Cage* (Toronto, 1970).

[28] Confidential source.

[29] J. Schull, *Laurier* (Toronto: 1965), pp. 444-50.

[30] Public Archives of Canada, Manion Papers, Vol. XLV, memoranda, 2, 7 January, 1935.

[31] LaMarsh, *Memoirs*, pp. 93-4.

[32] *Ibid.*, pp. 165-7; P. C. Newman, *The Distemper of Our Times* (Toronto, 1968), pp. 390-99.

the most prominent Quebec Liberal after himself; Mackenzie King reliev-
ing the popular J. L. Ralston as Minister of National Defence in 1944. The
Prime Minister's powers seem very presidential indeed.

These incidents have to be examined more closely, for the displays of
power were indications of a pathological condition in the Canadian political system. Laurier's two autocratic outbursts entailed the loss of two of the
strongest pillars in his Cabinet about whom he had once remarked, "So
long as I have Tarte and Sifton with me, I shall be master of Canada."[33] In
the Alberta and Saskatchewan schools controversy, he not only lost Sifton
but, in a humiliating retreat, allowed him to rewrite the legislation.[34] Bennett, continuing his practice of one-man government, was taking a desperate, eleventh-hour policy initiative which did not prevent one of the party's
worst election defeats. Mr. Pearson's changes of policy, which were presented to a Cabinet battered with crises and increasingly demoralized with
reversals and retreats, brought several Ministers to the point of resignation.[35] Lastly, the firing of Ralston, though brilliantly conducted, was carried out by a Prime Minister whose own position was desperate and whose
Government several times threatened to collapse over a seven-week period. It was saved more by Ralston's forbearance and St. Laurent's courage
than King's command.[36] Historically the great examples of prime ministerial autocracy have come either when the Government was already in
perilous circumstances or they have produced a decisive descent in the
Government's fortunes. In quieter, happier times, a Prime Minister has
played the role of moderator, the firm but careful persuader,[37] the cabinet-
maker who realizes the necessity of leaving aside some of his personal
preferences when he forms his ministry,[38] the man who hesitates to fire a
colleague.[39]

Probably the most important key to a Canadian Prime Minister's success lies in his being able to attract into his Cabinet, men of outstanding
ability and great political weight. The difficulty of finding and keeping
such men was a recurring problem for MacDonald[40] and, after his death,

---

[33] Quoted in Schull, *Laurier*, p. 412.

[34] *Ibid.*, pp. 452-3.

[35] LaMarsh, *Memoirs*, pp. 94, 167; Newman, *The Distemper of Our Times*, p. 398.

[36] R. MacG. Dawson, *The Conscription Crisis of 1944* (Toronto, 1961).

[37] Schull, *Laurier*, p. 340; R. MacGregor Dawson, *William Lyon Mackenzie King* (Toronto,
1958), I, 443-5; Neatby, *Mackenzie King* pp. 274, 313-15.

[38] H. N. Macquarrie, "The Formation of Borden's First Cabinet", *Canadian Journal of Economics and Political Science*, XXIII (1957), pp. 90-104; Dawson, *King*, p. 373; B. Hutchison, *Mr.
Prime Minister, 1867-1964* (Toronto, 1964), p. 151. It should be noted that a Prime
Minister's rivals for the leadership of his party are almost always included in his Cabinet
whereas that almost never happens in the U.S. In Canada, six Prime Ministers have been
elected to the leadership of their parties by conventions. They faced opposition from 20
other serious candidates; all but four were subsequently members of the winners' Cabinets and at least one other—Robert Winters—was offered a portfolio but declined.

[39] Hutchison, *Mr. Prime Minister*, p. 160.

[40] D. Creighton, *John A. Macdonald: The Old Chieftain* (Toronto, 1955), pp. 389-90, 429-30,
504-5, 523.

made the search for new leadership that much more difficult. Laurier's first Cabinet was by contrast a stellar one and under him the notion of a "lieutenant", to complement the Prime Minister's leadership of his own linguistic group, was developed into more of a system of regional lieutenancies: Fielding, the strong man from the Maritimes; Sifton, the West; Cartwright and Mulock for Ontario; and Tarte, the second-in-command in Quebec. They looked out for the interests of their regions in the Government and for the interests of the Liberal Party in their regions. Such Ministers may have been opinionated men who "fought like blazes" (to use Tarte's words), but they provided the ministry with a firm, national basis. Electorally, 1904 was the high point for the Government. As both the Government and the Prime Minister aged, Laurier came to dominate more but his Government grew weaker. One by one many of his giants grew restive and departed until only Fielding was left. Laurier was prepared to get along with these weaker men;[41] but without men of political weight to direct it, the party's organization declined and, in the end, Laurier lost touch with public opinion throughout English Canada and Quebec.[42] Mackenzie King was unique in having a succession of politically influential Cabinet Ministers throughout his 21½ years as Prime Minister. If anything, his Governments grew stronger as time went on: from the Maritimes came Fielding, then Ralston and Ilsley; Lapointe from Quebec was succeeded by St. Laurent and, on the English-speaking side, Claxton and Abbott followed Power; in Ontario, Graham and Murphy were followed by Howe, Martin, and Pearson; and from the West came Dunning, Crerar, and Gardiner. King's biographer observes that he was not afraid to promote a rival, particularly after his early years as Prime Minister. "He knew what less successful men forget: that his own career depended on the support of strong colleagues."[43] The system of regional lieutenants was continued under St. Laurent but, according to Miss Judy LaMarsh, these responsibilities were never defined in the Pearson Cabinet (apart from the Quebec lieutenancy) and questions of the welfare of the Liberal organization throughout the country were ignored.[44] The West had no effective voice in the Cabinet and, to the Government's great cost, the Government was consequently unable to communicate with Western voters.

A successful Canadian Prime Minister, then, must find Cabinet Ministers who can not only run departments, but who can give effective representation to their regions in Ottawa and effective leadership to the party in their home regions. It is not easy to find men who can do all well, particularly the last. As Chubby Power remarked to Mackenzie King:

The difficulties of a party in power were much greater than when in opposition, in that the [party] organization must be left in the hands of the Ministers since otherwise there would be an almost continual clash of interests. Unfortunately, it is not

[41] Schull, *Laurier*, p. 458.
[42] *Ibid.*, p. 529.
[43] Neatby, *Mackenzie King*, p. 92.
[44] LaMarsh, *Memoirs*, pp. 144-7.

always possible to make a good organizer out of a good Minister, and some of your
best colleagues in the Cabinet were utterly incapable of understanding anything
whatsoever about practical party organization.[45]

If he is to attract the paragons that he needs, a Prime Minister cannot override their views too often. He cannot be a one-man government. As King's friend Violet Markham advised him in his first year as Prime Minister, "Delegation is the secret of all successful work."[46] On the other hand, his Government will drift aimlessly if he hopes to achieve unanimity as Mr. Diefenbaker was apparently inclined to do.[47] A Prime Minister has to demand a decision from his Cabinet and, when his Ministers are in disagreement, his power as dispute-settler is considerable. Canadians have sometimes been disappointed that their Prime Ministers have often appeared to be just grey compromisers and conciliators, while the great initiators on the federal scene have usually been Cabinet Ministers: Sifton, Hughes, Howe, Hamilton, Hellyer. A Prime Minister has occasionally become the protagonist for some policy—Laurier on separate school rights in Alberta and Saskatchewan, Mr. Trudeau with his Bill of Rights—but in each case, when opposition arose (from within the Cabinet and from provincial governments respectively), there was no one and no institution to work out the necessary compromise. In Canada, that is the pre-eminent function of the prime ministership. Two other examples from the same ministries illustrate how much more smoothly the system works when Ministers take the initiatives: Mowat dealing with the Manitoba government on the explosive schools controversy;[48] Mr Benson proposing controversial and wide-ranging reforms to the tax structure. The retort could be made that a Minister, then, is simply a lightning rod attracting the charge away from the Prime Minister; but sooner or later the Prime Minister must come to his defence— as Mr. Trudeau came to Mr. Benson's—or the Cabinet becomes demoralized—as when Mr. Gordon's first budget was scuppered.[49] On the other hand, when the initiatve succeeds, the Prime Minister usually sees his cabinet colleague get most of the credit. The Prime Minister's role in the system is not as advantageous as has sometimes been suggested.

The checks on prime ministerial power in Canada come from different sources and operate in very different ways from those on presidential power in the United States. In a very general sense, it is true that any head of government is subject to Theodore Sorensen's list of "five ever-present limitations. He is free to choose only: (1) within the limits of permissibility; (2) within the limits of available resources; (3) within the limits of available time; (4) within the limits of previous commitments; (5) within the limits of available information."[50] Perhaps, even within the Canadian public service,

---

[45] N. Ward, ed. *A Party Politician: The Memoirs of Chubby Power* (Toronto, 1966), pp. 273-4.
[46] Dawson, *King*, p. 452.
[47] Newman, *Renegade*, pp. 92-4.
[48] Schull, *Laurier*, p. 329.
[49] *Ibid.*, pp. 65-6.
[50] *Decision-Making in the White House* (New York, 1964), p. 23.

"dissent, inertia, incompetence or impudence" can bridle a Prime Minister as much as they do a President.[51] Sorensen adds that two potential sources of presidential constraint are minimal: party platforms, which are usually vague and easily evaded,[52] and Cabinet Secretaries, who can rarely separate their own departmental interests from the advice they give.[53] Canadians might add a third restraint which is not nearly as great as in Canada: a federal system which has become increasingly centralized over the last four decades.

The little regard that most recent Presidents have had for the Cabinet as an institution is well known. Mr. Nixon's recent reorganization of his executive further downgrades the Cabinet *vis-à-vis* his Executive Office. President Kennedy, Sorensen says, "with few exeptions . . . had Cabinet meetings only because 'I suppose we should—it's been several weeks since the last one', and with few exceptions these meetings bored him. . . . No decisions of importance were made at Kennedy's Cabinet meetings and few subjects of importance, particularly in foreign affairs, were even seriously discussed. The Cabinet as a body was convened largely as a symbol, to be informed, not consulted, to help keep the channels of communication open, to help maintain the *esprit de corps* of the members and to prevent the charge that Kennedy had abolished the Cabinet." With a few exceptions "he usually had little interest in the views of Cabinet members on matters outside their jurisdiction" and "much the same was true of the large formal meetings of the National Security Council". That is not to say that Kennedy did not have close communication with his cabinet officers and rely on them a great deal in their particular areas of responsibility and competence, for according to Sorensen he did.[54] Although ethnic, regional and interest-group considerations may have some part in the choosing of American Cabinet Secretaries,[55] these factors are much less important than they are in Canada.[56] Furthermore, cabinet officers sometimes have no past political experience, take no part in partisan politics, and may even be hardly known by the President when asked to join his administration. Small wonder that the Cabinet cannot assist the President in looking at the problems of government as a whole.

The President himself has to be the great initiator, the "voice of the people," the man in the "bully pulpit"[57] because the Cabinet and even the President's closest advisers lack credibility[58] and Congress lacks organized

[51] *Ibid.*, pp. 25-6.
[52] *Ibid.*, pp. 32-3.
[53] *Ibid.*, pp. 68-70.
[54] *Kennedy* (Toronto, 1966), pp. 317-20.
[55] See, for example, J. MacG. Burns, *Roosevelt: The Lion and the Fox* (New York, 1956), p. 150; Sorensen, *Decision-Making*, p. 68 and Sorensen, *Kennedy*, pp. 281-8, 297-311.
[56] Dawson, *Government*, pp. 193-200; P. Fox, "The Representative Nature of the Canadian Cabinet", in his *Politics: Canada* (2nd ed.) (Toronto, 1966), pp. 206-10.
[57] C. Rossiter, *The American Presidency* (2nd ed.) (New York, 1960), pp. 32-4.
[58] R. E. Neustadt, "White House and Whitehall", in (ed.) A. King *The British Prime Minister* (London, 1960), p. 140, and appearing in this volume, pp. 344-55.

leadership. But once the President makes his demands, he loses control. Sectional interests find their most effective voice in Congress rather than in the Cabinet. By the often slow and painful progress through bottlenecks, by means of coalitions and saw-offs between petty baronies, the opposing forces are brought to rest in a compromise solution. The President's programme is only one of the "inputs" into the balance and there is very little that he can do to speed up the process if, as so often happens, it threatens to grind to a halt.[59] A President does have scope for bypassing Congress and, during emergencies and in the field of foreign affairs, he is often given a free hand. However the troubles that President Johnson and President Nixon had with Congress over their conduct of the war in Viet Nam indicate what happens when a President takes congressional acquiescence for granted.

If the President's initiatives are going to carry any weight, if he is going to be a strong President, he must, as Richard Neustadt says, have the power to persuade.[60] A Canadian Prime Minister, if he is to be successful, must have the ability to conciliate and, what has perhaps not been sufficiently noted, he must have something within his Cabinet worth conciliating. From these considerations comes also a differing relationship with the political party. The President as the pleader for a programme is tempted to find support wherever he can. Every President has to choose between being a partisan leader who attempts over the long term to unify and reform his party and being a short-term opportunist who takes congressional support wherever he can find it. Most Presidents have chosen the second alternative except, perhaps briefly, at election times. A Canadian Prime Minister will have every reason to try and build up his party, to listen to its views, and to reward those who have served well. According to Peter Newman, the party's 1960 Study Conference on National Problems at Kingston was "the most important single source of Lester Pearson's lieutenants and advisers".[61] Mr. Pearson's addition of Messrs. Marchand, Trudeau, and Pelletier to his Cabinet was the necessary first step in dealing with the Quebec problem. The strong stand taken by the 1966 Liberal Policy Conference against any further postponement of medicare was apparently an important factor in the Government's decision not to consider a second postponement.[62]

A "separation of power" exists not just in Washington, but in Ottawa and London as well; in each country, however, these constraints on the power of the Head of Government operate in different ways. As Neustadt says, a President tends to "manoeuvre around" congressional leaders as carefully and gingerly as a British Prime Minister "tiptoes" around his Cabinet.[63] But Neustadt argues, what really preserves Cabinet Government

---

[59] J. MacG. Burns, *The Deadlock of Democracy* (Englewood Cliffs, 1963).

[60] R. E. Neustadt, *Presidential Power* (New York, 1962).

[61] *The Distemper of our Times*, p. 62.

[62] Confidential source.

[63] Neustadt, "*White House*", pp. 349-52 of this volume.

in Britain is the necessity for Downing Street to treat senior civil servants with due respect, to bring them along.[64] "They are loyal to a 'Government Decision' but that takes the form of action in Cabinet, where the great machines are represented by their minister".[65] The civil service elite in turn have a stake in preserving the independence of their departments from being overridden by Downing Street; they have "every incentive . . . to keep their fights below his [the Prime Minister's] level—below Cabinet level".[66] In Canada, the relationships are different; the Prime Minister apparently listens more seriously to the views of Cabinet Ministers than to Deputy Ministers.[67] The difference is due to the fact that a Canadian Prime Minister has to respect a regional point of view—both from within the Cabinet and from M.P.s' regional caucuses—and that, more than Parliament or the civil service, provides a check to prime ministerial power and preserves cabinet government in Canada.

The American system does have the advantage that much (though not all) of the bargaining takes place in full public view and a sectional interest can at least be satisfied that its case is being put forcefully. In Canada, caucus and Cabinet secrecy have allowed doubts to be raised in voters' minds about how effectively their views have been represented. The main disadvantage to the American system is that the President is the only participant who has to take the national view. Elsewhere in Washington, power and responsibility are much more diffused than they are in Canada. (Our counterpart is the buckpassing that often takes place between federal and provincial levels of government.) All the unwritten rules for representing geographical, ethnic, and religious interest in the Cabinet have frequently been deplored because "merit is disregarded";[68] but they can be interpreted as one of the great strengths of the Canadian cabinet system. Not all Ministers are really effective spokesmen for the interests they are supposed to represent, but when they are, they contribute a viewpoint in the making of governmental policy which is separate from departmental considerations. The more a Minister can really speak for his region or group, the better is his advice to the Prime Minister and Cabinet, and the less a Prime Minister can ignore this advice without suffering the consequences. When a Canadian Cabinet is strong and working well, it is the institution in the country which, *par excellence*, represents the many aspects of the nation and, most importantly, can take a national point of view in settling the conflicts of interest which inevitably arise. Individual Ministers are, within limits, expendable; but the fortunes of the Cabinet rise and fall together, so the best interests of the nation *have* to come out of the amalgam of sectional elements which go into a Canadian Cabinet. Getting the amal-

[64] R. E. Neustadt interviewed by H. Brandon, "10 Downing Street", in (ed.) A. King, *The British Prime Minister* (London, 1969), p. 123.
[65] Quoted in Neustadt, *"White House"*, p. 355 of this volume.
[66] Brandon, "10 Downing Street", pp. 128, 126.
[67] Confidential source.
[68] Quoted in Dawson, *Government*, p. 193.

gam right is primarily the responsibility of the Prime Minister and, when the system is working well, he shares it with his cabinet colleagues.

What about the present Prime Minister? Professor Smith claims that "he has taken the system further, faster, more self-consciously, than it would otherwise have gone"[69] in the direction of a presidential system. Mr. Trudeau's expansion of the Prime Minister's Office is a case in point. Isn't it the equivalent of the White House Office, and isn't the Privy Council Office our counterpart to the Executive Office of the President?

The role of adviser to the Prime Minister is a shadowy one, whose outlines are more difficult to discern than that of Cabinet Minister. Mr. Jack Pickersgill is often described as having been a considerable power behind Mackenzie King's throne, but he himself denies that he was "one of his principal advisers" during the War.[70] St. Laurent's biographer remarks of Mr. Pickersgill that "watching over every aspect of political and administrative activity, Jack Pickersgill proved an invaluable aide and counsellor. 'Check it with Jack' became a watchword on Parliament Hill";[71] but there are no examples of how that influence operated. Peter Newman claims that Mr. Diefenbaker did not try to find an equivalent *chef de cabinet* and that the only man in his office to have any impact on him was Mr. John Fisher whose "functions were never clearly defined, though one of his main assignments was to act as troubleshooter and supplier of Canadiana."[72] Mr. Tom Kent is described as having been Mr. Pearson's "policy co-ordinator" and "an absolutely brilliant idea man" who was closely involved in formulating the Canada Pension Plan and election campaign strategies.[73] In the present Prime Minister's Office, Mr. Marc Lalonde is described as being "most influential" in "constitutional policy and federal-provincial relations" and "a troubleshooter with regard to Quebec".[74] "It may be questioned whether any Cabinet Minister has as great day-in and day-out influence with the Prime Minister as Lalonde has".[75] [This referred to Mr. Lalonde's influence in his capacity at that time as Principal Secretary of the P.M.O.] Mr. Ivan Head, the Prime Minister's Legislative Assistant, has been described as "Trudeau's alter ego".[76] It is hard to imagine that the Prime Minister's Office as a body outweighs in influence the Cabinet and the civil service as does the White House Office. For one thing, P.M.O. assistants never attend cabinet meetings as do presidential assistants.[77] Nor can one imagine, for instance, that any Canadian prime ministerial assistant

---

[69] *Ibid.*, p. 29.

[70] J. W. Pickersgill, *The Mackenzie King Record* (Toronto, 1960), Vol. I, p. x.

[71] Thomson, *St. Laurent*, pp. 263-4.

[72] Newman, *Renegade*, pp. 83-4.

[73] Newman, *The Distemper of our Times*, pp. 84, 306-15; LaMarsh, *Memoirs*, pp. 60, 79-133.

[74] L. Seale, "Marc Lalonde: the shadow beside Pierre Trudeau", Toronto *Globe and Mail*, February 1, 1969.

[75] J. Bird, "Who are the men on Trudeau's inside team?", *Financial Post*, July 5, 1969.

[76] J. Bird, "Meet Ivan Head, lawyer and Trudeau's alter ego", *Financial Post*, November 30, 1968.

[77] Sorensen, *Kennedy*, p. 294.

340 APEX OF POWER

would have responsibilities as broad as those ascribed to Mr. Arthur Burns, Counsellor to President Nixon. "One of his tasks, as he sees it, is to detect and resolve disputed issues of policy and administration before they become the President's problems. It is a conception that requires high officials, Cabinet Ministers included, to recognize his primacy and to accept his intervention without appeal to President Nixon".[78]

The duties of the Prime Minister's Office are described in the official *Organization of the Government of Canada* as keeping the Prime Minister "aware of all significant developments throughout the country", "liaison with various party organizations", correspondence, appointments, public appearances, and press releases.[79] The P.M.O. assists the Prime Minister in attempting to keep the Government's (and the P.M.'s) broad policy objectives clearly in focus, to work closely on problems which involve more than two or three departments and are highly sensitive politically—such as the Arctic. The Office specializes in trying to keep an overall view of where the Government is going, and in this sense it resembles the White House Office. However, it also has a coordinating function which is different from its Washington counterpart. While there is undoubtedly some rivalry with departments and the Privy Council Office, the P.M.O. appears to work more closely with them than the White House Office, which often acts in competition with the departments or supersedes them completely. For example, a P.M.O. assistant undertaking a special task for the Prime Minister, as when Mr. Head went to Nigeria, will be briefed by the relevant department; new policy ideas coming from the P.M.O. are not developed there, but are passed on to normal departmental channels. Responsibilities with the P.C.O. are ideally shared on the basis that the P.C.O. does the theoretical work on a proposal, while the P.M.O. attempts to determine how public opinion would react. The attempt to tap grass roots thinking involves the largest manpower in the P.M.O. and the information is gathered, in part, from correspondence to the Prime Minister. His Office claim to have a sophisticated method of analyzing and tabulating the "beefs" that lead people to write to their P.M. This is passed on to the Minister and chairmen of regional caucuses. Recently two members of the P.M.O. have been given full-time responsibility for researching governmental appointments. Getting the right man for the right job is of crucial importance, but this apparent development of prime ministerial influence is qualified by the fact that appointments are now also a regular item on cabinet agenda.[80]

The personnel of the P.M.O. also give an indication of how its duties lie more in the political than the policy sphere. Mr. Pearson's Office contained a number of journalists and advertising men and a number of the assistants in the present P.M.O. were part of the nucleus that organized

---

[78] J. Osborne, "Nixon's Home Guard: Discipline and Order But an 'Open' Image", *New Republic*, February 22, 1969.

[79] 3-CP-4, January 1970, January-July 1969.

[80] Confidential sources.

Mr. Trudeau's campaign for the leadership. They were largely bright, young people in their 20's and early 30's who, with one or two exceptions, had no pre-eminent expertness in particular policy fields. The exceptions would seem to have been Mr. Marc Lalonde and Mr. Ivan Head, both lawyers, both about 40 years of age at the time and both backing up the Prime Minister's interest in constitutional and legal matters. Generally in Canada, the job of executive assistant to the Prime Minister or to a Cabinet Minister is a good way for a young man to get some experience, which can often be pretty hectic odd-jobbing, rather than being the sort of professional "in and out" expert who advises American Presidents.[81]

The Privy Council Office is a kind of cabinet secretariat whose main duties are the handling of agenda, documents, and decisions for the Cabinet, Cabinet committees, and inter-departmental committees.[82] Apart from these rather mechanical, secretarial functions, it has recently been given responsibility for long-term planning and can undertake special studies. The establishment of a Federal-Provincial Relations Secretariat in 1968 indicates its special responsibility in this sphere. With its control over the circulation of documents, the Office has the opportunity to insert its own ideas alongside departmental ones.[83] However, it is not as large as the Executive Office of the President nor would it appear to have the preponderant influence of such Executive Office components as the Budget Bureau or the national Security Council. In any case civil servants in the Privy Council Office are said to treat Cabinet Ministers with more deference than their rivals in Finance and External.[84] Does that mean that it is as loyal to the idea of cabinet collectivity as the British Cabinet Secretariat is?[85] The answer to that question is only one of the things we need to know about these two somewhat mysterious, but fascinating bodies.

In his relations with the Cabinet, Mr. Trudeau would appear to be more committed to cabinet government than some of his predecessors. According to Miss LaMarsh, the Pearson Cabinet did not discuss foreign or military policy.[86] Mr. Martin "usually got the decisions he needed through private conversations with the Prime Minister, and fully expected the Cabinet to do little more than rubber stamp his proposals".[87] By contrast, the Trudeau Government's foreign policy review brought forth prolonged debate and divided opinions from members of the Cabinet.[88]

The fuller use now made of cabinet committees no doubt brings Canada closer to British practice, which J. P. Mackintosh has described as

---

[81] Neustadt, "White House", p. 348 of this volume.

[82] Organization of the Government of Canada (Ottawa, 1964).

[83] Confidential source.

[84] Ibid.

[85] Neustadt, "10 Downing Street", p. 122.

[86] LaMarsh, Memoirs, p. 31.

[87] Ibid., p. 327.

[88] A. Westell, "Trudeau facing Cabinet division on NATO policy", Toronto Star, April 1, 1968.

replacing government by cabinet with government by committee.[89] "Group decision-making" as described by J. K. Galbraith is the hallmark of the modern "Technostructure"[90]—just as much a feature of governmental as of corporate organizations and not least of American presidential government. Canadian Cabinet Ministers, however, occupy a much more central position in our Federal Government and in the organization of the cabinet committees. Mr. Trudeau is chairman of only two of the so-called co-ordinating committees—Priorities and Planning and Federal-Provincial Relations. The other two co-ordinating committees—Legislation and Government Priorities in Parliament, and the Treasury Board—are chaired by other Ministers, as are the four functional committees—External Policy and Defence; Economic Policy and Programmes; Communications, Works, and Urban Affairs; and Social Policy.[91] Mr. Trudeau has certain very definite policy preferences in areas in which he is keenly interested—Federal-Provincial Relations, the Constitution, Quebec, relations with France, and regional development—and the Cabinet have followed his lead in these areas. Elsewhere, one suspects that he is more interested in an orderly, well-reasoned dispatch of business and that meetings which he chairs do not ramble as did those of his predecessor.[92] His key committee, Priorities and Planning, while it obviously gives the Prime Minister a chance to get a broad outline for his Government's future policy, is also concerned with providing an orderly time-table for Government projects within the resources of the nation. Presidents usually ascribe to themselves grander occupations than that!

Mr. Pearson attempted to use a similar committee system, but Ministers often failed to attend committee meetings, and the full Cabinet frequently insisted on going over the same ground that had been covered in the committees.[93] A properly functioning committee system effectively distributes responsibility more widely and eliminates that peculiarly Canadian phenomenon, the independent Minister who runs his department largely without interference from either the Prime Minister or Cabinet. In the previous administration, it is said that when a Minister presented the Cabinet with a proposal, a threat was implied that, unless Cabinet agreed, the Minister would resign. Mr. Hellyer's plan to unify the armed forces was not really discussed in Cabinet and, when close scrutiny was given to his housing ideas by cabinet committee, he became impatient and that was one of the factors leading to his resignation.[94]

Once an item of cabinet business has found its way through the Committee on Priorities and Planning and the appropriate functional committee, it goes before the full Cabinet and here the Prime Minister's traditional

---

[89] *The British Cabinet* (Toronto, 1962), p. 451.

[90] *The New Industrial State* (New York, 1967), 71-82.

[91] A. Westell, "Trudeau streamlines his Cabinet with a new system of powerful committees", Toronto *Globe and Mail*, May 1, 1968.

[92] Confidential source.

[93] *Ibid.*

[94] *Ibid.*

powers—setting the agenda, promoting discussion, voicing his own opinion, and drawing a conclusion from the discussion—come into play. However, it is indicative of the smooth functioning of the present Cabinet that one Minister can recall no decision which has been taken by the Prime Minister without full discussion in Cabinet. For example, when a foreign take-over of the uranium Denison Mines was threatened, a full cabinet meeting was called on short notice.[95] Another indicator which suggests that Mr. Trudeau sees his role, in some degree at least, as being a coordinator and arbitrator is the wide spectrum of conservative and radical viewpoints which he has put into his cabinet.

Under Mr. Trudeau, more attention is being given to party matters than formerly. The so-called "political Cabinet" is an innovation which attempts to "politicize" the Cabinet and includes Ministers and party officials. It meets about once a month and has discussed such questions as Western alienation, student unrest, and party finance. In addition, there are provincial advisory groups composed of the caucus chairman, Cabinet Minister, and president of the party organization of each province; they are intended to be a channel between the constituencies and the Government.[96] The crucial question is—how well *does* the Government communicate with voters? As we have seen, this is essential for the political well-being of any Canadian Cabinet and Prime Minister. Quebec and Ontario, with roughly ten and 11 Ministers respectively since the advent of the Trudeau Government, have never had such strong representation; the quality of the Quebec contingent is even more impressive than its size. The other provinces each have one representative, except for British Columbia which has three and Prince Edward Island which has none. From the point of view of political weight and effective party leadership in their respective provinces, there are notable weaknesses outside Central Canada. The creation of the regional desks in the Prime Minister's Office is a partial attempt to correct this weakness. At first there was no Ontario regional desk and the Quebec regional desk is primarily responsible for Mr. Trudeau's duties as M.P. for Mount Royal. The regional desks, when they were first set up, were seen by many (including this writer) as a slightly sinister, super-information network which competed with the M.P.s as the traditional party link with the constituencies. The regional desks appear now to be more like a stop-gap measure that attempts to improve the Government's communication with those areas where the party is weakest, and the Ministers are still recognized to have primary responsibility for the Liberal party's organization in their respective regions. But even in this more modest role, the regional desks find it difficult to keep from stepping on established toes.[97]

In the end, a Canadian Cabinet is only as strong as its provincial components within the Cabinet. Professor Smith, in his conclusion asks, "Who is there, I wonder, to play Senator Fulbright to Pierre Trudeau's Lyndon Johnson?"[98] The answer is: he and several like him are in the Cabinet—and, if they are not, Mr. Trudeau's regime is in trouble.

---

[95] *Ibid.*

[96] *Ibid.*

[97] *Ibid.*

[98] Smith, "President and Parliament", p. 325 in this volume.

27

White House and Whitehall*

RICHARD E. NEUSTADT

'Cabinet Government', so-called, as practised currently in the United Kingdom, differs in innumerable ways, some obvious, some subtle, from 'Presidential Government' in the United States. To ask what one can learn about our own machine by viewing theirs—which is the question posed for me this morning—may seem farfetched, considering those differences. But actually the question is a good one. For the differences are matters of degree and not of kind.

Despite surface appearances these two machines, the British and American, are not now at opposite poles. Rather they are somewhat differently located near the centre of a spectrum stretching between ideal types, from collective-leadership to one-man rule. Accordingly, a look down Whitehall's corridors of power should suggest a lot of things worth noticing in Washington. At any rate, that is the premise of this paper. . . .

What I shall do [here] is to raise two simple points of difference between their machine and ours, with an eye to implications for the study of *our* system:

First, we have counterparts for their top civil servants—but not in our own civil service.

Second, we have counterparts for their Cabinet ministers—but not exclusively or even mainly in our Cabinet.

If I state these two correctly, and I think I do, it follows that in our conventional comparisons we students all too often have been victims of semantics. Accordingly, in our proposals for reform-by-analogy (a favourite sport of this Association since its founding) we all too often have confused function with form. I find no functions in the British system for which ours lacks at least nascent counterparts. But it is rare when institutions with the same names in both systems do the same work for precisely the same purpose. We make ourselves much trouble, analytically, by letting nomenclature dictate our analogies. Hopefully, this paper offers something of an antidote.

---

* Abridged from *The Public Interest*, Vol. II (1966). © National Affairs Inc., 1966, by permission of *The Public Interest* (New York).

For the most important things that I bring back from my excursioning in Whitehall are a question and a caution. The question: what is our functional equivalent? The caution: never base analysis on nomenclature. With these I make my case for a comparative approach to American studies. These seem to be embarrassingly obvious. But that is not the way it works in practice. By way of illustration let me take in turn those 'simple' points of difference between Whitehall and Washington.

I

'Why are your officials so passionate?' I once was asked in England by a bright young Treasury official just back from Washington. I inquired with whom he had been working there; his answer 'Your chaps at the Budget Bureau.'

To an American those 'chaps' appear to be among the most dispassionate of Washingtonians. Indeed, the Budget staff traditionally prides itself on being cool, collected, and above the struggle, distant from emotions churning in the breasts of importunate agency officials. Yet to my English friend, 'They took themselves so seriously . . . seemed to be crusaders for the policy positions they thought made sense . . . seemed to feel that it was up to them to save the day . . . ' If this is how the Budget Bureau struck him, imagine how he would have felt about some circles in our Air Force, or the European Bureau of the State Department, or the Office of Economic Opportunity, or the Forest Service, for that matter, or the Bureau of Reclamation, or the National Institutes of Health!

His question is worth pondering, though that is not my purpose here.[1] I give it you gratis to pursue on your own time. What I should rather do is to pursue two further questions which his inquiry suggests. First, out of what frame of reference was he asking? And second, is it sensible of him (and most of us) to talk of our own budgeteers as though they were his counterparts? I ask because I think that we are very far from candid with ourselves about the way we get *his* work done in *our* system.

This young man was a Principal-with-prospects at the Treasury. By definition, then, he was a man of the Administrative class, elite corps of the British civil service. More importantly, he was also apprentice-member of the favoured few, elite-of-the-elite, who climb the ladder *in* the Treasury. With skill and luck and approbation from his seniors he might someday rise to be a Mandarin. And meanwhile he would probably serve soon as personal assistant to a Cabinet minister. In short, he had the frame of reference which befits a man whose career ladder rises up the central pillar of the whole Whitehall machine toward the heights where dwell the seniors of all seniors, moulders of ministers, heads of the civil service, knights in office, lords thereafter: Permanent Secretaries of the Cabinet and Treasury.

---

[1] I have suggested at least a partial answer in 'Politicians and Bureaucrats', *The Congress and America's Future* (New York 1965), pp. 115-16.

English civil servants of this sort, together with their Foreign Office counterparts, comprise the inner corps of 'officials', civilian careerists, whose senior members govern the United Kingdom in collaboration with their ministerial superiors the front-bench politicians, leaders of the Parliamentary Party which commands a House majority for the time being. Theirs is an intimate collaboration grounded in the interests and traditions of both sides. Indeed it binds them into a Society for Mutual Benefit: what they succeed in sharing with each other they need share with almost no one else, and governing in England is a virtual duopoly.

This is the product of a tacit treaty, an implicit bargain, expressed in self-restraints which are observed on either side. The senior civil servants neither stall nor buck decisions of the government once taken in due form by their political masters. 'Due form' means consultation, among other things, but having been consulted these officials act without public complaint or private evasion, even though they may have fought what they are doing up to the last moment of decision. They also try to assure comparable discipline in lower official ranks, and to squeeze out the juniors who do not take kindly to it. The senior politicians, for their part—with rare and transient exceptions—return the favour in full measure.

The politicians rarely meddle with official recruitment or promotion; by and large, officialdom administers itself. They preserve the anonymity of civil servants both in Parliament and in the Press. Officials never testify on anything except 'accounts', and nobody reveals their roles in shaping public policy. Ministers take kudos for themselves, likewise the heat. They also take upon themselves protection for the status of officialdom in the society: honours fall like gentle rain at stated intervals. They even let careerists run their private offices, and treat their personal assistants of the moment (detailed from civil service ranks) as confidentially as our department heads treat trusted aides imported from outside. More importantly, the politicians *lean* on their officials. They *expect* to be advised. Most importantly, they very often do what they are told, and follow the advice that they receive.

This is an advantageous bargain for both sides. It relieves the politicians of a difficult and chancy search for 'loyal' advisers and administrators. These are there, in place, ready to hand. And it relieves officials of concern for their security in terms both of profession and of person. No wonder our careerists appear 'passionate' to one of theirs; they have nothing at stake [in Britain] except policy!

So a Treasury-type has everything to gain by a dispassionate stance, and nothing to lose except arguments. Since he is an elitist, ranking intellectually and morally with the best in Britain, this is no trifling loss. If parliamentary parties were less disciplined than they now are, of if he had back-benchers who identified with him, he could afford to carry arguments outside official channels, as his predecessors sometimes did a century ago, and *military* officers still do, on occasion.[2] But party discipline calls forth its

---

[2] Regarding civil servants of an earlier era, when aristocratic patronage opened the way to careers, it is delightful to note that Sir Charles Trevelyan, one of the creators of the

counterpart in his own ranks. And party politicians on backbenches have
no natural affinities for *civil* servants—quite the contrary. He really has no
recourse but to lose his arguments with grace and wait in patience for
another day, another set of ministers. After all, he stays, they go. And
while he stays he shares the fascinating game of power, stretching his own
mind and talents in the service of a reasonably grateful country.

The Treasury-type is a disciplined man, but a man fulfilled, not frustrated. His discipline is what he pays for power. Not every temperament
can take it; if he rises in the Treasury he probably can. Others are weeded
out. But there is more to this than a cold compromise for power's sake.
Those who rise and find fulfilment in their work do so in part because
they are deliberately exposed at mid-career to the constraints, the miseries,
the hazards which afflict the human beings who wield power on the political side. They know the lot of ministers from observation at first hand.
Exposure makes for empathy and for perspective. It also makes for com-
fort with the civil servant's lot. Whitehall's elitists gain all three while
relatively young. It leaves them a bit weary with the weight of human
folly, but it rids them of self-righteousness, the bane of *our* careerists—
which is, of course, endemic among budgeteers.

A Treasury-type gains this exposure through that interesting device,
the tour of duty in a minister's private office as his personal assistant
('Dogsbody' is their term for it). The private secretary, so called, now
serves his master-of-the-moment as a confidential aide, minding his business, doing his chores, sharing his woes, offering a crying towel, bracing
him for bad days in the House, briefing him for bad days in the office.
Etcetera. Remarkably, by our standards, the civil service has pre-empted
such assignments for its own. (Do not confuse these with mere *parliamentary* private secretaries.) Still more remarkably, the politicians feel themselves well served and rarely dream of looking elsewhere for the service. I
know an instance where a minister confided in his private secretary a
secret he told no one else save the Prime Minister, not even his Permanent Secretary, the career head-of-department, 'lest it embarrass him to
know'. The Permanent Secretary was the private secretary's boss in career
terms. Yet the secret was kept as a matter of course. This, I am assured, is
not untypical: 'ministerial secrets' are all in the day's work for dogsbodies.

Accordingly, the one-time private secretary who has risen in due
course to be a permanent secretary of a department, knows far more of

modern civil service, was accustomed to 'sound off' on issues of the day, with which he
was concerned as an official of the Treasury, in letters to the Press. See Cecil Woodham-
Smith, *The Great Hunger* (New York, 1962).

Regarding the military, I am indebted to Hugh Gaitskell, in a conversation three years
ago, for the observation that the Opposition was the target of confidential griping from
senior service officers to a degree 'absolutely unknown' on the civilian side, 'perhaps for
the reason that the Army and Navy are so much older than the Civil Service and quite a
lot older than Cabinet government. This gives a certain confidence.... They still rather
regard themselves as "servants of the Crown" *apart* from the Government. The civil servants wouldn't dare; theirs is a "junior" service ... under Cabinet from the start.'

348 APEX OF POWER

what it feels like to perform as politician than his opposite number, the department's minister, can ever hope to fathom in reverse. . . .

Our budgeteers imagine that they are the nearest thing to Treasury civil servants. For this no one can blame them. Much of our literature suggests that if they are not quite the same as yet, a little gimmickry could make them so. Many of our colleagues in this Association have bemused themselves for years with plans to borrow nomenclature and procedures from the British side on the unstated premise that function follows form. But it does not.

Functionally, our counterparts for British Treasury-types are *non*-careerists holding jobs infused with Presidential interest or concern—'in-and-outers' from the law firms, banking, business, academia, foundations, or occasionally journalism, or the entourages of successful Governors and Senators—along with up-and-outers (sometimes up-and-downers) who relinquish, or at least risk, civil service status in the process. Here is the elite-of-the-elite, the upper crust of *our* 'Administrative class'. These are the men who serve alongside our equivalents for ministers and share in governing. One finds them in the White House and in the *appointive* jobs across the street at the Executive Office Building. One finds them also on the seventh floor of State, and on the third and fourth floors of the Pentagon: these places among others. If they have not arrived as yet, they probably are trying to get in (or up). If they have gone already, they are likely to be back. . . .

Every detail of our practice is un-English, yet the general outline fits. One of our men appears on television; another testifies against a bill; a third and fourth engage in semi-public argument; a fifth man feeds a press campaign to change the President's mind; a sixth disputes a cabinet member's views in open meeting; a seventh over-turns an inter-agency agreement. So it goes, to the perpetual surprise (and sometimes envy?) of the disciplined duopolists in Britain. Yet by *our* lights, according to *our* standards, under *our* conditions, such activities may be as 'disciplined' as theirs, and as responsive to political leadership. The ablest of our in-and-outers frequently display equivalent restraint and equal comprehension in the face of the dilemmas which confront our Presidential counterparts for Cabinet politicians.

The elite of our officialdom is not careerist in the British sense (although, of course, our in-and-outers have careers); why should it be? Neither is the President with his department heads. They too are in-and-outers. We forget that the duopoly which governs Britain is composed of *two* career systems, official and political. Most ministers who will take office through the next decade are on the scene and well identified in Westminster. The permanent secretaries who will serve with them are on the Whitehall ladders now; a mere outsider can spot some of them. Contrast our situation—even the directorships of old-line bureaus remain problematical. Who is to succeed J. Edgar Hoover?

We have only two sets of true careerists in our system. One consists of senators and congressmen in relatively safe seats, waiting their turn for chairmanships. The other consists of military officers and civil employees who are essentially technicians manning every sort of speciality (including 'management') in the Executive establishment. Between these two we leave a lot of room for in-and-outers. We are fortunate to do so. Nothing else could serve as well to keep the two apart. And *their* duopoly would be productive not of governance but of its feudal substitute, piecemeal administration. We can only hope to govern in our system by and through the Presidency. In-and-outers are a saving grace for Presidents.

II

Since 1959, English commentators frequently have wondered to each other if their government was being 'Presidentialised'. In part this stemmed from electoral considerations following the 'personality contest' between Harold Macmillan and Hugh Gaitskell at that year's general election. In part it stemmed from operational considerations in the wake of Macmillan's active Premiership—reinforced this past year by the sight of still another activist in office, Harold Wilson.

Despite their differences of style, personality, and party, both Macmillan and Wilson patently conceived the Cabinet Room in Downing Street to be the PM's office, not a mere board-room. Both evidently acted on the premise that the PM's personal judgment ought, if possible, to rule the day. Both reached out for the power of personal decision on the issues of the day. Macmillan did so through off-stage manoeuvre, while avowing his fidelity to cabinet consensus as befits a man beset by the conventions of committee government. With perhaps a bit more candour, Wilson does the same. But what alerts the commentators is that both have done it. Hence discussion about trends toward Presidential government.

Yet between these two Prime Ministers there was another for a year, Sir Alec Douglas-Home. And by no stretch of the imagination could his conduct of the office have been characterised as Presidential. On the contrary, by all accounts he was a classic 'chairman of the board', who resolutely pushed impending issues *out* of Number 10, for initiative elsewhere by others. He managed, it is said, to get a lot of gardening done while he resided there. I once asked a close observer what became of the initiatives, the steering, the manoeuvring, which Home refused to take upon himself. He replied:

When ministers discovered that he really wouldn't do it, they began to huddle with each other, little groups of major figures. You would get from them enough agreement or accommodation to produce the main lines of a government position, something they could try to steer through Cabinet. Or if you didn't get it, there was nothing to be done. That's how it began to work, outside of Number 10, around it.

That is how it would be working now, had there been a slight shift in the popular vote of 1964.

The British system, then, has *not* been Presidentialised, or not at least in operational terms. For as we learned with Eisenhower, the initiatives a President must take to form 'the main lines of a government position' cannot be kept outside the White House precincts. Toss them out and either they bounce back or they do not get taken. A President may delegate to White House aides ('ok, S.A.'), or to a Foster Dulles, but only as he demonstrates consistently, day-in-and-out, that they command his ear and hold his confidence. Let him take to his bed behind an oxygen tent and they can only go through motions. Eisenhower's White House was a far cry from 10 Downing Street in the regime of Douglas-Home. That remains the distance Britain's system has to travel towards a Presidential status for Prime Ministers.

But even though the system did not make an activist of Douglas-Home, his predecessor and successor obviously relished the part. The system may not have required it but they pursued it, and the system bore the weight of their activity. In externals Number 10 looks no more like the White House under Wilson than it did a year ago. But in essence Wilson comes as close to being 'President' as the conventions of his system allow. He evidently knows it and likes it. So, I take it, did Macmillan.

How close can such men come? How nearly can they assert 'Presidential' leadership inside a Cabinet system? Without endeavouring to answer in the abstract, let me record some impressions of concrete performances.

First, consider Britain's bid for Common Market membership four years ago, which presaged an enormous (if abortive) shift in public policy, to say nothing of Tory Party policy. By all accounts this 'turn to Europe' was Macmillan's own. The timing and the impetus were his, and I am told that his intention was to go whole-hog, both economically and politically. As such this was among the great strategic choices in the peacetime politics of Britain. But it never was a Government Decision. For those, by British definition, come in Cabinet. Macmillan never put the issue there in terms like these. Instead he tried to sneak past opposition there—and on back-benches and in constituencies—by disguising his strategic choice as a commercial deal. The Cabinet dealt with issues of negotiation, *en principe* and later in detail, for making Britain part of Europe's economic union without giving up its Commonwealth connections (or farm subsidies). One minister explained to me:

Timing is everything. First we have to get into the Common Market as a matter of business, good for our economy. Then we can begin to look at the political side. . . . Appetites grow with eating. We couldn't hold the Cabinet, much less our back-benchers, if we put this forward now in broader terms. . . .

Accordingly, the move toward Europe had to be played out in its ostensible terms, as a detailed negotiation of commercial character. This took two years, and while the tactic served its purpose within Tory ranks these were the years when France escaped from the Algerian war. By the time negotiations neared their end, Charles de Gaulle was riding high at home. Macmillan tiptoed past his own internal obstacles, but took so long about it that his path was blocked by an external one, the veto of de Gaulle.

Second, take the Nassau Pact of 1962, which calmed the Skybolt crisis between Washington and London even as it gave de Gaulle excuses for that veto. Macmillan was his own negotiator at the Nassau Conference. He decided on the spot to drop his claim for Skybolt missiles and to press the substitution of Polaris weaponry. He wrung what seemed to him an advantageous compromise along those lines from President Kennedy. Then and only then did he 'submit' its terms to the full Cabinet for decision (by return cable), noting the concurrence of three potent ministers who had accompanied him: the Foreign, Commonwealth, and Defence Secretaries. With the President waiting, the Cabinet 'decided' (unenthusiastically by all accounts) to bless this virtual *fait accompli*. What else was there to do? The answer, nothing—and no doubt Macmillan knew it.

Third, consider how the present Labour Government reversed its pre-election stand on Nassau's terms. Within six weeks of taking office Wilson and his colleagues became champions of the Polaris programme they had scorned in Opposition. Their back-benchers wheeled around behind them almost to a man. It is no secret that the PM was the source of this reversal, also its tactician. So far as I can find, it was his own choice, his initiative, his management, from first to last. He got it done in quick-time, yet he did it by manoeuvring on tiptoe like Macmillan in the Common Market case (with just a touch of shot-gun like Macmillan in the Nassau case). When Wilson let Polaris reach the Cabinet for 'decision', leading ministers, both 'right' and 'left', already were committed individually through things they had been led to say or do in one another's presence at informal working sessions. By that time also, Wilson had pretested back-bench sentiment, 'prematurely' voicing to an acquiescent House what would become the rationale for Cabinet action: keeping on with weapons whose production had already passed a 'point of no return'.[3]

Superficially, such instances as these seem strikingly *un*presidential. In our accustomed vision, Presidents do not tiptoe around their Cabinets, they instruct, inform, or ignore them. They do not engineer *faits accomplis* to force decisions from them, for the Cabinet does not make decisions, *Presidents* decide. A Kennedy after Birmingham, a Johnson after Selma, deciding on their civil rights bills, or a Johnson after Pleiku, ordering the bombers north, or Johnson . . . taking off our pressure for the multilateral force, or Kennedy confronting Moscow over Cuba with advisers all around him but decisions in his hands—what contrasts these suggest with the manoeuvres of a Wilson or Macmillan!

The contrasts are but heightened by a glance at their work-forces: Presidents with twenty-odd high-powered personal assistants, and a thousand civil servants in their Executive Office—Prime Ministers with but four such assistants in their Private Office (three of them on detail from departments) and a handful more in Cabinet Office which by definition is not 'theirs' alone. Differences of work-place heighten the effect still more: 10 Downing Street is literally a house, comparing rather poorly with the

---

[3] From the Prime Minister's statement to the House of Commons, defence debate, 23 Nov. 1964.

White House before [Theodore Roosevelt's] time. The modern White House is a palace, as Denis Brogan keeps reminding us, a physically-cramped version of the Hofburg, or the Tuileries.[4]

Yet beneath these contrasts, despite them, belying them, Americans are bound to glimpse a long-familiar pattern in the conduct of an activist Prime Minister. It is the pattern of a President manoeuvring around or through the power-men in his Administration *and* in Congress. Once this is seen all contrasts become superficial. Underneath our images of Presidents-in-boots, astride decisions, are the half-observed realities of Presidents-in-sneakers, stirrups in hand, trying to induce particular department heads, or congressmen, or senators to climb aboard.

Anyone who has an independent power-base is likelier than not to get 'Prime Ministerial' treatment from a President. Even his own appointees are to be wooed, not spurred, in the degree that they have their own attributes of power: expertise, or prestige, or a statute under foot. As Theodore Sorensen reported while he still was at the White House:

In choosing between conflicting advice, the President is also choosing between conflicting advisers. . . . He will be slow to overrule a Cabinet officer whose pride or prestige has been committed, not only to save the officer's personal prestige but to maintain his utility. . . . Whenever any President overrules any Secretary he runs the risk of that Secretary grumbling, privately, if not publicly, to the Congress, or to the Press (or to his diary), or dragging his feet on implementation, or, at the very worst, resigning with a blast at the President.[5]

But it is men of Congress more than departmental men who regularly get from Pennsylvania Avenue the treatment given Cabinet ministers from Downing Street. Power in the Senate is particularly courted. A Lyndon Johnson when he served there, or a Vandenberg in Truman's time, or nowadays an Anderson, a Russell, even Mansfield, even Fulbright—to say nothing of Dirksen—are accorded many of the same attentions which a Wilson has to offer a [Roy Jenkins].

The conventions of 'bipartisanship' in foreign relations, established under Truman and sustained by Eisenhower, have been extended under Kennedy and Johnson to broad sectors of the home front, civil rights especially. These never were so much a matter of engaging oppositionists in White House undertakings as of linking to the White House men from either party who had influence to spare. Mutuality of deference between Presidents and leaders of congressional opinion, rather than between the formal party leaderships, always has been of the essence to 'bipartisanship' in practice. And men who really lead opinion on the Hill gain privileged access to executive decisions as their customary share of 'mutual deference'. 'Congress' may not participate in such decisions, but these men often do: witness Dirksen in the framing of our recent Civil Rights Acts, or a spectrum of Senators from Russell to Mansfield in the framing of partic-

---

[4] Sir Denis Brogan, 'The Presidency', in *American Aspects* (London, 1964) pp. 5-6.
[5] Theodore Sorensen, *Decision-Making in the White House* (New York 1963) pp. 79-80.

ular approaches to Vietnam. Eleven years ago, Eisenhower seems to have kept our armed forces out of there when a projected intervention at the time of Dien Bien Phu won no support from Senate influentials. Johnson now manoeuvres to maintain support from 'right' to 'left' within their ranks.

If one seeks our counterparts for Wilson or Macmillan as Cabinet tacticians one need look no farther than Kennedy or Johnson manoeuvring among the influentials both downtown *and* on the Hill (and in state capitals, steel companies, trade unions, for that matter). Macmillan's caution on the Common Market will suggest the tortuous, slow course of J.F.K. toward fundamental changes in our fiscal policy, which brought him only to the point of trying for a tax cut by the start of his fourth year. Macmillan's *fait accompli* on Polaris brings to mind the South-East Asia Resolution Johnson got from Congress after there had been some shooting in the Tonkin Gulf—and all its predecessors back to 1955 when Eisenhower pioneered this technique for extracting a 'blank cheque'. Wilson's quiet, quick arrangement for the Labour Party to adopt Polaris has a lot in common with the Johnson coup a year ago on aid to education, where a shift in rationale took all sorts of opponents off the hook.

British government may not be Presidential but our government is more Prime Ministerial than we incline to think. Unhappily for thought, we too have something called a Cabinet. But that pallid institution is in no sense the equivalent of theirs. Our equivalent is rather an informal, shifting aggregation of key individuals, the influentials at both ends of Pennsylvania Avenue. Some of them may sit in what we call the Cabinet as department heads; others sit in back rows there, as senior White House aides; still others have no place there. Collectively these men share no responsibility nor any meeting ground. Individually, however, each is linked to all the others through the person of the President (supported by his telephone). And all to some degree are serviced—also monitored—by one group or another on the White House staff. The 'Bundy Office', and the former 'Sorensen Shop', which one might best describe now as the Moyers 'sphere of influence', together with the staff of legislative liaisoners captained until lately by Lawrence O'Brien—these groups although not tightly interlocked provide a common reference-point for influentials everywhere. This is the White House calling. . . .

The functional equivalence between a British Cabinet and our set of influentials—whether Secretaries, Senators, White House staffers, Congressmen, or others—is rendered plain by noting that for most intents and purposes their Cabinet members do the work of our congressional committees, our floor leaderships, and our front-offices downtown, all combined. The combination makes for superficial smoothness; Whitehall seems a quiet place. But once again appearances deceive. Beneath the surface this combine called 'Cabinet' wrestles with divergences of interest, of perspective, of procedure, personality, much like those we are used to witnessing above ground in the dealings of our separated institutions. Not only is the hidden struggle reminiscent of our open one, but also the results are often similar: 'bold, new ventures' actually undertaken are often few and far between. Whitehall dispenses with the grunts and groans of Washington, but both can labour mightily to bring forth mice.

It is unfashionable just now to speak of 'stalemate' or of 'deadlock' in our government, although these terms were all the rage two years ago and will be so again, no doubt, whenever Johnson's coat-tails shrink. But British government is no less prone to deadlock than our own. Indeed I am inclined to think their tendencies in that direction more pronounced than ours. A keen observer of their system, veteran of some seven years at Cabinet meetings, put it to me in these terms:

The obverse of our show of monolithic unity behind a Government position when we have one is slowness, ponderousness, deviousness, in approaching a position, getting it taken, getting a 'sense of the meeting'. Nothing in our system is harder to do, especially if Press leaks are at risk. You Americans don't seem to understand that . . .

In the Common Market case, to cite but one example, the three months from October to December 1962 were taken up at Brussels, where negotiations centred, by a virtual filibuster from the British delegation. This drove some of the Europeans wild and had them muttering about 'perfidious Albion'. But London's delegates were not engaged in tactical manoeuvring at Brussels. All they were doing there was to buy time for tactical manoeuvring back home, around the Cabinet table. The three months were required to induce two senior ministers to swallow agricultural concessions every student of the subject knew their government would have to make. But Britain could not move until those influential 'members of the government' had choked them down. The time-lag seemed enormous from the vantage point of Brussels. Significantly it seemed short indeed to Londoners. By Whitehall standards this was rapid motion.

One of the checks-and-balances in Britain's system lies between the P.M. and his colleagues as a group. This is the check that operated here. A sensible Prime Minister, attuned to his own powerstakes, is scrupulous about the forms of collective action: overreaching risks rejection; a show of arbitrariness risks collegial reaction; if they should band together his associates could pull him down. Accordingly, the man who lives at Number 10 does well to avoid policy departures like the plague, unless, until, and if, he sees a reasonable prospect for obtaining that 'sense of the meeting'. He is not without resources to induce the prospect, and he is at liberty to ride events which suit his causes. But these things take time—and timing. A power-wise Prime Minister adjusts his pace accordingly. So Macmillan did in 1962.[6]

Ministerial prerogatives are not the only source of stalemate or slow motion in this system. If members of a Cabinet were not also heads of great departments, then the leader of their party in the Commons and the country might be less inclined to honour their pretensions in the govern-

---

[6] A man who seems to have made every mistake in the book on these scores, among others, is Anthony Eden, before, during, and after the Suez invasion of 1956.

ment. A second, reinforcing check-and-balance of the system lies between him and the senior civil servants. To quote again, from the same source:

The PM has it easier with ministers than with civil servants. The ranks of civil servants do not work for him. They have to be brought along. They are loyal to a 'Government Decision' but that takes the form of action in Cabinet, where the great machines are represented by their ministers.

The civil servants can be his allies, of course, if their perceptions of the public interest square with his and all he needs is to bring ministers along. Something of this sort seems to have been a factor in the Labour government's acceptance of Polaris: Foreign Office and Defence officials urged their masters on; Treasury officials remained neutral. The PM who first manages to tie the civil servants tighter to his office than to their own ministries will presidentialise the British system beyond anything our system knows. But that day is not yet. For obvious reasons it may never come.

So a British Premier facing Cabinet is in somewhat the position of our President confronting the executive departments and Congress combined. Our man, compared to theirs, is freer to take initiatives and to announce them *in advance* of acquiescence from all sides. With us, indeed, initiatives in public are a step toward obtaining acquiescence, or at least toward wearing down the opposition. It is different in Downing Street. With us, also, the diplomatic and defence spheres yield our man authority for binding judgments on behalf of the whole government. Although he rarely gets unquestioning obedience and often pays a price, his personal choices are authoritative, for he himself is heir to royal prerogatives. In Britain these adhere to Cabinet members as a group, not the Prime Minister alone. Unless they stop him he can take over diplomacy, as Neville Chamberlain did so disastrously, and others since, or he can even run a war like Winston Churchill. But Chamberlain had to change Foreign Secretaries in the process, and Churchill took precautions, making himself Minister of Defence.

Still, despite all differences, a President like a Prime Minister lives daily under the constraint that he must bring along *his* 'colleagues' and get action from *their* liege-men at both ends of the Avenue. A sensible Prime Minister is always counting noses in Cabinet. A sensible President is always checking off his list of 'influentials'. The P.M. is not yet a President. The President, however, is a sort of super Prime Minister. That is what comes of comparative inquiry!

28

Some Canadian Notes on "White House and Whitehall"*

THOMAS A. HOCKIN

If Professor Neustadt is accurate in suggesting that the machines of British cabinet government and American presidential government are "not now at opposite poles" but are "differently located near the centre of a spectrum stretching between ideal types, from collective-leadership to one-man rule", it is difficult not to place the Canadian system near the centre of the spectrum as well. Some of Professor Neustadt's themes suggest to the Canadian observer, however, that there are some singular variations of the Canadian system from the British and American systems and these are worth noting.

First, the question of "passion". Canadian public servants resemble their British counterparts more than their American counterparts because of their official political neutrality. However, some "americanization", some increments of crusading passion can be injected by a Canadian Prime Minister into the generally mandarin neutrality of the Canadian public service. Prime Minister Trudeau's explicit attempt to fill a number of deputy ministerial and various quasi-independent agency and commission headships with appointees from outside the normal public service pattern who are noted for clear policy inclinations or administrative competence is one important example. (See the comments by Mr. Pitfield in this volume.) This technique is not so much a "party partisan" way of infusing passion and energy as a technique which seeks to infuse a kind of policy and administrative passion from experience of those outside of government. Appointments of public servants from the provincial public services can also help to leaven the federal bureaucracy by broadening its experience and perspective.

Partisan passion can be injected into the Canadian system without involving the public service, however, by the use of executive assistants. (See the article by Mr. Lenoski in this volume.) The duties of the Minis-

---

* Written for this volume and revised for this edition.

ter's private secretary in Britain, which Neustadt describes, are filled in large part by the Minister's Executive Assistant in Ottawa. Unlike Whitehall, this person is not appointed from the public service and is, therefore, not subject to public service rules on pay, holidays, etc. A large number of these appointments are filled by young men who are party members and look to a career in politics. (Occasionally, however, an "E.A." will decide to pursue a career in the public service after his stint as an E.A. and usually his years of service will be calculated as experience in the public service for the purpose of placing him in the public service.) Before Executive Assistants became ubiquitous in Ottawa, these duties were usually filled — as in Whitehall today — by a member of the department. Ottawa's practice may keep public servants out of much of the Minister's purely personal political ambitions and strategies. Yet because of this lack of involvement, the senior members of the public service are less likely to know "what it feels like to perform as a politician" in the way that Professor Neustadt suggests a British public servant feels after a stint as a private secretary. (Mitchell Sharp and Gordon Robertson have emphasized how the Canadian system could not work if top Canadian public servants were totally naive on these types of political questions, however. Mr. Chrétien's comments in this volume ruefully confirm this suspicion as well.)

There is also the question of the locus of power in Ottawa. The "collaboration" in Whitehall of the senior "inner corps of officials . . . with their ministerial superiors" amounts to a "virtual duopoly" of power according to Professor Neustadt. This assessment may broadly reflect realities in Ottawa as well, but two important and obvious qualifications remain. First, various Ministers or public servants in the provinces have not only an interest in, but considerable power to frustrate, the effectiveness of many decisions by the Ottawa duopoly. This "collaborating duopoly" can easily be punctured or stalled by inputs from provincial officials. This contrast reflects not only that Canada has a federal, and Britain a unitary, system of government, but also the fact that an increasing number of federal initiatives even within exclusive federal jurisdiction necessitates rather close collaboration and advance consultation with provincial officials. On a vast array of provincially-sensitive questions, such as conditional grants, resource conservation and development, and transportation, the attitude and power of provincial officials may be as important as the designs of any "duopoly" in Ottawa. The second qualification is more recent. The Prime Minister's Office under Mr. Trudeau has included many key advisors who are not "career" public servants and both Ministers and public servants must on occasion "collaborate" with the P.M.O. and keep it informed. At times members of parliamentary committees and the government's caucus committees can claim some right to be consulted.

However this duopoly — the top public servants and the executive — may dominate in most cases. For example, a key element of presidential control in the U.S., as Professor Neustadt indicates, is the Bureau of the Budget which interprets the President's overall priorities for the U.S. budget. The Bureau is part of the presidential machinery. In Canada, however, most of the work of the Bureau of the Budget is done in the Treasury Board with significant help from the Department of Finance. Neither of these key budget forums are in the Prime Minister's Office, nor does the Prime Minister seem to have an institutionalized way of dominating either body in detail. The Treasury Board is made up of Ministers with key staff help from mandarins (many of whom are rotated through the Treasury Board for two or three year stints). The Prime Minister does not sit on the Treasury Board. The Treasury Board's recommendations may be affected by the Cabinet Committee on Priorities, but when it comes to applying general priorities to a host of specifics, the Prime Minister's influence through a cabinet committee is no doubt far more diluted than the President's influence in the Bureau of the Budget, where all the key policy-makers are direct presidential appointees and are responsible directly to the President not to secretaries of departments. In Canada, Ministers on the Treasury Board and on the Cabinet Committee on Priorities are responsible not to the Prime Minister alone, but to the Cabinet.

The second set of forces examined by Professor Neustadt in assessing the locus of power is the extent to which a British Prime Minister can be either a Chairman of the Board (such as Sir Alec Douglas-Home) or "presidential" in his relations with the Cabinet (such as Harold MacMillan and Harold Wilson). Various perspectives on this are considered in this volume. However it is important to recognize that in Ottawa, unlike Washington (but like Sir Alec's premiership in Britain), "the main lines of a government position" can be worked out by cabinet committees or by the complete Cabinet or sometimes by Ministers alone with little or no prime ministerial input *if* the Canadian Prime Minister wishes. In contrast to the U.S. President, there is nothing inherent in the office of Canadian Prime Minister that implies that issues cannot be pushed out of the Prime Minister's Office and settled elsewhere. As Schindeler's, Wright's and Wearing's articles show, some issues may invite reconciliation by the Prime Minister; but Ministers, Cabinets and cabinet committees can settle the "main lines of a government position" if a Prime Minister wants them to be so settled, as indicated by Mr. Pearson's comments in this volume and Mr. Schultz's article.

Professor Neustadt's reminder that a President, like a Prime Minister, must give "prime ministerial" treatment to various power-men in his administration and in Congress explains the restraints against "bold, new ventures" by Presidents. This reminder should also help Canadians to see reflections of similar patterns in the conduct of Presidents and Canadian Prime Ministers; the necessity for manoeuvering, for deference to those who disagree, the need to induce support and so on. The key difference is that these activities of a Canadian Prime Minister are less public than the activities of an American President. The mistake Canadians usually make is to confuse public revelation with actual activity. A Canadian Prime Minister by use of the P.C.O. and P.M.O. must work hard in cabinet, in its committees and elsewhere to insure that his intentions are not ignored. The articles by Mr. Schultz and Mr. Lenoski reflect on this. The difference is that most of this activity in Ottawa and Whitehall is secret, out of public view, whereas in Washington so much of it is public. In the last analysis, however, as Mr. Schultz clearly intimates, the Canadian must remember that no matter how large and aggressive the Prime Minister makes his P.M.O. or P.C.O. these two offices will never be able to supplant the policy network of departments on a vast array of policy areas. And since the civil servants in each department are not working directly for the Prime Minister but report to their Minister, they are not directly tied to the Prime Minister. They are tied to a host of other influences equally compelling in most instances: to the department's preferred way of doing things, to departmental politics and past policies, to the Minister, to the agreements in cabinet committees, to their own notion of the public interest and to the Prime Minister. Sometimes all these converge, sometimes not. For example the Department of External Affairs 1969 Task Force on Europe and NATO did not produce a report remotely similar to the Prime Minister's eventual decision on NATO. This helps us to understand how far the perceptions and direction of departments can be from those of the Prime Minister. Perhaps the same was true during the air controllers' strike a month before the Montreal Olympics in July 1976. Professor Neustadt warns students of British Government that in order to presidentialise the British system of government, the Prime Minister would have "to tie the civil servants tighter to his office than to their own ministries". This is a large task for any Prime Minister in Britain or in Canada. Such a task may be so large that no Prime Minister has—with iron fist—ever tried it or ever will. If this attempt is never made, or is never successful, then the Canadian system cannot really be called presidential in the American sense. Even a strengthened cabinet committee system with substantial P.C.O. staff and co-ordination roles would not tie the departments directly to the Prime Minister.

To turn the Canadian Government into the American type of presidential system, a Prime Minister would have to choose all of the top policy advisors in the departments (deputies, assistant deputies, directors of divisions etc.) and make them responsible to him personally and in consequence make all ministers mere secretaries reporting to the P.M.O. or P.C.O. This would be an enormous undertaking. There is little evidence that a Prime Minister has ever tried it. And until he tries and succeeds, we cannot—with accuracy—call Pierre Trudeau's or anyone's system of government presidential. But the political impact (voting behaviour and media concentration for example) of Pierre Trudeau or any prime minister is something else. This, however, is more an indicator of public political appeal than an indicator of a type of governmental system.